COMMUNICATING IN INTERPERSONAL RELATIONSHIPS

Bobby Burby
26967 Burkhart Lane
Ingleside, 60041-933

940 - 3226
W 937 - 3086
Fax 938 - 3191

COMMUNICATING IN INTERPERSONAL RELATIONSHIPS

BLAINE GOSS   DAN O'HAIR
New Mexico State University

MACMILLAN PUBLISHING COMPANY

New York

Macmillan Publishing Company
866 Third Avenue, New York, New York 10022

Collier Macmillan Canada, Inc.

Library of Congress Cataloging-in-Publication Data

Goss, Blaine.
  Communicating in interpersonal relationships.

  Includes index.
  1. Interpersonal relations. 2. Interpersonal
communication. I. O'Hair, Dan. II. Title.
HM132.G667 1988   302.3'4   87-12245
ISBN 0-02-345280-3

5 6 7   Year: 1 2 3 4

Photo Credits:
Chapter 1, Ellis Herwig/The Picture Cube; Chapter 2, Charles Milligan/Camera Press-Photo Trends; Chapter 3, Therese Frare/The Picture Cube; Chapter 4, Ulf Sjoestedt/FPG International; Chapter 5, Horst Schaeper/ Photo Trends, and Laimute Druskis/Taurus Photos; Chapter 6, Ellis Herwig/The Picture Cube; Chapter 7, Hays/Monkmeyer Press Photo Service, and Richard Wood/The Picture Cube; Chapter 8, Carolyn A. McKeone/FPG International; Chapter 9, Laimute E. Druskis/Taurus Photos; Chapter 10, Ulf Sjoestedt/ FPG International; Chapter 11, Sholik/FPG International; Chapter 12, Paul Conklin/Monkmeyer Press Photo Service; Chapter 13, Mimi Forsyth/Monkmeyer Press Photo Service, and Shirley Zeiberg/Taurus Photos.

ISBN 0-02-345280-3

This book is dedicated
to
Carol
Mary John
Angela
Missy
&
Erica

PREFACE

Communicating in Interpersonal Relationships is the kind of book we wish we had had when we first started our careers in the field of communication. When we took our first classes in interpersonal communication, we used social psychology texts written by psychologists. The writers knew a lot about attitude change, small group behavior, and human relations, but not much about such things as relational development, conversations, nonverbal communication, family communication, and conflict management. Furthermore, we had to buy several different books to cover the topics that a good course in interpersonal communication should contain. Today, you no longer have these problems. This book, for instance, is written by two active teacher/scholars of human communication who have relied heavily on current research in human communication (not just social psychology) in preparing this text. For more than 20 years, we have been teaching and conducting research in interpersonal communication. We have covered all the critical topics of interpersonal communication in this one volume. In addition, the comprehensiveness of the book makes it a flexible partner in learning. Teachers may choose whatever chapters they wish to make required reading and arrange the chapters to fit their course plans.

Currently, interest in interpersonal communication is burgeoning. We have more communication specialists and researchers studying interpersonal communication than ever before. Furthermore, other professionals such as physicians, lawyers, editors, supervisors, educators, account executives, engineers, social workers, ministers, and counselors are realizing the importance of interpersonal skills in performing their jobs effectively. The fact that you are reading these words suggest that you, too, feel that improving your interpersonal communication would make your life a little easier, more satisfying, and perhaps more profitable.

The popularity of interpersonal communication, though, is not sufficient justification for writing a book on the topic. Why, then, did we write this book? One reason is that many other interpersonal communication books ignore the importance of the relationship in interpersonal communication. This is a mistake. Your relationship with your conversational partner affects how you communicate. You communicate differently with your neighbor than you do with your boss. You talk to your parents differently than you talk to a child. In this book, you will learn how interpersonal communication is affected by and affects the underlying relationships between people. Another reason we wrote this book is that we feel that many other books on interpersonal communication depend too much on what other writers think about the subject and are not concerned enough with what we can learn from the current research findings. As a review of our references will demonstrate, we use current research findings and apply them to everyday interpersonal communication. We have done this because the research going on now is simply too exciting and important to ignore. Communication experts now know more about how interpersonal communication works than in any time in our history. Thus, we wanted to write a book that would reflect the very latest knowledge we have available. Furthermore, the timeliness of this literature made it easy for us to write an enjoyable and readable book that you will immediately understand and identify with.

We would like to thank several people for helping make such a book possible. The most important of these are our colleagues whose work we have cited. Because of their enthusiasm and willingness to publish their ideas and findings, we had much of the material used to write this text. Also, we would like to thank our colleagues who read various portions of the manuscript and made outstanding recommendations for improving our work. Specifically, these include Malcolm Parks, University of Washington Seattle; Larry Nadler, Miami University; Barbara Bullard, Orange Coast Community College; Judy Goldberg, Arapahoe Community College; William Robinson, Purdue Calumet; Rex Gaskell; Lloyd Goodall, University of Alabama; and David Brenders, Indiana University.

Finally, we recognize the fine support we have gotten from Macmillan Publishing Company, especially from Lloyd Chilton, who originally latched on to the project, and to Julie Alexander, who saw it through the reviewing and production processes. Also, the quality work of the production people is obvious as you thumb through the finished product.

B.G.
D.O'H.

BRIEF CONTENTS

CONTENTS

UNIT 2   INTERPERSONAL COMMUNICATION IN ACTION   99

SETTING A
PERSPECTIVE

1

> "Of all those qualities we can point to that permit us to assume the lofty position we enjoy above all other life forms, the ability to communicate is probably our crowning achievement. It enables us to translate what we are thinking, feeling, and sometimes only sensing into a verbal or nonverbal language that connects us with other people. It makes our encounters with others possible."
> Don Hamachek, Encounters with Others (Holt, 1982)

In our rapidly changing world the need for effective interpersonal communication is greater than ever. As John Naisbitt has so cogently observed, our society has changed from an industrial society to an information society.[1] Satellite technology, microchips, lasers, and other developments allow us to mass produce and distribute information at incredible speeds across great distances. Consequently our options for communicating have expanded. Today, people communicate face-to-face, write letters, use electronic mail, do their banking on personal computers, monitor current events on television, and watch their city councils "spin their wheels" on cable television. Technology has provided us more channels of communication, but it has not changed our basic way of communicating. Our society still runs on encounters between people. Technology will not replace one-on-one, or interpersonal, communication.

We sometimes take for granted how much our world depends on interpersonal communication. Certainly our professional success depends on our communication skills. Yet television often presents to viewers inappropriate images of professionals and their lives. For instance, we see the excitement of a busy executive racing across town in a fancy car, making large financial deals, talking on the phone with important people, always in the middle of a crisis situation. Or we see a physician quickly and completely responding to a pressure-packed emergency case in surgery. If all goes well, the patient lives, and the surgeon smiles as though it has just been another day at work. But we see little of the nuts-and-bolts, everyday communication activities of these professionals. In reality, physicians and executives spend hours tending to everyday communication chores. They write reports, attend meetings, mend relationships, answer the phone, meet new potential clients and colleagues, make vacation plans, listen to their children tell about school, talk to the clerk as they stop at the store on the way home from work, etc. These are the communication activities that make up most of their lives and the communication skills that must be mastered. Ironically, many professionals are not as well trained in everyday communication as they are in their chosen profession. Thus, professionals, as well as all of us, need to study interpersonal communication carefully. We cannot depend on our intuition or past experience.

WHAT'S AHEAD

In this chapter, you will learn how interpersonal communication functions in a number of different relationships that we are all familiar with. Then we will explore how interpersonal communication can be conceptualized and defined.

Next, you will be asked to complete a test asssessing your feelings about your own interpersonal communication skills. You will be shown how to score the test so that you can analyze your own results. Finally, we will close with an explanation of how the subsequent chapters are organized.

RELATIONSHIPS AND INTERPERSONAL COMMUNICATION

Most students who enroll in an interpersonal communication class already have some understanding of the important role of communication in interpersonal relationships. Unfortunately, most of us do not focus much attention on the importance of interpersonal communication until there is some type of breakdown. When parents and children argue, communication is usually blamed as the cause of disagreement. When lovers have a falling-out, it is attributed to a lack of understanding and communication in the relationship. And when nuclear disarmament negotiations and SALT II (Strategic Arms Limitation Treaty of 1979) talks break down, communication is seen as the culprit. As amazing as it seems, all of these parties are basically right. Interpersonal communication is a troublesome activity for many people primarily because it is taken for granted much too often. If individuals in relationships could understand and utilize the appropriate principles and practices of interpersonal communication, fewer breakdowns would occur.

Some One way of developing a notion of the importance of interpersonal communication is by describing the various contexts that rely so heavily on it. While the following sections do not describe all the situations or contexts that are dependent on effective interpersonal communication, they do represent a healthy sample of those that research has pointed out as important areas. Undoubtedly, you could suggest other situations that require a comprehensive knowledge of communication in interpersonal relationships.

Close Personal Relationships

One of the most important functions of communication is to help us establish close personal relationships with others. By reaching out to others and building relations, we avoid loneliness and develop happier lives. Such relationships can be found in families, among roommates, among classmates, in churches, lodges, and clubs. They even occur at work. No matter where they are formed, these relationships are often the mainstays of our lives. In these relationships people turn to one another in times of trouble. In these relationships people accept you for who you are. Yet these same people may be your stiffest critics. Most of us realize that our best friends, parents, spouses, and other intimates fill these important roles of confidant and critic. Most of this book is about personal relations, but since you will be learning a lot about personal relationships in later chapters, little more need be said now. Instead, let's review some common professional relationships.

w̶o̶r̶k̶

Relationships in Business

Communicating in interpersonal relationships in business or occupational contexts requires more than intuitive judgment. Functioning effectively in these relationships entails an understanding of the motives, perceptions, and skills of relationship partners. Countless surveys and studies have suggested that the number one priority in preparing for a successful business career involves interpersonal communication training. In fact, a recent issue of the *Journal of Business Communication* reports that business executives are now more convinced than ever that the development of interpersonal skills is a prerequisite for success in a growing information-oriented society.[2] Several specific relationships can be illustrated in the business arena.

Superior-subordinate relationships.   This type of communicative relationship is one of the more important ones in a business environment. The communication between superior and subordinate determines whether tasks are complete and goals are achieved and also influences employee motivation and satisfaction. All of these factors are directly related to productivity and profits.[3] Effective superior-subordinate communication also has a direct impact on the morale and esprit de corps of those in an organization. Superiors who are trustworthy, approachable, and open to workers' ideas engender a greater sense of satisfaction and more positive attitudes in workers than bosses who are less interpersonally inclined. Human nature teaches us that we will voluntarily work harder for individuals whom we like and respect. The following example illustrates this point.

> **Mr. Flannery:** Mike, I've called you in today to discuss a problem in your department.
>
> **Mike:** A problem? In my department?
>
> **Mr. Flannery:** It seems that since you became the department supervisor—what has it been, eight months now?—the employees in your department have raised more complaints about your management style than that of any other supervisor or of any supervisor who previously held your position!
>
> **Mike:** I know that some of the workers are mad that I'm pushing them too hard, but production has fallen and I have to stay on top of them to get our rates back up.
>
> **Mr. Flannery:** Mike have you stopped to think that maybe your relationship with the workers could be part of both problems?
>
> **Mike:** What do you mean, *both* problems?
>
> **Mr. Flannery:** Mike, I know you are young and haven't had a lot of opportunity to adjust to a managerial position, but one of the things you will learn is that if you can get your workers to feel comfortable around you it won't be necessary to "stay on top of them." They will be willing

to go the extra mile for you. Our workers are not like the machines that they run and repair. They are humans and have feelings. Communicate with them on a personal level and I think you will be surprised at the results. There won't be as many complaints about you and production will go up.

Mike: I'll give it my best shot!

Sales relationships.   Selling is one of the most dynamic and rewarding professions in the business environment. As you have probably heard many people say, it takes a particular kind of person to be successful in sales. Maybe that's true, or maybe it simply takes *particular kinds of skills* for a person to be successful in sales. Salespersons are some of the best paid and most admired of business professionals, yet many of them will tell you that effective selling is nothing more than establishing a relationship with a client and gaining his or her confidence. After that, the actual sale is simply a minor issue. Obviously, the most effective method of establishing relationships and building confidence is through interpersonal communication.

Sales relationships are both similar and different to the friendships and intimate relationships that we have with other people. Sales relationships are different in that they are based on an assumption by both parties that one person is buying and the other is selling. The parties also assume that one will deliver a service or product and the other will provide compensation. Basically, that is where the differences end. Sales relationships are similar to other relationships in methods of acquaintanceship, building rapport, exchanging information, establishing trust, and forming a bond between individuals. When a relationship is established through effective methods of interpersonal communication the closing or actual sale is simply an agreement that any two partners in a relationship would make with one another. A highly successful power machinery and ball bearing salesperson once told one of the authors:

> When I became an experienced salesman I learned that you really don't have to ask customers to buy anything. If they like and trust you and your product they *will close the deal for you!*

Peer relationships.   Maintaining harmonious relationships with coworkers or peers is an important element in any career plan. Many appraisal forms, which are used to evaluate an employee's progress, include categories involving interpersonal relations (such as whether the employee gets along well with others or works well in groups). A common misconception among workers is that as long as they do their job they will advance and succeed in their careers. As the example above illustrated, supervisory and management positions are relationship-oriented. If a person wants to advance in an organization, that person must almost necessarily demonstrate effective interpersonal skills with his or her coworkers.

Coworkers can communicate more effectively with one another on the job by gaining a greater understanding of each other's perspective. Communication with peers often revolves around the specific tasks assigned to each indi-

CITIZEN
cout ele eredit

vidual. Many workers fail to see the whole picture when communicating with peers and make the mistake of considering only their own position. A friend of ours who works at a Fortune 500 company once remarked,

> *Gaining the trust, confidence, and friendship of coworkers is just as important as the skills that are learned. Uppermanagement is looking for people who can establish good relations, because they will have to do the same thing when they are promoted to higher positions.*

Many of the strategies in this book (such as persuasion, conflict management, compliments, accounts, etc.) can provide skills in maintaining successful relationships with coworkers.

As we mentioned previously, these examples of interpersonal relationships in business are only some of the more obvious ones. Many other interpersonal relationships in this context could be identified. The primary purpose was to illustrate how important communication can be in determining the outcomes of business and professional relationships.

Relationships in Education

By now you are probably already predicting the various types of educational relationships you think we will discuss. You are probably right on target. The most obvious are the teacher-student, parent-teacher, teacher-teacher, and principal-teacher relationships. We will discuss the first two, since much of the material in the superior-subordinate section could also apply to principal-teacher relationships, and the material in the peer relationships section could also apply to teacher-teacher relationships.

Teacher-student relationships.   You probably will be able to identify with this type of relationship quite well. Teacher-student relationships are some of the most common involuntary relationships you will experience. While much of the communication that takes place in a classroom setting is not exactly what we would term interpersonal, interaction that takes place before and after class, in the hallway, and in the teacher's office usually involves interpersonal communication. Not all students, or teachers for that matter, are interested in developing an interpersonal relationship much beyond the classroom environment. However, teachers and students who do communicate in more informal contexts report that such communication is a very worthwhile endeavor. In fact, student learning and teacher evaluation scores can increase as a result of this type of interpersonal communication.

Of course, interpersonal communication is also evident in the classroom itself. Much of the learning process comes in the form of question and answer sessions, directed feedback, informal conferences, and behavior regulation episodes. Research has found that teacher-student communication, although sometimes varying from one context to another, is the primary impetus for learning. Certainly the manner in which material is presented is important to learning. For instance, when dramatic nonverbal gestures and vocal inflections are used during lectures, students are more satisfied and learning is increased.[4] Even the types of influence teachers use to get students to comply greatly affect the teacher-student relationship (see Chapter 12). Obviously, the types of interpersonal strategies that students use on teachers can have a similar impact on the relationship. In the next class period, ask your instructor how, in the classroom environment, the interpersonal communication strategies he or she uses as a teacher differ from the strategies he or she used as a student. (Don't tell him/her we suggested it!)

Parent-teacher relationships.   While many of you reading this book probably haven't had the occasion to participate in this type of relationship, it is nonetheless a common and important interpersonal relationship to consider. In most school settings, the parent-teacher relationship is quite formal, with the parties interacting mainly over report cards, at open houses, and at PTA meetings. However, research has suggested that although *direct interpersonal communication* between teacher and parent is not that common, parents believe this method is most effective in communicating with the school.[5] It is ironic that the most efficient and forceful method of ensuring open lines of information exchange between school and home is infrequently utilized. Unfortunately, teachers and parents are not the only ones in interpersonal relationships who prefer less direct methods of communicating. We hope that the ideas presented in this book will provide convincing arguments that direct forms of interpersonal communication are not only the most effective forms of relating with others, but also can become the most preferred methods as well.

Medical Relationships

Communicating with medical personnel—such as doctors, dentists, nurses, and pharmacists—can be one of the most important yet least satisfying relational experiences. Undoubtedly, the most written about and discussed medical relationship is that between physicians and patients. A great deal of evidence suggests that the doctor-patient relationship suffers from a lack of effective interpersonal communication.[6] Doctors blame patients for withholding information, and patients blame doctors for being insensitive to their needs. As with most interpersonal relationships, when communication breaks down, a number of problems can ensue. The problems associated with a strained doctor-patient relationship can have very serious implications for both parties.

    One of the negative outcomes of a poor doctor-patient relationship involves mistrust and noncompliance on the part of the patient.[7] Research reveals that patients actually judge a physician's technical competence based on his/her communication skills.[8] When physicians demonstrate care and understanding, patients are more likely to view their technical competence in a positive vein. When communication breaks down between doctor and patient, the patient has a tendency to resent the physician and believe that he/she doesn't really know what he/she is talking about in the first place! According to numerous accounts, patients stop taking their prescribed medications when they no longer place confidence in the doctor "because he doesn't know how to communicate with me." Severe medical problems can result from a patient's failure to take the medicine prescribed by a doctor. Obviously, patients can be harmed by a lack of effective interpersonal communication with their physician.

Physicians, on the other hand, may also suffer from a poor doctor-patient relationship. Not only can doctors become dissatisfied that patients do not recover from illness because of their unwillingness to take prescribed medicine, physicians may also face malpractice action as a result of ineffective interpersonal communication. Studies have shown that physicians who enjoy interpersonal relationships with their patients are also those who have a lower malpractice record. Are the doctors with the best medical skills also those who have the best interpersonal skills? Probably not. Two issues explain this phenomenon. Evidence suggests that patients are reluctant to sue those people whom they like and trust. It stands to reason that we are less likely to sue our friends than we are strangers or those whom we do not care for. Physicians who take the time to communicate effectively with patients and establish interpersonal bonds with them are less likely to be sued for medical malpractice.

As you can tell, relationships are critical determinants of how people use interpersonal communication. Different relationships call for different communication tactics. If nothing else, the relationship influences the topics discussed and the manner in which we choose to talk about them. In short, the relationship sets the context in which we regulate our interpersonal communication and adapt our message strategies to fit the current situation.

DEFINING INTERPERSONAL COMMUNICATION

Most interpersonal communication textbooks begin with a definition. The authors generally attempt to describe how they see communication operating in dyadic (two-person) relationships. Our goal will be a little different. College students are at a point in their intellectual careers where they are able to make choices among theoretical concepts and advance some very convincing arguments of their own. To some extent we will be asking you to decide among competing alternatives in reaching a definition of interpersonal communication. We feel that it is naive to suppose that only one definition of interpersonal communication exists or that only one conceptualization is possible. Don't get us wrong. We have our own idea about the definition of interpersonal communication, and we will not hesitate to present our point of view. But we feel as Bochner does, that communication in interpersonal relationships is a phenomenon dynamic enough to consider different perspectives:[9]

> . . . interpersonal communication shall be viewed as a subject that can be legitimately approached in several different ways, described in several different vocabularies, and studied with several different purposes in mind.

With this goal in mind, we will briefly offer a few of the perspectives that have attempted to conceptualize interpersonal communication, and then summarize with our own ideas. Again, you must eventually decide which perspective seems appropriate for you and your relationships.

In an article in *Human Communication Research*, Miller suggested that the field of interpersonal communication had been conceptualized according to four different perspectives: situational, laws, rules, and developmental.[10] Since that time many theories about communication in relationships have been advanced, but only a few have gained the same prominence as distinct categories that these four have. Therefore, we will present these four concepts as alternative perspectives of interpersonal communication.

Situational Approach

The situational approach proposes that determining whether or not communication is interpersonal depends on context, or on the number of people involved in the interaction. This perspective also supposes that direct and immediate feedback is a prime ingredient in determining whether or not communication is of an interpersonal nature. The following helps to explain the situational idea.

	Intrapersonal	"Interpersonal"	Group	Public
Number of People	1	2	3–20	Over 20
Type of Feedback	Instantaneous	Direct & Immediate	Less Direct/Immediate	Delayed & Indirect

As the number of people communicating increases, their speed in responding to each other decreases and their ability to provide and obtain feedback becomes less certain. Therefore, the situational perspective relies on the number of interactants as a way of distinguishing interpersonal from other types of communication.

Laws Approach

The law-governed approach states that environmental conditions (two strangers meeting for the first time) precipitate or cause certain behaviors (they do not talk about their sexual relations), except under unusual circumstances (for instance, when they are drunk). This perspective presumes that the laws of nature can apply equally well in interpersonal relations. A common analogy from physics is that water boils at 212 degrees Fahrenheit. Interpersonal communication laws abound:

Women are more easily persuaded than are men.

Highly credible speakers are more persuasive than less credible speakers.

Children imitate their parents.

The law-governed approach takes advantage of seemingly inherent tendencies of human behavior and calls these regularities "laws." As long as these laws are not broken, this approach to interpersonal communication can remain valid. However, once these laws begin to show even infrequent violations, something other than laws are being used to describe interpersonal communication. Fisher suggested that only two explanations are possible if exceptions to a law are found. Either we are incorrect in believing there is an exception, or the law is invalid.[11] The law approach is very rigorous in its treatment of interpersonal communication and may hold true in very few cases.

Rules Approach

The rules approach to defining interpersonal communication does not presuppose that behavior is regulated according to inherent environmental and social conditions. Rather, rules are more like guidelines, and communicators have a choice in deciding whether or not to follow a rule. Furthermore, rules are basically generated from consistent social behavior and could change depending upon social norms and mores. Some people have even suggested that rules are formed through our self-concepts, which means that we will behave in a certain fashion depending upon how we feel about ourselves.

It has been suggested that rules help to govern and regulate the back-and-forth nature of conversation. We all know most of the rules of conversation. "It is impolite to interrupt someone while he/she is speaking." "It is rude to 'hog' the floor by not allowing others to speak." We also know that these rules are sometimes broken. In fact, conversations are frequently interrupted, especially those among friends or people who are exchanging arguments over an issue. Other interpersonal rules include:

Don't talk with your mouth full.

Don't ask someone to stay the night with you on the first date.

Always say "please" and "thank you."

Don't ask recent acquaintances how much money they make.

Don't ask teachers to raise your grade for no reason.

Use eye contact when listening to someone else talk.

Always knock before entering someone's office.

How often are these rules violated? It depends on the situation and the people involved in the interpersonal relationship at the time. In fact, you may not have even considered some of the items on the list as rules in the first place. They may not even serve as guidelines for your own behavior. However, there may be other interpersonal communication rules that you consider and abide by from time to time. Think about the last time you felt embarrassed or angry at yourself for communicating in a way that seemed to surprise or offend someone else. You may have violated a rule that you generally adhere to.

Developmental Approach

One of the most popular perspectives on interpersonal communication is the developmental approach. According to this perspective, interpersonal relationships are understood and described by identifying which developmental stage the parties are in at a particular time. The developmental approach assumes that in the early stages of a relationship certain types of communication are most evident (small talk, safe topics, etc.). As a relationship develops, communication moves toward more personal and intimate topics, with very private information being communicated only between those who are in the latter stages of development. Chapter 9 of this textbook relies a great deal on the developmental approach in describing how relationships become more intimate.

Each of the approaches to understanding the process of communicating in interpersonal relationships has distinctive characteristics, and all have some element of validity. Some of them seem more readily applicable to relationships in our own lives. Furthermore, there is probably some overlap among the perspectives. We want to remind you of our guiding perspective—there is more than one way of defining interpersonal communication.

Our Definition

Since the "right" definition is impossible to produce, we offer the following definition, which is workable and serves our immediate purposes. Interpersonal communication is *the process of exchanging verbal and nonverbal messages in order to understand, develop, and influence human relationships.* We believe that whenever people interact directly with one another they affect one another (laws perspective). They might understand each other better, might persuade each other, or could simply feel closer because they talked. Whatever the effects, the way we communicate with others can make a difference. Much of what we witness on television sitcoms such as *The Golden Girls* or *The Bill Cosby Show* reminds us of how dialogue affects and is affected by relationships. For instance, the character portrayed by Bill Cosby displays an open and supportive relationship with his sitcom family. He does this through his style of interpersonal communication—his warm, loving, and humorous manner. This style produces warm, loving, and humorous relationships. Thus, Cosby illustrates the commonly believed notion (law?) that you get from others what you give to others. Or said another way, people will communicate with you in a manner similar to which you communicate with them.

We also believe that relationships are altered by interpersonal exchanges (developmental perspective) and that communicators make their message choices (rules perspective) based on how they perceive the underlying relationship. Thus, how you interact with someone is affected by your purposes, by your understanding of who you are talking with, and by the relationship and the level of trust that exists between you and your conversational partner. Consider the problem that arises when interpersonal trust is broken by one incident, such as an unkind word or a careless act. History is full of stories about public figures (politicians in particular) who probably would like to erase brief moments of history in which they made costly mistakes. Most of us can think of moments in our own histories that we regret. When these moments cause changes in our relationships, we learn that we cannot go back in time to repair the past and that we must alter our current communication strategies to accommodate the changed relationship. Thus, a person trying to restore a strained relationship has a different task than one who is enjoying a harmonious relationship.

All told, interpersonal communication is people interacting within the context of relationships. You can understand more about a particular relationship by studying the interaction upon which the relationship was built, and you can learn more about how to interact effectively by understanding the relationship. Now, let's look at how you see yourself as an interpersonal communicator.

ASSESSING YOUR INTERPERSONAL COMMUNICATION SKILLS

Most of us have been communicating for most of our lives. From the first day you entered the world, you made movements and gestures that others paid attention to. Even as an infant you were cast into the world of interpersonal relationships. At first you were unaware of how your actions affected others in your environment, but eventually you discovered that your actions influenced others. When you smiled, others smiled. When you laughed, others laughed. When you accomplished new physical or mental feats, others responded. Friends, relatives, and visitors took note. Thus, you learned at an early age that your actions can cause reactions. You become a force in your world of interpersonal relationships.

Now that you have reached adulthood you have accumulated many skills, and you realize even more now than before that the quality of your interpersonal life is directly related to the quality of your communication skills. Even the success of something as straightforward as asking someone for a date is dependent on your past experience and your communication skills.

Testing Yourself

While few doubt the personal and social significance of effective communication skills, we often don't take stock of how we feel about ourselves as communicators. We don't often ask, "How do I feel about myself as a communicator?" To answer this question, take the test "Exploring Your Feelings about Communicating in Interpersonal Relationships" on page 13. It is important that you complete this test before reading the subsequent chapters of this text. The test will reveal those areas of interpersonal communication that you are most comfortable with and least comfortable with. The test is also organized according to the topics to be presented in subsequent chapters. Thus, your answer to each item will set the stage for your reading of the chapters.

Take a moment to respond to each item. Read each one carefully, and then circle one of the answers to the left, indicating whether you strongly agree (sa), agree (a), are neutral (n), disagree (d), or strongly disagree (sd).

EXPLORING YOUR FEELINGS ABOUT COMMUNICATING IN INTERPERSONAL RELATIONSHIPS

sa (a) n d sd   1. I have a pretty good attention span.

sa (a) n d sd   2. I am forgetful.

sa (a) n d sd   3. I like myself.

(sa) a n d sd   4. I am a good judge of character.

sa (a) n d sd   5. I have a good vocabulary.

sa a n (d) sd   6. I am not a particularly good writer.

(sa) a n d sd   7. I watch how others use their hands, eyes, and facial expressions when I'm talking with them.

sa a n d (sd)   8. I am not very animated when I talk.

(sa) a n d sd   9. I enjoy talking with people.

sa a (n) d sd   10. I usually think before I speak.

sa a (n) d sd   11. I am a better-than-average listener.

sa a n (d) sd   12. I ignore speakers who don't make much sense.

(sa) a n d sd   13. I make new friends easily.

sa (a) n d sd   14. I try to get to know better each person I meet.

sa a n d (sd)   15. I conceal my feelings when I talk to others.

(sa) a n d sd   16. I am open and honest with others.

sa a (n) d sd   17. I am equally comfortable talking with women as well as with men.

sa a n (d) sd   18. I believe that men should talk like men and women should talk like women, without exception.

sa (a) n d sd   19. I communicate freely with members of my family.

(sa) a n d sd   20. I find it easier to talk with my sisters (and/or brothers) than I do with my parents.

sa (a) n d sd   21. I am more argumentative than other people.

sa a n (d) sd   22. I never interfere in my friends' lives, even if they are hurting themselves.

(sa) a n d sd   23. I hold positive values about life.

sa a (n) d sd   24. I am often unsure about my attitudes on issues.

sa (a) n d sd   25. I use different strategies when trying to convince my friends to do something.

Now that you have completed the test, reflect back on some of the items. Are you an effective interpersonal communicator? Why did you answer certain items as you did? What do your answers tell you about yourself? Do others feel the same way about themselves? Compare your answers with others who have completed the test.

Scoring the Test

Now, let's score the test so that you can learn more about your feelings on interpersonal communication. For all items (except items 2, 6, 12, 15, 18, 21, 22, and 24) give yourself 5 points for circling *sa*, 4 points for *a*, 3 points for *n*, 2 points for *d*, and 1 point for *sd*. To score items 2, 6, 12, 15, 18, 21, 22, and 24, reverse the scoring so that *sa* earns 1 point, *a* earns 2 points, and so forth.

You can now calculate your overall score by summing the points earned on all 25 items. The highest possible score would be 125, the lowest, 25. Most people will score in the 75–105 range. If your overall score exceeds 110 points, you have a very positive outlook on communicating in interpersonal relationships. You are to be congratulated. On the other hand, if your total score falls below 70, you may need to work especially hard on developing your understanding and skills in interpersonal communication. No matter how you scored, though, all of us need to continually develop our interpersonal communication abilities.

Now that you have calculated your total score, you can see how you did on specific areas of interpersonal communication covered in this book. The items are grouped according to some of the topics covered in this text. For your convenience, the item numbers, topics, and upcoming chapter numbers are listed here:

Items	Topic Areas	Chapters
1–4	Human information processing, and self concept	2 3
5–8	Verbal and nonverbal communication	4 5
9–12	Conversational skills, and listening	6 7
13–16	Interpersonal relations	9
17–20	Male/female communication, and family communication	8 10
21–25	Conflict management, and interpersonal persuasion	11 12

By summing your points in each group of items you can discover your strengths and weaknesses in each of the specific areas. For instance, if your total score on items 1–4 exceeds 18, you have a lot of confidence in yourself and in your ability to process information. On the other hand, if your score falls below 10, you may need to pay special attention to improving your self-concept and your ability to handle information. The materials in Chapters 2 and 3 will help you understand more about these things. For instance, you will learn how your perceptual biases may be enhancing or interfering with your ability to understand others. We will also see how your self-concept is developed and how it affects your interpersonal life.

The statements numbered 5–8 cover verbal and nonverbal communication. If you score greater than 18 on these items, you are confident in your language skills and are sensitive to nonverbal communication. Those who score below 10, on the other hand, may need to work on language skills and become more aware of the nonverbal messages that others are sending. Even in the most long-standing relationships, people may find out, often much too late, that what they said to someone was taken offensively and they were not alert enough at the time to notice the verbal and nonverbal cues indicating trouble. To help you meet some of these challenges, Chapters 4 and 5 demonstrate how symbols and meanings are learned and used in communication and how people vary in their ability to send and receive nonverbal messages.

Ever have difficulty starting a conversation with a stranger? If you have, you recognize the idea in items 9–12. If your score on these four statements surpassed 18, you apparently feel in control of your conversation skills and listening ability. A score below 10 suggests a need for special attention to speaking and listening skills. Chapters 6 and 7 explore how conversations are enacted and illustrate how human listening works.

Representing the focal point through which we are studying interpersonal communication, items 13–16 inquire about your abilities to build interpersonal relationships. If your total score on these exceeds 18, you are managing your interpersonal relationships pretty well. On the other hand, if your score falls below 10, you need to work on your understanding of interpersonal relationships. Chapter 9 (along with most of the rest of the text) will be addressing this issue.

Communicating with members of the opposite sex can often be an awkward experience. Likewise, many people report problems communicating with their family and relatives. Statements 17–20 address male/female communication and family communication. As before, we can note meritorious skill through a score of 18 or more, while observing difficulties when the score is less than 10. Your communication with your family may not be as spirited or rocky as illustrated on some TV sitcoms, but all of us have had both good and bad communication with those we care the most about. Chapters 8 and 10 will bring you the most up-to-date information available on male/female communication and family communication. In these chapters you will learn how women and men can use their gender-specific communication skills to the fullest, and how communication differences between the sexes is often only folklore! You will also see how communication patterns in dating affect communication in marriage.

Finally, items 21–25 consider your encountering skills. Looking primarily at conflict management and persuasion strategies, these questions explore your feelings about direct and indirect attempts to convince others. Many of us are not "fighters" and thus do not enjoy conflicts. Others are Machiavellian enough to enjoy talking others into doing things. A high score on these items shows that you are in command of your ability to influence people. Chapter 11 will demonstrate the different ways in which people can manage conflict. Chapter 12 will present research showing the effects of the many different interpersonal strategies people use on one another.

PLAN OF THE BOOK

The study of interpersonal communication requires an understanding of both theory and practice. Theory allows you to know the principles that underlie human communication, and it also arms you with useful insights that will help you adapt to a number of communication situations. Practice, on the other hand, is skill development. Good theory is important, but without effective practice, good theory goes wasted. Consequently, each chapter in the book is a careful blend of theory and practice. In preparation for writing the book, the authors reviewed the literature in each topic area with the goal of reporting to you what scholars know about each area at this time. By comprehending the research, you gain theoretic understanding, which should enhance your own interpersonal communication skills.

The book is divided into two major sections: The Basics of Interpersonal Communication, and Interpersonal Communication in Action. In the first section, you will learn about the principles that guide all kinds of human communication. This section focuses on people and how their personal abilities affect interpersonal communication. Without these basics, the materials in the second section would not make as much sense. The second section targets seven key areas of interpersonal communication. In essence, section two looks at communication in action. Our topic choices for these chapters have been governed by the current research activities as reflected in our journals and textbooks.

In all of these chapters, we have provided up-to-date reviews of the literature, along with practical suggestions for using this new knowledge. This is especially noted in the "Improving Your _____" sections, which are found in nearly every chapter. We have also included in the following chapters a number of exercises ("Theory into Practice"), which you can use to assess and develop your own interpersonal communication skills. You are encouraged to glean from your reading whatever helps you become a more successful interpersonal communicator. But be careful. Significant gains in one's understanding and application of any field of knowledge call for serious study. Be ready and willing to work at it. This book, along with the guidance of a competent instructor, should help you learn more about yourself and your communication behavior.

Finally, at the completion of each of the following chapters, the reader will notice a visual model (a drawing) that depicts how each chapter fits into the study of communication in interpersonal relationships. The outer circles display the chapter titles. The inner figure represents the book's theme of "communication in interpersonal relationships." Since each chapter adds to our understanding of interpersonal communication, the inner figure becomes larger as each chapter is added. With the addition of the last chapter, the inner figure encompasses all the chapters to denote a completed blending of communication in interpersonal relationships with the different aspects of the study of interpersonal communication.

Unit 1

THE BASICS OF INTERPERSONAL COMMUNICATION

2

INFORMATION PROCESSING

It may seem a little odd to you to find a chapter on information processing in an interpersonal communication book. Yet whenever people communicate interpersonally, they must create conversations on-the-spot, relying on their perceptions and memories for data. Sometimes what we say to others is accurate and fair. Other times, our messages are subject to distortions because we have difficulty remembering our own ideas and what the other person has said, yet to continue the conversation we have to say something sensible. So we may "wing it," hoping not to be too far off base.

Even when we are not very confident in what we are talking about, we rely on the cognitive baggage that we carry with us. In short, we use information processing every time we engage in interpersonal communication. Thus, it's a good idea to know more about how human information processing works.

WHAT'S AHEAD

In this chapter, we will be looking at both the psychological and physiological aspects of human information processing. First, we will explore some basic principles of perception. Then you will learn how the brain and the sensory mechanisms of hearing and vision influence your ability to process information. The research in human memory will be covered and will be followed by a section on improving your memory.

MENTAL ECONOMY

At any time, humans are capable of storing and retrieving a lot of information. Yet, there seems to be a tendency in humans to prevent information overload and simplify the process. In other words, the "human computer" strives toward efficiency by minimizing the number of complexities necessary to understand things. This is called mental economy. It is observable in three ways.

Closure

Closure is the mental tendency to see things as whole rather than incomplete. It is an inferential process of finishing what your senses have sent to the brain. Thus, most people view the following inputs as a circle and a square, even though the figures are incomplete.

Familiarity

This refers to our tendency to interpret inputs in their most familiar or common forms rather than as unusual. For instance, most people see the following as a rectangle overlapping a circle rather than three irregularly shaped figures.

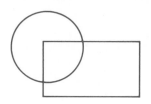

Expectations

The final feature of mental economy, expectations, refers to our tendency to "think ahead" of the input. Relying on closure and familiarity, people read into the input what should be there even if it isn't there. The popular illustration below is an example of expectations. Many people read the words in the triangle as "a bird in the hand," failing to notice the duplication of the word "the."

Because closure, familiarity, and expectations work together to speed up the perceiving process, they make perception efficient. Unfortunately, they also can make perception inaccurate, as the "bird in the hand" example illustrated. Clear perception requires a careful analysis of the input. When we fail to perceive accurately what is "there," we make mental errors in judgment. This occurs not only when we make judgments about the examples shown above, but also when we judge people. Your prior feelings about a particular person will affect how you view that person. Consequently, you may not be able to find fault with someone you admire because your mental image of that person does not include any known shortcomings. This would be particularly true for hero worship. Furthermore, additional experience with the object of perception may not help. Generally, the more prior experience perceivers have with a particular form of input, the more they depend on their memories for interpretation, and the less they scrutinize the input itself. Experienced perceivers often see what they have seen before, and little more. For this reason, they may be quick to respond but not always sensitive to changes in the input. Because they lack experience, new learners pay more attention to the input. They are "data driven" in their analysis of it. They are also more likely to be overloaded with input, since it is so new. On the other hand, experienced perceivers would be less likely to be overloaded with input.

Sometimes when people have known each other a long time, they can become perceptually lazy in that they think that they know each other "like a book." They may think they have little to learn about each other, that they have no particular need to pay close attention to what they are saying to each other. Consequently, the quantity and quality of interpersonal communication may decline. Commenting on this point, a friend of ours once observed that if you go into a restaurant and watch the couples seated at different tables, you can tell how long each couple has been together by how animated their conversations are. Likewise, married couples who have settled into their relationship may have developed poor listening habits. They have gotten so used to one another's voices and ideas that they may not notice subtle changes in one another. As with perceiving other inputs, experience in a relationship is helpful in sharpening one's perceptions, but too much experience can actually dull our awareness. Be careful that you have not become perceptually lazy in some of your most cherished relationships.

PHYSIOLOGICAL BASES OF PERCEPTION

As mentioned earlier, human perception is a dynamic, not a static, process. How people "see" something is dependent on the information presented and on what goes on between input and output as information is processed. Since human perception depends heavily on brain functions and on the auditory and visual receptors (ears and eyes), it is worth your time to learn more about the physiological bases of perception.

Brain

The human brain is a grayish, spongy mass weighing approximately 3 pounds. Compared to the average elephant brain, which weighs 13 pounds, the human brain is small. This compact information processing system, though, is amazing in terms of its functions. It serves as the main response center for motor functions as well as for cognitive functions. Containing somewhere between 10 and 14 billion nerve cells, the human brain monitors, directs, and coordinates your behavior, even making it possible for you to carry on a conversation with your passengers as you drive your car. The cerebral cortex, the largest part of the brain system, is made up of an interconnected network of neurons that facilitates thought processes, thereby making it possible for you to tell stories, talk on the phone, or relate to a friend what happened to you last night.

At birth, the human brain is not yet fully developed. Consequently, newborn babies cannot walk or talk or execute many mental functions until the brain matures along with the rest of the body. By comparison, a newborn horse

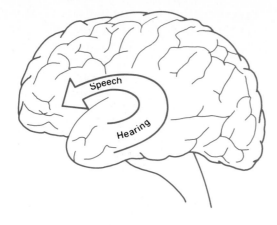

FIGURE 2.1   **Hearing to Speech in the Cerebral Cortex**

can stand up after birth and begin walking. Humans require 10 to 12 months before they walk. This temporary deficiency is caused by a lack of myelination of some of the neurons. Myelin refers to the coating that encases the exterior of neurons. Until a neuron is sufficiently myelinated (coated with myelin), it will not function to its capacity. Myelination is a large part of the first year of brain growth.

Neurons vary in size. Some are one millimeter in length, others are much larger. In fact, one nerve cell extends from your head to your foot. When a neuron dies, it does not replace itself. The information stored in that neuron is lost. Fortunately, one dead neuron may not lead to a loss of memory, since information is often handled by many neurons within an immediate network. If memory loss does occur because of neuron decay, relearning must take place to reestablish the information in memory.

The brain stores both verbal and nonverbal information, with the left hemisphere (for 90 percent of the population) controlling verbal responses and the right hemisphere controlling nonverbal responses.[1] Although researchers are still learning how the brain functions during speech and hearing, figure 2.1 illustrates what is generally believed to happen when someone hears a message and then takes a turn at speaking. As you can see, humans are especially equipped for these basic communication activities.

Ears and Eyes

The brain cannot function well without external information, and the ears and the eyes serve as the main conduits through which the brain receives such information. Realistically, the brain does not "hear" or "see" anything. It receives electrical-chemical impulses sent by the sensory receptors. With these signals the brain processes information. Thus, it is crucial that the impulses sent to the brain are representative of the external input. If the signals sent are impaired or inaccurate, processing errors will occur. The fidelity of these signals is dependent on the proper functioning of the ears and eyes.

The accuracy of human hearing is governed by the strength of the trans-

120 — Some rock concerts
        Pain threshold

100 — Jackhammer

80 — Noisy city traffic

       Vacuum cleaners

60 — Conversations

40 — People rustling about in
       a room

20 — Whispers

0 — Hearing threshold

FIGURE 2.2 **Common Sounds in dB**

mitted signal and by the signal conduction capacity of the hearing organs. Signal strength is a function of loudness and pitch. Loudness refers to the amplitude of the signal, measured in decibels (dB), whereas pitch refers to the cycles per second (cps) of the wavelength of the signal. Fortunately, most normal conversational speech falls nicely within our normal hearing range in terms of both loudness (50–60 dB) and pitch (1000–1500 cps). Figure 2.2 presents some common environmental sounds with which you can compare dB levels.

In terms of signal conduction capabilities, the human ear is unusually strong. Human hearing is a high fidelity operation that involves four different signal forms. For instance, a sound that starts out as air movements is ultimately translated, with very little distortion, into electrical-chemical impulses. This allows hearing to be remarkably accurate. Given a clear signal and properly functioning ears, hearing should present few problems in interpersonal communication. But as you will learn in Chapter 7, accurate listening does not automatically follow accurate hearing.

Although it is certainly possible to communicate without the benefit of vision, visual inputs are significant to communication, particularly in perceiving nonverbal messages. Seeing speakers as well as hearing them helps listeners understand the message.[2] Similar to auditory signals, visual signals can be measured in terms of amplitude and cycles per second. With vision, amplitude (brightness) refers to the amount of light reflected off an object. If there is not enough reflected light, we cannot see. In terms of cycles per second of visual signals, the visible light spectrum ranges from 400,000 cps (red color) to 800,000 cps (violet color). From a comparative point of view, humans are not particularly gifted in vision. Some animals can see well in the dark; humans cannot. Some animals can see in all directions (front, back, left, right); humans are stuck with frontal vision, and limited peripheral vision.

From an interpersonal communication perspective, the importance of hearing and vision is in how their inputs are coordinated by the brain. In face-to-face interaction, the brain simultaneously stores the speaker's words and actions to create a complete account of the exchange. Information stored both auditorily and visually is easier to recall later. In fact, it is possible to recall what someone said by having only the visual actions as a reminder. Woodall and Folger discovered this in their two experiments. They had 72 students watch videotapes of speakers who used gestures as they spoke. Later the students were shown the same videotapes with the sound turned off and were asked to write down what the speaker was saying. Since they could not hear what the speaker was saying, they had to rely solely on the visual cues to help them remember the speaker's words. Woodall and Folger found that the recall rate was particularly good when the gestures were meaningfully related to the words spoken. For instance, if the speaker gestured with circling hand and arm motions while talking about birds flying overhead, the spoken message would be pretty obvious. Even when the gestures were not meaningfully tied to the specific words, students could still recall (with a modest amount of accuracy) what the speaker said.[3] All in all, communicators use both auditory and visual inputs (when they are available) to make sense of messages.

In retrospect, it is clear that human perception cannot be understood well without some appreciation for its physiological aspects. If humans were constructed differently, physiologically speaking, they would perceive differently. This is especially easy to notice if you have a physiological deficiency such as a hearing loss or a visual impairment. Those who do not have normal hearing or vision live in a perceptual world that is limited, and the limitations of that world affect what such people know and understand about it. Likewise, if people had expanded auditory and visual capabilities, they could know the world in more elaborate ways. These same considerations could be applied to brain capacity as well, but such speculation is unnecessary here. The next step is to consider the role of human memory in communication.

HUMAN MEMORY

Recent research into human memory is rekindling the beliefs of the classical Greek rhetoricians who held memory to be one of the five *essential* parts of rhetoric.[4] Since written records were scarce, the classical communicator had to have a good memory in order to be an effective speaker and defender of his/her rights. Today, we have many methods for filing information other than mental storage. Perhaps this has caused some people to develop lazy habits of memory. But given the spontaneity of modern interpersonal communication, people must be able to speak and listen on-the-spot with little hesitation. In a conversation, communicators rely on their memories as they call up ideas and encode and decode messages.

Short-Term Memory

Memory researchers typically divide human memory into two kinds: short-term memory (STM) and long-term memory (LTM). The difference between the two consists of more than time: it is a matter of functions.

STM is an "immediate" memory. It serves to suspend information long enough to use it or to store it in long-term memory. You use STM when you rehearse a phone number as you are dialing it. STM is needed when you take notes in class. Specifically, you must mentally preserve what the professor said while you write it down. Furthermore, you have to listen to what is coming up as well. All of these activities require STM.

STM is a temporary, rapidly changing memory system. STM lasts as long as it needs to, but most estimates range from 10 to 30 seconds.[5] The contents of STM change quickly, so you must be alert so that you do not forget information. Breakdowns in STM can occur when there is too much information coming at you at one time or when the information is too complex to handle quickly. In such cases, the information needs to be preserved for a longer time. To extend the life of information in STM, rehearsal is necessary. By rehearsal we mean mentally repeating the information to yourself to postpone forgetting. Since information fades rapidly without rehearsal, people need to rehearse information until it is used or else stored in long-term memory. College students taking notes in class often rehearse silently the teacher's ideas as they are writing them down. Once they get the ideas on paper they can suspend rehearsal. When a woman discloses her phone number to a man at a social gathering, the man will need to rehearse the number and perhaps write it down, so that he may use it later.

STM is crucial for everyday conversations. For instance, when you are listening, you need to rehearse in STM what the speaker is saying while you store what the speaker said earlier. When you are speaking, you need to monitor what you are saying while you plan your next utterance. In one case, you are rehearsing with STM; in the other case, you are monitoring with STM. Figure 2.3 illustrates these functions.

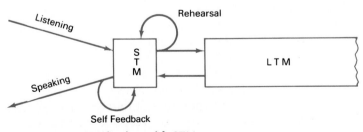

FIGURE 2.3   **Monitoring with STM**

The importance of STM for interpersonal communication cannot be overlooked, but it is just the beginning. People need draw on long-term memory for past learned experiences in order to speak and to listen. Long-term memory is a mental library of experiences that helps us make sense when we talk and understand others when they talk.

Long-Term Memory

LTM is what most people think about when they refer to memory. LTM is a permanent storage system. It contains information that has the potential to last a lifetime. Tulving suggests that there are two divisions of LTM.[6] *Episodic LTM* contains memories of events, places, songs, and so forth. It is organized according to time and space. Memories of your first car, your lines in a school play, and the combination to our lock will be stored there. Anything that has order in time and space will be handled by episodic LTM. The other side of LTM, *semantic LTM,* is a conceptual, category-based memory system. Meanings are stored there. Semantic memory contains your conceptual understanding of ideas, which allows you to properly encode and decode messages. Many of your language skills are part of semantic LTM.

Categories in semantic LTM are organized by schemata.[7] Schemata are bundles of knowledge about concepts. The items in these packages of information are linked together by association.[8] Thus, a schema about "Hawaii" might include beaches, vacation, expensive, high-rise hotels, suntans, etc. If asked to talk about Hawaii, you would use the information in your schema to weave a story about this topic. If you did not have schematic packages in semantic LTM, you couldn't produce sensibly organized utterances about the topic. So semantic LTM is a major data base from which encoding and decoding emanate.

The roles of STM and LTM in interpersonal communication are not insignificant. STM works to keep us in a conversation, holding information so that you can store it or encode it into a sensible utterance. LTM is your data bank, giving you things to talk about. When STM and LTM work properly, you can function effectively. When you experience breakdowns in one or both of these memories (for example, when you forget something), your communication competency suffers. Let's consider the problem of forgetting.

> *"Why is it that when I play Scrabble my memory for words seems to be limited to only 3- and 4-letter words!"*
> *Signed: Forgetful*

FORGETTING

Human memory, per se, cannot be directly observed. It is studied through recall research. With the exception of the neurological probe studies of the cerebral cortex, memory is always studied through post hoc recall.[9] In a typical recall study, subjects are given a body of information to remember. They are then tested later for recall. As you would expect, subjects have difficulty remembering everything they were taught. In fact, what they fail to remember often reveals more about human memory than what they remember. Thus, much of our understanding of human memory is garnered from what people forget!

What People Forget

What kinds of information do people forget most easily? Herrman and Neisser asked a number of people to judge what things they have the most difficulty remembering, things such as where they leave belongings, people's names, people's faces, and information learned by rote.[10] Their results revealed that people had the least difficulty with recognizing faces and recalling conversations and the most difficulty with rote memorization and remembering people's names. Most of us can empathize with the last two.

Why is it that people have trouble with rote memorization and people's names? Is it that we don't work hard enough to store the information properly? Or is it that most of us are either socially inept or too self-centered to remember any name but our own? Certainly rote memorization is difficult, but the answers to these questions lie not so much in our willingness to learn such information as in the nature of the information itself. Items for rote memorization and people's names are unique forms of information. Both require exact recall: paraphrases will not work. Both, typically, are not meaningful. Take people's names, for instance. A name is not a word in the usual sense. It is not something found in a dictionary. Whereas words have definitions, names do not. Words refer to classes of things. A name refers to one person or object. You can talk about "*a* loan officer" as a role that a person fills. But you cannot talk about "*A* Paul Tyler." It doesn't make any sense to do so. Names are not generalizable to many objects as words are. Consequently, a name goes with *one* object of memory, and that specific connection must be learned well enough for later recall. Remembering names, then, is another form of rote memorization, the most difficult kind of memory and often the least meaningful. With normal language you don't have to work as hard. In Chapter 4, you will learn more about this property of language that makes words easier to recall than names.

Not all problems of forgetting are a function of failures in rote memorization. Sometimes forgetting occurs because the previously learned information has decayed from memory. Other times, forgetting occurs because of conceptual confusions. These are problems of decay and interference, our next topic.

Decay and Interference

Forgetting previously learned information occurs in two ways. One is through item decay, the other is by interference. Decay occurs when an item once stored in memory is no longer available because it wasn't used or because of a change in the neuron structure in the brain. Decay occurs over time. Thus, it is not uncommon to hear people say that they can't remember something because they "learned it so long ago." But the passage of time alone does not account for decay; inactivity, or failing to recall the information often enough, also contributes to it. When you do not use an item in memory, it will not be reinforced, and decay may set in.

Interference occurs when one item of information keeps you from remembering another. We can observe interference in many of the word games that people play. In a game such as *Password* one person gives the other a verbal clue. The respondent must guess the secret word using the clue as a reminder. Respondents frequently get stumped because they get locked into one line of thought and cannot think of other options. Their immediate line of thinking is interfering with their mental search for the secret word.

Interference can also make learning information difficult, especially when two similar stimuli compete for your attention. Dissimilar stimuli cause less interference. Thus, we more easily understand a speaker while a noisy fan is rattling than we understand the speaker while another person is also talking. The noisy fan creates less interference because its signal is unlike the speech signal of the speaker. Similarity and dissimilarity can also affect memory. Many people more easily recall two different items than two similar ones. The color of your car and your shoe size will not interfere with each other during recall, but keeping track of which professor said what on a common topic in two of your classes may give you fits at exam time. These examples show how similarities can lead to confusion. The more two items are alike, the more difficulty people will have keeping them separate in memory. This is one reason that you as a student should not study notes from similar classes consecutively during finals week. It is better to arrange your study schedule so that you do not confuse what one teacher said with another. To do this, study notes from dissimilar classes in between those from similar classes.

Sometimes interference is caused by communication itself. In other words, the flow of a conversation directs memory, causing people to think of some things but not others. This can produce distortions in memory. Loftus and Palmer report that people's memory of an event can be shaped by the questions they are asked about it. A question about an automobile accident phrased as "how fast were the cars going when they smashed into one another?" brings higher speed estimates than if phrased as "How fast were the cars going when they collided?" The difference in verbs (smashed versus collided) affects the answers.[11] Likewise, Loftus, Burns, and Miller found that memories do not remain stable over time. When people discuss topics with one another, they often leave the conversation with adjusted memories about the topic based on what was said in the conversation. Thus, if witnesses to an accident talk about the accident before they testify in court, their final versions of the event will be affected by their prior conversations.[12] If these conversations cause distortions in memory, the accuracy of the testimony will suffer. So communication can be detrimental to accurate recall.

Visual and Auditory Inputs

Have you ever heard the expression, "A picture is worth a thousand words"? There is some truth to this popular notion. Information recall is affected not only by the ability to remember, but also by the way in which the information is acquired. This is especially true for children. Hayes and Birnbaum found that when preschoolers were shown televised cartoons, they paid more attention to the visual aspects of the cartoons than they did to the dialogue. Consequently, they recalled more of what they saw than what they heard. Adults, viewing the same cartoons, recalled equally well the visual and auditory information.[13] Thus, for children, visual inputs may be more important than auditory inputs. This conclusion is further solidified by Levin and Berry, who found that fourth-grade children remembered more of a news story when pictures accompanied the reading of the stories.[14] In this case, the pictures helped reinforce the information in the story, thus making recall better. Apparently, visual aids help people remember information. This applies to adults as well as to children. For example, adults tend to retain more information from televised news than they do from radio new broadcasts.[15] When the inclusion of visual data reinforces what is said, recall is easier. So a picture may be worth a thousand words when it comes time to recall information.

The quality of recall is a function of many things. You have seen how recall is affected by the type of information being recalled and by the degree to which decay and interference have taken place. You have also learned how auditory and visual information can reinforce one another to enhance recall. Still, some people are better at recalling information than others. In other words, recall is influenced by capabilities of the recaller. More specifically, recall is affected by a person's level of cognitive complexity.

COGNITIVE COMPLEXITY

Cognitive complexity refers to the level of complexity by which people mentally organize their world. As Kelly pointed out years ago, people develop personal constructs about life, and they use these personal constructs to categorize such things as events, people, and objects.[16] As our understanding of the world matures, so should the complexity of our thinking about it. For example, young children tend to think about the world more simplistically than do adults. Likewise, people just learning some new task tend to think more globally about it than specifically, which would allow them to see nuances and fine details. With more experience, their thinking should become more complex.

Schroeder, Driver and Streufert view cognitive complexity as a matter of integrative complexity.[17] In other words, cognitively simple thoughts typically stand alone in a person's mind. They are not nested with a lot of other thoughts that might modify the basic idea. Thus, if you believe that "child beaters are despicable," and if you maintain this idea as standing by itself, your level of integration about child beaters would be low. On the other hand, if you view child beaters along with other ideas such as "they have rights," "they should be helped," and/or "they are nice in other ways," then your thinking about child beaters is more complex, involving more levels of integration. Your levels of integration affect how you process information. As Littlejohn notes:

With low integration the person's thinking is quite programmed, and little creativity or self-initiative is possible. Thinking tends to be black and white; conflict among competing stimuli is minimized since differences are not noted; conclusions are concrete; and compartmentalization is rife. With high integration comes freedom of choice, high levels of behavioral adjustment and adaptation, and creativity (p. 128).[18]

Cognitive complexity manifests itself in one's perceptions of the world. Highly complex people see the complexities of life. Simple people perceive ideas, objects, and other people in stereotypical ways. Thus, different levels of cognitive complexity lead to different degrees of cognitive differentiation.

Cognitive Differentiation

Whenever people observe something, they do so with different levels of discrimination. Some people can look at an object and see many facets of it. Others see only the most apparent features of the object. For example, a recruiter for a professional basketball team may pay little attention to the final score of a college basketball game that she is scouting but be able to describe in detail a number of skillful moves that a particular prospect displayed during the game. Likewise, an artist looking at an art exhibit would see many features about the exhibit that an untrained tourist would miss. In essence, cognitive differentiation refers to the number of variables that a person uses to make sense out of a stimulus object. Those who are more cognitively complex use more variables to categorize objects and thus would be more differentiating in their judgments (compared to those who are less complex).

This carries over into our interpersonal relationships. Hale observes that the more complex a person's thinking is, the more he/she will see both good and bad qualities in others.[19] This can be illustrated by the child beater mentioned earlier. If you are like most people, your negative feelings about child beaters would make it difficult for you to see any good qualities in such a person. In this case, you would be operating with low cognitive complexity. If, on the other hand, you were able to view the child beater with high cognitive complexity, you might notice some of the child beater's positive qualities. As Crockett reminds us, cognitively complex individuals view others more open-mindedly than do those who are cognitively simple.[20] Given that everyday interpersonal communication can provide opportunities to meet many different kinds of people, a good dose of cognitive complexity is not a bad idea.

Traits and States

Whenever you categorize others or attempt to explain why they do what they do, you can approach the task from two different theories about human behavior. One is called the trait approach and is a popular method of identifying different kinds of people. This theory posits that people behave according to innate or learned personality traits. A trait is simply an enduring personality characteristic that is identified with a person. Physical traits include height, weight, hair and eye color, build, shoe size, etc. Psychological traits might include shyness, aggressiveness, temperament, frugality, honesty, and so forth. Since traits are considered to be a potentially permanent part of one's personality, they are useful in explaining why a person acts in a particular way. Thus, people who have high IQs may be labeled as "smart." Taller people may be seen as having "more leadership potential." If we are not careful, though, the trait approach can lead us into a cognitively simple frame of mind, thereby producing inaccurate stereotypes about people, such as that taller people make better leaders than shorter people.

The second theory is called the state approach. This method explains human behavior not so much based on personality characteristics as on the situations in which behaviors are performed. Thus, a person in a financially desperate situation might break the law to relieve the financial pressures he/she is experiencing. Or an individual might become dangerously inebriated during a celebration or party. In either case, the action could be explained in part by the respective situations. If either condition recurs frequently, then we might conclude that we have a criminal on one hand and an alcoholic on the other. When we make these judgments, we have returned to the trait approach, and we must be careful to check the accuracy of our perceptions.

> *"This past weekend I went to a bar with a few friends. As the evening wore on, one of my friends who is normally quiet and reserved began to open up and talk about his emotions and some of his frustrations. He wasn't particularly loud or obnoxious, but he wasn't the guy I knew before. Can alcohol (he had a number of drinks) bring about such a change? Also, how honest is someone in this condition? After being so intimate in the bar, will he be more willing to do so later on when he is sober?"*
> *Signed: Sober*

It is probably safe to say that in viewing others we get our most accurate perceptions by considering both traits and states. A good example of this is communication apprehension, commonly called stage fright. Many people have a fear of speaking to others, a trait that they carry with them. But the trait may not manifest itself in all communication situations. A person may have an intense fear of standing up in front of an audience and giving a speech, but have considerably less apprehension about talking on the telephone or chatting with a friend over a cup of coffee. Though not necessarily caused by stage fright, the country-western singer Mel Tillis suffers from stuttering, but only when he is talking, not when he is singing. In either case, we see how certain behaviors can be explained as traits and states.

The trait-state comparison can be applied to a number of interpersonal communication situations as well. For instance, a person might be seen as a "caring" person, but exhibit that trait more openly when dealing with children than, say, when dealing with adult strangers. Likewise, people who are seen as "talkative" may be more verbose at work than at a party. Thus, the manifestations of traits are affected by the contexts (states) in which they can be performed. A cognitively complex interpersonal communicator realizes this and judges others accordingly.

IMPROVING YOUR MEMORY

One of the things that we know about human memory is that sometimes STM can interfere with your ability to process additional new information. In other words, people who are unable to transfer information in STM to LTM (or to somewhere else) quickly will have to repeatedly rehearse the information in STM so that it is not lost. If you are too busy rehearsing data in STM, you cannot devote much energy to currently available input. The key to avoiding this problem is to dump the information that is in STM. How you do it, though, makes a difference. Some people write themselves notes, then proceed to lose the notes! Others try to actively memorize the information, then discover later that they have forgotten it.

Writing yourself a note is probably the best way to remember something for later use. But your method for leaving yourself notes is crucial. You must place your notes in the vicinity of the place you will be at when you need to remember the information. For instance, if you need to call a colleague before you leave home for work the next morning, don't lie in bed the night before worrying about it. Place a note in your drawer containing your socks, or put it on top of your shoes in the closet. Do not place it in the shower unless you have a well-grounded, waterproof telephone in your shower. If you need to stop at the television repair shop on the way home from work, place a note on your car's speedometer. In either case, you should anticipate where you are going to be and then set your reminders in their best place. If you do so, you will be able to set aside your concern and pay attention to current inputs.

Another suggestion for improving your memory is related to LTM. If it is true that the brain can store anything presented to it, then the key to recalling something at a later time is in the cues used for recall. In other words, you could probably remember any particular day of your life if I could provide the right memory cues for you. Memories always have cues associated with them. This is best illustrated by the "that reminds me of" phenomenon. Suppose I said to you, tell me a joke. You might be hard-pressed to come up with a decent joke. On the other hand, if I tell you a joke first, it might remind you (cue you) of one that you know. The same thing happens in everyday conversations. We remind each other of what we know. To enhance your ability to remember ideas, seek the input of others. Get them to talk to you about the thing you are trying to remember. They might cue your memory when you cannot do it alone.

SUMMARY

People communicate what they know, experience, and sense. Knowing, experiencing, and sensing are all part of perception. How people filter information and how well their memories work help determine what they talk about and how they listen to others. Without STM and LTM it would be difficult to speak and listen or remember what was said or who said it. Unfortunately, we still forget information. How much we forget is dependent on how much we use the information learned and how well we have it stored in memory. Furthermore, the research in cognitive complexity reminds us that people differ in their perceptual skills. Since we vary in cognitive complexity, we don't perceive the world in exactly the same ways, and thus we don't all communicate exactly alike.

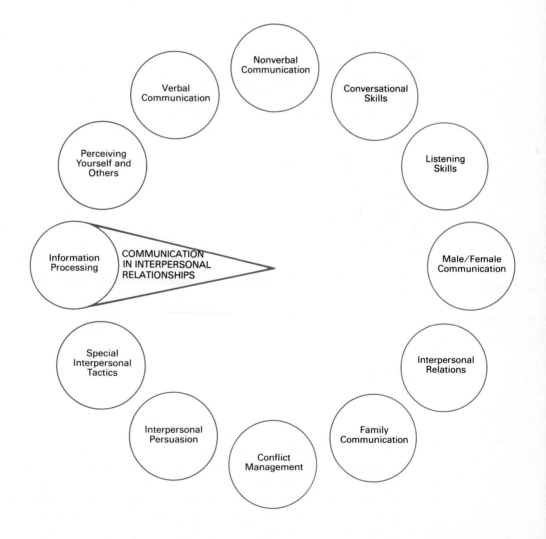

THEORY INTO PRACTICE _____

Here are some exercises that will demonstrate how perception works in your personal and interpersonal lives.

Exercise 2.1: What Can You Remember?

Purpose: To discover what kind of information people remember best.

Materials: Paper and pencil.

Time Required: 30 minutes.

Procedure: This is an exercise in memory. Divide into groups of two. One person should find a paragraph in one of the subsequent chapters of this book that the class has not yet been assigned. Look for a paragraph that has approximately 3–10 sentences. Read the paragraph aloud to your partner. When you are finished your partner is to write down as much of the paragraph as he/she can remember. Then you are to switch roles. Have your partner choose another paragraph for you to recall after it is read aloud. When both of you have completed this recall test, discuss what you recalled and didn't recall, and draw conclusions about the kind of information that is easiest to remember and hardest to remember. After everyone has done this, the instructor will conduct a class discussion which will focus on the factors that determine what is recalled and what is not.

Questions to Ask: (1) Which parts of the paragraph (beginning, middle, end) were the easiest to recall? the hardest? (2) How does the writing style or word choice affect memory? (3) What should writers do to make information more memorable to readers? (4) What did you learn about memory and recall doing this exercise?

Exercise 2.2: How to Strike a Match

Purpose: Human information processing occurs when a listener processes a speaker's message based on what he/she already has stored in memory. The purpose of this exercise is to demonstrate how simple instructions can be impossible to follow without prior knowledge.

Materials Needed: None.

Time Required: 15 minutes.

Procedure: This is a role-playing exercise requiring two people. One person will be the "instructor," the other the "student." The instructor is to explain, orally, to the student how to strike a match taken from a book of matches. The student is to play someone who has never seen or used matches. The instructor cannot use an actual book of matches, but can use hand gestures and drawings during the instructions. The student should ask questions when he/she doesn't understand the instructions. The exercise is over when the student feels that all questions have been answered and when he/she could actually perform the task.

Questions to Ask: (1) What assumptions about the student did the instructor make that caused problems? (2) Which questions were most fruitful for the student? (3) Under what circumstances would it be possible to teach people something new, something with which they have had no prior experiences?

3

PERCEIVING
YOURSELF AND OTHERS

The term "interpersonal" is comprised of two parts: "inter," meaning between, and "personal," meaning people. Thus, interpersonal communication is about communication between people. As such, communication is affected by the thoughts, emotions, and intentions of the people communicating. To understand interpersonal communication, then, you need to know more about people.

WHAT'S AHEAD

In this chapter, we will explore several dimensions of the communicator. A major focus will be the self-concept and how people monitor themselves. Then we will discuss self-esteem, self-disclosure, and interpersonal trust. Each of these plays a significant role in determining how people communicate with each other. In the section on communicator competence, you will learn the basic communication skills that all competent communicators should possess. Finally, we will offer advice on improving your self-image.

SELF-CONCEPT

Of all the psychological variables available for consideration, perhaps none is more important than the self-concept. The self-concept is your attitude about you as a person. It is how you see yourself and how you see others seeing you.[1] For instance, you might see yourself as a good dancer. Because others have complimented you on your dancing skills, "good dancer" becomes part of your self-concept. Likewise, you may have discovered that people are persuaded when you talk. This observation leads you to believe that you are an effective communicator. Your self-concept, however, is not simply one attitude about yourself. It is comprised of many perceptions, some positive, and some negative.

People are not born with attitudes about themselves; they must be learned. This means that the environment, as well as your personality characteristics, influences your self-concept. Part of your self-concept is related to innate personality traits, but these are also related to your attitudes about your self. In other words, people learn their self-concepts within the confines of their personality traits, but these traits do not add up to self-concepts. Consequently, some of us will not be very good chess players because our abstract thinking skills are not developed enough to help us become good chess players. Personality traits may influence self-concepts, but they do not define them. Such definition must come from experience. Given that it is more than an exercise of personality traits, the self-concept must be acquired socially. In other words, it must be discovered, developed, maintained, and changed through social interaction. People learn about themselves by observing themselves in action, especially as they relate to others. As Mead pointed out years ago, the self is comprised of roles and attributes and is learned through interacting with others.[2] Thus, a person may see herself as a successful lawyer who is attractive and plays an above-average game of racquetball. Such a healthy self-concept comes from the roles (lawyer) and attributes (attractive, above-average racquetball player) that this person is recognized for. In essence, people learn their self-concepts through social interaction, in which communication is central.

Conditioning

How does social interaction provide people with self-concepts? It is a matter of conditioning and reinforcement. Conditioning, whether classical or operant, occurs when the learner associates two events as "going together." In classical conditioning, this association occurs when the learner responds a certain way to the presence of a stimulus that previously did not cause such a response. Pavlov's dog is the best-known example of classical conditioning.[3] Pavlov was able to get the dog to salivate to the ring of a bell before the meat powder was injected into the dog's mouth. The dog learned to associate the ringing bell with the expectation of food, thereby initiating a response long before the presence of the food. Similarly, many people associate certain upcoming situations with feelings of nervousness or inadequacy. For example, students who experience a lot of test-taking anxiety can be made uncomfortable when someone mentions an upcoming test. The words alone seem to produce negative reactions, and such apprehension can inhibit one's ability to study effectively for the exam. Furthermore, these undesirable feelings of apprehension become part of a person's self-concept.

People can also learn their self-concepts through operant conditioning, in which learners associate their performance with subsequent outcomes. In this type of conditioning, people realize that their behavior has social consequences, some of which are pleasing, others of which are not. People learn to fear public speaking in this manner. If you have had positive experiences giving speeches (audience approval, good feedback, etc.), you will have good feelings about public speaking. On the other hand, if giving speeches has been painful for you, you will have negative attitudes about public speaking and about yourself as a public speaker.[4]

Reinforcement

This brings us to the concept of reinforcement, which is most closely related to operant conditioning. Reinforcement refers to the rewarding or punishing nature of reactions to your behavior, reactions which increase or decrease the likelihood that you will repeat a particular behavior. Rewards can come in many forms, such as praise, pay increases, prizes, or seeing that your friends are persuaded by your arguments. Rewards can also occur through removing some pain you are experiencing (medication to treat an illness, reassigning you to a less stressful job, etc.). Punishment, on the other hand, occurs when your behavior results in pain, such as a penalty for tardiness or a scolding for making a mistake. Punishments can also occur when something you like is withheld from you, such as a promotion at work or a driver's license because of your accident record.

In interpersonal communication, rewards and punishments come in the form of positive and negative feedback. Nods of agreement or smiles of approval can be rewarding to a speaker. Likewise,negative feedback can be devastating to a speaker, especially when the speaker interprets this kind of feedback as an indication of personal weakness. Interpersonal feedback is one of the main vehicles for reinforcing a person's self-concept. People who receive a lot of positive feedback for their communication behaviors typically have high self-concepts. People who experience little positive feedback can develop low self-concepts.

A good self-concept is, according to Maslow, what people naturally strive to attain. Through self-actualization (becoming all you can be), people develop healthy attitudes about themselves. Healthy self-attitudes supposedly affect how people look at themselves and the world. A fully actualized person, then, accurately perceives reality, acts spontaneously, accepts herself/himself, has a sense of humor, is not defensive, and willingly explores the environment to try new things.[5] These behaviors can be facilitated (or thwarted) through interacting with others. To some degree, then, everyone's self concept is in the hands of his/her colleagues. The more they reinforce you, the more you can become what you want to be.

In sum, a healthy (or unhealthy) self-concept is learned by observing your own behavior and observing how others react to you. The image that you ultimately construct about yourself may be influenced by your innate personality characteristics, but it will also depend on your social effectiveness. If people reward you with positive feedback, your self-concept can grow. If you experience a lot of negative feedback from others, your self-concept can suffer. In any event, people are not born with self-concepts, they learn them over time.

SELF-MONITORING

How much people understand about themselves comes from their assessments of their own behaviors. This is where self-monitoring comes in. Self-monitoring occurs when people pay close attention to their immediate actions. Thus, a man asking a woman for a date may be very conscious of how well he is performing the task. Likewise, when you are giving a public speech, you are likely to be very aware of your voice, your appearance, and how you are coming across.

A certain amount of self-monitoring is necessary to develop a self-concept that can be confirmed socially by others. If you cannot observe yourself, you cannot develop a socially based self-concept. For most of us, this is not a problem. In fact, people may be too self-conscious and overly concerned about their images and social acceptance. This is especially true of teenagers, who often conform to the demands of peers to be accepted.

Individual Differences in Awareness

Some people are better at self-monitoring than are others. Theater performers, for instance, are known for observing their own behaviors, both on and off the stage. Lawyers in a courtroom or ministers in their pulpits would be very aware of their actions as they attempt to persuade others. Such awareness can be good, because the more people are skilled at self-monitoring, the more adaptive they will be when they communicate.[6] They will be able to adjust their communication behavior to fit the needs of the occasion.

It is important to realize, though, that self-monitoring is not a steady activity. In some circumstances (such as asking for a date or giving a speech) people are very aware of themselves. Other times they seem to float along without much concern for their self-concepts. Berger and Roloff label periods of low self-monitoring as functioning on "automatic pilot."[7] At such times, behavior is primarily habitual and typically not very memorable. If you have ever driven to work, home, or school and, after arriving there, wondered how you made it because you don't remember what you saw along the way, you know what Berger and Roloff are talking about. Just how much of your interpersonal communication behavior is automatic rather than well planned and monitored is unknown to researchers at this time. But it is clear that people will be differentially aware of themselves and their behaviors in different circumstances.

Vulnerability to Influence

Whenever a situation causes discomfort and makes us more self-conscious, we become vulnerable to the influence of others. King observes that, for the most part, when people are socially anxious they will be more easily persuaded then when they are not so aroused.[8] The reason for this is that when people feel a high degree of uncertainty about themselves, they look to others for guidelines on how to act. Furthermore, the influence from others may be unintended and indirect. Thus, when a 14-year-old girl wears a particular brand of jeans, she may not be doing it to persuade her friends to do the same, yet many will follow suit, particularly those who are unsure of their social acceptance.

Likewise, people who have healthy self-concepts are more likely to enjoy observing their own behavior. In fact, Gibbon and Wicklund report that when people receive positive feedback about themselves, they subsequently enjoy listening to their own voices, without the typical embarrassment that often comes from hearing our own voices.[9] People who are good at self-monitoring can actually use the information provided by different situations to help them adapt successfully to their changing world.

CASE STUDY _____

Sometimes we don't realize just how much influence others have on us. One evening a college student named Kate was taking stock of herself when she realized that much of what she said and did was a function of her sorority's influence. She noticed a lot of similarities in her life and in the lives of her sorority sisters. For instance, she talked like her sisters, drove a 2-door hardtop car like many of them did, listened to the same music and patronized the same restaurants they did, and dressed similarly to them. She also sat at the football games with them and went to the same parties afterwards. Although she was having fun, she wondered about her individual identity. Her doubts came to a head when she decided that her major was no longer satisfying to her. She remembered that her father insisted she choose a major with lucrative job opportunities. Kate's mother, on the other hand, wanted her to be happy and choose a major she enjoyed. Her sisters in her sorority were predominantly business majors, and many of her sorority sisters dated men from fraternity X who were business majors. All signs pointed to a business major for Kate, but she wasn't sure. Given Kate's current state of uncertainty, we would expect her to be especially vulnerable to influence. What would you advise her to do?

SELF-ESTEEM

Closely related to self-concept is the notion of self-esteem. Whereas self-concept refers to attitudes about yourself, self-esteem refers to how you value yourself—how much you think you are worth as a person. Self-esteem is more evaluative than self-concept, which is a more descriptive, involving your mental description of your roles, attributes, and attitudes about these things. Self-esteem, on the other hand, is a more general estimate of your intrinsic value as a human being. People with high self-esteem like themselves and have confidence in their abilities. People with low self-esteem don't think that they are important and may question their ability to "do anything right."

As with self-concept, self-esteem must be learned. Childhood experiences can make a difference in one's self-esteem. A child who is overly criticized and constantly compared to others who are "better" could develop low self-esteem; a child who is raised in a supportive home and encouraged to explore the environment will probably develop positive self-esteem. These feelings of self-worth will help the child cope with the demands of life. Developing a strong sense of self-esteem is a need that everyone possesses, and we never seem to outgrow the need for "positive strokes." When your self-esteem needs are not met, it can affect your communication behavior, which is why self-esteem is so important in interpersonal communication.[10]

In a classic study of self-esteem and social influence, Arthur Cohen discovered that the way in which people responded to success and failure was dependent on their self-esteem.[11] People with high self-esteem tended to respond to failure by evaluating themselves more highly than did people with low self-esteem, who took failure more personally and looked to others for ways to improve. Furthermore, Cohen found that people with low self-esteem were more susceptible to influence from others, particularly if the others were people with high self-esteem. People with high self-esteem were not so easily influenced by others. The implications of this study are clear: people need a sufficiently high level of self-esteem if they wish to develop some independence from the influence of the crowd. Whenever people are unsure about their self-worth, they are subject to the influence of others, thereby giving over control of their behavior to others.

Our interest in self-esteem as a variable in interpersonal communication stems from the fact that how communicators feel about themselves affects how they communicate and react to communication. You have already seen that people with low self-esteem are more susceptible to persuasion than people with high self-esteem. There is even evidence that self-esteem is related to communication apprehension. Those who experience unusually high levels of communication apprehension tend to have low self-esteem.[12] Such people not only feel that they are poor communicators, they don't like themselves very much either. Such feelings may inhibit one's professional success, as well as interpersonal success. Obviously, low self-esteem and high communication apprehension are undesirable.

Self-esteem even affects one's outlook on messages. Leventhal and Perloe report that subjects with high self-esteem were more influenced by optimistic messages than by threatening messages, while subjects with low self-esteem showed the opposite pattern.[13] This study shows that because people with low self-esteem have a negative attitude, they are more receptive to negative messages. This creates an undesirable cycle of negativeness that simply reinforces low self-esteem. Furthermore, people with low self-esteem are not likely to interact with others much if they are burdened by these poor evaluations of themselves. Low self-esteem will manifest itself in the amount of self-disclosure that such people will engage in. It is to this concern that we now turn.

SELF-DISCLOSURE

Sidney Jourard defines self-disclosure as the act of revealing personal information to others.[14] Within intimate relationships, such communication is common. In fact, some researchers use the amount of self-disclosure as a measure of how interpersonal a conversation is. To some degree Miller and Steinberg do so when they suggest that a conversation becomes more interpersonal as the participants talk more about psychological information (attitudes, values, personal experiences, etc.) and less about sociological information (hometown, occupation, etc.).[15] As John Powell maintains, people talk to one another on different levels. His five-level system ranges from the shallowness of clichéd talk ("Nice day, isn't it?" "Yes, it is") to peak communication, in which people talk openly, exposing their self-concepts.[16] As people become more intimate with each other their style of talk changes. Self-disclosure is one way that conversations shift as perceived intimacy levels shift. Differences in self-disclosure, however, are a matter of degree rather than kind. Some conversations have more self-disclosure than others. To illustrate this, Figure 3.1 shows self-disclo-

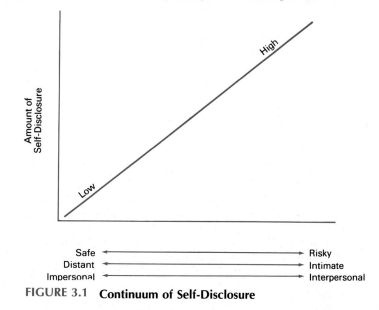

FIGURE 3.1   **Continuum of Self-Disclosure**

sure as a continuum rather than as an all-or-none variable. High self-disclosure, as the figures shows, is riskier than low self-disclosure. Furthermore, it implies more intimacy and a more interpersonal relationship.

Reciprocity

Reciprocal self-disclosure occurs when *both* communicators share personal information. If one discloses while the other does not, there is no reciprocity. For example, if I tell you that my oldest child is having difficulty in school and you do not respond by disclosing how you or your children had troubled times in school as well, my disclosure was not reciprocated by you. Recent research into self-disclosure suggests that its success may depend in part on reciprocity. For instance, Hosman and Tardy found that people who shared personal information, after someone shared first with them, were viewed as better communicators than those who did not reciprocate.[17] Apparently, people expect reciprocity when they reveal things about themselves; when it doesn't happen, they take a dim view of the other person. However, the amount of self-disclosing, even when reciprocating, is a function of the level of intimacy between the people. Archer and Berg found that the limits of self-disclosure depended on the discloser's judgment of how much would be appropriate under the circumstances.[18]

Although self-disclosure is desirable under the proper circumstances, one cannot expect equal reciprocity of another person when revealing something of oneself. In a well-designed experiment, Lynn found that people were more willing to reveal something of themselves to those who also revealed something of themselves than to those who did not.[19] Lynn also discovered that people disclosed less when responding to other people who disclosed little. However, people did not necessarily disclose more when responding to people who disclosed a good deal. In other words, a high degree of self-disclosure by one communicator will encourage the other communicator to disclose more as well, although the other communicator may not necessarily disclose a comparable amount. Apparently, people find self-disclosure sufficiently painful to want to regulate how much they do it even if the other person seems to be disclosing more openly.[20] In addition, another person's self-disclosure can cause discomfort for some people. Lange and Grove found that when given a choice of who they would like to interact with, most people chose others who were moderate self-disclosers rather than high or low self-disclosers.[21] Finally, it is possible that too much self-disclosure may be bad for your mental health. Chelune and Figueroa present evidence that people who use self-disclosure too much are just as neurotic as those who refuse to use self-disclosure at all. The least neurotic people are those who use self-disclosure in moderation.[22]

Traditionally, openness has been seen as a necessary condition for moving a relationship into intimacy. Recently, however, Rawlins has questioned the value of open communication. He finds that people need to learn to be more restrained about revealing personal information, as well as to learn to be honest. Indeed, he concludes that "we cannot mandate a specific style for relational interaction, and scholars should be cautious in stressing open communication as the hallmark of intimacy" (p. 13).[23] Openness and self-disclosure, then, are not categorically beneficial to interpersonal communication. Sometimes, it is prudent to restrain such activity.

In sum, self-disclosure, though desirable in intimate relationships, does not ensure effective communication. Honesty and openness have value, but people cannot expect equal treatment when revealing something of themselves to others. Self-disclosure is worked out between communicators within the context of the relationship and the topic of discussion. Competent communicators will be sensitive to the need for self-disclosure and will employ it at an appropriate time and place.

Dimensions of Self-Disclosure

Self-disclosure is not simply "spilling out" your innermost feelings. According to Wheeless, acts of self-disclosure can be assessed by at least five criteria:

1. The amount of disclosing done.
2. The honesty/accuracy of the information disclosed.
3. The positiveness/negativeness of the information disclosed.
4. The degree of intent to disclose.
5. The depth of disclosed information.[24]

Each instance of self-disclosure can be evaluated by these criteria. Thus, some acts of self-disclosure will fall short on one or more of the above criteria when compared to other acts of self-disclosure. The validity of these criteria is reinforced by Wheeless, and by Tardy, Hosman, and Bradac, who found similar criteria in subsequent research.[25] Self-disclosure, then, is something that can be controlled by the discloser. Because of this, communicators could choose to use self-disclosure when they engage in interpersonal communication. Although there are some differences of opinion among scholars as to the value of self-disclosure in interpersonal communication, a review of the literature on self-disclosure led Bochner to conclude that, although people believe it is appropriate to use self-disclosure with those they like, self-disclosure does not cause people to like one another.[26] In fact, he found that liking someone may actually inhibit self-disclosure, since people would not want to offend those they like by getting too personal or saying things that others might find offensive. This leads to the issue of trust, an important component of interpersonal communication.

> *"I have trouble communicating with my 15-year-old daughter. I've always encouraged her to be open and honest with me, and I've tried to be open and honest with her. I used to trust her, but lately I've caught her in some lies, and I don't trust her very much anymore. She still tells me some things, but how can I get her to be more open and stop the lying?"*
> Signed: *Concerned Mom*

INTERPERSONAL TRUST

Effective self-disclosure calls for a certain amount of trust between the disclosers. Without trust, self-disclosure would be risky. Consequently, as a relationship matures between two people, so should the bond of trust between them. Intimate confidants must be able to assume that their partners will not use disclosed personal information to say and do things that will place them in a vulnerable position.

Trusting is risky, and in relatively new relationships it is sometimes difficult to trust the other person. The reason for this is that there may not be any real evidence that the other person has your welfare in mind. Sometimes we have to trust unknown others or else not do business with them. For instance, when you check your luggage with an airline porter, you must assume that your bags will get on the plane and be at your destination when you arrive. As many of us have experienced, this will not always be the case. If you have a lot of baggage and cannot carry it with you on the plane, you have to trust the airline personnel to do their job properly. Trusting, under such circumstances, is always a gamble.

In most interpersonal relationships, trust is earned. It grows over time. Usually you can trust your close friends and your parents because they have shown that they will not hurt you. Trusting is learned from past experience and is correlated with self-disclosure. The more you trust someone, the more likely you will share personal information with that person.

Disclosing information, without a certain amount of established trust has its dangers. For instance, the information you disclose to another may be used against you later. Or you might say the wrong thing and offend your partner without intending to do so. Trust should provide security and a cushion for error, so that you do not pay a horrendous social price for revealing your feelings to someone else. When trust is broken, a relationship suffers. That's why it is important for people to work toward building trust in others. Had Richard Nixon kept this principle in mind, he might have completed his second term in office without having to face the disgrace of resigning. Unfortunately, his handling of the Watergate scandal cost him the people's trust.

COMMUNICATION COMPETENCE

As mentioned in chapter 1, success in life often depends on how competent you are as a communicator. Communication skills, then, are as important for a student of communication as is communication theory.[27] Such a concern has stimulated a number of researchers to explore in detail the elements of communication competency. Generally speaking, communication competency is a proficiency notion, a measure of your communication skill and effectiveness as manifested in your conversations with others.

People are not born with communication competency. They must learn it, and sometimes the road to competency takes amusing turns. Most of us as children said things we shouldn't have and were corrected by our parents or caretakers with such admonishments as, "Stop interrupting when we are talking," or "You shouldn't say things like that to other people," or "Where did you learn *that* word?" These familiar instances remind us that competency is often acquired through trial and error. In fact, communication competency is rarely learned through organized teaching—you pick it up as you go along.

According to Berger, effective communicators "must learn to enact behavioral routines which are deemed appropriate to the particular individuals and social situations where they are interacting."[28] Communication competency depends on the choices that communicators make as they interact. These choices are based on the communicators' knowledge of the rules of language, the accepted procedures for enacting a conversation, and the immediate situation. Competent communicators, then, have mastered the rules for effective interaction and can execute them successfully—often without being able to recite the rules they are following.[29]

In one sense, everyone possesses communication competency. As situations change, though, so may a communicator's competence. People are not equally competent in all situations. Thus you might perform quite competently talking with a friend on the telephone, but not do as well in a job interview. Those who are skilled at handling a wide range of situations are seen as more generally competent than those who do not have this flexibility.

Strategic Acts and Desired Outcomes

Competency involves many things, but based on the works of Shimanoff, Frentz and Farrell, Delia, Searle, and others, communication competence seems to be a matter of strategic acts and desired outcomes.[30] Strategic acts can be identified by the messages that communicators employ. Strategic messages are not simply ceremonial or habitually uttered words and sentences. They are deliberately phrased messages to accomplish particular goals. For instance, a competent parent knows how to reprimand a teenager who has just wrecked the family car so that the child does not lose all sense of self-esteem but still understands the parent's anger.

Desired outcomes refer to meeting one's goals, such as creating understandings with others or persuading them. Since people accomplish many of their goals through interacting with others, they must possess some degree of communication competence. Thus, communication competence may be formally defined as *one's ability to manage interaction through performing speech acts and enacting conversations that will produce understanding and/or influence.* Competency, then, depends on how you act and what effect you have on others. You are a competent communicator when your speaking and listening skills (along with your social skills) are effective with others.

Other-Oriented

To successfully combine actions with desired outcomes, competent communicators have to be both good conversationalists and socially sensitive people. Competent communicators fit their strategies within the perspective of their listeners. As Wiemann notes, "the competent communicator is one who is other-oriented, while at the same time maintaining the ability to accomplish his own interpersonal goals."[31] To be a competent communicator you need to combine your communication skills with an understanding of your audience to accomplish your goals. For instance, a competent husband will know his wife well enough to adapt his communication behaviors to fit her and the goals of the interaction. On the other hand, an incompetent communicator will plunge ahead without thinking about these things. Likewise, a teacher that has communication competence will not only be a clear and effective lecturer and discussion leader, but will also choose and present material that fits the level of the students. Being other-oriented is an important part of being a competent communicator.

General Signs of Competency

Since competency is largely related to our effectiveness in interpersonal relations, a good measure of our communication competency can come from how others view us. People seem to know a competent communicator when they see one. But what do they see? Let's consider an example. The popular TV sitcom *The Mary Tyler Moore Show* involved a vivacious woman who worked in a TV newsroom for an often grumpy boss named Lou Grant. In the first episode, Lou interviews Mary for the newsroom job, and after observing her communication style, he says "You've got spunk!" Mary smiles in assent. "I hate spunk!" Lou says, and Mary's face drops. Mary obviously expected Lou to be pleased with her effervescence, but he wasn't. Mary thought she had a competent communication style; Lou did not.

Competency manifests itself in a number of ways, of which enthusiasm or effervescence are only a few. Numerous research reports tells us what competent communicators do.[32] As an example, let's consider the findings of Spitzberg.[33] According to him, competent communicators:

1. Speak fluently
2. Know when to take turns talking
3. Look at the other person when talking
4. Show approval by nodding their heads and saying "uh-hmm", etc.
5. Compliment the other person
6. Refer to the other person often
7. Smile and laugh occasionally
8. Use many gestures when speaking

If you apply the items in this list to people that you judge to be competent interpersonal communicators, you should find that they meet these standards. These are not the only things that competent communicators can do, but they are general signs of competence that apply to many different communication situations and goals. Certain situations will demand more, or less, of each of these behaviors, but in most circumstances these behaviors will be evident. As you look at the above list, notice that communication competence requires both verbal and nonverbal skills and calls for an other-orientation that facilitates the development of empathy and influence.

Skill Areas for Competency

The items listed above represent general signs of communication competency. In order to develop competency as a communicator, you need to develop skills in certain areas. If you are interested in developing your own communication competency, Glaser suggests that you practice the following skills:[34]

1. Describing feelings
2. Initiating and maintaining conversations
3. Giving and receiving compliments
4. Clarifying perceptions
5. Requesting behavior change
6. Responding to criticism
7. Paraphrasing
8. Pinpointing and documenting
9. Stating intentions and purpose
10. Saying no

These skill areas are only some of the possible interpersonal skills that you can work on. And, as with any set of skills, you may be quite good in some and weak in others.

IMPROVING YOUR SELF-IMAGE

There are many things you can do to improve your self-image. But first of all, you must get out of automatic pilot and become an accurate monitor of your own actions. People know you by what you say and do, so it's a good idea to work at seeing yourself as others see you. This can be accomplished through self-disclosure. In other words, you can learn about yourself by tactfully engaging others in conversations about topics important to you.

You can also enhance your self-image by promoting positive feedback from others. This can be accomplished by being a positive person yourself. If you talk positively, you can make people feel better for talking with you. If you act like a sourpuss, others will help you realize that self-image by treating as one.

Finally, you can use communication to learn more about yourself and enhance your image. By becoming an active communicator, not a shy one, you can engage others in conversations, probing their thoughts and learning how you feel in the process. Talking with others with an open mind can do wonders for your understanding of yourself and your world. If interpersonal communication frightens you, seek help through your instructor.

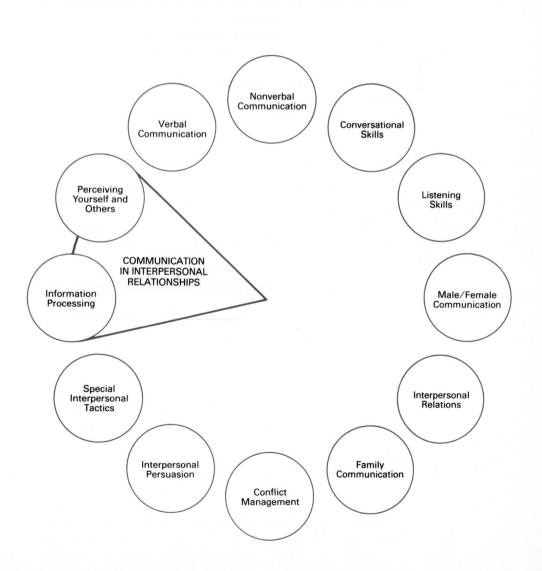

SUMMARY

In this chapter we have explored the dynamics of the self-concept. You learned that the self-concept is learned through interacting with others. In many ways, our feelings about ourselves are dependent on how others react to us. If people confirm our positive feelings about ourselves, we develop healthy self-concepts. Likewise, positive feedback helps people develop high self-esteem, i.e., feelings of self worth. The desirability of high self-esteem is made clear when we realize that self-esteem not only affects how we value ourselves but also how we interact with others. Low self-esteem is correlated with high communication apprehension, and highly apprehensive people tend to avoid communication. The consequences of unhealthy self-concepts, low self-esteem and high communication apprehension are both personal and societal. A society containing nothing but people with low self-esteem would not function well because the people would not be able to create the kind of interpersonal interdependence that makes societies work.

THEORY INTO PRACTICE

Here are some exercises that will help you understand how the self-concept operates in your daily life.

Exercise 3.1: How I See My Partner

Purpose: To show how people project a self-image to others.

Materials Needed: A pencil and the following questionnaire:
Circle the word in each of the following word pairs that best describes the person you have been talking with.

optimist   pessimist
dogmatic   open-minded
liberal   conservative
traditional   nontraditional

Using percentages (100% = absolutely yes, 0% = absolutely not), estimate the probability that your partner would:

[%] 1. Cheat on an exam.
[%] 2. Stop someone who is robbing a store at gunpoint.
[%] 3. Scalp a football ticket for twice the printed price.
[%] 4. Sign a petition to legalize marijuana.

Time Required: 40 minutes.

Procedure: Form groups of two and spend 10-15 minutes getting to know one another in terms of personal background and interests. Be sure to divide your shared time so that each person can learn about the other person. Then complete the questionnaire without letting your partner see your answers. When both of you have completed your questionnaires, swap questionnaires, and explain why you answered the way you did. Afterwards, the instructor will lead a class discussion with the following questions.

Questions to Ask: (1) How accurate were you in filling out the questionnaire? (2) Which questions were the most difficult? Why? (3) What specific things did your partner say or do to lead you to answer as you did on the questionnaire? (4) How accurate was your partner in predicting you? (5) Do you need to make any changes in your behavior to reflect the image you desire?

Exercise 3.2: Self-Esteem

Purpose: To identify those social situations that affect one's self-esteem.

Materials Needed: Paper and pencil.

Time Required: 35 minutes.

Procedure: In groups of five, develop lists of events that cause an increase in one's self-esteem (column 1) and things that result in a decrease in self-esteem (column 2). After about 15 minutes, the class will be reconvened to report and discuss the groups' lists.

Questions to Ask: (1) How many common items were there between the groups? (2) What are the implications of the commonly acknowledged items? (3) What can people do to maximize those things that enhance self-esteem?

Exercise 3.3: How I See Myself

Purpose: To help people identify their self-concepts.

Materials Needed: Pencil.

Time Required: 10 minutes.

Procedure: This is a private exercise in which you evaluate yourself on the following scales. Place an X in the space that most accurately describes you.

```
        happy :  :X:  :   :   : sad
       strong :  :X.  :   :   : weak
        quiet :  :   :   :  :X: talkative
         slow :  :   :  :X:   : fast
        brave :X:  :   :   :   : cowardly
 disorganized :  :  :X.  :   : organized
     reliable :X:  :   :   :   : unreliable
        timid :  :  :   :X.  : aggressive
         sure :  :X:  :   :   : unsure
         warm :  :X:  :   :   : cold
     dishonest :  :   :   :  :X: honest
        smart :X:  :   :   :   : dumb
     punctual :  :X:  :   :   : tardy
        short :  :X:  :   :   : tall
      graceful :  :   :  :X.  : awkward
```

Questions to Ask: (1) What did you learn about yourself doing this exercise? (2) Which items are you most sure about? least sure about? (3) In your opinion, which items are most obvious to others?

Exercise 3.4: Student Perceptions of the Instructor

Purpose: To show how students develop perceptions about their instructors.

Materials Needed: Paper and pencil.

Time Required: 40 minutes.

Procedure: Perceptions that people have of each other strongly affect interpersonal communication. By now, you have had a little time to learn about your instructor through contact in class and perhaps outside the class. Let's see how you perceive your instructor. Form groups of 5, and develop group answers to the following questions. Take about 15 minutes for your discussion.
1. Is your instructor married, single, engaged, or what?
2. Is he/she politically liberal, conservative, or moderate?
3. Would your instructor prefer to go bowling, golfing, fishing, or snow skiing?
4. How old is your instructor? *46*
5. Is he/she on a diet? *NO*
6. Would he/she prefer to travel in Mexico, Greece, or Japan?
7. In what profession could your instructor be, if he/she were not a teacher. *politican*
8. (Create your own question and answer here).

After each group has answered the above questions, reconvene the class and share the groups' answers.

VERBAL COMMUNICATION

4

When we were young children we used to retaliate when someone called us a name by saying, "sticks and stones may break my bones, but names will never hurt me." This retort may have made us feel better, but the names still hurt us psychologically. Even as adults, we know that words make a difference, and at times we may say something that we later regret. On the other hand, a well-chosen, well-timed word of praise can make someone's day. Language is important in everyday life, and it is a powerful interpersonal vehicle for establishing, maintaining, and changing relationships. Consider how carefully adolescents distinguish between the verbs "love" and "like" when talking about their feelings of affection for one another. Teenagers even develop ways of modifying "like" to suggest that they are nearing but not totally to the point of "love."

One cannot underestimate the role of verbal communication in human relationships. Without the ability to express ourselves through language, we would not be able to form the kinds of relationships we have become accustomed to. For instance, language is used to formalize wife-husband, landlord-tenant, agent-client, manager-ballplayer, and union-worker relationships. Even more informal relationships depend on the spoken word.

WHAT'S AHEAD

Verbal communication is probably the main staple in interpersonal communication, and because of its prevalence in human interaction, we may have unrealistic expectations about verbal communication. For instance, we tend to assume when we speak that our words are clear and that any misunderstanding that may occur is a problem with the receiver, not the speaker. Such an attitude may reflect some unrealistic expectations about the role of language in everyday discourse. In this chapter, we will look at the parameters of language that help us define language. Then you will learn about meanings—the area of verbal communication that causes us the most trouble. To help you understand how verbal communication functions in everyday interpersonal communication, we will review a number of studies in language research. Then we will offer some advice on how to improve your verbal communication. By the end of the chapter, you should have a greater appreciation for the complexities of verbal communication and acquire some additional insights about language in communication.

PARAMETERS OF LANGUAGE

Language is a symbol system. People use words, phrases, and sentences to stand for meanings that they are trying to communicate. People can talk about yesterday, today, and tomorrow whenever they want to. For instance, you can tell your friends about last summer's vacation. Likewise, you can talk about your future, speculating where you want to be and what you want to be doing. If language was not symbolic, you could not do these things. The symbolic nature of language is, indeed, fundamental to understanding language, but these facts explain what language does more than what language is. To understand what language is, you need to know its basic parts. Languages have three major components: a set of sounds, a grammar, and a set of meanings.[1]

3Ss: Sounds, Syntax, and Semantics

What makes a language? Many people believe a language is simply words formed from an alphabet. Such a point of view, though, is only applicable to writing. Languages are not based on writing; they are based on *speech.* Consequently, the basics of language are sounds, not letters. When particular sounds are identified as the building blocks of a language, they are called phonemes. The study of sounds used in a language is called phonology. The English phonological system contains vowel sounds and consonants sounds, which Table 4.1 illustrates. When phonemes are combined into sets, they form words. Thus, the word "cat" is comprised of three phonemes (k, æ, t).

Syntax is the way in which sentences are organized to make sense, the grammatical rules used for constructing correct sentences. Oddly enough, most

TABLE 4.1:   Some Common Phonemes in English

Consonants			
Plosives or Stops	/p/ *pea, pan*	/t/ *tea, tan*	/k/ *cat, kite*
	/b/ *bat, bill*	/d/ *date, dog*	/g/ *gas, golf*
Nasals	/m/ *man, mill*	/n/ *now, nice*	/ŋ/ *sing, hung*
Fricatives	/f/ *fat, phone*	/v/ *vat, vice*	/s/ *sip, soup*
	/z/ *zoo, xylophone*	/š/ *shall, sugar*	/ž/ *pleasure, seizure*
	/ð/ *thy, either*	/θ/ *thigh, ether*	
Liquids	/r/ *run, ring*	/l/ *let, list*	
Glides	/y/ *you, use*	/w/ *win, wet*	/h/ *hit, house*
Affricates	/č/ *chew, chum*	/ǰ/ *judge, jury*	
Vowels			
	/i/ *key, me*		
	/ɪ/ *did, hit*	/ʊ/ *full, could, hook*	
	/e/ *late, rave*	/u/ *fool, true, moon*	
	/ɛ/ *pet, neck*	/a/ *father, hot*	
	/æ/ *cat, fast*	/o/ *hope, soak*	
	/ʌ/ *cut, putt*	/ɔ/ *ought, caught*	
Diphthongs	/au/ *house, plow*		
	/oi/ *boy, oil*	/ai/ *mice, right*	
Word Examples			
	/kɔt/ = caught		
	/klač/ = clutch	/saicalogɛ/ = psychology	
	/siŋk/ = sink	/intɛlɛjɛnt/ = intelligent	
	/manapolɛ/ = monopoly	/yuniform/ = uniform	

adult speakers know the rules of grammar but cannot list all of them.[2] In other words, we can produce grammatically correct sentences and most of us can identify an incorrect sentence, even if we cannot specify the precise language rule broken. This implies that competent speakers of a language develop a sense of correctness about their language. This sense is called language competence (more on this later).

Semantics, the third major element of language, refers to the meanings that people have for words, phrases, and sentences. As you will learn later, meanings have many different levels. Furthermore, meanings differ as people differ. Two people can be using similar words yet be talking about different things. This is because meanings are in people, not in words.[3] I remember my youngest daughter's reaction to an announcement over the public address system in a nearby airport. The announcer said, "Would Mr. Smith please meet this party at the information desk in the main lobby?" My daughter turned to me and asked if she could go to the party too! Between adults, such obvious misunderstandings do not often occur because they use words conventionally so that their listeners will not be misled. But the words themselves do not have meaning, only the people do. It is up to the people to supply meaning to what they hear.

The elements of language (sounds, syntax, and semantics) are what define a language. Languages are built on speech, not on writing. Speech is primary to language, writing is secondary. Furthermore, meanings are in people, not in words. As long as people do not use words idiosyncratically, a reasonable level of understanding can be expected in verbal communication.

Language Universals

If you have ever studied a foreign language you know that each language is unique. Different languages have different vocabularies and grammars. Yet all languages have some common features, and a knowledge of these features can help you understand how language functions in interpersonal communication. The features are called language universals, and they are numerous.[4] For our purposes here, we will consider three of them.

Arbitrariness.   To say that a language is arbitrary is not to say that it is accidental, rather it is to acknowledge the fact that the words used in a language are symbolic and not necessarily tied to the things they refer to. For instance, there is nothing in the word "offspring" that makes it a better word to use to refer to our daughters than a word like "paper." That "offspring" refers to daughters or sons is arbitrary. Consequently, to know the meaning of "offspring," the listener must understand the concept of children and realize that the word "offspring" can be used to talk about this concept. The word is simply a convention for talking about the concept. And as long as people speak conventionally, the arbitrariness of the language is no problem.

Openness.   Words have a portability about them. They can be used at many different times and in many different circumstances. Furthermore, ideas can be expressed in many different ways. People can use many different words, phrases, and sentences to say essentially the same thing. Hockett calls this quality of language "openness"[5] and uses it to refer to the flexibility of language that enables people to put together different combinations of words and create an infinite number of different sentences. Consider the following exchange:

> **Terry:** What classes are you taking this semester?
>
> **Jan:** I've got 15 hours . . . most of them in my major.

Compared to:

> **Terry:** What's your class schedule like this term?
>
> **Jan:** A full load . . . mainly classes in my major.

Each exchange communicates similar information, but uses different words to do so. The openness of language, then, means that we don't have to use only certain words to express our thoughts. This flexibility makes language easier to enact, but as Foss and Hakes observe, "one consequence of this openness of language is that no one has ever heard more than a very small proportion of the sentences that could occur. Similarly, no one has ever produced more than a very small proportion of the sentences he or she could produce."[6] This is the beauty of language. It is a creative tool that people use to engage one another in communication. Its openness allows people to adjust their communication to fit many circumstances and many listeners.

Sensibleness.   Have you ever gotten lost in a conversation and had to ask, "What's your point?" Such a question illustrates the third language universal, the sense of the utterance. An utterance, to be sensible, has to have propositional content and illocutionary force.[7] Simply stated, propositional content is the assertion being made in the utterance—what the speaker is trying to say. It can usually be deduced from the words themselves by noting how the subject and object of the sentence are related. Thus, if Barry says "Pauline is a good athlete," he is connecting the idea of "Pauline" with the idea of "good athlete." The propositional content is evident.

The illocutionary force of the statement, or what the speaker is doing by making the statement, can be surmised from the context in which the utterance occurred. Why did Barry even say that Pauline is a good athlete? Was it a compliment? Was he arguing with someone who doesn't believe that Pauline is a good athlete? Or was he warning the listener, who is overconfident about defeating Pauline in a competitive match? Whatever the reason, you cannot accurately understand the utterance until its illocutionary force is made evident by its context.

Both propositional content and illocutionary force apply to whole conversations as well as to individual sentences. Most dialogue takes place within an ongoing context, and observers need to know the context to make sense out of the conversation. If this were not true, you could turn on your television set and immediately understand what's going on in a show that started 15 minutes earlier. As most of us realize, we have to watch the show for a while before we understand enough to make sense out of it. The relevance of the ongoing context is reinforced by Ellis when he writes that "naturally occurring interaction that is situated in a pattern of communicative events is not an abstracted form but a correlate of situation" (p. 36).[8] Natural language usage is "about" something, and by paying attention to the words and to the context of the utterances, you should be able to determine what the speaker is driving at.

The universal features of arbitrariness, openness, and sensibleness are found in all languages, which means that these features are necessary conditions for utterances to be called language. As such, language is something that must be understood and known by the users, otherwise people could not adequately communicate with it. This brings us to the topic of competence and performance.

Competence and Performance

Competence in communication is, in part, dependent on competence in language. In other words, the competent communicator understands the rules of language. This is *language competence*. It is distinguished from language performance, which is also a significant part of communication competency. Whereas language competence refers to the speaker's knowledge of language, *language performance* refers to the speaker's linguistic behavior, the actual sentences the speaker produces. For example, the words you are reading right now are part of my language performance. My mental ability to produce these sentences in a coherent fashion is my language competence. As you can see, language performance is readily observable. Language competence must be inferred. In other words, given my language performance, you can make judgments about my language competence. The tacit understanding of the rules of language (linguistic competence) simply cannot be observed. People do not exhibit the rules of language, they use the rules of language to speak correctly. Rules, then, are rarely communicated directly, yet they underly all utterances.

Language rules are learned by observing others use the language. They are not often taught to someone in an explicit manner. For instance, children learn language by observing it in action. By the time most children are five years old, they have mastered language well enough to begin formal education. This process of acquiring language knowledge is not simply a matter of imitation. Dale points out that it would be impossible to learn a language by imitation, since the learner would have to wait to hear all possible utterances before being able to perform them.[9] The rules that make up linguistic competence, then, must be inferred by the learners as they encounter the language in action. As with values (see Chapter 10), the rules of language underly verbal behavior and are thus not communicated in a formal sense.

In sum, language competence is the knowledge of the language that a speaker possesses. This knowledge is tacit and discovered by learners as they hypothesize about the underlying rules that seem to govern spoken utterances. Language performance, on the other hand, is the actual message produced, the utterance itself. We observe language performance to learn about language competence.

MEANINGS

In everyday interpersonal communication, people often understand one another without any great effort. For instance, most of us have little difficulty responding to a request such as "Please hand me the pencil." As long as we understand the speaker's intentions, we can respond appropriately. How does this occur? Do listeners add up the separate meanings of each word in an utterance to determine the intended meaning? Of course not. Listeners do not need to analyze the utterances word-for-word when trying to determine meanings. What listeners do, though, is determine the illocutionary force of the complete utterance. In other words, they respond to the assertion more than to the individual words, which are merely vehicles for communicating ideas. Thus, words serve as symbols standing for the concepts being communicated.

Meanings are mental concepts based on learned experiences and on the linguistic units used to describe those experiences. By definition, then, meanings are all the learned experiences that you have associated with the usage of words, phrases, gestures, and so on.[10] In a practical sense, meanings are not definitions found in a dictionary. Whereas formal definitions are needed in textbooks and at exam time, in everyday interaction, they are rarely present. Meaning, then, refers more to conceptual understanding than to formal definitions and depends on people making the appropriate connection between the words spoken and the ideas associated with those words. The meaningfulness of any utterance is determined by the responses of the listeners. The words in the utterance serve only as cues to help listeners make the correct conceptual decisions.

Suppose we said to you, "It's time to call in the knackers." Would you know what we meant? Until recently, the authors of this book were unfamiliar with the word. Do you know what a "knacker" is? Unless you have had some experience handling animal carcasses, you probably wouldn't know that a knacker is someone who buys deceased or worn-out animals for use as animal food or fertilizer. The example may seem usual, but it calls attention to the fact that meanings are not in the words themselves but in the minds of the listeners. Until you realize that certain words are connected with certain concepts, the words are meaningless. Now that you know the word "knacker" refers to a particular occupation, you can make the proper conceptual decision the next time you encounter it.

Now let's expand our understanding of meaning. Often we think of meaning only in terms of denotation and connotation. This is a little too simple. Let's consider meaning at four different levels—formal, functional, affective, and prototypical.

Level 1: Formal Meaning

Often called denotative meaning, the formal level of meaning refers to the class inclusion and property relations of a concept.[11] Formal meaning is a person's understanding of what something *is* (class inclusion) and what characteristics it *has* (property relations). A hat is an article of clothing ("hat" is included in the class of objects called "clothing"). It has a brim and a band (brims and bands are properties of hats). A parakeet is a bird (a member of the class called birds) or a pet (a member of the conceptual class called pets) and has wings, feathers, and legs (parakeets have these identifiable properties). Obviously, formal meaning is essential for recognizing what people are talking about. Without it, we could not classify objects into different categories. Formal meaning, then, serves important categorizing functions and allows us to distinguish between different concepts.

Level 2: Functional Meaning

Understanding anything depends not only on knowing what something is and what properties it has, but also on knowing what it *does* or how you relate to it. Functional meaning refers to what something does. For instance, a hat serves as a covering for the head, a parakeet flies and chirps and provides company for people. Often the functional meaning of a concept is momentarily more important that its formal meaning. For instance, if I need a doorstop to prop open a door and can only find a hammer, my understanding of all the possible uses for hammers will determine whether I used it for a doorstop. Some people wouldn't think of using a hammer for a doorstop, but as a temporary solution to the problem it could work fine. Whenever you think about what something does or what you do with something, you are considering its functional meaning.

Level 3: Affective Meaning

As a means of illustrating affective meaning, consider what happens to your reactions to the word "knife" when it is modified to "surgical knife." By itself, "knife" may evoke a neutral feeling, but "surgical knife" is another matter. For many people, the thought of surgery generates feelings of concern and perhaps fear. This is the affective side of meaning. It is sometimes called connotative meaning. Affective meaning is anchored in the emotions and attitudes of the listeners. Although not always a defining quality of a word or expression, it is an important part of how people conceptualize objects.[12] Think about how you conceptualize "college education." You can define it formally, functionally, and affectively. Your affective meanings might include attitudes about the joys and pains experienced as you listened to lectures and pounded out term papers and your recollections of college parties and football games. Whatever your attitudes are about college, they will be part of how you conceptualize "college education." The effective level of meaning is difficult to avoid.

Level 4: Prototypical Meaning

Meanings not only have formal, functional, and affective levels, they also seem to have prototypes. A prototype is an example of a typical member of the class of objects being referred to. People create prototypes or "most typical examples" for conceptual clarity.[13] By having a model or prototype in mind, people can assess any object in terms of its goodness of fit with the prototype. Let me explain. Most of you have a meaning for the concept of vacation. A vacation for you must have certain qualities before you classify it as a vacation. But more than this, you have an idea about what a typical vacation would be like. It may or may not include visiting relatives or camping out in a tent. The point is this: you will judge any trip or excursion according to your personal prototype for the concept. Prototypes, then, serve as standards by which people can decide *how well* a communicated idea fits their prior understanding of the idea.

Combining the Levels of Meaning

Taken together, the four levels of meaning represent a rather thorough analysis of how people conceptualize ideas into meaning clusters. Look at Figure 4.1, which illustrates how "camera" can be conceptualized. Notice that by understanding all four levels, you know what something is, what it has, what it does, how you feel about, and what a typical example would be. Notice also that there is no dictionary-type definition in this structure. The reason for this is that people do not naturally store definitions in memory. They don't need to. If asked to produce a definition, they would use their conceptual frame-

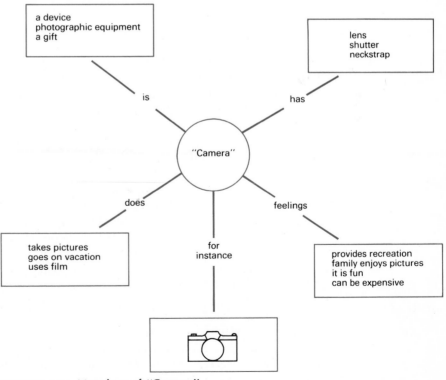

FIGURE 4.1   Meanings of "Camera"

work for constructing one. The four levels of meaning provide a pretty clear picture of the conceptual nature of meaning. As such, it is more useful to think of meaning in these terms rather than in terms of definitions.

LANGUAGE RESEARCH IN COMMUNICATION

As mentioned at the beginning of the chapter, language is one of the main tools people use to accomplish many of their interpersonal goals. Through verbal communication, you can exchange information, influence others, establish new relationships, or enlist the cooperation of others. The potential for verbal communication is seemingly endless. For this reason, communication researchers have shown an unflagging interest in how language affects interpersonal communication. In this section, we will consider language style and language distortion.

Language Style

Although communicators may speak the same language, they have many options for encoding messages. These options, when exercised, produce messages that vary in style. Language style is a general term that refers to how a message is structured. When you are concerned about the specific wording of a message, you are talking about lexical style, which seems to affect interpersonal communication. We will review three forms of lexical style: lexical intensity, lexical diversity, and convergence.

Lexical intensity.   Bowers defines lexical intensity as "the quality of language which indicates the degree to which the speaker's attitude toward a concept deviates from neutrality" (p. 345).[14] Consequently, speakers may use words that not only talk about concepts but give some indication of the speaker's feelings as well. A statement such as "The concert was packed with enthusiastic fans" is more intense than "Many people attended the concert." Similarly, "Mary and Ted exchanged pointed barbs" is more intense than "Mary and Ted had an argument."

On a well-known TV talk show, a movie star recently lamented the fact that her latest film received an "R" rating. She claimed that the rating was due to the film's language, not to its sexual content or violence. She went on the say that the profanity seemed appropriate for the characters being portrayed, but that in her opinion the movie should have been given a "PG" rating. "I've heard worse language in the stands at a football game" she said. Still, the reviewing board felt that the film deserved an "R" rating. What is the impact of profanity? Let's consider some of the research in this area.

Bradac, Bowers, and Courtright present a copious review of the literature dealing with the effects of intense language usage.[15] Among their conclusions is the finding that the use of obscenity (an extreme form of language intensity) produces negative consequences. For instance, Mulac found that the use of obscenity caused people to form negative judgments of the speaker's credibility.[16] Likewise, obscenity does not seem to facilitate persuasion.[17] Swearing, then, does not seem to serve any interpersonal purpose other than to allow speakers to ventilate intense feelings. On the other hand, positive talk has been found to increase one's social attractiveness.[18] So if you want to be found attractive by others, avoid obscenity and talk about positive things.

Increasing the language intensity of a message can communicate the speaker's enthusiasm, and listeners may enjoy a little "spice" in the messages they hear. Language intensity increased in a nonobscene manner can have positive social effects. This is especially true for highly credible sources, as observed by Burgoon, Jones, and Stewart.[19] They found that highly credible sources were able to induce more attitude change in their listeners using high-intensity language than using low-intensity language. Listeners accept and may even enjoy high levels of language intensity if it comes from the right speakers. Similar findings came out of the Yale studies conducted in the 1950s and 1960s. These studies reported that messages intended to evoke fear in listeners could be used most successfully by highly credible speakers. Less credible speakers were less successful when they tried to scare their listeners.[20] High levels of language intensity can be effective if exercised with care.

These studies suggest that although highly intense language may be more exciting to listen to, it can backfire on speakers if they carry it too far. As such, the best insulation against a negative reaction to highly intense language is to be a highly credible source and to avoid obscene language.

Lexical diversity.   Bradac, Bowers, and Courtright define lexical diversity as the "manifest range of a source's vocabulary" (p. 263).[21] Diversity in this context means variety of word choice. Diverse messages contain many different words rather than the same words used repeatedly. Supposedly, the more lexically diverse a message, the more the listeners will judge the speaker to be intelligent.

Barbara Jordan, John F. Kennedy, and Adlai Stevenson, Sr., are or were politicians famous for their "way with words." Their speeches display a command of the language and often are spiced with interesting word choices and beautiful sentences. And although you may not want to be famous for your lexical diversity, it is important to vary your language usage.

Variety in word choice is not only a function of the speaker, it is also a function of the mode of communication. For example, people generally use a more diverse vocabulary when writing than do they for everyday speech. As DeVito observes, we repeat ourselves more when we talk than when we write.[22] We tend to use plainer, more repetitious language when we speak than when we write.

Sometimes the situation can determine the lexical diversity in a message. Street and Jordan had students give formal speeches, then participate in an informal interview about the speech topic.[23] The speeches were given publicly (in class with the audience seated at least 12 feet from the speaker), and the interviews were conducted privately (two people in a small private office seated 3 feet apart). The students' messages were recorded and later analyzed for lexical diversity. As expected, the formal speeches were more lexically diverse than were the statements made in the interviews. Apparently public speaking made the students more aware of their speech and facilitated more variety in their word choice.

The role of linguistic variation becomes more complicated when we consider the persuasive intent of the communicators. You would expect that if someone were trying to persuade you that he/she would vary his/her word choices to maximize the potential persuasive effect. Actually, the opposite occurs. Sherblom and Reinsch, in their study of persuasion in conversations, found a decrease in lexical diversity when the speaker was attempting to persuade his/her listener.[24] Why do speakers narrow their word choices when trying to convince others? We are not sure about the reasons, but it is possible that the persuasive mindset is so goal oriented that communicators fail to vary their language and repeat themselves more than they realize. Perhaps you have noticed that you repeat yourself when engaged in a lively discussion about something you really believe in.

All things considered, lexical diversity is seen as an attractive feature by listeners. A series of studies conducted by Bradac and his associates revealed a positive correlation between speakers' lexical diversity and their listeners' judgments of their credibility and the effectiveness of their messages.[25] This means that communicators who, in speaking, exhibit a diverse vocabulary will be more effective than those who do not display such a vocabulary. Therefore, if you want to be a more effective interpersonal communicator, strive for more variety in your vocabulary.

Convergence.   Even though convergence follows diversity in this discussion, the two terms are nearly opposite in meaning. Diversity refers to linguistic variety, while convergence, as an interpersonal phenomenon, refers to linguistic similarities. Convergence occurs when two or more people communicate often or long enough to begin to talk alike. It is apparent in long-standing relationships and can also be observed in newer relationships when the two parties are highly attracted to one another and wish to demonstrate their interest in each other. Specifically, convergence refers to two or more communicators developing a common language style, involving the use of similar words and sentence patterns, over the course of an interaction or a relationship.[26]

> *"Help! My kids are starting not only to act like me but to talk like me as well. Last week I overheard my son teasing his playmate the same way I tease him. Do kids really pay that much attention to how you talk? If so, I better pay more attention to my style of communication."*
> Signed: Copied

Convergence occurs for a number of reasons. Among them the need for approval, the need for developing a sense of belonging to a group, and a desire to increase one's social standing.[27] A young executive will act and sound like "one of the team" to increase the likelihood of being promoted in the organization; a college sorority sister will act "as she should," so that there will be no doubt about her commitment to the sorority. These examples make clear that communicators desire to fit into a conversation and be accepted by others, even if they are unaware that they are doing so. To some extent, then, linguistic convergence is a natural outcome of conversations.

Since communicators adjust their verbal messages through lexical intensity, lexical diversity, and convergence to meet personal and interpersonal goals, language style is an integral part of interpersonal communication. A competent communicator will be aware of these stylistic variations and will control them for positive social outcomes.

Language Distortion

Since words can stand for many different meanings and because people distort information as they process it, everyday language usage is sometimes not clear. All of us have experienced this problem at one time or another. Language's lack of clarity can be a problem of meaning or a problem of inferences. When it is a meaning problem, the listener will have difficulty assigning the meaning intended by the speaker. When it is an inferential problem, the listener may be assigning more meaning to the utterance than the speaker expects.

Ambiguity and vagueness.   Whenever a word or expression has more than one interpretation, ambiguity is present. For example, the word "bark" can refer to a covering on a tree or a sound made by animals. Fortunately, this simple form of ambiguity can be avoided by referring to the word's immediate context to determine which meaning is intended. If we are talking about gardening and I say that I'm having problems keeping bugs off the bark, you should not hesitate to think of tree bark instead of an animal's bark. The context clarifies the ambiguity. Such is not the case for vagueness, which is different from ambiguity.[28] Ambiguity occurs when the listener has two or more different (but clear) referents from which to choose. The confusion is over which referent to choose. On the other hand, vagueness results from conceptual fuzziness. Vagueness occurs because the boundaries that encompass the referential field are unclear. For instance, a term such as "middle-aged" is vague. It is difficult to specify when it begins and when it ends. Likewise, "a peaceful settlement" is vague. So could be "a reasonable price." Such expressions need further clarification in order for mutual understanding to occur, and the immediate context may be of no help.

Vagueness is more common in interpersonal communication than is ambiguity. The conversational context helps regulate ambiguity, but people interact all the time using vague words and sentences, and the context does not seem to alleviate the problem. Most of the time, people don't even realize that they are being vague, but then their vagueness may not be causing any immediate problems in a particular conversation. In fact, a certain amount of vagueness is desirable. It prevents many disagreements that might otherwise emerge. For instance, in political communication, deliberate vagueness (equivocation) would be a good rhetorical strategy for candidates who do not want to lose credibility by clearly disclosing their opinions on controversial issues.[29] On the other hand,

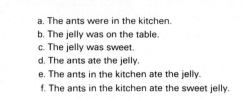

a. The ants were in the kitchen.
b. The jelly was on the table.
c. The jelly was sweet.
d. The ants ate the jelly.
e. The ants in the kitchen ate the jelly.
f. The ants in the kitchen ate the sweet jelly.

FIGURE 4.2   **Bransford and Frank's Sentences**

vagueness is counterproductive when precise communication is essential. But for most everyday conversations, vagueness can go uncorrected without great harm.

Inferences.   Another key source of distortion in language usage is related to inferences. People have a tendency to go beyond the data given when they react to messages.[30] They infer ideas and thoughts that the speaker did not say or intend. According to Bransford and Franks, making inferences is a natural and inevitable part of processing information.[31] In their study, Bransford and Franks gave subjects sets of sentences (as in Figure 4.2) to remember. Later the subjects were tested for recall. The recall test contained the sentences presented earlier but also contained sentences that were not in the original set. Each subject had to decide whether or not a sentence was one of the original ones. Overall, the subjects performed well. But the most interesting finding was the regularity with which some of the sentences that were not in the original set were recalled as being *in* the original set. These were integrative sentences, such as "The ants ate the sweet jelly, which was on the table in the kitchen." Without realizing it, people made the inference that such integrative sentences (one sentence that combines two sentences from the original set) were part of the original list when they were not.

The Bransford and Franks study, along with many others, reminds us that listening is a creative process, wherein listeners fill-in obviously missing ideas to make their understanding more complete. To do this, they must know what was said and infer the rest to complete the picture. (For those of you interested in perusing this topic further, read Elizabeth Loftus's book.[32])

Leveling, sharpening, and assimilation.   Distortion in interpersonal communication is caused not only by the language, but also by the interaction between people. The more people talk to one another about a topic, the more the details of the topic can be altered. Allport and Postman's well-known work on rumors demonstrates that rumors are models of distortion.[33] People passing messages to others have a tendency to adjust the message. They do this in three ways. The first is by leveling, which refers to making the message shorter and simpler in structure. Next is sharpening. This occurs when people highlight certain parts of the story at the expense of others. It often results in a minor point becoming a major point. Finally, messages can be reorganized at each telling to fit the personality and biases of the teller. This is known as assimilation. With rumors, each person in the chain can customize the message through leveling, sharpening, and assimilation, and in doing so, produce a unique message at each exchange.

Even though Allport and Postman's work focused on rumors (the most fertile ground for message distortions), distortions can be expected in simple everyday interactions as well. Whenever people talk, they create their messages on the spot, and such spontaneity is bound to lead to some leveling, sharpening, and assimilation of the ideas being presented. No matter how you try to control it, there will be some form of distortion in human interaction.

IMPROVING YOUR LANGUAGE

As most of you know, our society not only values literacy, it rewards it as well. People who are viewed as excellent communicators can even make a living with their verbal communication skills. You may not want to become a professional communicator, but you probably want to improve your verbal communication abilities. You can improve your skills in a number of important areas. Some people engage in vocabulary studies, others join professional speaking clubs such as the Toastmasters, others travel or increase the number of books they read a year, thereby expanding their vocabulary and experiences. These are all worthy plans for improvement, and you are encouraged to do such things.

All of us, however, should be especially attentive to some common errors that people make when using language in interpersonal communication. One is the problem of "word fixedness." As discussed earlier, words don't mean, people mean. Words have a degree of portability that makes them applicable to a number of different contexts. Some words are used to mean many different things. The skilled communicator takes advantage of the flexibility of our language. For fun, look up the word "run" in a dictionary. You might be surprised to learn how many definitions are associated with it.

Another error is the problem of "I told you so." This is related to the belief that words are the carriers of meaning and that if I make myself clear, you should understand what I'm saying. If you don't, it's because you are stupid. After all, "I told you so." If this is a problem for you, be reminded that words are often vague in their referents. Just because you and I have a word for something does not insure that we understand it or have the same meaning for the word we use. A competent communicator is never surprised when his/her words are misinterpreted. Expect to be misunderstood occasionally.

Finally there is the problem of jumping to conclusions. As you learned earlier, people naturally make inferences when they listen to a speaker. They cannot avoid doing so. Your task, as an informed communicator, is to realize that you do make inferences and to monitor them, so that your conclusions don't cause you interpersonal problems. Many people jump to conclusions without realizing it. Informed students of communication should at least realize that they do this.

SUMMARY

We have covered a lot of territory in this chapter, but verbal messages are the mainstays of human communication, so they deserve full coverage. In this chapter, you learned that languages are built on sounds, syntax, and semantics. We discovered that all languages have certain commonalities called language universals, and that people need both language competence and language performance skills in order to engage in interpersonal communication. Since

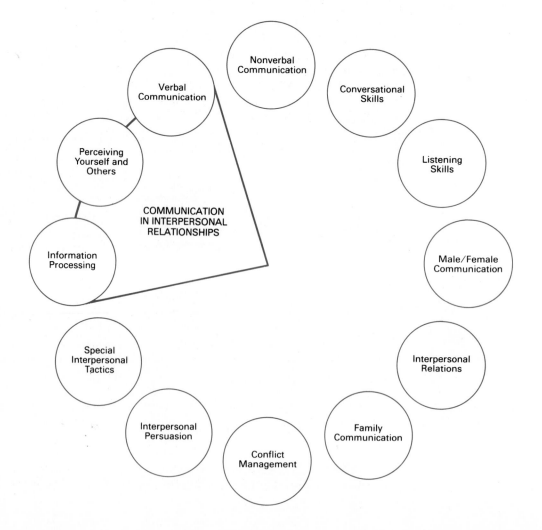

verbal communication is usually "about" something, we spent a lot of time talking about meaning. Meaning has at least four levels: formal meaning, functional meaning, affective meaning, and prototypical meaning.

The material reviewed under the heading of language research in communication taught us that humans are guided by the rules of language but that they are quite capable of adapting our language to different people and situations. Language style is something that everyone has and it too can be modified occasionally. Furthermore, you learned that precision in language is not always present, nor is precision in the language user always possible. Language distortions, then, are inevitable when people communicate.

THEORY INTO PRACTICE

These exercises should help you understand better that role of language in interpersonal communication.

Exercise 4.1: Word Associations

Purpose: To illustrate how concepts are interconnected and can be classified by the four levels of meaning.

Materials Needed: Paper and pencil.

Time Required: 30 minutes.

Procedure: In dyads, you will be participating in three rounds of a word association exercise. One person will say aloud a word and the other will say aloud as many different words that he/she associates with the given word. Each associator will have 30 seconds to say the associations that come to mind. Before you begin, you need to come up with three stimulus words that you can use on your partner. To find the words, go to any page in this book (other than this one) and locate a noun that begins with the letter *r*. Then go to another page and find a noun that begins with the letter *h*. For the third word, go to another page and look for a noun that begins with the letter *n*. These three words will be the ones that your partner responds to. (Your partner will follow the same procedure to locate three stimulus words to give to you.) After each of you have determined your stimulus words, begin the exercise by taking turns giving the word and responding to it. The person who is giving the stimulus word should write down the associates that his/her partner says. When you have completed three rounds of the exercise (after each person has associated to three different words) categorize the associates given by your partner according to the four levels of meaning discussed on pages 61–64. When all groups have completed their associations and categorization of the responses, the instructor will conduct a class discussion.

Questions to Ask: (1) Were there any associates that could not be classified into one of the four levels of meaning? (2) Why does this occur? (3) Which level of meaning was used the most? the least? (4) Which level of meaning seemed to occur earliest?

Exercise 4.2: Facts and Inferences

Purpose: To determine the differences between statements of fact and inferences.

Materials Needed: Pencil and paper.

Time Required: 30 minutes.

Procedure: Working independently, read the following story and write down on a piece of paper whether each of the statements that follow are true (T), false (F), or undetermined (?). Use only the information given in the story to determine your answers. When everyone has completed the test, the instructor will list everyone's answers on the board and discuss each item with the class.

It was a cold, wet day when the boss called Charlie in for a talk. Charlie was not as productive as he used to be. He was often late for work and was having difficulties getting along with the factory line workers. During the meeting, the company psychologist asked about possible family problems. None were indicated. After talking for more than an hour, it was agreed that Charlie would take a leave of absence and get some rest. One month later, Charlie sought other employment.

_____ 1. Charlie was never late for work.
_____ 2. Charlie was a factory line worker.
_____ 3. The meeting took place in the winter.
_____ 4. The meeting was held in the boss's office.
_____ 5. Charlie was a man.
_____ 6. There are at least three men involved in this story.
_____ 7. The psychologist asked if Charlie was having family problems.
_____ 8. During the meeting everyone talked.
_____ 9. The boss suggested that Charlie take a leave of absence.
_____ 10. Eventually, Charlie went to work for another company.

Questions to Ask: (1) On which items were your answers different from others in the class? (2) When is something a fact? (3) What is an inference? (4) What causes people to make inferences? (5) Are inferences false?

5 NONVERBAL COMMUNICATION

While few students have received formal training in nonverbal communication, everyone has thought about nonverbal behavior. How many times have you said to yourself, "Her face was telling me that something was wrong," or "I could tell he was lying because he wouldn't look me in the eye"? Nonverbal behavior is a very important part of interpersonal communication. Most of what we communicate emotionally is done through nonverbal symbols. Many experts believe that, in communicating, when verbal and nonverbal behavior contradict each another, the nonverbal behavior reflects our true feelings and intentions. While the verbal message is what speakers worry about most in forming the right impression, nonverbal behavior is a very important part of what listeners rely on to determine true emotions, intentions, motives, and behavior. Furthermore, a significant proportion of communicating in interpersonal relationships involves nonverbal behavior. Relationships can suffer from a lack of nonverbal communication.

WHAT'S AHEAD

This chapter examines the nature and importance of nonverbal behavior to interpersonal communication in general, and specifically how it affects interpersonal relationships. In order to understand nonverbal communication, we must learn to recognize the types of nonverbal behavior and the effects of nonverbal behavior on day-to-day interactions. After reading this chapter, you should have a firm grasp of why nonverbal communication has been regarded as the behavioral system of true feelings and intentions.

DEFINITION OF NONVERBAL COMMUNICATION

While many communication experts have attempted to define it, no clear consensus exists regarding the exact nature of nonverbal communication. Knapp has offered a broad definition: "Nonverbal communication designates all those human responses which are not described as overtly manifested words."[1] More simply put, we define nonverbal communication as *the process of signaling meaning through interpersonal behavior that does not involve spoken words*. Communication takes place in many contexts where a person may or may not consciously signal meaning. For example, all of us have said before, "I really didn't mean to say that," or "That's not what I intended." Furthermore, in your own past you may have been asked by an annoyed parent or roommate, "Would you quit drumming your fingers on the table, it bothers me." How many times were you intending to communicate a message to this exasperated receiver? What was the message? Of course, it is possible that you were trying to reveal your boredom. But behavior that signals meaning in another person, intended or not, communicates certain ideas to that person. Obviously much of our interpersonal behavior involves nonverbal actions, and the rest of this chapter will be spent describing what is known about communicating interpersonally through nonverbal behavior.

FUNCTIONS OF NONVERBAL COMMUNICATION

Nonverbal communication serves many functions. Argyle believes that the primary uses of nonverbal behavior in communication involve (1) expressing emotions (crying, laughing), (2) revealing one's personality to others (smiling, gesturing expressively), (3) indicating interpersonal attitudes (frowning, hugging), and (4) accompanying speech to manage conversation (nodding, raising one's hand).[2] Ekman has another view of the functions of nonverbal behavior. From his perspective, nonverbal behavior can best be described by the following terms: *repeat*—nonverbal behavior that mirrors the verbal message (saying, "There are only two sections of this course open," while holding up two fingers); *contradict*—verbal and nonverbal messages that contradict each other ("It won't bother me if you go out with other guys" said with sad eyes); and *substitute*—nonverbal behavior that takes the place of verbal communication (thumbs up, indicating "good job"). In addition, nonverbal behavior can *complement* (when nonverbal behavior coincides with the verbal message, such as when waving as salutations are exchanged,) *accent* (when nonverbal behavior reinforces the verbal message, such as when a professor pounds the lecturn as she makes an important point), and *regulate* (when nonverbal behavior helps to manage interaction, such as when one raises one's hand while speaking to prevent another from butting in).[3] Given these functions, it is obvious that nonverbal behavior is a very important part of interpersonal communication. Managing an interpersonal relationship would be difficult if we relied only on words to explain our true feelings. Getting a point across would be frustrating without the use of nonverbal behavior, especially when we become emotional.

Nonverbal behavior may also serve the function of tension release. Many nonverbal behaviors are exhibited during highly emotional or stressful situations as a means of coping with the arousal involved. For example, many people are reticent or apprehensive about communicating. This reticence causes tension or stress, which in turn causes abnormal nonverbal behavior. For example, increased touching of oneself and covering one's face, reduced eye contact and head nodding, and tense posture are just some of the nonverbal behaviors associated with the tension release related to communication reticence.[4] Other types of emotions and their related nonverbal behaviors will be discussed throughout the chapter.

TYPES OF NONVERBAL COMMUNICATION

Many different types (categories) of nonverbal behavior directly affect interpersonal communication between individuals. In this section we will discuss paralanguage (how we use our voice), facial expressions, occulesics (eye behavior), kinesics (body movement), proxemics (personal space), territoriality (use of space), and tactile behavior (touching). The distinctions made among the types of nonverbal behavior are important because if we as interpersonal communicators know how to classify a behavior, we can better ascertain the meaning of its message. Just as the study of entomology is useful for classifying insects and knowing how the various groups affect us, so too the classification of nonverbal communication is useful in understanding how it affects us in our interpersonal relationships.

Paralanguage

Paralanguage refers to not what is said, but how something is said. How we use our voice to communicate interpersonal messages is very important. In fact, our vocal characteristics may enhance or inhibit the content of our message. It is always distracting to hear a big, burly man speak with a Mickey Mouse voice. On the other hand, strong, lower tone voices such as Tom Brokaw's or Dan Rather's add to the credibility of the message being sent. The voice is an important nonverbal communication source. The elements of paralanguage have been delineated in a widely quoted article by Trager.[5] We will discuss two of Trager's categories of paralanguage.

Voice qualities is the term Trager employed to characterize the manner in which a voice can be used and abused. Eight different voice qualities are listed below:

1. Pitch range—the actual range of pitch of a voice.
2. Vocal lip control—the degree of rasp or hoarseness evident in a voice.
3. Glottis control—the sharp or smooth transitions in pitch.
4. Articulation control—whether speech is precise or slurred.
5. Rhythm control—the level of smoothness in our vocal activity.
6. Resonance—the thickness or thinness of vocal tone.
7. Pitch control—the ability to maintain and vary the range of pitches.
8. Tempo—the rate of speech.

Vocal qualities can affect the interpretation of the verbal segment of the message. For example, the emotional state of a speaker can be determined from vocal qualities. Listeners may wonder what is wrong when they hear rapid and broken vocalizations from individuals who ordinarily talk at moderate and consistent rates. Listeners can become so preoccupied with the unique vocal qualities of the speaker that the content of the message is not heard.

Paralanguage also includes a category termed *vocalizations*.[6] This category is broken down into three types: vocal characterizers, vocal qualifiers, and vocal segregates. Vocal characterizers include such nonverbal sounds as laughing, snickering, whimpering, crying, moaning, and yawning. Obviously, emotional or physical states can be associated with each of these sounds. Vocal qualifiers include the intensity of the voice (loudness, softness), its pitch height (high and low), and the extent of a vocal sound (duration). Again, the emotional state of a communicator could be inferred from these paralanguage qualities. Vocal segregates are vocalizations that are not actual words, but provide connotative meaning. Examples of vocal segregates are "uh-uh" for no, "uh-huh" for yes, "uh" for hesitation, and "umm" for recognition.

The ability to accurately decode nonverbal messages is an important component of interpersonal communication. Studies have indicated that listeners are more accurate in identifying negative expressions of emotions than positive ones.[7] In fact, anger was the most accurately identified emotion, and love was the least accurately identified. Why would negative emotional cues be more easily defined than positive ones? Perhaps one reason is that angry communicators want to leave no doubt about their intentions and emotional state. With positive emotions such as love and pride, communicators may not be as preoccupied with ensuring accurate paralanguage cues, and they may not be as eager to open up this type of communication to public scrutiny.

Paralanguage can also be used as a tool for managing conversation. When we are engaged in a conversation with another person or persons we may intentionally raise our voice and begin talking faster in order to prevent someone from interrupting us. On the other hand, a lower inflectional tone at the end of the sentence is an indication that we are willing to give up the floor of conversation to someone else.

Facial Expressions

Facial expressions are the second type of nonverbal behavior that we will discuss. Several research projects in nonverbal communication have indicated that the face may be the most important body area through which nonverbal cues are conveyed. However, the face's importance in communication can be problematic because of the complexity of facial expressions. Because of the numerous muscles in the human face more than a thousand different facial expressions are possible.[8] However, with only a limited number of known emotions (happiness, sadness, anger, fear, disgust, surprise), a large variety of facial expressions can be used to express each emotion. Even more importantly, as decoders we may interpret certain nonverbal behaviors to represent emotions that were not intended. For example, some people can look as if they are smiling when in fact they are grimacing in pain (those people may think we are sadistic or rude when we smile back at them). Since facial expressions primarily reflect emotions, it is important to understand their role in interpersonal communication.

One of the interesting aspects of facial expressions is that different facial areas are involved in emotions. In an interesting study, Boucher and Ekman cut photographs of faces into distinct facial areas (eyes/eyelids, cheeks/mouths, brows/foreheads) and asked participants in the study to indicate what emotions they perceived from different photos of each of the facial areas. Surprise was judged accurately from all three facial areas; happiness was observed in the cheeks/mouth and eyes/eyelids areas; sadness and fear were best determined from the eyes/eyelids area. Anger was not accurately predicted from any one area of the face, implying that "anger differs from the other five facial expressions of emotions in being ambiguous to the viewer unless the anger is registered in at least two and usually three areas of the face."[9] This is an intriguing finding, since, as the reader will recall, anger was easily identifiable from vocal qualities.

Apparently, different emotions produce different displays or expressions of nonverbal behavior. Anger is an emotion that is more observable in the voice, and if the voice is not available for scrutiny, then the whole face must be viewed to determine accurately if someone is angry. When interpersonal communicators do not have both visual and auditory channels available to them such as in telephone conversations or when large distances separate communicators, accurate decoding of emotions will be limited. In these circumstances, concentrating on those areas of facial expression that best reflect the felt emotion may be our safest bet for understanding the emotional state of the other communicator.

Smiling is a facial expression that has received considerable study. Unlike other facial expressions, only one facial muscle is involved in the expression of smiling: the zygomatic major muscle "which reaches down the cheekbone to the lip corner,"[10] and as such, is easily identified by others. Smiling is generally associated with communicating attraction, liking, and intimacy.[11] Smiling is also displayed more with friends and with those whom we are trying to impress or obtain a favorable response from.[12] Smiling has been studied in conjunction with assertiveness. Researchers have suggested that smiling is a nonassertive, submissive behavior,[13] and reductions in smiling behavior are related to perceptions of enhanced assertiveness.[14] Smiling may compromise an otherwise strong position and cause an opponent or adversary to perceive weaknesses. On the other hand, smiling may provide the opportunity to increase relational closeness with another person or demonstrate that we are open to others' interpersonal communication.

Ekman and Friesen, two prominent researchers in the field of nonverbal behavior, have suggested that there are three types of smiles.[15] *Felt smiles* reflect positive emotion, such as happiness, amusement, or delight. This type of smile is probably an automatic reflex, especially when we are in a good mood. *False smiles* are used to convince others that we are experiencing positive emotion when we actually aren't. There are three types of false smiles: (a) phony smiles are used when no emotion (positive or negative) is felt, such as when we smile at jokes we do not understand; (b) masking smiles are used when we experience negative emotion but attempt to smile in order to cover up our true feelings; and (c) dampened smiles are expressed when we experience positive emotions, but attempt to conceal or tone down the expression of our emotions, such as when we avoid a display of extreme joy when a car dealer finally meets our price on a new car.

Miserable smiles are exhibited when negative emotion is experienced and no attempt is made to cover up our feelings. Miserable smiles are used to convey unhappiness. In some instances miserable smiles may be fairly reflexive, like felt smiles. We simply respond nonverbally to the way we feel emotionally. In other instances, we may display miserable smiles rather obviously, hoping that someone will catch on and provide us with some needed sympathy.

Both felt and miserable smiles are intentional expressions of our true emotions, whereas false smiles are meant to conceal our emotions. It has been suggested that false smiles can be detected as such by carefully monitoring the smiling individual.[16] First, false smiles may not involve a changed movement of the eye areas as with felt smiles. Second, false smiles are likely to be more asymmetrical than a felt smile (stronger on the left side of the face if the person is right-handed). Third, false smiles, if expressed too early or too late, are out of sync with the interaction taking place. Detection of false smiles is important because many individuals who need emotional support may not want to request help deliberately. If we can detect others' emotional feelings through false smiles, we can be in better position to offer our support and help.

Obviously, smiling is a nonverbal behavior that can be perceived in a variety of ways, depending on the situation. Formal situations involving task achievement (arguing for a point in a small group discussion) may constrain smiling behavior. Smiling in such a situation would appear nonassertive and hamper effectiveness, whereas, in informal situations, smiling can be used as a means for getting to know someone better. Taking note of the various dimensions and perceptions associated with smiling can tell us when smiling is appropriate and when it is not.

One of the methods of studying facial expressions in interpersonal encounters is through the use of display rules. *Displays rules* are modifications of facial expressions that occur as a result of the social situation.[17] That is, as the social situation dictates, normal facial expressions, those which reflect our true emotions, become altered or modified in order to suit the situation. For example, the old adage that "men do not cry in public" has caused a widespread display rule among males of being stone-faced when experiencing grief and despair. Likewise, showing pleasure (false smile) at a meal of undercooked fish prepared by new acquaintances or acting surprised at a birthday party that you knew about for days are examples of display rules.

An important consideration of display rules is that modification or control of the face during felt emotion is best achieved around the lower part of the face.[18] This implies that facial expressions that are best determined from the eye/eyelid area (sadness, fear) may be more difficult to cover up than emotions that are displayed from the lower face. It is difficult to obey a display rule that demands faking a difficult emotion. This can be illustrated with the following example:

George and Sam were graduate students together at a large university in the Southwest. They were very close friends, but were also very competitive, especially since the graduate program they were involved in encouraged competition. George and Sam had the same adviser, a famous research professor who was at the time writing a textbook. The professor told them that he would select one of them to write the instructor's manual for the text. This was considered an honor and a privilege for many reasons, and the one selected would also get $1,000 for writing the manual. Sam was selected for the job. George was extremely disappointed, hurt, and somewhat embarrassed for losing to Sam, but felt that he should congratulate Sam on his good fortune. When George did congratulate Sam, his smile was weak, his jaw was tense, his forehead was slightly wrinkled, he used very little eye contact, and his voice had very little of the emotion it normally did when the two men spoke together. George was going through the motions in congratulating Sam, but his display rules were fairly weak, especially since Sam knew George well and could tell when his nonverbal behavior was not genuine.

Occulesics

Occulesics refers to eye behavior, which involves what we do with our eyes during speaking and listening. Much of how we regulate conversation and how we manage relationships with strangers, acquaintances, and intimates depends upon eye and visual behavior. Argyle and Ingham have conducted studies into eye contact and conversation and have found that we do twice as much looking when listening as we do when we are speaking.[19] Social norms may dictate that it is good manners to look at people when they are speaking rather than looking into space as if we are not interested. However, the authors know several people who can constantly look at people while they are speaking and still ignore them (all the while watching movies on the inside of their eyeballs).

On the other hand, individuals avoid eye contact in interpersonal communication situations for several reasons. Embarrassment,[20] sorrow,[21] and emotional arousal[22] are primary reasons for eye avoidance (the example of George congratulating Sam is pertinent here). Each of these reasons for avoiding eye contact can be traced to emotional arousal, and two hypotheses are suggested for explaining this phenomenon. First, individuals may be attempting to maintain privacy during heightened emotional states—turning inward with their thoughts and perceptions. For many people, maintaining this sort of mental privacy is necessary to cope with the nervousness, tension, or exhilaration associated with a stressful situation. We have observed students avoiding all eye contact just before giving an oral presentation. Students later report that the arousal or stress they experienced before speaking induced them to maintain privacy before the speech.

A second alternative is that eye avoidance is a result of increased cognitive load. That is, as individuals feel arousal, they attempt to cope with the arousal mentally. Increased mental functioning causes the eye to focus on an area of reduced stimuli and to attempt to block out other stimuli (much as we do when pondering an answer to a test). A colleague of ours, when asked a difficult question, frequently looks down at the floor while he is contemplating an answer. While some may regard this behavior as eccentric or as an avoidance, he seldom has an odd or inappropriate response. By reducing the visual stimuli around him (avoiding eye contact), he has the opportunity to focus completely on what his answer will be and thus avoids distractions.

As mentioned previously, eye behavior is an important component of conversation regulation. Studies have shown that while individuals differ in their eye gazing behavior, they have a tendency to reciprocate eye gaze.[23] Individuals tend to match the duration of the eye gaze of their conversational partner. This phenomenon may be due to the desire of conversationalists to make their partner feel comfortable during the interaction. In contrast to what happens in dyadic exchanges, members of groups will look more while speaking than while listening. In a group situation there is no social obligation to engage in direct eye contact with a speaker because you are only one listener and others can pick up the slack. On the other hand, as a speaker you would want to carefully scan the group in order to determine if you are being successful and understood.

Eye and visual behavior are very important elements in interpersonal relationships. Included in this area of eye behavior is the Like-Look paradigm.[24] Essentially this implies that we look longer at those whom we like, and those who look more are liked better. Along similar lines, familiarity with someone causes more eye gaze. Strangers or newly acquainted individuals may feel uncomfortable engaging in extended direct eye contact, but increased eye contact probably does not bother most friends. In addition, an attempt to demonstrate friendliness has been associated with increased looking.[25]

> Think about the last time you were trying to become friendly with a member of the opposite sex whom you found attractive. What was your eye contact strategy? Did your strategy produce the desired effect?

Status differences perceived by two people in relationship can cause varying levels of eye contact. For instance, low-power individuals will look more when listening than when speaking, while high-power individuals will look more while speaking than when listening. Again, social norms may dictate that those who have more authority and power deserve more respect and as such receive our undivided attention (through eye contact). On the other hand, people with lower status receive the least amount of eye contact.[26] You may recall a conversation among several people that you took part in. You could tell how much status you had in the conversation by how much others looked at you when they spoke. You may have even nodded at them to obtain more eye contact. On the other hand, you may recall how you excluded others with low status from your eye contact in order to look at people with higher status.

Staring is a form of eye behavior that affects interpersonal relationships. By most standards staring is considered rude and socially unacceptable. Several interesting studies have confirmed that staring is not the best nonverbal method for making friends and influencing people. Research by Ellsworth and colleagues found that pedestrians waiting at a corner for the lights to change tended to cross the street much faster after someone had stared at them.[27]

Altruistic or helping behavior seems to decrease among strangers after they have been stared at. In one study subway passengers would help pick up dropped papers much less often after they had been stared at by the individual.[28] Apparently, staring is considered an intrusion of privacy or a threat to the individual, and he or she enacts appropriate sanctions against such behavior. Staring is not usually the most effective way of establishing meaningful relationships, although students have told us that this method is sometimes helpful in showing someone that they are interested in establishing a relationship.

Kinesics

Kinesics, is a Greek word meaning body motion or movement. In nonverbal behavior terms, it refers to how movement of the body sends messages to others. According to Ekman and Friesen there are five different categories of kinesic behavior: emblems, illustrators, regulators, adapters, and affect displays.[29]

Emblems are instances of nonverbal behavior that can stand alone in that no verbal behavior is necessary for understanding the message. A thumbs up sign is generally meant to convey success or appropriateness of behavior, and most people do not confuse the meaning of this behavior. Photo A displays an emblem commonly used in interpersonal behavior when words are not necessary to convey meaning. What is being communicated with this emblem?

Illustrators are nonverbal behaviors that accompany speaking in order to illustrate what is being said. Wiping your forehead as you say "Boy, is it hot today" is an example of an illustrator, and this nonverbal act helps to get the

A

B

C

D

(Photos by
Brian Patterson)   E

point across much more dramatically than using words alone. Photo B represents an illustrator being used as someone speaks. What is the intent of the illustrator being used in this photograph?

Regulators accompany speech for the purpose of regulating conversation. For example, raising one's hand to gain the floor, opening one's palm to relinquish the floor, and turning away from a speaker to indicate lack of interest are instances of regulators. Many times, nonverbal regulators are more effective in managing conversation than verbal communication. For example, leaning forward, raising our eyebrows, and lifting our heads may be better mechanisms for gaining the floor in a conversation than simply butting in with words. Photo C illustrates the use of a regulator during conversation.

Nonverbal behaviors used in response to emotional arousal are termed *adapters*. As our emotions become aroused or heightened, our body tends to try to dissipate this arousal, many times subconsciously, in order to maintain an emotional balance. Adapters are therefore release mechanisms for emotional arousal and include such behaviors as scratching, rubbing, massaging, etc. A friend of ours has a unique way of adapting to emotional pressure—rubbing his nose and pushing his glasses up simultaneously. You can probably think of idiosyncratic nonverbal behaviors that your friends or relatives use when they are emotionally aroused. These behaviors can serve as a means for you to more readily understand their state of mind and could give you the opportunity to help them with their situation. Photo D represents an adapter.

The final category is *affect displays*. These behaviors are primarily used to convey an emotional or affective state. Often, they are facial expressions which communicate happiness (smiling), sadness (frowning), anger (scowling), boredom (blank look), and other affective behavior. Sometimes the entire body can be observed to indicate an affective state, such as slumping or a slouching body, indicating boredom and fatigue. These are important nonverbal behaviors to understand since knowing the emotional or affective state a person may be experiencing affects our communication with them. Photo E is an example of an affect display. What is being communicated in this picture?

If you think about it, emblems are the most conscious and intentional of the kinesic behaviors. Illustrators, regulators, and affect displays are used many times without conscious thought, and adapters would be the least likely kinesic behavior to be consciously used to communicate our emotions. In fact, as we will discuss later, adapters are unintentional nonverbal behaviors that can give us away when we tell lies.

Proxemics

In face-to-face interpersonal communication, proxemics refers to how closely communicators are positioned as they interact. Hall's categorization of spatial zones included *intimate* (0–18 inches), *personal* (18–4 feet), *social* (4–12 feet), and *public* (12 feet and beyond).[30] Close proxemic distance has been associated with attraction for others and intimacy.[31] Closer distances are reserved for our friends and those whom we like, while larger distances are intended for those we dislike and those who view us negatively.[32] A recent study indicated that close proximity can also convey greater dominance, persuasiveness, and aggressiveness.[33]

Research shows that people use interpersonal space not only to define the intimacy of the conversation but to leave impressions and to imply certain roles. Seating preferences in a meeting are good examples. Riess and Rosenfeld found that people would choose seats in a group situation according to their desires to lead, to avoid interaction, or to show attraction for another. Specifically, those who desired to be leaders chose seats in a head position. Those who wished to withdraw from talking chose seats of low visibility with the greatest distance from others. Those who wished to impress another chose seats close to that person.[34] By strategically choosing particular seats, the subjects were sending messages to help define their intentions.

Spatial distance between two communicators must be mutually determined. If you have ever avoided closeness by someone you didn't like you know what we mean. The distance between communicators is interpersonally negotiated according to the desires of the communicators. Just how close people permit others to get is a function of many factors. One of these is the relative attractiveness of the other person. Unattractive people who invade our personal space might be annoying. On the other hand, we might enjoy an invasion from an attractive person. Another measure of physical closeness involves whether we are interacting with someone of the same or opposite sex. Research has shown that male-female pairs interact more closely than do female pairs, and females pairs interact at closer distances than male pairs.[35] Social stigma is one reason that same-sex communicators do not interact at close distances.

Invading one's personal space is a means of crowding. When people feel crowded, they may react differently than when they do not. One's personal space is considered exclusive territory. This space "serves a protective function and expands in response to perceived threat."[36] As we feel intimidated or threatened by others we wish to expand the spatial distance between ourselves and the source of threat. A student once reported that every time she argued with her father she always recoiled and leaned backwards in order to get away from him. In situations where she anticipated a hostile encounter with her father, she would always look for a seat that would position her as far away from him as possible. Her concern for an expanded spatial distance was related to her negative feelings for these hostile encounters.

Concerns for privacy, intimacy, dominance, role-enactment, status, and persuasion all govern how people position themselves during interpersonal encounters. When the participants have settled on the distribution of space in any given situation, they have defined the roles and relationships in that situation and have implicitly agreed to act accordingly. Because of the potentially binding nature of proxemic decisions, people often position themselves strategically to be sure they end up where they want. Such spatial game playing is evident in international negotiations, at social events, and in the classroom.

There is an old adage among professors that students who wish to avoid speaking or being called on in class will sit at the back, on the sides, or near the door. This impression is so widespread that many professors we know (including ourselves) deliberately call on those students sitting in those positions!

Tactile Communication

Tactile communication, or haptics, refers to touching behavior. While particular types of touching mean different things to different people, touch is one of the primary types of nonverbal communication. Touch was one of the first means of consolation in our lives. Many times, the desperate cries of babies cannot be quieted without the reassuring touch of an adult, Likewise, the wrenching sobs of a heartbroken lover cannot be soothed without the touch of another. Although everyone reacts a little differently to touch, depending on the person touching and the relationship involved, touch is basic to human existence.

Richard Hesler developed a classification system of the types of touch that correspond to the relationship of the interactants.[37] The most formal type of touch was termed *functional-professional*. This category refers to touching that is intentionally impersonal and that is used to perform a specific activity unrelated to any interpersonal relationship between two people. Dentists, physicians, chiropractors, and hair stylists all engage in functional-professional touching. Those who are touched generally know that the purpose of the touch is simply to perform a job.

The second category of touching is termed *social-polite*. When we touch others in order to greet, congratulate, or otherwise recognize them in some way we are engaging in social-polite touching. While this type of touching is more interpersonal than functional-professional, it does not connote a great deal of information about the definition of the relationship. Many adversaries shake hands (Reagan-Gorbachev) or kiss, depending on the culture. These behaviors are simply ways of carrying out social functions.

Friendship-warmth touching is the third category and involves physical touch that conveys liking and nonintimate affection for another person. Back patting, putting an arm around another's shoulder, and arm squeezing are examples of touch that indicate friendship and warmth, but not necessarily love. However, these touching movements can be misinterpreted by those who would want to read more into them than is meant.

The fourth category of touching behavior is termed *love-intimacy*. Examples of this type of behavior include hugging, kissing, caressing, and idiosyncratic nonverbal behaviors (such as pats or pinches), which can become common in intimate relationships. These behaviors are used to communicate intimate affection and emotional attraction. They can be misinterpreted, but this is not likely except when one is trying to deceive another.

The fifth category of touching behavior involves *sexual arousal*. Touching of this type may or may not involve individuals with close, intimate relationships. For most individuals, touching behavior involving sexual arousal is a very important part of intimate relationships, and for others (for example, prostitutes), sexual arousal is important in nonintimate relationships.

More recently Jones and Yarbrough[38] developed a system of categorization for the meanings of interpersonal touches. Through their research they identified 12 categories of touch. The following figure displays the category label, the type of touching behavior, and the meaning usually assigned to this type of touch.

Category	Meaning	Behavior
1. Support	Serves to nurture, reassure, or protect ("You'll be all right")	Hand and arm touches
2. Appreciation	Expresses gratitude ("Thanks!")	Hand-to-body; hand hold
3. Inclusion	Draws attention to act of being together ("I'm glad to be with you!")	Holding/pressing against
4. Sexual	Expresses physical attraction or sexual interest ("You feel so good")	Holding; caressing, touching of intimate body parts
5. Affection feelings for another	Expresses positive caressing ("I like you")	Hugs, kisses, holding
6. Playful affection	Serves to lighten interaction ("Why are we being so serious?")	Intimate body contact; wrestling; tickling; punching; pinching; patting
7. Playful aggression	Serves to lighten interaction ("You didn't need this head anyway")	Mock strangling; mock wrestling; slapping; grabbing; standing on toes
8. Compliance	Attempts to direct behavior and attitudes ("I want you to get to work!")	Holding; patting; spot touches to body parts
9. Attention-getting	Serves to direct recipient's perceptual focus ("Look at that!")	Spot touches by hand to nonintimate body parts
10. Announcing a response	Calls attention to the feeling state of the toucher ("I'm really happy")	Hand contact with body parts; hugs
11. Greeting	Serves to acknowledge another at the opening of an encounter ("Good to see you")	Handshake; spot touch; pat
12. Departure	Serves as part of the act of closing an encounter ("Have a nice life")	Hand contact to one body part; pats; caresses

(Adapted from Jones and Yarbrough)

Hesler's category system differs from Jones and Yarbrough's only in degree, with the latter system breaking the types of touch down into more specific categories. The two symptoms are similar in their explanation of touch as a very intentional and important component of interpersonal communication. Touch carries a great deal of meaning for communicators, especially when opposite-sex and same-sex touches are compared and contrasted.

The meaning of touch for men and women can differ according to who is touching and who is touched. While men and women agree on the type of touch that conveys sexual desire, they differ in their reactions to such tactile stimulation.[39] For example, men perceive touch that signifies sexual desire as pleasant, warm, and playful, while women do not have the same perceptions. This difference is especially noteworthy when we consider that men, much more than women, anticipate or consider romantic involvement during initial encounters with a person of the opposite sex.[40]

Heslin and his colleagues conducted research that identified preferences, or perceived pleasantness, that men and women have for touch depending upon what part of the body is touched, whether the toucher is a stranger or close friend, and whether the toucher is of the same or opposite sex.[41] By examining Figure 5.1, you can determine what their research says about the preferences

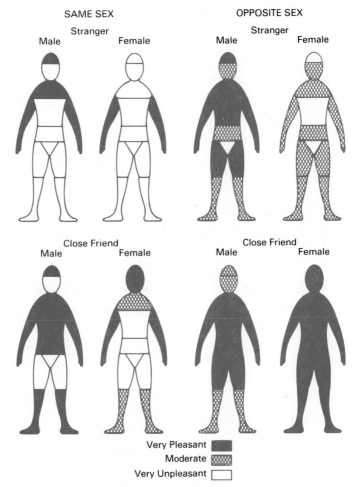

FIGURE 5.1 **Areas of Touch**
After Heslin, R., Nguyen, T. D., and Nguyen, M. L. "The Meaning of Touch: Sex Differences." *Journal of Nonverbal Behavior* 7 (1983) 147–157.

we have for interpersonal touch. Touches from same-sex strangers were least preferred, while touches from close, opposite-sex friends were most preferred. Furthermore, males indicated that female touch to their intimate areas was pleasant regardless of whether the female was a stranger or close friend. Women, on the other hand, were more restrictive in their preference for intimate touch, so that only close friends provided them with a sense of pleasantness for this type of touch. In fact, females demonstrated a general lack of preference for touch by an opposite-sex stranger. This research suggests that some gender differences exists regarding the perception of tactile communication when the toucher's sex and relational status are considered. Consider the following example of opposite-sex touch that happened to a friend of ours.

> Fred was a faculty member in a communication department, and each year Lance, his department chair, invited the faculty to his house for a Christmas party. The year before Ruth, Fred's wife, was repulsed when, upon leaving the party, Lance kissed her on the cheek as a way of showing holiday affection. Ruth told Fred that she did not want to go to the party this year and be kissed by her husband's boss even though it was only a Christmas ritual. Fred pleaded with Ruth that it was something quick, and he needed Ruth's cooperation because he was coming up for reappointment this year and needed Lance's blessing. Ruth finally acquiesced, and according to plan, as Fred and Ruth were leaving the party Lance leaned over to kiss Ruth good-bye. As he leaned, Ruth, wanting to get it over with, also leaned (rather quickly) and unavoidably smashed her face into Lance's nose, causing it to bleed. Needless to say, this episode of interpersonal touch was a disaster. How could this situation have been handled better by Ruth? by Fred? or by Lance?

Other conceptions of touch have considered the meaning of touch in terms of status, dominance, and power.[42] For example, when touch is reciprocated, perceptions of closeness and solidarity are evident, whereas when touch is not reciprocated, perceptions of status and dominance are conveyed. The toucher enjoys more status and dominance relative to the person being touched. Individuals initiating touch are also seen as being more assertive, confident, and independent than those who are touched.[43] Nonreciprocated touch seems to convey certain positive interpersonal messages to those touched and to those who observe touch. Of course, these perceptions put some communicators in an awkward situation. When people who are highly sensitive to touch and who generally do not touch others much are touched by others, they are placed in a perceived subordinate and uncomfortably submissive position.

Tactile communication is very important to human interaction and communicates very salient information about the nature of the relationship between individuals. While it is difficult to predict how accurate tactile communication usually is, it is easy to understand how different interpretations can be made about such gestures. Some people just naturally touch others a great deal. However, when their touch is meant to communicate friendliness, but is perceived by an eager individual as an invitation to romantic involvement or as a dominant move, an awkward situation may result.

Territoriality

Territoriality refers to action or behavior that is associated with the claim of territory or space and the defense of it.[44] Altman claims that territoriality is used as a method for matching desired and achieved privacy levels. He has classified the types of territories into three groups, according to the degree of control or ownership of the territory by an individual or group.[45] The first group of territories is termed *primary territories*. This group includes things over which individuals exercise exclusive ownership, things such as hairbrushes, underwear, wallets, bedrooms, and offices. *Secondary territories*, which comprise the second group, include territories that are not controlled exclusively by any one person but that others generally relate to one person or group. Examples include church pews, desks in a classroom, and favorite tables at bars that people regularly occupy. The third group of territories is termed *public territories*. This group includes areas that are available to anyone. These could include public beaches, libraries, and general admission seating.

The negotiation of each of these territories affects the interpersonal relationships we have with other people. For example, while most people would not think of using our toothbrush (primary territory), some would not hesitate to take our regular desk in class (secondary territory) or grab our seat during the halftime of a ball game (public territory). How many roommate conflicts have erupted because of unauthorized use of hair spray, deodorant, or peanut butter? An individual's perceived territory can be very important to him/her, and interpersonal relationships can be affected by how others treat this territory.

Encroachment of another's territory has been studied by Lyman and Scott, and they have identified three categories of territorial encroachment.[46] The first is termed *violation* and refers to the unauthorized use of another's territory. Examples of violations include taking up more than your share of available space, cutting in front of another motorist to turn, and talking loud during a movie. *Invasions* comprise the second category of territorial encroachment and constitute a more comprehensive and on-going type of takeover. Of course, unilateral military action would qualify as an invasion, as would a daughter constantly taking over the family car in order to "cruise the Sonic" and a mother-in-law permanently moving into a guest room. The final category of territorial encroachment, *contamination*, refers not to the presence of another, but the aftereffects or remains of another's encroachment. For instance, food left on a restaurant table that was missed by the busboy, cigar smoke residue, and someone else's clothes left in a washer in the laundry room are examples of contamination.

Privacy is an experience directly linked to territoriality. Most people desire some privacy in their lives from time to time, and some people need more privacy than others. The reasons for seeking privacy are varied. Some people seek privacy because the strain of everyday life produces too much verbal and visual stimuli. Solitude is a way of reducing those stimuli. Others may desire privacy in order to collect their thoughts and engage in introspection. Still others may require privacy to avoid communicating with other people.

Methods for obtaining privacy vary, depending upon the reason for seeking it, the available territory to be used for it, the time sought for it, and resistance by others to the attempt to obtain it. Westin[47] has suggested that four different types of privacy exist: (1) solitude, in which a person attempts to be completely alone (finding a quiet place in the library); (2) intimacy, in which a small group of people attempt to exclude themselves from others to communicate privately (a couple moving away from the rest of the crowd); (3) anonymity, in which a person attempts to lose his/her identification (attempting to appear as an innocent bystander); and (4) reserve, in which a person attempts to construct psychological barriers to avoid communicating with others (avoiding eye contact to avoid conversation).

Privacy can have an important effect on interpersonal relationships. If someone desires and obtains too much relative to a relational partner's desire for social interaction, a strain in the relationship may evolve. Of if someone needs privacy for introspection and others refuse to allow that solitude, relational decay may again occur. Furthermore, two friends who always seek privacy apart from their other friends may be seen as snobs or as too exclusive. Some roommates are perceived as bookworms because they insist on their privacy for studying. Perhaps roommates should negotiate to set aside certain hours for undisturbed studying and other hours for socializing.

Territoriality, encroachment, and privacy are important considerations in interpersonal communication. The manner in which we perceive and maintain territories considered ours reveals a lot about us as social actors. If we insist on always sitting in one location in class or in a lunchroom, we may be perceived as rigid and inflexible. Others may view this behavior as a sign of immaturity or dogmatism, which may cause them to react to us in a similar manner or avoid us altogether. In addition, the manner in which we seek privacy reflects our style as an interpersonal communicator, and our negotiation of privacy is crucial to our success as effective interpersonal communicators.

NONVERBAL COMMUNICATION IN INTERPERSONAL RELATIONSHIPS

By this time, you should have a firm background in the various types of non-verbal communication that play important roles in social interactions. It is appropriate at this point to discuss specifically how nonverbal behaviors communicate relational messages. In an important study, Judee Burgoon and her colleagues discovered the relationships between certain nonverbal behaviors and relational message themes.[48] To summarize their findings, personal space was the most important nonverbal cue in revealing relational intentions, with smiling, eye contact, forward body lean, and touch playing influential roles in communicating the nature of the relationships. The table on the next page displays many of the findings of their research more specifically.

These findings confirm much of the material already presented in this chapter. However, one of the interesting aspects of this line of research concerns the combination of nonverbal behaviors when communicating in interpersonal

Nonverbal Behavior	Communicates	Relational Message
1. Close personal distance and	convey	greater intimacy, attraction, trust, and caring
2. Direct eye contact		less detachment and coldness greater dominance, persuasiveness, aggressiveness
3. Forward body lean	expresses	greater intimacy less interpersonal distance
4. Smiling	demonstrates	greater intimacy, relaxation, involvement, and composure less arousal
5. Touch	conveys	greater intimacy less interpersonal distance

relationships. Rarely are only one or two nonverbal behaviors used when communicating with others. Rather, when we communicate we use several nonverbal behaviors simultaneously.

Burgoon and her colleagues discovered that behavioral combinations can affect the meaning conveyed to others. For example, a level of low intimacy seems to be communicated when a backward body lean and little smiling occur, while high intimacy is displayed when high eye contact and close proximity occur. Furthermore, greater interpersonal immediacy appears to be more clearly communicated when two, rather than one, nonverbal behaviors are used. Specifically, direct eye contact and close proximity communicate greater interpersonal involvement, whereas, backward body lean and decreased smiling give the opposite impression. In addition, the absence of touch, a lack of smiling, and a backward body lean express a high degree of interpersonal detachment.

While these results are limited to those behaviors which Burgoon studied, they do suggest that nonverbal communication has a significant influence on how relationships are managed. If an individual wants to become more intimately involved with someone and knows that close physical distance can help to communicate those intentions, the individual could also increase eye contact with the target person, assume a more forward body position, and smile more in order to more clearly convey his/her feelings.

SENDING AND RECEIVING NONVERBAL COMMUNICATION

In previous sections of this chapter we have discussed elements of nonverbal communication and their influence on interpersonal relationships. In this section we want to develop a discussion on the nonverbal encoding (sending) and decoding (receiving) abilities of interpersonal communicators. Just as human beings differ in social interaction skills generally, individuals differ in their nonverbal encoding and decoding skills as well. The sources of these differences have been explained in two ways. First, individuals seem to develop nonverbal sending and receiving skills associated with expressiveness according to family expressiveness styles.[49] When in a family the level of expressiveness is low (when the display of emotions is subtle and low-key), family members must pay careful attention to the indirect and subtle nonverbal cues that display the emotions of other family members. Individuals in this type of family environment have a greater opportunity to develop a keen sensitivity toward nonverbal behavior and consequently can become more effective decoders of nonverbal expression. On the other, they also learn that emotional expressiveness is downplayed and are less likely to develop highly expressive encoding skills.

The other side of the coin involves families who display a very expressive emotional atmosphere in the family environment. In this instance, family members do not develop a high level of sensitivity to nonverbal cues because the high degree of expressiveness leaves little doubt about the emotional state of other family members. The opportunities for becoming a skilled nonverbal decoder are limited because there are fewer chances for practice. However, encoding abilities should be more precisely developed because of the role models in the family.

A second consideration in the discussion of encoding and decoding skills involves the influence of nonfamily members. Friends, for example, are more similar in their understanding of facial expressions (decoding) than strangers.[50] As friendships develop, individuals will discuss social behavior and its meaning by comparing and contrasting normal and abnormal displays of nonverbal behavior ("Did you see the look on his face when we told him!" or "Did you think she was about to cry when she heard the news?"). As discussion of others' behavior unfolds, friends develop similar perceptions of the meaning of nonverbal behavior.[51]

Our previous discussions have revealed the importance of effectively encoding and decoding nonverbal behavior during interpersonal communication. Through accurate nonverbal encoding we convey our true meaning more appropriately. Less confusion results with accurate encoding, and we may be perceived as more competent. Effective decoding allows us to respond to others in sympathetic and supportive ways, especially when there is no overt display of emotions. The next section provides material that can help you determine what type of nonverbal sender and receiver you are.

IMPROVING YOUR NONVERBAL COMMUNICATION

By now, you have learned that nonverbal communication plays a very important part in creating meaning in interpersonal contexts. If you were to guess, what type of a nonverbal communicator do you think you are? Can others readily understand what you intend to communicate nonverbally? Or do you send conflicting verbal and nonverbal signals? One method of determining the accuracy of your nonverbal behavior is to have a friend consciously observe your behavior with the intent of determining your nonverbal style. Ask the friend to observe you when you are communicating in a natural setting and you are not aware of observation. Have the person rate you on various kinds of nonverbal behavior: eye contact, touch, proxemic distances when communicating, facial expressions, etc. Do such behaviors amplify the verbal message or contradict it? Are you an expressive nonverbal communicator?

Another method of estimating your nonverbal encoding ability is by testing your perceptions of nonverbal communication. This can be accomplished by reading and responding to the items on the scale called "Encoding Ability." The directions for completing the scale are provided at the top, and the instructions for scoring the scale are at the bottom.

ENCODING ABILITY

Please respond to each item by writing in the blank a (5) if you strongly agree with the statement, a (4) if you agree, a (3) if you are neutral or undecided, a (2) if you disagree, and a (1) if you strongly disagree with the statement.

_4_ 1. People can usually tell when I am angry from my tone of voice.
                                                  5 A   1 D
_4_ 2. People can usually tell when I feel hostile from my facial expressions.
_5_ 3. When I feel confident, people can usually tell from my facial expressions.
_5_ 4. I usually share my feelings with other people.
_3_ 5. When I'm nervous my voice shakes, even if I try to control it.
_4_ 6. When I am surprised, people usually can tell from my tone of voice.
_3_ 7. People can usually tell when I feel guilty from my facial expressions.
_4_ 8. When I am surprised, people can usually tell from my tone of voice.
_5_ 9. I almost always burst out laughing when I hear a good joke.
_4_ 10. I can hardly tell a lie with a straight face.

15
20
6
41

(Adapted from Zuckerman and Larrance) [52]

Add up the numbers to get a composite score. If you scored between 40–50 you perceive yourself to be **especially aware** of your nonverbal encoding abilities. If you scored between 30–39 you perceive yourself to be **relatively aware** of your encoding abilities. If you scored between 20–29 you perceive yourself to be **relatively unaware** of your encoding abilities. If you scored below 20 you perceive yourself to be **quite unaware** of your encoding abilities.

The ability to encode nonverbal behavior related to our feelings openly and expressively has its advantages. Other people can be more accurate in reading our emotions and intentions when we encode our nonverbal behavior openly. We may not have to reinforce what we are saying verbally or repeat ourselves if our nonverbal communication can provide much of our intended meaning. Relationships may more easily develop if others can readily observe our nonverbal display of invitation and openness. The ability to effectively encode nonverbal behavior can be improved by becoming more consciously aware of how our nonverbal system of communicating is in step with our verbal system.

Encoding ability is only part of the process involved in interpersonal communication. It is also important to be an accurate receiver or decoder of nonverbal signals. Misunderstanding another's message can occur because of the inaccurate decoding of nonverbal behavior. Another scale is available to test your perceived decoding ability. The scale, "Decoding Ability," is provided to give you an estimation of the awareness you have of decoding others' nonverbal communication.

DECODING ABILITY

Please indicate how you feel about each statement by writing a (5) if you strongly agree, a (4) if you agree, a (3) if you are neutral or undecided, a (2) if you disagree, and a (1) if you strongly disagree.

_4_ 1. When someone is afraid, I can usually tell from that person's tone of voice.

_4_ 2. I can usually tell when someone is grateful from his or her tone of voice.

_3_ 3. When someone tries to please me, I can usually tell from his or her facial expression.

_5_ 4. I am usually aware of other people's feelings.

_4_ 5. I think I'm better than most people I know at picking up on subtle cues.

_4_ 6. I can usually tell when someone is lying from his or her facial expression.

_4_ 7. I can usually tell when someone is surprised from his or her tone of voice.

_4_ 8. I am often surprised that I pick up on nonverbal cues that other people seem to miss.

_5_ 9. I can usually tell when a person approves of something from his or her tone of voice.

_5_ 10. I can usually tell someone feels hostile from the person's facial expression.

(Adapted from Zuckerman & Larrance)[53]

Add up the numbers to get a composite score. If you scored between 40–50 you perceive yourself to be **especially aware** of your nonverbal decoding abilities. If you scored between 30–39 you perceive yourself to be **relatively aware** of your decoding abilities. If you scored between 20–29 you perceive yourself to be **relatively unaware** of your decoding abilities. If you scored below 20 you perceive yourself to be **quite unaware** of your decoding abilities.

Just as the ability to openly encode nonverbal behavior has its advantages, so also does the ability to decode has it benefits. Detecting the concealed emotions of others can provide us with the opportunity to comfort and support them in their time of need. The ability to precisely understand someone who was verbally ambiguous can prevent us from asking stupid questions. And, knowing when someone is nonverbally inviting you to become an intimate friend can increase your social life. We can become better nonverbal decoders by more carefully observing how someone's nonverbal behavior repeats, contradicts, substitutes, accents, or complements his/her verbal behavior.

SUMMARY

This chapter has discussed how important nonverbal behavior is to interpersonal communication. Each type of nonverbal behavior has a unique impact upon how we understand and relate to other individuals. Paralanguage is nonverbal behavior that deals with how something is said. Tone of voice, pitch, and rate are some examples of how the use of the voice can modify the verbal component of a message. Facial expressions reveal a great deal about our emotional state. Most people are aware of this fact, and some may attempt to cover up the emotion with a fake facial expression. This is known as display rules. Smiling is an example of how we cover our emotions with an appropriate nonverbal response.

Occulesics refers to eye behavior, which helps us to regulate conversation and manage interpersonal relations. Kinesics is the nonverbal category that refers to body motion or movement. Emblems, illustrators, adapters, affect displays, and regulators are kinesic behaviors that send nonverbal cues which can amplify, elaborate, contradict or otherwise affect the verbal signal. Proxemics refers to the use of personal space. How closely we interact with another individual can have a great impact on the interpersonal perceptions of the relationship. Tactile communication is revealed through our touching behavior. Certain types of touch are reserved for special people. Territoriality involves the consistent use of space or property presumed to be under the control of an individual. The unwarranted use of another's territory can have severe implications for the relationship.

Many times verbal and nonverbal behavior are inconsistent with one another. However, an individual's true motives, intentions, and feelings are more readily seen through the nonverbal channel. Therefore, the ability to accurately encode and decode nonverbal behavior is important in becoming an effective interpersonal communicator.

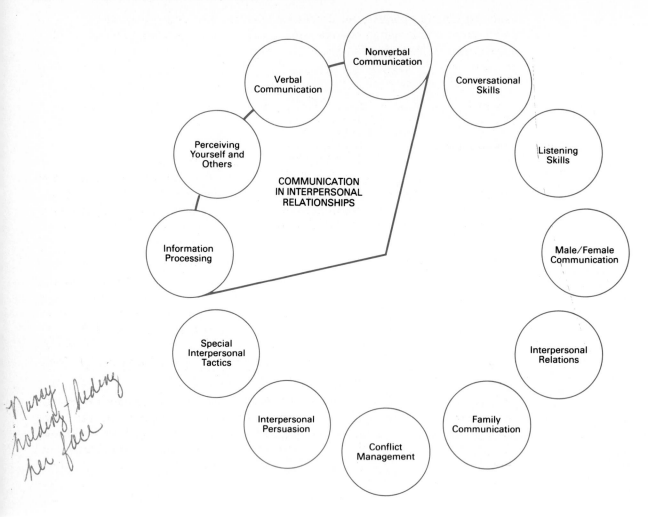

Nancy holding + hiding her face

THEORY INTO PRACTICE _____

Exercise 5.1: Identifying Nonverbal Behavior

Purpose: The purpose of this exercise is to demonstrate many of the nonverbal behaviors discussed in the chapter. By observing nonverbal behavior in action, you will obtain a fuller understanding of how these behaviors are used to communicate meaning.

Materials needed: None.

Time required: 20 minutes.

Procedure: As a class, list the various nonverbal behaviors discussed in the chapter. Suggest famous people who consistently demonstrate each of the behaviors (such as Chevy Chase, who demonstrates kinesics). Have volunteers demonstrate how these behaviors look in action (role play) and then discuss the importance of these behaviors to the person's image.

Questions to Ask: Do the behaviors demonstrated and discussed make the person more famous or noteworthy than if that person did not demonstrate such obvious behaviors? Do the behaviors complement, contradict, accent, or modify the verbal behaviors of the person?

Exercise 5.2: Don't Invade My Space!

Purpose: The purpose of this exercise is to determine the proxemic distance at which you feel comfortable when interacting with different individuals. Comfortable distance will vary depending upon the type of person being perceived.

Materials needed: Yard stick, ruler, or tape measure.

Time required: 20 minutes.

Procedure: Each student should be paired with another student. The pair should negotiate the proxemic distance at which both students feel comfortable when interacting with one another. Measure this distance, and write it down. Next, each student should physically move the other person to a distance that he/she would feel comfortable at when interacting with: (a) a close same-sex friend, (b) a teacher, (c) a clergyman, (d) a same-sex sibling, and (e) a salesclerk. Measure each of these distances, and write them down.

Questions to Ask: What were the distances for the pairs originally? Were the distances easily negotiated? How do the distances differ depending upon the various persons we interact with? Why is personal distance such an important component of interpersonal communication? Why are we so conscious of interacting distances with other people? How do other cultures handle personal distances?

Exercise 5.3: Successful Behavior

Purpose: This exercise is designed to make you aware of those nonverbal behaviors that contribute to more effective interpersonal communication behavior. Such situations as persuasion, relational development, assertiveness, and kindness could be used as discussion topics.

Materials needed: None.

Time required: 20 minutes.

Procedure: The class as a group should attempt to identify those nonverbal behaviors that are indicative of successful interpersonal communication. For example, the class should generate ideas and suggestions about which nonverbal behaviors enhance and inhibit successful persuasion. Likewise, the class could discuss what behaviors are most helpful in being assertive. Many different types of interpersonal communication are available for discussion.

Questions to Ask: How do successful nonverbal behaviors differ depending upon the situation? Are some nonverbal behaviors consistently successful across most situations? Do other types of nonverbal behavior consistently inhibit success in interpersonal communication situations?

Unit 2

INTERPERSONAL COMMUNICATION IN ACTION

6

CONVERSATIONAL SKILLS

How do you feel about talking to others? Rank the following communication situations in terms of difficulty for you. Use 1 for the most difficult situation and 7 for the easiest one for you, ranking the others in between.

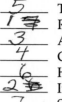

_5_ Talking on the telephone
_1 7_ Reading aloud to a group
_3_ Asking a person for directions
_4_ Giving a speech
_6_ Having a conversation with a friend
_2 5_ Interviewing for a job
_7_ Starting a conversation with a stranger

If you are like many others, you probably ranked giving a speech or interviewing for a job as the hardest to do. But which was the easiest? One of the authors asked one of his classes to take the above test, and, as expected, the most troublesome situation was giving a speech while the easiest situation was talking with a friend. How do you compare? Is having a conversation with a friend so much easier than giving a speech? If it is, why?

Apparently, conversations are less threatening and easier for us because we engage in conversations daily. And if our past interactions have been sufficiently satisfying, we can develop confidence in our ability to talk with others. Furthermore, when conversing with others, especially friends, we can be assured that we are not being graded as we may be when giving a speech in class.

In spite of these things, though, conversations are incredibly complex acts that call for the cooperation of all participants to be meaningfully enacted. In essence, a good conversation depends not just on you, but on your conversational partners as well.

In any given day, you probably spend more time talking and listening than you do reading or writing. Yet most of us do not understand how we accomplish this interpersonal act of conversation. Through conversation we process ideas with others and come to understand ourselves and others better. Yet it is interesting to note that most conversations are unplanned. They just happen. For instance, you probably don't know who you will be talking with or what you will be talking about in an hour from now. Even though you may not know when your next conversation will be, past experience gives us some expectations of what it will be like. As with other facets of life, conversations have predictable patterns. Some conversations are so routine that they seem trivial, such as the well-worn greeting, "Hi, how are you". Other conversational patterns are more related to the task at hand, such as asking for directions, expressing gratitude, and agreeing with a point made by your conversational partner.

WHAT'S AHEAD

This chapter explores the structure and nature of human conversations. To properly understand how conversations are managed, you need to know more about the act of speaking and how natural speech takes place. Then, you will learn both the theory and practice of conversations. By the end of the chapter you should have a pretty good understanding of how conversations function to help people process ideas together.

THE ACT OF SPEAKING

Since most people have been speaking most of their lives, they don't often think about the process of speaking. As with listening, we tend to take this fundamental skill of communication for granted. The speech act is the basic staple of interpersonal communication—the "stuff" of conversations. Consequently, you should have a basic understanding about how it is produced.

Speaking is superimposed over breathing, and most of the sounds that humans utter occur during exhalation. This fact gives speech rhythm. The pattern is one of sound, silence, sound, silence. These sound/silence patterns form breath groups of vowels and consonants commonly known as syllables. With these, people form words, phrases, and sentences.

Listeners no doubt process complete words, phrases, and sentences, but the smallest unit of analysis is probably the syllable. Syllables are acceptable sets of phonemes defined by the language. They contain enough phonemes and context to be meaningfully understood. For example, the word "interaction" is composed of four syllables "in-ter-ak-shun." You can understand this word by identifying its four-part syllabic structure. The problem with a syllable (and the rest of the speech signal) is that it fades. Consequently, listeners must work quickly to understand what is said. Likewise, speakers must work quickly when they talk. Speakers must monitor their own speech to be sure that it comes out correctly. Motley, Baars, and Camden claim that at the onset of speech, speakers edit their output to correct for errors.[1] In other words, to prevent embarrassing speech errors, speakers rapidly review what they are about to say, then say it. The majority of the time, they are successful and say what they intend. Occasionally, however, speakers slip up and produce ungrammatical speech.

Given the rhythmic structure of speech, one would expect that utterances would be nicely segmented according to word breaks, but this is not often the case. Most conversational talk is *not* neatly articulated into separate sounds and words. People do not talk in a word-by-word-by-word fashion. Brown and Deffenbacher observe that sounds and words blend together in everyday speech.[2] The sounds and words in speech tend run together. Thus, speech, to be properly understood, must be decoded in context. In other words, the listener needs the context of the prior sounds and words before the current sounds and words are decodable. For instance, if we were to tape-record a conversation and then erase all but one word, most listeners would not be able to understand the word when it was played back to them. People can, and do on occasion, carefully articulate their speech, but this is rare in everyday discourse. Speech flows like a stream, and stepping into the middle of the stream can be difficult.

Given the sloppiness of the speech signal, listeners have to be pretty flexible in handling speech. Sometimes people have difficulty understanding a speaker. This happened frequently to Jimmy Carter when he was running for President of the United States in the late 1970s. Carter's speaking style, primarily his rhythm, caused problems for many people. But once the public got used to his unique style of speaking, the difficulties subsided. This problem also occurs on American college campuses between American students and international students. Some U.S. students avoid interacting with international students because they are uncomfortable with foreign speech patterns. Both Carter's speaking style and the international speech styles remind us that all speakers sound different and that a competent communicator will adapt immediately to each different style.

THOUGHT INTO LANGUAGE

In Chapter 4 you learned about the nature and structure of language. Now we will see how language and speech work together in interpersonal communication. Speech is spoken language. When people speak they are translating non-linguistic materials (ideas and thoughts) into linguistic messages. To produce a sensible utterance, the speaker makes a number of decisions. Before saying a word, the speaker must know what he/she wants to assert and decide how to say it. Foss and Hakes suggest that the speaker must decide about three things: the content of the sentence, its structure, and which particular words to say.[3] These decisions, though, must be coordinated by some organizing principle so that sentences can be meaningfully spoken. This is where language production comes in.

Language Production

When speaking, you rely on your memories for thoughts and ideas and on your linguistic competence for producing understandable sentences. If you have a deficiency in either, your speech will be affected. To speak coherently, you need some sort of gameplan for producing sentences. Elsewhere, we have argued for a language production model that has the verb as the central point of organization.[4] It goes something like this. When planning an utterance, your initial concern is with the main point of your utterance (your assertion). People don't often speak without asserting something, and, by definition, an assertion links together two or more thoughts. Grammatically speaking, the verb is the part of speech that we use to link ideas. Consequently, sentences are best planned with the verb as the focal point. Furthermore, the intentions of the speaker can be best understood by referring to the linking point of the sentence. Consider the sentence, "Paul is waiting outside the professor's office." The sentence links three ideas: who (Paul) is doing what (waiting) where (outside the professor's office). The force of the sentence is centered on what Paul is doing. How about this sentence? "The dogs are wildly chasing the cat." Once again, the thrust of the utterance is on the action. Not all sentences are as action-oriented, but most of our utterances link ideas together through verbs. To test this for yourself, refer to any sentence in this book and see how the verb phrase ties together the main ideas to give the sentence a point.

Translating thought into speech is, indeed, a complicated process, and the verb-as-the-center model presented above may be an oversimplification. But it does provide a convenient way to look at language production. To date, researchers are still exploring how thought is translated into speech. We don't have all the answers yet, but we are confident that people do not simply regurgitate memorized sentences. That would be too much work, requiring an enormous amount of memory. In order to create sentences as they talk, people engage complicated information-processing mechanisms. Future research may will help solidify our knowledge about this fascinating human capacity to rapidly translate thought into speech.

EVERYDAY SPEECH

Because everyday speech is made up on-the-spot, it is less formal than public speaking. When you are chatting with your friends you don't worry too much about word choice and sentence length. In more formal situations, communicators control their output more carefully. In spite of its informality, everyday speech has some interesting characteristics that are common to many conversations. Let's quickly review some of them.

Brevity

James Deese conducted an interesting study of informal interaction when he tape-recorded one of his college seminars.[5] Deese discovered that spontaneous interaction is quick, with many speaker changes. Most of the utterances were quite short. Of the 20,000 utterances recorded, 20 percent lasted one second or less, and 90 percent were completed within ten seconds. Apparently, when most people talk spontaneously, they do not hold the floor very long. Obviously, we all know people who are consistently long-winded, but most turns at talking are brief. In fact, Lashbrook and Lashbrook argue that if a turn at talking lasts more than 45 seconds, it is no longer a spontaneous interaction but a speech![6]

Errors

Spontaneous speech is also remarkably free from errors. As the Motley, Baars, and Camden study mentioned earlier discovered, people are able to correct their utterances before they say them.[7] Deese's data show that fewer than 2 percent of the utterances he recorded were left uncorrected. If we make a mistake, we typically correct it before going on. Speakers, then, closely monitor their output to prevent serious problems. It is interesting to note, though, that listeners do not prefer totally error-free speech, especially not speech that is perfectly fluent. Miller and Hewgill found that if a speaker was so smooth as to never have a nonfluency (such as an occasional "ah" or other hesitation), he/she was not awarded the highest credibility ratings.[8] Listeners seem to believe and trust speakers who occasionally have nonfluencies compared to the smooth talker who is without error.

Lexicon

The vocabulary (lexicon) of everyday speech tends to be simpler than those of formal speaking and writing.[9] Communicators display different vocabularies depending on which kind of communication they are engaged in. For instance, our vocabulary is the largest when we are reading, and the smallest when we are speaking informally. Compared to writing, people engaged in face-to-face interpersonal communication use less lexical diversity—shorter words, fewer qualifiers, and more action-oriented words. In short, informal speaking is bolder and more assertive than writing or more formal forms of public speaking.

Speech Rate

Radio disk jockeys and television newscasters speak at a fairly rapid pace because time is money in broadcasting. But people in everyday interaction speak at a rate of around 150 words per minute (wpm), unless they are excited or bored. Dividing 150 wpm into 60 seconds, there will be 2 to 3 words per second, or 4 to 5 syllables per second. Place this into a rapidly moving conversation with lots of turn taking, and you have a lot of oral data to process. Your speech rate may even be saying things about you. Street and Brady find that speech rates lead listeners to make inferences about speakers.[10] More specifically, they find that speakers who talk slow are not perceived to be as credible

CASE STUDY

Recently, a rash of new TV programs that focus on television outtakes have become popular. *TV Bloopers and Blunders* is one program that shows the mistakes that actors, actresses, and newscasters make while the show is being taped. As these programs demonstrate, sometimes several trials (takes) are necessary before a scene is accurately portrayed by the actors. The outtakes are often entertaining not because of the miscues themselves, but because of the reactions of the people trying to do the scene. As viewers, we can empathize with their problems and enjoy the malaprops and mistakes.

Why do these problems occur? One answer lies in the fact that TV programs are driven by scripts, not by spontaneous speech. Thus, the speakers do not have any choices in the words they utter. They must speak according to the predetermined script. Such an unnatural act upsets our natural speech-producing abilities to the point where even professional actors, actresses, and newscasters have difficulty. Speaking from cue cards is more difficult than many realize.

as speakers who talk faster. Furthermore, speakers whose speech rates were significantly different from their listeners' rates of speaking were not viewed as favorably as those who fell into the listeners' acceptable rate of speech. Street and Brady also point out that faster speech rates may be associated with higher competency ratings but that more moderate speech rates lead to higher trustworthiness ratings. This suggests that faster rates leave one impression while moderate rates leave another. Apparently, a balanced speech rate that periodically varies (becoming faster or slower) seems to be the best style in terms of overall social impact.

IMPROVING YOUR SPEECH

Now that you understand how speech is produced, you might be wondering how you can improve your own speech. The direction that speech improvement should take depends mainly on the problem you are trying to correct. If you have a speech disorder, such as stuttering or lisping, go to a speech pathologist for special assistance. On the other hand, if you simply want to improve your speech to increase your social effectiveness, then you can do so by applying some of the research findings mentioned earlier. For instance, if you speak at a slow rate (say, 100 wpm), you should work to speed up your rate. Likewise, if you talk too fast, slow down. You should also check to see if you talk too long when you take a turn at talking. Remember that most turns at talking last less than ten seconds. So make your point, and let others talk. Develop an attitude that you can make your points over several turns rather than having to do so in one turn. You may also want to consider the possibility that you talk too often or too little in conversations. Either extreme is socially undesirable.

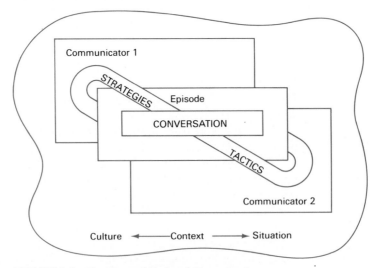

FIGURE 6.1 **The Central Role of Conversations**

How about specific vocal qualities? How does your voice sound? Is it pleasing, effective? Professional answers to these questions can come only from a voice and diction specialist who can listen to your voice and then make judgments. There are, however, some vocal qualities you can develop by practicing. For instance, many speakers have thin voices. They don't take deep breaths when they talk. Their speech seems to come more from the upper respiratory cavities (sinuses) than from the lungs and diaphragm. This makes the voice sound weak, sometimes nasal, and doesn't allow it to project. To produce a full-sounding voice, practice speaking from your lower chest area. Focus on coordinating your breathing with projecting your voice far across the room. In doing so, be sure that your mouth is open enough, and work also on varying your speed, rhythm, and volume. Projection, combined with varying speed, rhythm, and volume will result in an effective speaking voice that will serve almost any communicative situation you may encounter.

THE THEORY OF CONVERSATION

Conversations are strings of utterances that are relevant to one another. When people converse, they manage the conversation as well as their own utterances in order to create meaningful discourse. As with language, conversations have conceptual order. Ellis and other researchers claim that, though it is not as rigid as a linguistic grammar, there is an implicit grammar for conversations that gives coherence to interaction.[11] This coherence is similar to illocutionary force in sentences. In other words, as an interaction progresses, it becomes more sensible. It develops coherence that allows us to understand any utterance in the context of the conversation. In a conversation, a competent communicator will produce utterances that fit the gist of the conversation, thereby reinforcing the coherence of the interaction. Think what would happen if people cared only about their own utterances and did not participate cooperatively in managing dialogue. Irving Lee calls this "talking past each other."[12] For adults, this is not permissible. For children, though, it is quite common, as even a casual observation at a preschool will show.

Meaningful Dialogue

Modern conversation theory assumes that competent speakers keep track of their own speech behavior, while at the same time seeing to it that the conversation they are participating in makes sense. Discourse, then, is produced by people who know the rules for personal utterances and understand how to engage in a meaningful dialogue. H. Paul Grice contends that people engaged in conversations must make certain assumptions about one another's utterances.[13] In essence, any remark made in a conversation will be informative, truthful, relevant, and clear. Without these presuppositions, conversations would not be sensible.

All four presuppositions of utterances are important for interpersonal communication, but the notion of relevance is particularly crucial for extending a conversation. In other words, if people want to continue the topic of discussion, they have to know what it is and make remarks that are relevant to prior utterances. When conversations have themes that are organized around issues and events, people can respond relevantly by reacting to the main point of the conversation or by responding to the last thing said. If we are talking about the high cost of automobiles, at any point in the conversation you can extend it by picking up where I leave off or by reinforcing my feelings about the price increases. Karen Tracy finds that most of the time people extend a conversation by referring to its ongoing issue or theme, rather than by responding to the last thing said.[14] She goes on to observe that when people have difficulty following a conversation, they will likely respond to the last thing said, since they do not understand the issue. In many ways, responding to the issue of a discussion shows that you are "with it," whereas responding to the last thing said indicates that you heard the other person. And for some of us, that is quite an accomplishment!

CASE STUDY

Below are utterances taken from a coherent conversation involving Jan and Lynn who are discussing their weekend plans. Based on what you have read so far in this chapter, see if you can reconstruct the conversation by putting the statements in their meaningful order.

(15) 1. Jan: How about noon?
(1) 2. Jan: Hi, what are you doing?
(13) 3. Jan: Then let's do it.
(9) 4. Jan: That's OK. It's a big job, and I'm the one who is stuck with it.
(3) 5. Jan: Yea, me too. I saw that the weather is going to be rainy.
(5) 6. Jan: That's why I am expecting to stay home Saturday and give my apartment a thorough cleaning—sort of a spring cleaning.
(7) 7. Jan: I know, but I have put if off way too long.
(11) 8. Jan: That's a nice offer. If you think you could stand my dirt, I'd love some help.

(16) 9. Lynn: See you then.
(14) 10. Lynn: Great! What time?
(6) 11. Lynn: What a way to spend a Saturday, huh?
(12) 12. Lynn: I don't mind dirt. I get dirty when I go hiking in the mountains.
(2) 13. Lynn: Not much, just thinking about the weekend.
(4) 14. Lynn: Really? I was planning on hiking through Baylor Pass. I guess that's out of the question now.
(10) 15. Lynn: I really don't mind. Please, let me help.
(8) 16. Lynn: Could I help you with it? I could come over in the afternoon, and then we could take in a movie that evening.

Coordination of Dialogue

W. Barnett Pearce and his colleagues claim that as people interact their dialogue takes shape according to a coordination of meaning.[15] In other words, people exploit and explore a conversation to "get in the swing" with one another. At the beginning of a dialogue, there is little coordination of meaning because the participants have not had enough time to uncover one another's meanings. Once under way, dialogue becomes more and more understandable and unique, often producing one-of-a-kind conversations.

The context determines the rules by which people interpret one another's remarks. In a serious conversation, comments will be interpreted seriously. In a playful context, comments can be taken more lightly. Thus in the context of playfulness, an insult can be taken as a joke. In another context, the same insult will be a put-down. The choice of whether or not to articulate an insult, then, will be based on the context and the speaker's understanding of the interpretive rules. It will also depend on the speaker's goals. If you insult your friend at a time when you are not joking around, it will be taken negatively. If that's what you wanted, you got it. However, if you do tease someone with a playful insult, be sure that a humorous context has been set beforehand. Better yet, to avoid potential misunderstanding, insults may be best foregone.

The rules for communication get rather involved when we look at complete communication episodes. An episode is simply a sequence of utterances (a conversation) that form a completed set. Some episodes are lengthy, others are brief. Littlejohn says that communication episodes can be judged on three variables related to the coordinated management of meaning.[16] The first measure is coherence, the degree to which the participants understand the events in the episode. When an episode lacks coherence, the participants are confused and don't understand what happened. Secondly, control can be assessed. This refers to the communicators' feelings that they were effective in the episode, that their actions made a difference. It also refers to feelings of free choice (or that each person was not forced to interact in any particular way). The third criterion is valence, or feelings of satisfaction with the interaction. When people are happy with the interaction, the episode has positive valence. If they are not happy, the episode has negative valence.

Consider the following episode between a physician and a patient:

Physician: "We got the test results this morning and it looks like you need to check into the hospital tomorrow for surgery."

Patient: "But I thought that we could treat this without surgery."

Physician: "We could, but it would be better to do it in the hospital."

Patient: "Why?"

Physician: "The facilities are more complete at the hospital."

Patient: "But I'm not sure that I can afford the hospital bills."

Physician: "That's why you have insurance, isn't it?"

Patient: "Yes, but I don't like hospitals."

Physician: "A lot of people don't, but you have no choice in this case. I'll operate in the morning."

Obviously, the patient is unsatisfied with the conversation. He/she was ineffective in changing the physician's mind. Furthermore, the physician seemed to be in charge, refuting the remarks of the patient, rather than exploring the patient's feelings, which produced the comments. From the physician's point of view, the conversation met the criteria mentioned above. But from the patient's perspective, the interaction was out of his/her control and negatively valenced. The point is this: the coherence, control, and valence of a conversation must be cooperatively shared by the conversational participants. Whenever a conversation gets out of balance, the dialogue is not mutually coordinated.

THE PRACTICE OF CONVERSATION

What do communicators need to do to competently enact an episode? Most of you already know the answers even if you cannot systematically list the rules. There are dozens of rules of conversation that people employ when they interact.[17] Various studies of conversation management have confirmed some of the more obvious rules of conversation. For instance, we know that turn taking is expected and that people use eye contact as well as interruptions to take the floor.[18] We know that extended conversations often start with small talk and finish with different devices for leave-taking.[19] We know that distribution rules govern who talks next in an interaction, so that the phone caller waits for the answerer to say "Hello" before he/she talks.[20] Likewise, if someone asks you a question, you are expected to answer. We know that if you address someone by his/her first name that he/she will reciprocate and address you by your first name, unless social status differences dictate otherwise.[21]

Turn Taking

The most notable treatment of conversational conventions comes from Sacks, Schegloff, and Jefferson.[22] Look closely at Figure 6.2, which lists ten universal features of conversation in interpersonal communication that these researchers have observed. From the list you should notice how conversations are not preplanned, but that turn taking is expected even if turns are not equally distributed among the communicators. The technique for allocating turns is quite simple. The current speaker can select the next speaker, or the next speaker can select him/herself. These selections are often accomplished with questions. For instance, the current speaker can direct a question toward another, thereby giving the floor to that person. Or, a person may ask a question to gain the floor. Most of the time, the current speaker gives the appropriate cues (eye contact, questions directed to one person, etc.) to prompt the next speaker. If the current speaker does not choose the next speaker, anyone can take the

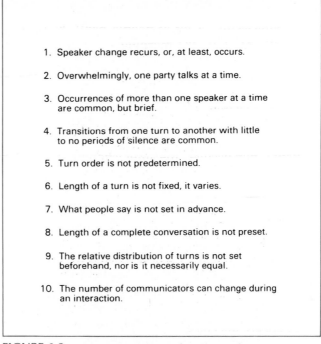

1. Speaker change recurs, or, at least, occurs.

2. Overwhelmingly, one party talks at a time.

3. Occurrences of more than one speaker at a time are common, but brief.

4. Transitions from one turn to another with little to no periods of silence are common.

5. Turn order is not predetermined.

6. Length of a turn is not fixed, it varies.

7. What people say is not set in advance.

8. Length of a complete conversation is not preset.

9. The relative distribution of turns is not set beforehand, nor is it necessarily equal.

10. The number of communicators can change during an interaction.

FIGURE 6.2   **Ten Conventions of Conversations**

floor. And, if no one speaks up after the current speaker is finished, the current speaker can continue talking until someone else wishes to speak.

In his fine review of conversational analysis, Malcolm Coulthard observes that in informal conversations, turn control resides with the current speaker.[23] That person determines who talks next. The current speaker, then, controls the conversation, but unfortunately has only short-range control. For example, if I am speaking, I can at the end of my turn choose you to speak next, but I cannot (in informal conversations) choose who will follow you. That's your privilege as the next speaker. Consequently, when a speaker gains the floor, he/she is granted two rights: the right to speak and the right to choose the next speaker.

Coulthard goes on to note that speaker changes take place at the ends of sentences when it appears that the current speaker is completing his/her turn. This makes it possible for speaker changes to occur frequently, with most turns being very short. The majority of turns are one sentence long, unless the formality of the situation calls for extended utterances.

Adjacency Pairs

Although conversations can vary in length from a simple two utterance exchange ("Where is the screwdriver?"; "Look in the drawer") to more extended dialogue (as in a group discussion over a topic), all conversations seem to be built on adjacency pairs.[24] An adjacency pair is simply two conjoint conversational acts of initiating and responding. Thus when people take turns talking, they often execute adjacency pairs. Typical adjacency pairs are: 1) question-answer (as in the screwdriver situation above; 2) request-comply ("Will you drive me to the hospital?"; "Sure"); 3) inform-acknowledge ("It's supposed to rain today"; "Thanks for reminding me; I'll bring my umbrella"); and 4) assertion-agreement ("Your credit rating should be good enough to get the loan"; "I think so too").[25] Many times an adjacency pair is simply one segment of a longer conversation, thus demonstrating that adjacency pairs are foundational units of conversations. Without them, there would be no conversation.

Silence

The above observations about turn taking and adjacency pairs may not be particularly insightful to you, since most of us already understand these things. There are, however, two areas of conversational practice that are often misunderstood and thus worth discussing more. The use of silence is one. Just as utterances contain pauses, conversations have periods of silence. It is interesting to observe how we respond to silence. Introverts use longer silences between utterances than do extroverts, so they might not find silence in dialogue as uncomfortable.[26] For others, noticeable periods of silence may cause uneasiness, and because of this, people will overestimate the amount of time that a period of silence lasts. Apparently, we don't like long periods of silence in conversations, nor do we like long speeches. People have a sense of tempo in conversations, which means that interactions (turns at talking) are expected to be frequent and brief. Thus if you and I are conversing, I expect to have a number of turns at talking and will not tolerate your hogging the floor. In other words, I expect that you and I will be able to synchronize our communication behaviors to produce a mutually satisfying conversation that is equitable. Furthermore, when there is no more to be said (a long period of silence) the conversation must be ended, or a new topic started. In sum, silence, like talk, plays an integral role in interpersonal communication. If it is properly managed, the conversation can be competently enacted.

Interruptions

Interruptions are another interesting area of conversational conventions. What does it mean when someone interrupts you? Is it a sign of rudeness or attempted dominance? Or an attempt to control the discussion? In the past, interruptions have been viewed negatively, but recent research shows that interruptions serve useful functions in communication. Kennedy and Camden tape-recorded and coded 255 interruptions taken from conversations.[27] They found five types of interruptions. The first was clarification ("What do you mean?"; "I missed your point"; etc.). This one type of interruption accounted for 11 percent of all the interruptions. Agreement, the second type of interruption ("You're right, this dog needs a bath," or "Our meetings do last too long," etc.), was the most popular type, accounting for 38 percent of the interruptions. Disagreement ("Hold it, you're wrong," or "I don't like that idea," etc.), the third type of interruption, occurred 19 percent of the time. The fourth kind of interruption was tangentialization. This kind of interruption picks up on the speaker's point but then makes light of the speaker's idea ("It's OK, but ugly," or "Let's eat here; I can get indigestion anywhere," etc.). Only 8 percent of the interruptions were of this type. Nearly one-fourth (24 percent) of the interruptions were subject changes ("Anyone seen my pencil?" or "Gee, it's hot in here," etc.). Such remarks have nothing to do with the speaker's point.

Looking back at the five types of interruptions, the last two (tangentialization and subject changes) are probably the most dysfunctional in a conversation. The others (clarification, agreement, and disagreement) can actually sharpen a conversation and assist the coordinated management of meaning. Furthermore, clarification and agreement combined make up nearly half of the interruptions (49 percent), and both serve to confirm the speaker's utterance. These findings lead the authors to conclude that interruptions do not always serve as acts of dominance and control, and that a conversation without interruptions may be no better than one with them.

Conversational Narratives

Sometimes a person takes a longer than average turn in a conversation to enact a narrative. By definition, a narrative is an extended turn at talking in which the speaker tells a story or offers an elaborated account of an event or idea. Narratives are typically driven by conceptual schemata (packages of information about an event or idea that are stored in memory). Studying narratives is currently popular in conversational research.[28] For instance, two German linguists have been analyzing conversational narratives for more than ten years, and they have identified a number of criteria for evaluating the quality of narratives.[29] Among the criteria are:

1. Both the speaker and listener must be at ease (in a leisurely mood), must know something about each other, and must not be busy otherwise.
2. The narrative must be about something that is reportable and interesting.
3. The narrative should be relevant to the ongoing conversation.
4. The narrative should contain listener-orienting information if the listener does not know about the setting and background of the event.
5. The story (narrative) must have a plan disruption (something unusual about it).
6. There should be enough details, but not too many, to fit the listeners.
7. The narrative should be well organized with the story sequence in order.

In sum, narratives are not to be enacted haphazardly. Although the motivation for enacting a narrative may be unplanned (i.e., the ongoing conversation may prompt you to tell a story), it is important to realize that you will be taking an extended turn, and so it should be timely, reasonably organized, and sufficiently interesting to warrant holding the floor. People who have nothing to say but enjoy hearing themselves talk soon bore their conversational partners. On the other hand, a well-placed, well-articulated narrative adds to the pleasure of a conversation.

IMPROVING YOUR CONVERSATIONS

Improving your ability to carry on conversations with people is a matter of knowing what makes conversations flow. Have you noticed that most social gatherings start out a bit sluggishly but soon pick up as the conversation rolls smoothly? What causes this?

Structurally, conversations are sequences of turns at talking, but the structure itself does not keep a conversation rolling: the content of the conversation does. Lively conversations are characterised by people who are in tune with each other's ideas and feelings. They have gone beyond the ceremonial, introductory talk about name, occupation, etc., and have engaged each other in a specific topic of mutual interest. How did they get to that point in a conversation? Someone had to start it. How, then, do people successfully start a conversation on a particular topic?

Alan Garner suggest that there are always three major topics that can be talked about at a social gathering.[30] They are the situation, the other person, and yourself. You can talk about these things in three ways: by asking a question, voicing a opinion, or stating a fact. Figure 6.3 illustrates a 3×3 matrix of

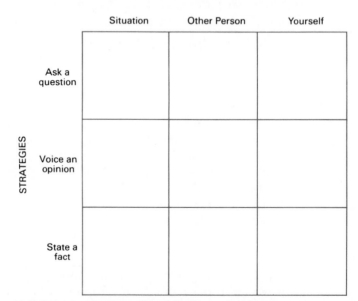

FIGURE 6.3   **Conversational Topics and Strategies**

the topics and strategies available for starting a conversation. As you can tell, you can start a conversation by asking a question about the situation, the other person, or yourself. Likewise, you can voice an opinion or state a fact about the situation, the other person, or yourself. Consider each square in the matrix, and see if you can come up with a possible conversation starter. You may be surprised to learn just how easy it is to do.

SUMMARY

Starting with the basic act of speaking and continuing to encoding conversational narratives, this chapter has attempted to explain how people conduct conversations. For most of us, speech is a natural activity, and conversations

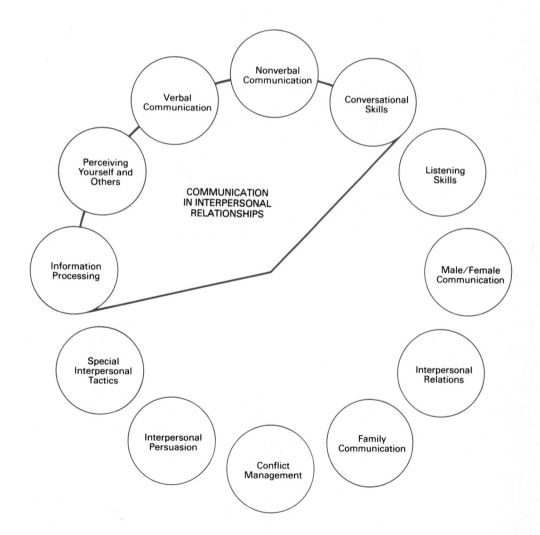

are simply the mutual enactment of speech skills through which people share and process their ideas with others. By engaging others in conversation, we come to know more about ourselves, others, and the world around us. Meaningful conversation depends on each speaker doing his/her part to produce meaningful, well-coordinated dialogue. This is accomplished through our implicit understanding of the social conventions of conversations. Effective conversationalists know these rules and practice the appropriate conventions of conversations. Furthermore, effective communicators realize that they can initiate conversations by talking about the situation at hand, the other person, or about themselves.

THEORY INTO PRACTICE

Here are some exercises that provide opportunities to study conversations in action.

Exercise 6.1: Examining the Conventions of Conversations

Purpose: To observe firsthand how conversations are patterned.

Materials Needed: Paper and pencil.

Time Required: 50 minutes.

Procedure: The instructor will divide the class into groups of six. In the groups, choose three members to discuss a topic of your choice. The topic should be one of interest to the members of the group and one the chosen communicators can talk about for 15 minutes. The other three members will serve as silent observers. Each observer should choose one of the communicators to observe during the discussion. The observers are to keep track (in writing) of the following:

1. How many times the communicator talked.
2. How many times the communicator talked for more than 45 seconds.
3. Who the communicator followed at each turn.
4. How many times the communicator interrupted a speaker.
5. What devices the communicator used to gain the floor.
6. Any other things that were relevant to the flow of the conversation.

When the discussion is completed, the observers should tally their records and share their findings with the group. At an appropriate time, the instructor will reconvene the whole class and lead a discussion about this exercise.

Questions to Ask: (1) Who talked the most? the least? (2) Who took the longest turns? (3) What consistent pattern, if any, emerged in the order of turn taking? (4) What rules of conversation where implicitly involved in the discussions? (5) What did you learn about conversations doing this exercise?

Exercise 6.2: The Content of Conversations

Purpose: To develop a sense of the relative frequencies of certain kinds of statements made in a conversation.

Materials Needed: A reproduction of the following chart and a pencil.

Time Required: 50 minutes.

Procedure: This is a repeat of exercise 6.1, with the exception that the observers will keep a frequency count on the communicators using the following categories:

1. Agrees with the previous speaker.

2. Disagrees with the previous speaker.

3. Gives an opinion.

4. Gives new information.

5. Jokes, laughs, etc.

6. Shows anger.

7. Clarifies a previous remark.

8. Asks the opinion of others.

9. Asks for information from others.

Notice that the above categories call for a content analysis of the communicator's statements. Sometimes more than one category will be needed to describe what the communicator did. For the most part, though, try to choose just one category as you are scoring your communicator's remarks. As before, the observers will share their tallies with the communicators at the end of the group discussion. The instructor will then lead the class in a discussion of the exercise.

Questions to Ask: (1) Which of the nine categories was used the most? the least? (2) What can you say about the group climate based on your observations? (3) Which kinds of statements are most beneficial for effective communication? Why?

Exercise 6.3: Analyzing Meetings

Purpose: To explore how conversations function in formal settings.

Materials Needed: Tape recorder.

Time Required: 5–10 minutes per report.

Procedure: You will be giving a 5–10 minute oral report to a class on how conversations operate in formal meetings. With permission, tape-record a small, but formal meeting that occurs outside of class. (Don't attempt to record a meeting involving a lot of people unless you have sufficient recording equipment to properly pick up all the voices.) Be sure to get the participants' permission, explaining that you will be using the tape in class as part of an oral report. Once you have recorded the meeting, take your recording home and identify three or four points in the tape that illustrate different aspects of conversational strategies. Your oral report, then, will be an explanation of the conversational strategies you discovered as illustrated by examples played from the tape recording.

Questions to Ask: (1) Are people more well mannered in formal meetings than in casual conversations? (2) Do turns take longer than in casual conversations? (3) Was anything done to insure that everyone had an opportunity to talk? (4) Did everyone talk? (5) How about interruptions and silent periods?

LISTENING SKILLS

7

When most people think about improving their competency in communication they think about bettering their speech skills. They don't worry much about their listening skills. This is because listening is taken for granted. Most people listen every day without much effort or attention to what they are doing. For many people, listening is similar to breathing—an automatic activity. In spite of the apparent ease and naturalness of listening, people have no dependable way of knowing how well they listen until their attention is consciously drawn to it.

Listening is also crucial for developing satisfying relationships with others. Effective listeners have many friends and usually participate in a variety of relationships. In fact, good listening skills are necessary to accurately monitor the development of any relationship. As you will learn in Chapter 9, interpersonal relationships can change in subtle ways, and sometimes these changes can be spotted early through effective listening.

WHAT'S AHEAD

The purpose of this chapter is to draw your attention to how listening operates in communication and how your own listening skills may be affected. This will be accomplished by looking at both the theory and practice of listening. First you will learn how listening works, beginning with a definition of listening and ending with the concept of forecasting. Then you will learn about the research in listening comprehension. Finally, we will offer some practical advice on how to improve your listening skills.

"I was recently promoted to a supervisor's job at work. Since I have taken over the job, I have had to train three new employees. One of them was easy to train. She caught on to the task quickly. The other two, however, have been a bear. I tell them something, and they act like they didn't hear me. They make lots of mistakes, which means I have to go over the instructions again. In short, they aren't listening. Why? What can I do to get them to pay more attention to my instructions?"
Signed: Repeating Myself

LISTENING DEFINED

Listening is an extension of hearing, but it is not the same as hearing. Whereas hearing is physiological, listening is psychological. Whereas your hearing transmits sounds, you need listening to interpret sounds. You need to hear to listen, but you do not listen simply because you hear. Thus, listening is a mental process that you direct and control.

By definition, *listening is a perception/comprehension process of taking what you hear and organizing it into units to which you assign meaning.* Notice that listening is defined as a process. Consequently, the definition focuses on the *act* of listening, drawing your attention to what you are doing when you listen. As such, listening is a psychological activity associated with making sense out of other people's speech. When you listen, you perceive, comprehend, organize, and assign meaning to what you hear. To help you understand this more completely, let's consider the Goss model of listening.

GOSS MODEL OF LISTENING

Listening is an auditory perception and comprehension task, in which listeners must not only hear what is said, but understand it as well. Given the fact that speech signals fade rapidly, listening must begin during the speaker's turn, not afterwards. In other words, listeners do not wait until the speaker has completed a turn before they process the utterances. Imagine what it would be like if we had to wait until the end of each turn before we analyzed a speaker's utterances. While it might be good for human relationships if listeners would wait until speakers finish talking, everyday listening doesn't work this way.

It is also important to realize that although spoken discourse unfolds in a linear, word-by-word manner, the listening process is not linear. Listening is a complex mental task that depends on the listeners analyzing the ongoing discourse while at the same time calling upon their own past experiences for assigning meaning to the messages. This means that listeners think as speakers speak and that listeners must often listen at different levels at the same time. To illustrate how this works, Blaine Goss recently presented a three-level model of listening.[1] Figure 7.1 shows that listening involves three phases: signal processing, literal processing, and reflective processing.

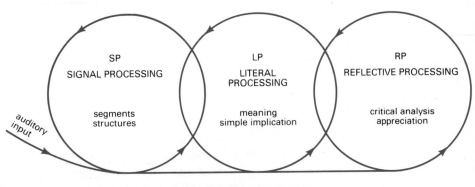

Goss Model of Listening

FIGURE 7.1   Goss Model of Listening
From Goss, B. "Listening as Information Processing." *Communication Quarterly* 30, no. 4, 304–307.

Signal Processing (SP)

The first stage of listening involves signal processing. SP is the act of scanning the signal and sorting it into discernible parts. In a conversation the communicators must discover the segments (words) and the structure (syntax) before assigning meaning. This signal partitioning task establishes the interpretable units of the utterance. An utterance that sounds like "Todaywewillgotothebank" must be mentally deciphered into its divisible units. This must occur while the speaker is talking. This rapidly occurring analysis of the speech signal requires language proficiency on the listener's part so that he/she will not get lost trying to decipher the speaker's message. If the listener has language comprehension problems, accurate listening is much harder to achieve. Thus, if you are listening to a group of foreigners speaking a language you do not understand, your signal processing of their speech will be very imprecise indeed. In fact, their speech may sound like a continuous flow of sounds rather than discernible words, phrases, and sentences. When you can't even make out when a word begins or ends, you have a signal processing problem. And if you have trouble at this early stage of listening, you're headed for more trouble in the next two levels.

Literal Processing (LP)

The next stage of listening is literal processing. LP occurs when the listener assigns the most obvious meaning to the utterance. This phase of listening is primarily referential, in that the listener is trying to figure out what the speaker is talking about. Denotative, rather than connotative, meanings are emphasized in LP. For very familiar messages, this stage of listening is quickly dispensed with. If a friend approaches you and says, "What time is it?" you can respond without too much thought. During LP, simple implications can be processed. For example, if your dinner host says, "Pass me your plate, and I'll give you some meat," you can safely assume that you have a plate to pass and that there is some meat to be served. LP essentially takes the message at face value and presupposes it to be true. According to Sanford and Garrod, listeners close in on the significance of an utterance early in the processing sequence.[2] They attempt to answer the question, "What is the speaker talking about?" This is the task of LP. Detection of other aspects of the message, such as humor, deception, and deeper implications of messages, requires the next level of listening.

Reflective Processing (RP)

The third phase of listening is reflective processing. RP is a deeper level of processing than LP. During this time, the listener is reflecting on the meaning of the message. As Lundsteen suggests, this level of message comprehension could lead to critical listening (listening for logical structures) and/or appreciative listening (listening for enjoyment, as in listening to poetry).[3] RP, then, is the most thoughtful phase of listening. During RP, the listener is likely to make extensive inferences about the topic and the speaker's intentions. And since

RP is a more thorough kind of analysis than LP, it takes more time and depends more heavily on the intellectual capabilities of the listener.

Although all three levels of listening are available for any message, they are not always engaged for each and every message. A selectivity factor will eliminate some messages after the LP stage. Still other messages may be processed only at the SP stage. As Craik and Lockhart note, information will be processed at different levels of analysis depending on the needs of the listeners, who determine how much they listen.[4]

In sum, listening can involve three stages of analysis, and each stage is more analytical than the previous one. As people perceive and comprehend messages to make sense out of the speaker's utterances, they choose how much to listen. And because the speech fades rapidly, listening is an ongoing process that occurs while the other person is talking. This means that listeners must anticipate where the speaker is going, which bring us to forecasting.

FORECASTING

In interpersonal communication, we do not wait until speakers are finished talking before we start processing the message. Listening is a spontaneous skill that occurs as people are talking. Listening, then, must be anticipatory in nature. This is where forecasting comes in. Forecasting is an anticipatory act of predicting the upcoming thoughts of the speaker. Given that speech is slower than thought, listeners are able to guess where the speaker is going before he/she gets there. For instance, if your friend says that "Mary signed the sales slip and placed her credit card back into her—" you should have little difficulty knowing what's coming up. Forecasting is a natural part of interpersonal communication. For instance, when a friend is stumbling for a word in the middle of a sentence, we can easily supply the missing word, because we are in the train of thought and we understand the language well enough to know what kind of word is needed.

The ability to forecast is facilitated by the maturity of the relationship between the communicators. In a pair of well-designed studies, Honeycutt, Knapp, and Powers tested 60 couples on their ability to predict their partner's answers to a *Password*-type game.[5] The couples were pretested for relational knowledge (how well they know each other) and categorized as couples with high, medium, or low degrees of knowledge about each other. As predicted, the couples with high degrees of knowledge had the best forecasting accuracy. Couples with low degrees of knowledge performed the poorest. Furthermore, the couples with high degrees of knowledge were able to take advantage of each other's nonverbal cues to increase their prediction accuracy. Couples with low degrees of knowledge did not benefit greatly from their nonverbal cues. To the degree that accurate forecasting leads to more effective listening, it is easy to see how people who have long, enduring relationships can be good listeners for each other (that is, as long as they are communicating in a predictable manner).

Forecasting also involves confirmation. As people listen to one another, they not only predict upcoming thoughts, they confirm their predictions as well. In

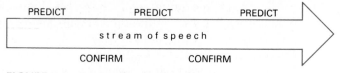

FIGURE 7.2   **Forecasting in Listening**

other words, I can check to see if you say what I expected you to say while we are interacting together. As Aronson observes, listening follows a very rapid predict-then-confirm pattern, and the amazing thing is that this occurs simultaneously.[6] This means that at any point in a conversation, people will be hearing the current utterance, predicting the next idea, and confirming a prior one. The stream of speech, then, is straddled by predicting and confirming. Figure 7.2 illustrates this.

Listening is a complicated cognitive act of perceiving and comprehending spoken messages as they are being transmitted. Different messages will be processed at different depths, and effective listeners will get in step with the speaker both to predict and confirm what is being said. What most people take for granted as a simple process is, in fact, a very complex one.

LISTENING COMPREHENSION

Research in listening comprehension has a spotty history. At the time when listening comprehension tests were being created, listening comprehension research flourished.[7] After sharp criticism of these listening tests and the research using them, interest in this kind of research waned.[8] But within the last few years, activity in listening comprehension has resurfaced. Much of this renewed interest can be attributed to the fact that researchers realized that listening comprehension was an extension of language comprehension and that both are based on information processing. As such, listening comprehension and reading comprehension, as offshoots of language comprehension, are governed by principles of human information processing (see Chapter 2). According to Sticht, learning by listening and learning by reading are both language decoding tasks, and thus would not differ much from each other.[9] The means of learning language (listening vs. reading) affect how information is perceived more than how it is comprehended. Sticht goes on to say that improving skills in one will result in an improvement in the other. The differences between listening and reading are minimized when we are talking about comprehending spoken language. Given this, the research in language comprehension is helpful in understanding listening comprehension.

Comprehending Discourse

In everyday interpersonal communication, listening is handled rather casually. People respond to one another without much effort and do not attempt to commit to memory anything said, unless a particular statement is unusual, funny, or offensive. In more formal situations, such as lectures or job interviews, listening becomes more systematic. Under these circumstances, you would expect people to comprehend more precisely the words spoken. For most people, these formal listening situations are not regular occurrences. The demands of the situation, then, determine much of what is comprehended. Since this text is about interpersonal communication, our attention will be on listening in informal conversations.

When people interact, what do they comprehend? For the most part, they comprehend the gist of the conversation more than the exact words spoken. By gist, I am referring to the main point or the main assertion being made. Tzeng, Alva, and Lee found "that under normal listening conditions memory for the meaning of a sentence is superior to memory for its form" (p. 132).[10] Hulse, Deese, and Egeth write that "when we come to meaningful material . . . it is meaning that is retained . . . not necessarily the linguistic form" (p. 417).[11] In interpersonal interaction, people listen for ideas, using the words as vehicles to discover the proposition that the speaker is asserting. It is possible, however, for people to recall the words spoken in a conversation, especially when they are given a multiple-choice type test to check their memories. O'Hair and Goss discovered that people could recall conversations with 80 percent accuracy when tested by multiple-choice exams. When the subjects had to recall the conversation on their own with minimal cues (cued free recall), their performance dropped dramatically.[12] Unless the situation calls for precise rec-

CASE STUDY

Attorney: What did Mr. Clausen say when he phoned you?

Witness: He said that Ellen was at the airport to catch a flight to Reno.

Attorney: Why was Ms. Franklin (Ellen) flying to Reno?

Witness: To meet with her financial adviser.

Attorney: How do you know that?

Witness: Mr. Clausen said so.

Attorney: Did they have business, or was she meeting him for other reasons?

Witness: A little of both, I suspect.

As you might expect, the last comment drew an objection from the other attorney. But what conclusions or understandings did the witness have from the phone conversation? Was it entirely factual? Or did he/she go beyond the information given while listening to Mr. Clausen? If more was added, where did it come from? Finally, is it possible to listen and process only the words spoken without distorting or adding information that wasn't heard?

ollection of the utterances, people in everyday conversations comprehend the gist of the conversation more than the exact words spoken. They can recall the exact words spoken, but they must be tested through recognition methods to perform well.

Foregrounding

The act of listening is a mental juggling task. The listener checks the input (oral discourse) against stored meanings as the speaker is talking. According to Marlen-Wilson and Welsh, normal speech processing by listeners requires that they process both the sentence input and the relevant meanings *at the same time*.[13] This means that listeners are constantly making decisions about meaning. Their task is simplified if the prior utterances have set the context so that they have a concept actively in mind. This is called foregrounding.

In everyday discourse, listening becomes easier as the conversation takes shape. If the context has been set (foregrounded), listeners will have little difficulty comprehending subsequent sentences. For example, "She was tired but continued anyway" is difficult to understand because it has not been foregrounded. If you knew that the sentence came from a conversation about a woman's mountain climbing experiences, it would make more sense. According to Lesgold, Roth, and Curtis, people store in memory the gist of an ongoing conversation and use this information to analyze subsequent remarks.[14] The context, then, plays a key role in accurate listening.

Listening becomes more problematic if the listener is lost in a conversation. Foregrounding works if the listener understands the information in the conversation, but should the material being presented be too difficult, the prior utterances may be of little help. Lindsay and Norman suggest that this leads to bottom-up processing, which occurs when the listener must laboriously analyze the message to find cues for assigning meaning.[15] Its opposite is top-down processing, wherein the listener recognizes immediately what the speaker is talking about and relies on prior knowledge to understand the conversation. For example, we could participate with ease in a conversation about the television show *M*A*S*H*, but we might have to struggle to listen to a lecture on nuclear physics. Since many of us would not have much prior knowledge of nuclear physics, we would have to depend heavily on the words spoken, hoping that they would be clear enough to assist our comprehension. Competent communicators learn to manage a conversation so that it is properly foregrounded, especially when dealing with uncommon topics.

Compressed Speech

Listening is affected by the speed at which the material is presented. In everyday conversations, the rate of presentation of most spoken messages is so slow that listeners have time to tune in and out while a speaker is talking. In interpersonal communication, people speak at an estimated 150 wpm, but think at about 500 wpm.[16] Given this discrepancy, listeners can become bored by the slow pace of speech.

Recent technological developments have produced machines that can compress speech, thereby doubling or tripling its normal rate. If information can be orally presented at faster rates, people might learn more quickly and not get bored along the way. Though still not widely accepted in schools, students are able to learn from speech compressors, which present information at rapid rates. Orr claims that the optimum rate of compressed speech is 275–300 wpm.[17] At this rate, speech is still intelligible to untrained listeners. Because more information is presented in a shorter time, students learn more sooner.

The development of speech compressors is, indeed, exciting. But the benefits of compressed speech seem to be mostly educational. Students can learn faster with speech compressors, but such learning does not assist everyday listening, which still lumbers along with a speech rate of 150 wpm. All of us have the capacity to listen faster; we just don't have much opportunity to do so.

The compressed speech research reminds us that people can comprehend speech at very fast rates, but the desirability of doing so depends on why they are listening. Usually, people listen for semantic understanding, which would call for all three stages of listening (SP, LP, and RP). However, if one is listening only to recognize a voice the signal processing task can be handled at extremely fast rates. If, on the other hand, one needs to listen to take notes and recall the information later, very fast rates of presentation would be detrimental. I would imagine that in everyday conversations, wherein people listen primarily for the gist of the talk, they could handle faster rates of speaking. However, when most people speak faster than 200 wpm, acoustical and grammatical production errors increase. The embarrassment from such errors prevents speakers from doing so. Therefore, listeners are usually stuck with slow inputs, even though they are capable of responding to messages at faster rates.

IMPROVING YOUR LISTENING

Now that we have considered how listening works and what effect it has on our social lives, let's review some steps that you can take to improve your listening skills. As you will discover, much of the task of improving listening involves altering your attitudes and habits associated with poor listening skills.

Recognition, Refusal, and Replacement

James Floyd, in his recent book on listening, recommends that people execute three steps in coping with ineffective listening habits.[18] They are recognition, refusal, and replacement. The first step in correcting bad listening habits is to recognize them. Until you realize that you have certain habits that inhibit your ability to listen effectively, you cannot map out a plan to correct them. As Floyd points out, recognizing a particular listening habit is not enough, you actually have to catch yourself in the act of doing it. Once you find yourself in the middle of an act of poor listening, you can proceed to step two, which is refusal. You realize that the act must be overcome by refusing to succumb to its influence on your life. It's a little like trying to stop drinking. While an alcoholic may know that he/she drinks too much, and while this bad habit may have had undesirable effects in the past, until the alcoholic is willing to refuse to "fall again," the road to recovery may be temporary at best. If you know that you have a bad listening habit, you need to say no and mean it. This leads to the third step, replacement. Once you have recognized the problem and have refused to let it dominate you, you are prepared for replacement. Replacement is simply substitution—substituting good habits for bad ones. For example, if you find yourself tuning out a person because he/she has unwittingly offended you, you should replace your distracting feelings of resentment with a deliberate effort to concentrate on what the person is saying. If you let your feelings interrupt your listening abilities, you might miss some information that would allay your feelings of offense.

Recognition, refusal, and replacement are steps that must be taken on the spot, while the act of poor listening is going on. As you begin to check your bad listening habits, you will discover that they will be replaced by more positive listening behaviors.

Positive Listening Behaviors

Let's look at some guidelines for better listening. These are the kinds of attitudes and behaviors that can lead to more effective listening.

1. Stop talking: Some people don't listen well because they take too many turns at talking and take too long at each turn. You can't learn much about a person if you are doing most of the talking.

2. Listen for ideas: Don't worry about the difficulties a person may be having when expressing ideas. Listen for the point. Discover what the other person has in mind.

3. Ask questions: Show the other person that you are interested. Ask questions that encourage the other person to develop his/her ideas.

4. Listen for unexpected information: By carefully listening to others you can discover unexpected topics of mutual interest. Pursue these. Your relationships with others will grow when you find that you have similar interests.

5. Don't argue until you really know what the other person means: It's always best to listen first, then make your point. Listen patiently. You won't forget your point if it's really important to you.

6. Avoid distractions: If some irrelevant thought is on your mind, dump it. Write yourself a quick note, then listen to the speaker. If there is too much noise in the room, move. Do whatever it takes to give the other person your undivided attention.

There is no magic in the above list, but if you were to work on mastering one of these behaviors every week, after six weeks you could be a very competent listener. One word of warning: if you master the skills of effective listening, be careful that your whole day is not taken up by people needing your ear. Effective listeners are sought out by others. If this happens to you, you will have to manage your time well so that you can be a good listener and still attend to other matters in your personal and professional lives.

SUMMARY

Listening is the important other half of interpersonal communication. Without it, interpersonal relationships would be nearly impossible to establish. As you have learned, listening is a complex process of perceiving and comprehending oral messages. It takes place at a number of levels and is something you can improve upon with conscious effort. Some writers believe that listening errors cost us time, money, and friendships. If this is so, it is a good idea to work on your listening skills as you become a more competent interpersonal communicator.

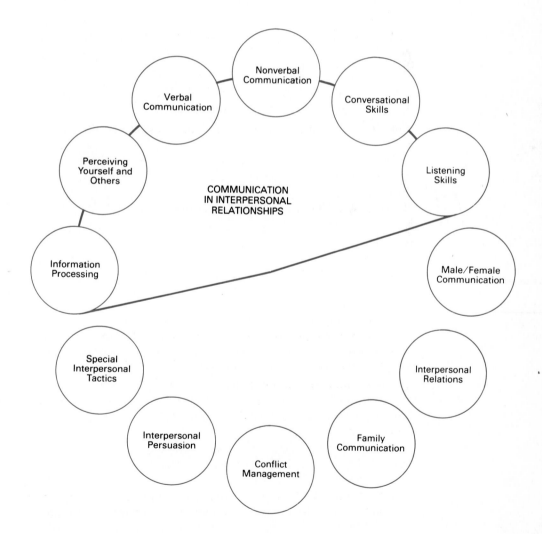

THEORY INTO PRACTICE

Here are some exercises designed to enhance your understanding and appreciation of listening.

Exercise 7.1: Listener Responsibilities

Purpose: To identify the responsibilities of the listener in achieving effective interpersonal communication.

Materials Needed: Pencil and paper.

Time Required: 40 minutes.

Procedure: Effective interpersonal communication requires that people understand their responsibilities when speaking and listening. This exercise asks you to specify problems and solutions in listening. To do this, the class will be divided into groups of five. In the groups, identify at least five specific reasons or causes of ineffective listening. Then specify those things that the listener can do to overcome these listening problems. When all groups have formed their lists, the different groups will report their findings to the class, and the following questions will be addressed in a class discussion.

Questions to Ask: (1) What are the most common causes of poor listening? (2) Which one occurs the most often? the least often? (3) Can the class develop a code of effective listening that all members will agree to strive to maintain? (4) Which item in the class code of effective listening do you need to work on the most?

Exercise 7.2: Three Levels of Listening

Purpose: To explore how listening involves signal processing (SP), literal processing (LP), and reflective processing (RP).

Materials Needed: None.

Time Required: 15 minutes.

Procedure: The model of listening presented in this chapter (p. 121) reminds us that when we listen to someone speak, we can process the message at three different levels of analysis. To demonstrate this, pair up with one other person. One of you read one of the quotations to the other. Then switch roles for the second quotation. (Quotation #1 can be found on p. 120 at the beginning of this chapter. Quotation #2 is on p. 47 at the beginning of Chapter 3.) The listener then should answer the following questions about the quotation:

1. What was said? (Repeat the quotation aloud.)
2. What does it literally mean?
3. What is implied by the quotation?

Question one tests your memory for signal processing, while questions two and three tap your literal processing and reflective processing skills.

Questions to Ask: (1) Did you have problems remembering the quotation word-for-word? (2) Why is it easier to recall the gist of the quotation than it is to recall its exact wording? (3) Do people interpret the quotations differently as they process them more deeply in reflective processing? (4) What accounts for these differences?

Exercise 7.3: Selective Listening

Purpose: To understand how we can direct our attention to one sound that we might not pay much attention to in our everyday lives.

Materials Needed: None.

Time Required: 5 minutes.

Procedure: Every day we hear sounds around us, but we often don't listen to them very carefully. As you leave class one day, conduct a personal experiment in which you deliberately listen for one of the following sounds:

> birds singing
> laughter
> footfalls
> car engines
> leaves rustling
> music

Questions to Ask: (1) Were you surprised to learn how often these sounds occur in a five-minute interval? (2) Why is it that we don't pay much attention to these sounds without being instructed to? (3) What other sounds do you often overlook?

Exercise 7.4: Listening Distractions from the Speaker

Purpose: To recognize distracting things that speakers do and to set some expectations about our responsibilities when we are speaking.

Materials Needed: Pencil and paper.

Time Required: 40 minutes.

Procedure: People sometimes develop speaking habits that are annoying to others. For instance, in a conversation you might become annoyed when the other person:

a. asks irrelevant questions
b. talks too much
c. gets confused when talking
d. repeats him/herself
e. talks down to you
f. fidgets nervously
g. interrupts you

    h. speaks too loud

    i. won't look at you when talking

    j. speaks in incomplete sentences

For fun, circle the three most annoying items listed above. Then the class will be divided into groups of five. In your group share with one another your feelings about annoying speech habits. From this discussion, develop a list of interpersonal speaking manners that would help prevent these problems. When all groups have developed their lists, the instructor will have each group report its findings, and a class list will be constructed based on the commonalities of the different group lists. The class list, then, will be the official code of speaking manners for the class.

Questions to Ask: (1) Do you have any of these annoying habits? (2) How might these habits interfere with effective interpersonal communication? (3) Which items in the class code of speaking manners will be the most difficult to achieve? Why?

MALE/FEMALE COMMUNICATION 8

Much has been written about the manner in which males and females communicate in personal, social, and professional settings. Obviously, males and females are biologically different, but are they also different in their communication patterns? It has been suggested that both similarities and differences exist in the way males and females interact with one another. The sources of the differences are difficult to define because biology is not an accurate barometer of behavioral distinctions. With this in mind we will examine the nature of female and male communication in our society.

WHAT'S AHEAD

This chapter will examine the nature of male and female communication. As interpersonal communicators, males and females demonstrate both similarities and differences in their communication behavior. These behaviors can be seen verbally and nonverbally. To accurately understand male and female communication we must consider several issues. It is very easy to apply our intuition about male and female communication, but as students of interpersonal communication we must avoid stereotyping. In some instances, you may be surprised at some of the research findings regarding male and female communication, and in other cases your original intuitions may be confirmed. By the end of the chapter you should have a good understanding of the nature of male and female communication. This understanding will facilitate effective interpersonal communication between females, between males, and between males and females.

ASSUMPTIONS ABOUT MALE AND FEMALE COMMUNICATION

In 1922, Otto Jespersen published a now famous book entitled *Language: Its Nature, Development, and Origin*.[1] In this book he wrote a chapter dealing with the differences between the sexes in the use of language, primarily directed toward women's use of language. Jespersen's contentions were that women and men differ in their language use and that men used more powerful language than women. While the chapter spawned a great deal of discussion, not to mention controversy, it set the stage for a program of research that attempted to confirm or deny the allegations and assumptions contained in it.

Basic assumptions about the differences in the ways males and females communicate revolve around two generalizations or stereotypes. Males are assumed to possess an instrumental view of social interaction and communicate in order to exchange information, attain goals, and influence other people.[2] Females, on the other hand, are assumed to view social interaction from a more passive and emotional perspective, such that they are more concerned with interpersonal relationships and the feelings of others. Furthermore, these stereotypes have been reflected in the perceptions of males and females. A survey of male and female college students generated adjectives that applied more to one sex than another.[3] The adjectives associated with males included ambitious, deliberate, witty, frank, aggressive, logical, stubborn, outspoken, and dominant. Words associated with females included sophisticated, tactful, sociable, gentle, kind, sentimental, lovable, submissive, touchy, and moody. Interestingly enough, both males and females agreed on the adjectives used for each gender.

In another study, males and females did not perceive themselves so differently. In fact, when asked about their own communications styles, males perceived themselves as more precise than females perceived themselves, and females reported that they were more animated.[4] No other communication style differences were reported by either gender. Males and females viewed themselves as similar on such communication style variables as contentiousness, openness, dramatic, dominance, relaxedness, friendliness, and attentiveness. As you can tell, no clear-cut conclusions can be drawn about the assumptions of male and female communication except that some communication differences do exist. Even when communication differences do exist, situations may cause females to adopt male communication characteristics and males to adopt female styles. While some communication traits may be primarily employed by males, and others by females, borrowing from the other gender's repertoire can occur.

DEVELOPMENT OF MALE AND FEMALE COMMUNICATION

Since we have assumed that some differences do exist between male and female communication we should discuss how these differences developed. In most discussions of human behavior the issue of nature vs. nurture surfaces in order to explain rationally why we act in certain ways. That is to say, are communication differences between the sexes attributed to physical differences (nature) or environmental differences (nurture)? If differences are physical (i.e., inborn or innate), then a change in behavior would be more difficult. However, if differences in communication are environmental (nurtured or learned), then changes in the way an individual communicates could be more easily accomplished.

Physical Differences

At birth, one of the first things communicated about you was your gender ("It's a girl," "You're the mother of a healthy son"). At that point only one thing indicated your gender; the sexual organ. As we develop we take on a few other distinctive physical characteristics. Only women can bear children. They must also endure menstrual cycles, which men do not experience. Other than these basic distinctions differences between the sexes are not so exact. For example, the hormones in men cause facial hair growth, but excessive facial hair on some women is not entirely uncommon. Female hormones cause more breast development, but some men appear voluptuous while some women are flat-chested. Men's and women's bone structures are usually different, but not always (hearty women and petite men). The point is, even physical differences between men and women are not always exact. Therefore, can we assume that females are born with genetic coding that requires that they are more expressive and emotional and that men are to be more instrumental or task-oriented?

Thus far, research has failed to demonstrate that physical differences account for the communication patterns of males and females,[5] although significant study in this area has not been accomplished. An important line of research has demonstrated that no differences in information processing capabilities appear to exist between males and females. Males and females appear to possess similar methods and rates of efficiency when solving tasks.[6] The myths that boys are quicker at math and girls are better at language may have to be recast. Perhaps evolving research by behavioral geneticists will provide more substantial information confirming or denying the existence of physical difference.

Environmental Differences

At this time, the most reasonable explanation for communication differences between males and females is environment. We learn as we grow that males communicate in certain ways that are different from the ways females communicate.[7] It is likely that we watched our parents and other adults communicate in ways that differentiate males and females. These role models provide us with information on how we are supposed to behave in our social interactions with others. Once we learn the appropriate behavior for our respective gender we are rewarded for it through satisfying interaction with others. In effect, we are socialized to perform our appropriate roles. These behaviors are difficult to change.[8]

Learned behavior accounts for the occurrence of gender differences in interpersonal communication. However, it does not answer the question of why differences exist. Birdwhistell has suggested that over time males and females, who are not very different physically, develop a desire to be different from one another.[9] That is, differences are interesting, sameness becomes boring. If he is correct, this would account for many behaviors that differentiate men and women. Hair style, clothing, and fragrance differences may exist because of their uniqueness for the other sex. Communication differences may also have evolved because of a desire to differentiate the sexes. If we assume that gender differences evolved as a desire for role distinctiveness, and we assume that these roles are perpetuated by socialization and learned behavior, then it is important to understand the nature of these roles as they are perceived in our society.

The male role has traditionally been associated with power and dominance. In the beginning of this chapter we discussed adjectives that are related to gender roles. These perceptions may be attributed to the value systems which we learn.[10] Males are thought of as dominant and females are perceived as submissive. Males are thought to be tough and females are considered gentle. These values may be manifested in communication behaviors. Division of labor may account for another cause of difference between the sexes.[11] In recent times, males have assumed those occupations which require brute strength (e.g., ditch-digging, construction, farming, etc.), while females have taken responsibility for less physically strenuous tasks (typing, filing, hair-styling, etc.). The perceptions of strength required to perform jobs may have translated into power and dominance attitudes affecting our communication behaviors. We are not suggesting that certain "female-related" jobs are not strenuous, and "male-related" jobs are, but rather, we are raising the issue that, in the past, perception of tasks may have influenced the attitude that males and females have had about traditional occupational roles. With more females assuming male-related occupations and males taking on female-related jobs, we suspect that these stereotypes are now weaker. Soon, the perspectives, "that's a man job" or "that women's work" will no longer exist. These changes subsequently may have an impact on the communication behavior of males and females.

VERBAL COMMUNICATION

Verbal communication patterns of males and females have been a point of interest in several fields of study. We have previewed some of the issues raised earlier in the chapter. Much of what has been written on the verbal tendencies of males and females indicates that several differences exist. This section will attempt to sort out the similarities and differences between males and females in their verbal communication. Such topics as language use, qualifying terms, tag questions, vocal fluency, conversational topics, and conversational behavior will be the focus of this section on verbal communication.

Language Use

Language use by males and females seems to differ most prominently in word choice. According to Eakins and Eakins,[12] females are more prone to select more intensive adverbs than males. Adverbial choices such as "really neat," "terribly nice," "awfully friendly," "completely sweet," and "wonderfully cute" characterize this aspect of female language use. Males rather than females may have a tendency to select words which are more descriptive and defining. In a study reported by Eakins and Eakins,[13] males used nouns and verbs which related more to objective determinations of photographs shown to them (fraction, centimeter, intersects, etc). Females, on the other hand, described the photos more indirectly using their own interpretations rather than describing them objectively (enjoying, confused, distasteful, etc).

In addition to the actual study of word choice by male and females, research has also studied how males and females are characterized by the media. One such study[14] examined the language use of children's cartoon characters. Female characters appeared to use verbs which connote less certainty. ("I guess," "I suppose"), words which are more polite, and more sentences beginning with adverbial phrases. Males used more vocalized pauses ("uhm," "ah") and more action-oriented verbs. Writers of children's cartoons may be stereotyping characters to conform to societal expectation, which may perpetuate the modeling effect we discussed earlier.

The qualities we attribute to individuals may be affected by the sex of the person who is communicating. Mulac and Lundell studied how people perceive male and female speakers.[15] Ratings of female and males speakers on several personality dimensions differed according to gender. For example, female speakers' language was more positively rated than males' language in general perceptions. Females' language was described as "pleasant," "attractive," and "sweeter," while the males' language was perceived as "stronger," "aggressive," and "louder." These differences were observed by four different age groups and by both male and female raters. Specific word selection by males and females do seem to differ, and males and females attribute different qualities to these distinctions.

The use of profanity in male and female speech seems to differ. Females report that they use less profanity in their speech and have a more negative view of profanity than males.[16] Men are more likely to perceive that the use of profanity is a demonstration of power and a way of obtaining control of situations. It is difficult to pinpoint why some individuals use profanity and others do not. Males and females report that fathers used profanity at home more than mothers, although females reported that mothers used profanity more than males did.[17] Male and female speakers were evaluated when using profanity, and apparently no differences along sex lines occur.[18] Male and female speakers who used profanity were not rated differently. Apparently, no sexual bias occurs for the use of profanity.

Qualifying Terms

Words and phrases that modify, soften, mitigate, blunt, or qualify the intent of our communication are qualifying words.[19] They are presumably used to make our language seem less omnipotent or absolute. Examples of qualifying words include "perhaps I can," "maybe," "I hope I'm right about this," "you know what I mean," "I guess you could say," and "it's only my opinion, but," to name just a few. Previous evidence had suggested that females use more qualifying words than males[20] and that the use of these words made female communication much weaker and less powerful.[21]

Subsequent study of qualifying words has found that females do not use this type of language device significantly more than males.[22] Females appear to communicate in language terms that are just as confident as those of males. It may be that the situation itself prescribes the use of qualifying terms for both males and females. The sex of the conversational partner was studied as a determinant of the frequency of the use of qualifying words.[23] In this experiment, male-male, female-female, and male-female conversations were studied for the effects of qualifying words. When talking to males, both females and males utilized approximately the same number of qualifying words. However, when speaking to females, males used fewer qualifying words while females used more. This contrasts with previous notions that females would be more likely to qualify their speech in the presence of males because of males' perceived dominance. Instead, females are more prone to qualify their communication when talking to other females. Of course, a mirroring effect may take place. Qualifying terms may be more appropriate with other females because speakers may be mirroring each other's language behavior. However, with males females may feel less inclined to use qualifying words because males are not prone to their use. We previously mentioned that females seem to be more person-centered. As a consequence, their language mirroring behavior may be more acute than that of males.

Tag Questions

Related to qualifying words is the notion of tag questions. Tag questions refer to questions, which usually occur at the end of the sentence, that ask the listener for confirmation of the statements being presented. Previous work in the area of tag questions suggests that they qualify or dilute the intensity of communication.[24] For example, "He always does the job right, doesn't he?" is much less forceful than if the speaker had not asked for confirmation at the end of the statement. In effect, declarative statements become interrogatives when tag questions are used. While this style of communication may be perceived as more polite,[25] it is much less direct and powerful. Looking for the listener to approve of our ideas is a weaker communication position than communicating confidently with powerful declarative statements.

Traditionally, tag questions have been associated more with females' speech than with males'.[26] Based on what we have already discussed regarding female communication, it is not surprising that this perception is widely held. However, specific research into tag question use by both males and females suggests that few sex differences exist and that males may be more inclined to use tag questions than females. In a professional setting, Dubois and Crouch found that 33 questions were tagged onto the statements made at a meeting. Males were responsible for all instances of tag questions.[27] Other research has confirmed that males use tag questions as often as females.[28] The use of tag questions may indeed weaken the communicative impact of a message, but it is not at all clear that these questions are the exclusive domain of a female's communicative repertoire.

Vocal Fluency

People commonly believe that females are more fluent speakers than males. Supposedly, females make fewer verbal errors, stutter less, have fewer false starts and filled pauses, and enunciate much more clearly than males. People also believe that females give more thought to their anticipated communication than do males, and consequently fewer verbal errors result ("engage brain before operating mouth"). Research has shown that these generalizations are not easily proven. Silverman and Zimmer indicated that women do not appear to be any more fluent in their communication behavior than men.[29]

One area of difference between men and women in vocal fluency is pronunciation. Women appear to use more standardized word pronunciations than men. Men have a tendency to shorten the ends of words ("-in" instead of "-ing"), whereas women will use the more proper pronunciation. Research suggests that since the shortening of words is considered masculine, males may be trying to live up to an image.[30]

Conversational Topics

Topics of conversation are an interesting source of study because almost everyone has an intuitive idea of what men and women talk about alone and together. Many students tell us that the general topics of discussion for men and women do not vary a great deal, while other students indicate that they would not dare bring up a certain topic in front of a member of the opposite sex. "They simply wouldn't understand," "That's in bad taste in mixed company," or "Men have no sensitivity for a topic such as that" are common statements made about conversational topics that could involve members of the opposite sex. These generalizations are not very informative, since they say little about specific topics (if there are any) that are predominantly discussed by same-sex conversationalists or about topics that are commonly discussed by mixed-sex interactants.

Research on topics of conversation has provided some insight into the kinds of topics men and women choose to discuss. In research conducted by Landis and Burt men reported that, when engaged in conversations with other men, they most frequently talk about business, sports, and other men.[31] Women reported that they talked to other women most frequently about men, clothes, and other women. When men and women talk to each other the topics reported by men were amusements, business, and money, while the topics reported by women were amusements, clothing, themselves, and men. This study also found that men were more likely to talk about themselves when talking to women than when talking to other men. Men may find it more difficult to disclose information about themselves in front of other men than in front of women, perhaps because of the male stereotype that it is not masculine to talk about yourself in front of other men. Men's self-disclosure in front of women may be due to the reciprocity effect or to males trying to impress members of the opposite sex.

Sports is an important topic of interest among male conversationalists. While some reports have suggested that discussion of sports among males is an attempt to keep the conversational topic depersonalized, it is also true that sports is a subject many males know a good deal about. Females who are more person-centered have a greater tendency to talk about family, relationship problems, and their own health.[32] It is interesting that men do not themselves report that they talk frequently on conversational topics, while women report that they talk about many topics with great frequency.[33] The art of conversing itself may hold greater value for females than for males. The question arises that, if women enjoy conversation and discuss a wide range of topics, why is sports not included as a topic, especially among other women? Women attend sporting events and watch sports on television in increasing numbers. The answer may lie in the fact that females do not place sports high on a hierarchy of interest when discussing topics with other women. While they can talk sports, they may not choose to do so.

Gossip is a topic that many people employ when talking to others. Gossip is generally defined as the discussion of a third person not present in a conversation. While people commonly assume that females gossip more than males, no proof has yet emerged to confirm this assumption. Lewin and Arluke studied the actual conversation of many male and female groups where gossip was a topic.[34] They found that women used more of their conversational time gossiping than did men and were more likely to gossip about close friends and family. Men gossiped most about sports figures and media personalities. Women were not found to be any more derogatory in their gossip than men. Topics discussed by both men and women were dating, sex, and personal appearance. These results support the contention that females are more person-centered than males in their communication behavior.

Before leaving the area of conversational topics, we should briefly discuss the issue of self-disclosure patterns among men and women. We mentioned before that men are reluctant to disclose very much information to other men. Men also find it more difficult to verbalize emotion.[35] Furthermore, when men do disclose information, it is significantly less intimate than information women disclose.[36] What accounts for these gender differences? Male behavior can probably be attributed to the masculine role model, which we discussed earlier. Females may use self-disclosure because they are more expressive and person-centered. However, females are careful (even more careful than males) in selecting the appropriate situation and person for self-disclosive communication.[37] Females find it important to use self-disclosure only to receivers whom they perceive as trustworthy, discreet, respected, warm, and open. Males do not report such restrictions on their self-disclosure. Apparently females are more concerned with the reaction to their self-disclosive information than are males.[38] Females appear to be more concerned that the information be positively received by the listener.

Conversational Behavior

In Chapter 6 we discussed the nature of conversation management. How males and females manage conversation is addressed more specifically in this section. Several differences have been reported in the conversational styles of males and females. Perhaps the most noteworthy difference between males and female involves interruptions. Males interrupt significantly more often than do females.[39] As you recall, interruptions involve the successful break-in on someone else's conversational turn such that the previous speaker has to relinquish a turn. Speakers must voluntarily give up the floor (their turn) in order for successful interruptions to occur. This implies that the interrupted speaker is allowing the interrupter to take control of the conversation. Obviously, males control more of the conversations they take part in if they interrupt more, and females allow this control. Consider the following example:

Wife: Just the other day Joyce said to me that . . .

Husband: (interrupting) Joyce doesn't know her head from a hole in the ground.

Wife: I thought you liked Joyce, I know she likes . . .

Husband: When's dinner, honey?

Wife: In twenty minutes.

Another male conversational characteristic is that they talk more.[40] The number of turns males take in a conversation and the length of time they speak per turn are higher than for females. Part of this verbosity on the part of male speakers may be due to the proactive nature of their social interaction (meeting situations head-on, aggressively solving problems, etc.). Female speakers are more reactive (waiting for others to act first).[41] Furthermore, males have been found to contribute more task-oriented information to discussions and conversations, and females communicate social and emotional support for other speakers.[42] It appears that gender differences in conversational behavior do exist. Males talk and interrupt more than females. The implication is that males attempt to control conversations more than females do, and females allow conversations to be controlled more than males do.

MALE AND FEMALE NONVERBAL COMMUNICATION

What would you say if you were asked, "What are the nonverbal differences and similarities between males and females?" Many of our students have readily focused on the gender differences in nonverbal behavior, rather than pointing to the similarities. The differences in behavior make males interesting to females and vice versa. While many nonverbal communication behaviors are similar (smiling, nodding, etc.), the differences between male and female behaviors have been the ones most noted in previous research. In this section we will examine some of the research that deals with gender differences and similarities in nonverbal communication.

Female Superiority in Decoding and Encoding Nonverbal Behavior

While a great deal of research has tried to prove otherwise, there is little doubt that females are better decoders of nonverbal behavior than males. That is to say, females are more sensitive than males to the various nonverbal cues that others communicate. One exception to this may be in the area of visual display. Fewer differences have been reported between females' and males' ability to detect dominance-related eye and visual cues.[43] In general, however, females seem more responsive to nonverbal behavior and appear to be more accurate in decoding this behavior.[44] For instance, females are more apt to detect that others are communicating certain emotions (fear, sadness, disgust) or intentions (dominance, approachability, persuasion). This is a decided advantage that females have over males. Knowing and predicting other's communication intent is a large part of being successful in social interaction.

There is some evidence to suggest that males may be accurate decoders of other males' nonverbal stimuli. One study asked participants to keep track of the number of different nonverbal facial expressions that were encoded by another participant in a simulated interview.[45] Males were found to be very accurate decoders of other males' facial expressions. Females were also found to be accurate decoders of other females' facial expressions and were able to decode males' facial expressions accurately. Thus, while males are effective in discerning some nonverbal stimuli from other males, females are sensitive to, and accurate to, decoding nonverbal stimuli regardless of gender. Enhanced sensitivity to nonverbal stimuli can provide additional communicative advantages for females. First, females are better at remembering faces than are males. As mentioned previously, they are also better able to tell one facial expression from another. Additionally, they are able to respond more empathetically to emotional expressions by adapting to or matching the expressions.[46] Although there is no certainty how increased sensitivity to nonverbal stimuli develops, it is clear that females have a decided advantage in this area.

Evidence also suggests that females are superior encoders of nonverbal expression.[47] Females appear to be more spontaneously expressive when experiencing emotion than males. As with other types of communication behavior, females are less hesitant in displaying their true feelings than males. As you recall from Chapter 5, display rules, which are culturally determined, prevent people from expressing true emotions in certain social situations. Display rules dictate that men should hide their emotions and appear masculine. These display rules are so well learned that they influence the nonverbal expression of many types of emotions by males.[48] Since display rules are not as prescriptive for females, their expression of emotion is more open and obvious. Hence, they are better encoders of nonberbal behavior.

Eye and Facial Behavior

It is generally thought that just as females are more sensitive decoders of nonverbal stimuli, they are also more expressive in their nonverbal behavior. If we tend to believe that females are more person-centered, emotionally honest, and empathetic, then it is not difficult to understand that their nonverbal expressions of feelings are more pronounced than those of males. While limited scientific research is available to confirm these beliefs, some evidence points to specific behaviors that are more generously communicated by females. One such behavior is smiling. Females have been observed to smile more while speaking and listening than males.[49] Smiling can be related to social pleasantries, and females may smile more in order to better manage conversation during social interaction. Smiling is a supportive form of nonverbal behavior while someone else is speaking, and females are generally thought of as more supportive communicators.

Eye gaze is another nonverbal behavior that females engage in more than males. Not only do females gaze more at other speakers, but they also gaze more while they are speaking. Females may look more during interpersonal communication because they are more interested in social and personal relations with others.[50] The more person-centered an individual is, the more that person may engage in eye contact in order to facilitate relationships. Increased looking may also partially account for why females are better at nonverbal decoding. They notice more about another's behavior because they look more. The more looking and observing a person does, the more practiced that person probably becomes at deciphering nonverbal stimuli.

As you recall from Chapter 5, women are more likely to exhibit their emotions through facial expressions than males. Males are thought to mask their expressions in order to live up to the masculine role of not displaying emotions in public. Since females do not have to conform to such a behavioral restriction, emotional displays are more common for females.[51] This is an unfortunate phenomenon in our culture. Males do not experience less stress or emotional arousal than females. However, their arousal is contained or bottled up entirely or released only at an appropriate time. The stress from this pent-up emotional arousal can be quite debilitating. It's no wonder that men die at an earlier age than women. In most cases, the open expression of emotions is healthy behavior.

Gestures and Posture

As we learned earlier, gestures belong to the kinesics category of nonverbal communication. Presently, we will discuss hand and arm movements generally instead of breaking them down into component parts (emblems, illustrators, adaptors, etc.) and term them *gestures*. Gesturing is not a behavior reserved for one sex. Obviously, both males and females gesture, especially when they speak. However, differences in gesturing behavior have been observed in males and females. Females have more of a tendency to use their fingers, wrists, and forearms when gesturing. Men, on the other hand, are more apt to gesture by holding their arm and hand as a solid unit.[52] The avoidance of "limp-wrist" gestures by males may account for some of their more stifled movements, but it is more likely that males do not express themselves with animated gestures because they are less prone to display their feelings and emotions.

Interacting with a partner of the opposite sex causes some interesting gestural modifications for both males and females. When females interact with males, their gestures appear to adapt to those of their male counterparts. That is, females seem to gesture more like males when communicating with males.[53] This is not surprising, since females are thought to be communicatively adaptive. However, while males do not take on female gesturing behavior when communicating with females, their gestures are even more masculine when interacting with other males. Masculine displays through gesturing may account for this behavior. In addition, males and females both appear more nervous in their gestures when interacting with members of the opposite sex than with members of their own sex. When talking to men, women handle their hair and clothing more than when talking to women.[54] Since, compared to facial expressions, gesturing is an obvious nonverbal display, we become more aware of what we are communicating by our gestures. Consequently, we can more easily adapt or modify them depending upon the situational requirements.

When interacting with each other, the posture of males and females seems to differ to some extent. Females are more willing than males to face their conversational partners directly.[55] Males assume more relaxed postural positions, while females seem more tense and rigid.[56] Males, more so than females, will sit with their legs crossed in a spread position and assume a more relaxed reclining position. Few females sit with their legs spread open. Rather, they assume a more parallel or symmetrical leg-cross position.[57] As conversational partners, females enhance the postural movements of males and other females. Males and females display more trunk (upper body) mobility when interacting with females.[58]

Touch and Personal Space

While only sparse evidence exists on touching differences, researchers assume that females are touched more than males and that males initiate touch more than females. You will recall this information from Chapter 5. One explanation for this behavior is that females react more positively to being touched than males.[59] Clay has suggested that this may be due to a female's upbringing, since mothers touch daughters more than sons.[60] Another explanation for gender differences in touch behavior involves the issue of dominance. Touching is perceived as communicating dominance, while being touched is associated with submissiveness. Males may believe that being touched by other males and females lowers their status and dominance level, and therefore they avoid being touched.[61] Of course, as we observed in Chapter 5, these gender differences may be modified depending upon the part of the anatomy being touched.

Males and females also show differences in how they view their personal space. Males prefer to interact with others at larger distances.[62] Women are more approachable than men and are more tolerant of personal space violations.[63] The space between interpersonal communicators reveals the nature of the relationship between the two parties. A smaller personal space usually means that the individuals are more intimate. Males may perceive physical closeness as an attempt to gain control over them relationally, and being in this position does not fit the masculine stereotype. Since females may be less concerned about control and are more emotionally honest and person-centered, they are not as sensitive about close personal distances.

Physical Appearance

Physical attractiveness or appearance is important to many people in our society. The number of dollars spent on beauty products increases every year, and few individuals are not concerned about making themselves appear younger or more attractive. Most people assume that females are more concerned about appearance than males.[64] This may be due to the fact that both males and females feel that physical attractiveness is more important for females.[65] The importance of physical appearance may diminish as a male-female relationship develops, but the early stages of the relationship are bound to elicit behavior intended to enhance or improve physical attractiveness.

Preening or grooming is intended to improve the appearance of an individual. Primping in front of a mirror is the most common form of preening. Daly and his colleagues conducted an interesting study of the preening behavior of a group of individuals in restaurants and bars.[66] Males and females were observed as they adjusted their physical appearance in the bathroom of these establishments. Later they were interviewed about the person they were with at the restaurant or bar. The results of the study showed that females preened more than males, indicating that females are more concerned with physical attractiveness than males. Furthermore, the more involved the relationship, the less the parties preened. Apparently we are more concerned with our appearance when relationships are just developing. Established relationships may not require the same level of attractiveness. Consider the conversation between two females in the bathroom of a restaurant:

Jill: Let's go back to the table.

Susan: Aren't you going to freshen your makeup and check your hair?

Jill: No.

Susan: I want to look my best for Craig. I really do want to make a great impression.

Jill: That's OK for you. You and Craig have just started dating. Steve and I have been going out for some time. He's already seen me at my best and worse. Why bother?

GENDER DIFFERENCES IN COMMUNICATION SITUATIONS

Social Influence

The ability to influence others or gain compliance from them is dependent upon several factors, including gender differences. We have already seen that females' language is sometimes different from that of males. Comparisons between male and female argumentative behaviors have shown that males are perceived more positively as arguers.[67] Evaluators consider argumentation to be a more masculine than feminine behavior. Perhaps those who were evaluating male and female arguers expected males to argue because argumentativeness is a male trait. The issue of expectations for behavior appropriate to the sexes was taken up by Burgoon and his colleagues in a study of persuasion.[68] They discovered that expectations have a significant impact on persuasiveness. Males are expected to persuade others in an aggressive manner, and if they do not, persuasion is inhibited. On the other hand, when females use aggressive strategies, they are less persuasive because they are not expected to behave in this way. Burgoon argues that the expectation of persuasive behavior is an important factor in persuasiveness.

Many argue that competence is all that should matter in situations involving social influence. If females, and for that matter males, are competent in their strategies, they should be successful in their attempts to influence. Indeed, this may be the case. Bradley reported that highly competent females were successful in exerting influence in male-dominated groups.[69] Highly competent females received more reasonable, submissive, and less hostile treatment from male groups than did less competent males. Bradley suggested that while males expect other males to behave competently, a highly competent female who argues her position in an articulate manner may violate stereotypical expectations and actually influence the group in a way intended by her. While Bradley's claims cast the typical male as egotistical and chauvinistic, there may some truth in the analysis of male responses to female persuasion. Males may be so surprised by a female's logical and competent argumentation, when they expect instead an appeal to emotions, that they become persuaded.

Dating Behavior

Students in interpersonal communication classes tell us that when two people meet and begin to date a great deal of positioning, game playing, and strategic maneuvering starts. It is as if one partner in the dating couple is concerned that the other will get the upper hand and control the relationship in a way that compromises him or her. Of course, not all dating couples go through this process, but usually some reflection on the status of the relationship and the control aspects of it will occur.

In an interesting study, males and females were asked about the power dimensions of dating relationships in an attempt to determine what perceptions and strategies (if any) were characteristic of males and females.[70] Females felt that they could gain power if they could control the reciprocation of love in the relationship. Males, on the other hand, felt that power was best achieved by having access to alternative dating partners. Traditionally, males have been in a better position to initiate new relationships on demand because of the societal norm that men ask women out and not vice versa. This stereotype seems to be changing to some extent, and the perception of power in the dating relationship may change as well.

Intimate Relationships

As with dating couples, communication differences exist between males and females engaged in intimate relationships. One of the striking differences between men and women who are intimate involves the expression of love. A great deal of research suggests that men do not express love as much as woman.[71] The reluctance of men in expressing love may result from the display rule that we discussed earlier. That is, men may not want to present themselves as too loving because it does not fit the masculine sex-role stereotype.[72] Men may prefer not to express love as openly as women because it would appear too feminine, but they may be just as romatically inclined.

Of course, the implications of this stereotype of the nonemotional male are far-reaching. A strain in a relationship may occur when the female cannot read her partner's feelings because he is living up to the macho image.

> A student once remarked that she felt the relationship she was involved was not rewarding because she was providing all the love in the relationship. Although she felt that her partner loved her, he rarely expressed his feelings openly. Her dissatisfaction with his behavior (or lack of) caused her many doubts where their relationship was leading.

Another student remarked:

> Even though I tell Tony how much I love him, he rarely tells me the same thing—even though I know he truly cares for me. Sometimes I mention to him how much I would love for him to openly express his love for me. He usually just shrugs off the suggestion and changes the topic. But, without fail, I soon receive flowers, or candy, or maybe just a card in the mail from him. He has a hard time telling me he loves me so he demonstrates it in his own way.

Gender Role Preference

In the past, relational partners gave little thought to gender roles. Men were assumed to enjoy their role as the dominant, masculine partner, and women were generally willing to assume their role as the submissive partner. Holter[73] referred to couples whose relationship adhered to distinct division of socially dictated roles as *traditional*. In traditional married couples, men played the masculine role of head of the household, were the primary wage earners, and performed household duties that were perceived as masculine (mowing the grass, washing and servicing the car, repairing the house, etc.). Women in traditional couples were cast in the role of homemakers and performed domestic duties such taking care of the children, preparing food, and cleaning the house.

More recently, couples have been less likely to assume traditional gender roles.[74] Intimate or marital partners who perceive traditional gender roles as more interchangeable are termed *modern* couples. Members of modern couples no longer perceive the division of labor in the home as falling into masculine and feminine roles. Rather, men perform domestic duties such as taking care of the children and cooking, and women mow the grass and paint the house. While changing societal norms may partly explains this shift in gender role preference, the increased number of women now working outside of the home is also partly responsible for a modified division of labor.

Discussions over decisions on household issues vary depending upon the type of couple involved. Traditional couples are likely to make decisions over household events easily because the gender roles associated with carrying out duties are already assumed ("you wash the car while I wash the dishes"). Likewise, modern couples may have a relatively easy time in making decisions because both members recognize that role interchangeability is expected when the situation calls for it ('George, if you'll watch the children this afternoon during my meeting, I'll have the car serviced"). However, what about couples where one partner has a preference for a traditional gender role and the other partner has a preference for a modern gender role?

Voelz suggested that couples with one traditional and one modern partner are more likely to "experience the kinds of opposition, resistance, and conflict that require negotiation when decisions are made."[75] Negotiation must occur because members of the relationship do not agree on which tasks go with which gender role. For example, if the male in a relationship is traditional and only wants to perform masculine duties, and the female assumes a modern role and wants household duties to be interchangeable, a negotiation about their roles must occur before a final decision can be reached about a certain task.

In her research, Voelz determined that the specific composition of the mixed couple affects the length of time required to reach a decision on household duties and the couple's degree of satisfaction with the outcome. Specifically, a traditional man/modern woman couple takes longer to reach a decision than a modern man/traditional woman couple. However, a modern man/traditional woman couple behaves much like a traditional couple in reaching decisions. Apparently, traditional women are comfortable in reaching decisions with either traditional or modern men. Voelz's research suggests that traditional men are the most determined in getting their way on decisions affecting domestic duties. They are followed in their level of determination by modern women, then traditional women, and finally modern men. These findings imply that negotiation between males and females is affected by the preferences they hold toward gender roles. Modern men and traditional women appear more flexible in their decision-making roles than do traditional men and modern women. Couples who are interested in becoming more intimate may want to discuss gender role preferences in order to understand each other's perspective. More will be said about gender roles in Chapter 10 (Family Communication).

Professional Relationships

Professional relationships between males and females and between females and females are just beginning to be studied in depth. Some of the research thus far has focused on the attitudes men and women have toward women managers or supervisors. Much of the research has indicated that females have more positive attitudes toward female managers than do males. Females also perceive female managers as more competent than males perceive them.[76] Other surveys have suggested that while female college students may report that they would prefer a female boss upon graduating, female graduates with work experience report that they prefer male supervisors.[77]

The values of female business students were surveyed in a study designed to determine how beliefs and values might affect decision-making behavior.[78] Females rated more highly social, aesthetic, and religious values and were less concerned with economic, political, and theoretical values. In a decision-making task females were more likely to spend their efforts in improving the human element of the workplace and less willing to spend money and effort on research and development. In other research, actual communication behavior was observed for male and female managers to determine if different styles were evident.[79] Male managers' communication behavior was characterized by dominance, challenges to others, and attempts to control conversation. Females were more informative, more receptive to ideas, stressed interpersonal relations, and showed concern for others. While we hesitate to perpetuate stereotypes, females in these studies did conform to the widely held belief that they are more person-centered than males. Many experts have argued that managers concerned about human relations are more effective in many business organizations. Females may have better managerial skills than males.

FEMALE COMMUNICATION IN A TRADITIONAL SOCIETY

Traditionally in our society men have enjoyed certain advantages. Even today, with over a hundred years of women's suffrage and liberation movements behind us, men still enjoy special status in several important facets of our society. Men are considered to be more dominant than women and so enjoy interpersonal and professional advantages. Men dominate conversations in our personal lives and control communication in our professional interactions. Furthermore, men attain leadership positions more easily than women, and their financial rewards are much greater, even when women complete the same tasks. Obviously some gains have been made in minimizing the differences in which society treats men and women. Yet, as this chapter has revealed, many real differences do exist in male and female communication. We have advanced the argument that, except for a few anatomical details, females and males do not significantly differ in their physical features. Role models and learned behavior contribute most to differences in communication behavior. If females communicate in submissive and less powerful ways, can't they just learn new communication behaviors and act more like males? This proposition involves several issues.

Female students have many times argued, "I'll never get the respect I deserve unless I look and act more like a male." The question is, what type of respect are they looking for? If they are looking to receive equal salaries or to gain the admiration of listeners as powerful communicators, taking on male-oriented communication behaviors is probably not the answer. Considerable research has pointed out that females who adopt male behaviors are not rewarded, but rather are considered to behave socially inappropriately by both males and other females.[80] Enacting behaviors that violate our expectations for a particular role is perceived as odd or awkward, and is therefore unrewarded. In addition, females who employ overly dominant behavior may threaten the power balance assumed in social interaction and cause her communication with males to be inhibited. This may seem like a Catch-22 situation ("Damned if I do and damned if I don't"), but role-adoption is difficult to pull off effectively.

Another problem with females adopting male communication behaviors is that relearning is not easy, especially not for nonverbal behavior. Much of what we communicate nonverbally is not cognitively processed.[81] Consequently, females who want to appear more assertive and dominant would have to learn first what their own nonverbal behavior communicates and then learn what behaviors are considered appropriate for their goals. Finally, they would have to learn to encode these behaviors so that they appear natural to others. This would be a long and tedious process, and many times one that would result in little or no observable change. In other cases the new behaviors may appear awkward and cumbersome.

A third consideration of behavior change is philosophical. Should females have to change their own behavior to obtain just rewards in social and professional interaction? As individuals studying communication, we would hope that behavior modification would not become necessary in order for females to obtain their goals. If we were to survey all of the females in the United States, I think we would find that most of them are proud of their communication behavior. Many of their behaviors (such as nonverbal sensitivity) are obviously superior to male behaviors. Our contention is that males and females communicate differently in some ways. Differences make life less monotonous. These differences do not actually affect competence, achievement, or task completion. Females may not need to change their behaviors so much as males may need to learn that communication differences are enjoyable and do not affect women's intelligence, resourcefulness, or abilities. We are further along in our quest to eliminate sexual stereotypes than we were earlier in the century. As perceived sex differences become smaller, the attitudes that were once held about men and women will weaken. However, what can we do in the meantime?

Eakins and Eakins have suggested several ways to reduce the effects of inaccurate stereotypes about sex differences in communication.[82] Some of these are general suggestions, and some are specific for males and females.

General Suggestions

1. More balance should be obtained in the use of language. Instead of using masculine pronouns in a generic sense, neutral pronouns or combinational pronouns such as he/she or him/her could be used.
2. Both men and women should become more informed on what is real and what is a stereotype regarding male and female communication differences.

Suggestions for Females

While we believe that permanent behavior change is difficult to achieve and perhaps inappropriate for females, we will pass along some ideas from Eakins and Eakins that females may want to try on a situational basis.

1. In formal settings, women should use less passive language and strive for stronger, more action-oriented language.
2. If you are someone who smiles a lot, you may want to adopt a more neutral facial expression when the situation calls for it.

3. Women need to speak up more in professional and social settings. Recognize that your comments and opinions are no less important than those of males.
4. Females should assume a more relaxed and open posture when interacting with males.
5. Females should not be afraid to touch males when to do so would be situationally appropriate.

Suggestions for Males

1. Males should avoid invading other people's personal space.
2. Males should avoid touching females when they suspect that it is unwarranted.
3. Do not interrupt females when they are talking in conversations.

4. Attempt to develop a more sensitive ability to decode nonverbal behavior. This could be very helpful in the future.
5. Respond to female speakers as you would for male speakers—in positive and supportive ways.

SUMMARY

This chapter took on a risky task. Discussing male and female communication is difficult because both similarities and differences exist in the communication behavior of men and women. Many of the preconceived ideas we have about male and female communication have been formed by traditional stereotypes. We hope we have dispelled some of the erroneous notions that our society has about male and female communication. We also hope that the reader will keep in mind that many of the differences in communication between women and men are positive, and these differences help to prevent boredom in our social interaction. Furthermore, even though much of this chapter reports on research which supports many of our intuitions of gender-related communication, it is hoped that the reader will understand that just as general behavior among a species can aclimate and change, so can the behavior of a gender. We are convinced that females are not as submissive in their communication as they once were. Only time will tell how far the evolution of male and female communication behavior will go. We hope that enough positive differences will exist so that men and women will remain interested in each other for reasons other than procreation.

THEORY INTO PRACTICE

The following exercises are designed to help you better understand the nature of male and female communication.

Exercise 8.1: Stereotypical Gender Communication

Purpose: To discuss and dispel the erroneous stereotypes that people have about male and female communication.

Materials needed: Chalkboard.

Time required: 30 minutes.

Procedure: The instructor will divide the class up into several all-male, all-female, and mixed-sex groups. The groups will be asked to generate as many stereotypes about male communication and female communication as they can. The stereotypes should be divided into those that are probably false for most people and those that are probably true for most people. After about 15 minutes the instructor should have a member of each group write on the board the group's stereotypes in each category. Subsequently, the instructor should point out any discrepancies in the generated stereotypes, especially from all-male and all-female groups. A healthy discussion of why such stereotypes exist should follow.

Exercise 8.2: Sexist Language in the Media

Purpose: To demonstrate that many instances of sexist language, which perpetuate gender myths, exist in the media.

Materials needed: Examples from TV, radio or print media that demonstrate a myth regarding male and female communication.

Time required: 50 minutes.

Procedure: In one class period, the instructor will ask students to bring to the next class examples of myths about males and females (especially about their communication behaviors) that are perpetuated by the media. The instructor can show a few examples of the types of myths that are supported by the media. In the next class period, each student can present and discuss the myths that they found about males and females. The class should take part in each discussion to determine if the myths are completely untrue and to discuss how these myths started and why they continue.

INTERPERSONAL RELATIONS

9

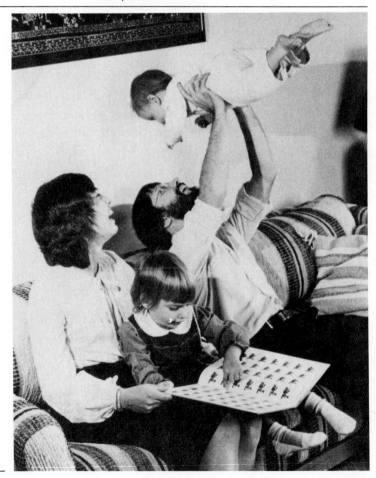

In 1959, a psychologist conducted a study involving electric shocks that a number of college women participated in.[1] The purpose of the study was to find out if high anxiety causes people to seek the company of others. Although never actually shocked, half of the women were told that the shocks they were about to receive were very painful. These women were therefore in a state of high anxiety. The other half were told that the shocks were more like a tickle or tingle. These women were therefore in a state of low anxiety. After the instructions were given, the experimenter left the room, telling the women that there would be a brief delay before the administration of the shocks. During this time they could wait in a private cubicle alone or with others involved in the study. The choice was theirs. As expected, the women who expected a painful shock requested to wait with others more often than did those who expected only a mild shock. Specifically, 63 percent of the women in a state of high anxiety chose to wait with others, while only 33 percent of the women in a state of low anxiety chose this option. The results demonstrate that when people are afraid of something, they prefer to have others around for reassurance and comfort. Thus, one reason for forming relationships with others is to reduce anxiety.

Actually, people seek relationships with others for several reasons. Reducing anxiety is only one. Others include avoiding loneliness, increasing the efficiency with which work can be accomplished, and meeting our basic needs for friendships. Concerning the last reason, plenty of scientific data supports the notion that intimate friendships provide much-needed social support, which enhances both our psychological and physical health. Well-adjusted people tend to have more intimate relationships with others.[2] Thus, relationships play a crucial role in our everyday lives.

As noted in Chapter 1, interpersonal communication always occurs within the context of a presumed relationship, even if the relationship is not well developed, as in initial contacts. Relationships can range in development from totally new ones, such as those with strangers, to intimate ones with special confidants. Pearson defines an interpersonal relationship as two or more individuals who are interdependent and who use consistent patterns of interaction.[3] Obviously, people would not have established much interdependence with strangers, nor would they have established a consistent pattern of interaction with them. Yet they could still communicate interpersonally with strangers. Thus, the reader should not assume that interdependency and consistency in interaction are prerequisites to interpersonal communication. They are not. We can communicate interpersonally with someone long before we build interdependence and predictable patterns of interaction.

To accommodate relationships ranging from those with strangers to well-established ones with intimates, interpersonal relationships can be more accurately defined in terms of interactional awareness. Initially, a relationship begins when circumstances cause people to sense that they are together and not alone and when they communicate with one another with that sense in mind. Thus, an interpersonal relationship exists when two or more communicators sense a "go-togetherness" between them and adjust their communication behaviors to account for each other's presence. Such a definition does not restrict relationships to previously established groups of two, three, or more. Furthermore, this definition emphasizes the role of communication.

WHAT'S AHEAD

This chapter is concerned with four major topics: interpersonal attraction, dominance and affection, relationship stages, and love in relationships. Each will be defined and analyzed as we go along.

INTERPERSONAL ATTRACTION

Some relationships, such as friendships and marriages, form voluntarily, while others, such as work groups and sibling groups, form out of circumstances. Whenever a relationship forms voluntarily, interpersonal attraction becomes a relevant concern. Interpersonal attraction refers to the degree to which the members in a relationship find each other desirable to be around or to affiliate with. In strong intimate relationships it is safe to assume that the parties are interpersonally attracted to each other.

Interpersonal attraction can occur mentally and behaviorally, and sometimes only in one of these ways. For instance, shy people can be mentally attracted to others but may never approach those people. Their shyness prevents them from putting their feelings into action. On the other hand, people may appear attracted to one another because they spend a lot of time together (such as in work groups), but there may be little mental commitment to one another. This suggests that the foundation for interpersonal attraction is more attitudinal than behavioral. Most of the time, though, our approach-avoidance behaviors toward others correspond with our feelings, so that people who like each other a lot spend a lot of time together, and people who do not like each other minimize contact with one another.

Attractiveness is a powerful variable in communication and in relationships. Highly attractive people reap social benefits from being attractive. Advertising depends on attractive models to display products, and the models are rewarded by being attributed positive personal qualities. This was demonstrated by Patzer's experimental study, which revealed that physically attractive models were judged to possess more expertise, to be more trustworthy, and to be more likeable than less attractive models.[4] Likewise, Benassi found that attractive people were attributed more competency than unattractive people by observers.[5] Thus when someone finds you attractive, you are attributed with a number of very positive characteristics. The benefits of being seen as attractive are undeniable.

Kinds of Attraction

Attraction comes in three forms.[6] **Physical attractiveness** is based on physical appearance. Although cosmetic firms and health spa owners would like us to believe that there are ideal types of men and women, physical attraction is relative, in the eye of the beholder. Depending on the perceiver's values and stereotypes, others will or will not fit desired images. Ironically, a person may be very attractive to one person but not to another. It all depends on what the perceiver is looking for. **Task attractiveness** is based on the relative expertise of the person being judged. People who are viewed as high in task attractiveness have good track records. They do a job well. These are the kinds of people you want to work with on important projects. **Social attractiveness** refers to one's apparent sociability and likableness. Those high in social attractiveness have many friends and can be the center of attention at social gatherings.

CASE STUDY

While it is probably true that "beauty is in the eye of the beholder," many people have standards or ideals of beauty that they look for in others. Is there a direct correlation between attractiveness and interpersonal attraction? In other words, do beautiful people hang around other beautiful people? Do men and women choose marriage partners who are equally attractive? Under which circumstances would such standards be irrelevant or minimized?

Now that we have established that attractiveness is socially beneficial and understand the three kinds of attractiveness, let's figure out what makes people attracted to one another.

Determinants of Attraction

What are some of the factors that determine who is attracted to whom? Berscheid and Walster find that such things as physical proximity, similarity in attitudes, complementary needs, and status similarity are significant predictors of interpersonal attraction.[7] This means that you will most likely make friends with those who live, work, or play nearby, those who have attitudes similar to yours, those who can help you achieve certain goals, and those who are similar to you in socioeconomic class and status. On a more romantic note, this means that your future marriage partner (for those of you who are looking) will be close at hand and will share common interests with you. As the old adage says, "like" attracts "like."

People demonstrate their feelings of attraction through interaction. Thus, people can, to some degree, control interpersonal attraction by their actions. Smiles, responsive gestures, and reacting to every point made by someone are ways to show your interest in fostering the relationship.[8] More specifically,

Matarazzo found that listeners nodding their heads as speakers spoke tended to increase the amount of time that the speaker talked.[9] (And keeping a speaker talking is a good strategy to encourage attraction.) Likewise, positive feedback in the form of positive statements produced more interpersonal attraction than did negative statements.[10] Interpersonal attraction is also increased when you discover through interacting with others that they share your attitudes and beliefs.[11] In sum, interpersonal attraction can be expressed by congeniality, supportiveness, saying the right things, and showing that you and the other person hold similar beliefs.

Supportiveness

Of all the factors that determine interpersonal attraction, none is more important to a relationship than supportiveness. According to Berger and his collegues at Northwestern University, supportiveness is comprised of the following:[12]

1. Understanding (how much the other person understands you).
2. Liking (how much the other person likes you).
3. Concern (how much the other person is concerned with your welfare).
4. Loyalty (the degree to which the other person will stand by you).
5. Reinforcement (the extent to which the other person does things to make you feel good).
6. Rapport (the relative ease with which you relate to the other person).
7. Helpfulness (how much the other person helps you attain your goals).
8. Similarity of interests and attitudes (how much you and the other person think alike and share the same avocations, hobbies, etc.).

This may seem to be a lot to expect from a relationship, but each of these qualities is important. People expect them from others, and if they do not get them, the relationship may be severed. For instance, in politics workers are often relieved of duties because in the eyes of the people in control they do not demonstrate enough of the above characteristics. Such expectations are prevalent in everyday relationships. Think how you would feel if you were married to someone or were in a business partnership with someone and did not receive liking, loyalty, reinforcement, and other positive responses from that person.

Supportiveness is especially important when people criticize one partner in a relationship and cause that partner to doubt his/her self-worth. For instance, if Jon complains to Merry that his colleagues on his bowling team tease him about his bowling style, Merry could be supportive of Jon by indicating that she thinks his style is methodical and effective. Furthermore, she might indicate that the others are merely jealous, since their styles do not lead to higher bowling scores than Jon's. Recent research by Swann and Predmore shows that if relational partners help dispel criticism from others, the impact of the criticism can be mitigated.[13] All in all, supportiveness counts, particularly in developing relationships. It is to this topic that we now turn.

THE DYNAMICS OF RELATIONSHIPS

Relationships are dynamic entities that are defined and affected by many variables. Each relationship is unique, and there are no fail-safe rules for forming and maintaining one. In spite of this, certain dimensions permeate all relationships. Let's consider some of them.

Dominance and Affection

Giffin and Patton suggest that relationships can be described by two principle factors—dominance and affection.[14] Their model of relationships includes a dominance-submission axis and an affection-hostility axis, as illustrated in Figure 9.1. Any relationship can be plotted on the axes. For instance, the example in the figure illustrates a parent-child relationship. The parent is strong in affection but more dominant than the child; the child is strong in affection but more submissive than the parent. The example in Figure 9.1 is only one possible relationship. Consider how you would plot a husband-wife relationship or a physician-patient relationship or a storeclerk-customer relationship. The possibilities are almost endless. Furthermore, few people have trouble imagining examples of relationships using these two factors. This suggests that, although the model presented in Figure 9.1 is simple, it seems to have some validity.

Although the concepts of dominance and affection may seem to be academic, they do manifest themselves in people's communication behavior. You don't often hear people say to one another, "I am dominating you," or "I am giving you affection," but people do express these intentions in other ways. Thus, when a father says to a child, "Clean up your room before dinner," he is not only giving a command but is exerting dominance. A professor announc-

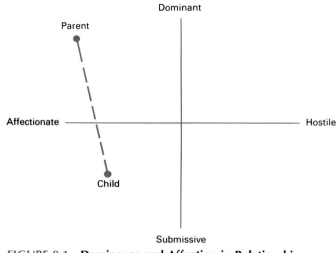

FIGURE 9.1 **Dominance and Affection in Relationships**

ing the date of the next exam is being dominating. A physician comforting a distraught patient is showing affection. A young couple embracing and holding hands is communicating affection. Villard and Whipple call these acts of affection relational currencies.[15] They are acts of giving and show that people care for each other. Whether the communication demonstrates dominance or affection, people have little difficulty recognizing them when they occur. More on this later.

CASE STUDY

> Leo Buscaglia explains that if people would become less self-oriented and more other-oriented their relationships would improve dramatically. Promoting the idea of togetherness, Buscaglia encourages people to think in terms of "us" and "we" instead of "me" and "I." By doing so, we demonstrate that we care for others. He writes, "Your relationships will be as vital and alive as you are. If you're dead, your relationship is dead. And if your relationships are boring and inadequate, it's because you are boring and inadequate. Liven yourself up!" Do you agree with this? Are relationships "dead" because people are "dead"?
> Taken from: *Living, Loving, and Learning* (Leo Buscaglia Inc., 1982)

THE DEVELOPMENT OF RELATIONSHIPS

Relationships are not static entities. They grow, change, and sometimes dissolve. Many relationships are similar to organisms in that they have "life" and pass through different stages over time. Several scholars in the field of interpersonal communication have proposed models of how relationships start, develop, mature, and dissolve.[16] Drawing upon several sources familiar with the communication properties involved in the stages of relationships, we have constructed *The Model of Interpersonal Communication Development* which was adapted from Altman and Taylor and Berger and his associates. As you can see from the model, movement in and out of the various stages is possible:

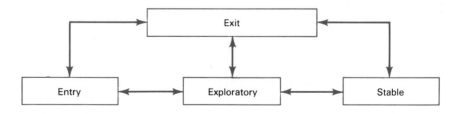

There are several important components which make up the model. For example, uncertainty about the other person, information-seeking behavior to reduce this uncertainty, making predictions about this person and their behavior, assessing rewards and cost of the relationship, testing the relationship, and communication components reflected in each of the relational stages are all factors which explain how a relationship can begin, grow, mature, and perhaps dissolve.

Stage 1: Entry

The entry phase of interpersonal communication development involves the types of communication which are typical when two people first meet and try to get to know one another. Since we do not have any history of the person we must base our perceptions of the person on what they look like and how they sound initially. Of course, interpersonal exchanges in this stage evidence the typical demographical exchange so characteristic of new acquaintances.

> *Hello, my name is Sue. I'm from Las Cruces. Where are you from? I am majoring in communication. What's your major? Are you pledging this semester? Are you going to buy football tickets this year?*

This type of communication behavior is role-oriented and appears ritualistic. That is, we are playing the roles of new acquaintances, and the reason we go through the ritual of exchanging information at this level is because social norms and mores dictate that we do not introduce topics of intimacy (sexual preferences, religious beliefs, our views of morality) in the earliest stages of a relationship. Violations of these norms of information exchange could cause sanctioning behavior by the other party (slapped face, withdrawal, verbal abuse, etc.).

Information at this level of a relationship is superficial.[17] While it may tell you a lot about this person's background there could be a dozen people you will meet with the same characteristics (20-year-old female marketing major from Chicago who is going to pledge and go to football games this year). This type of information is based on cultural and sociological data.[18] That is, what we know about the other person is based on superficial information that could apply to many people in our society and culture. In our eyes, this person is not yet a unique individual, at least not in this stage of relational development. Our *uncertainty* about this person is quite high because we do not have specific information available to us that demonstrates his/her individuality.

Uncertainty reduction.   Uncertainty reduction is an important dimension of relational development. When we are uncertain about another individual and the accompanying relationship we have with her/him we have less control over the relationship. When we have less control, we are less apt to obtain our goals in the relationship, whatever they may be.[19] According to Berger and his associates, we make sense out of the world and out of relationships by obtaining information that reduces our uncertainty.

Uncertainty reduction is achieved by obtaining information about other people that can be attributed only to them, information that makes these people unique from others—personalized information. When we can reduce uncertainty by obtaining personalized information, we can then make predictions about people, predictions about their behavior, their preferences, their values and attitudes, and their ideas about this particular relationship. The ability to make predictions about other people's behavior allows us to be more successful communicators in relationships. We can avoid saying the wrong things and emphasize communication strategies that are more appealing.[20]

The following model illustrates the series of steps that leads to more successful communication in a relationship.

Uncertainty ⟶ Information Seeking ⟶ Personalized Information ⟶ Better Predictions

Uncertainty about the other person is only one aspect of uncertainty in a potential relationship. Another facet of uncertainty involves ourselves. When interacting with others for the first few times, we probably have only a limited ability to predict how we will react to them. Their mere presence may make us uncertain about our own behavior. Therefore, acquiring information reduces our uncertainty about our relational partners as individuals and reduces our uncertainty about the relationship.

Quote from a forgotten movie:

> The best part of our relationships was the part of getting to know one another. Once I got to know you . . . Well . . .

Rewards and costs.   As we interact with another person in the entry phase of relational development we begin to assess whether we would like to continue developing our relationship with that person. We may ask ourselves such questions as, Is this person interesting (boring)? Is this person considerate of feelings? Does this person offer me opportunities I would not have otherwise? Am I attracted to this person? According to Altman and Taylor, our answers to these questions give us a *rewards/costs* determination. In other words, we size up the potential rewards of further interaction or relational development with the other person and weigh these against the costs we perceive to be related with a further association with the person.

For instance, we may determine that the person we are interacting with doesn't seem selfish, is witty, charming, and considerate of our opinions (such traits constitute rewards). On the other hand, that person does seem a bit conceited. At this initial stage of our relationship with the person we feel that the rewards exceed the costs associated with the relationship. Therefore, we decide to get to know this person better, and we move to the next stage of relational development. However, if we perceive that this person's conceitedness could really bother us and we feel that such wit and charm is not so unique, we could decide that the costs exceed the rewards and exit the relationship. As the model indicates, we can move in several directions depending upon where we are in a relationship.

The types of rewards and costs that relational partners deem important can vary from one person to the next. Furthermore, rewards and costs may vary for any one individual depending upon the stage of development the relationship is in. For example, physical attractiveness may be important in early stages of relationships, but less important in later stages. Communication and conversational skills may be important later in the relationship. It is difficult to hypothesize about how relational partners perceive and assess rewards and costs except to suggest the three general categories of relational rewards discovered by Rempel and his associates.[21]

We gain **extrinsic rewards** from a relationship simply because of our association with another person. Examples of extrinsic rewards can include elevated social status and respect, new opportunities, additional relationships, and personal gain. Being seen with certain people (important people, attractive people) may provide relational benefits that are important for some people.

Instrumental rewards are those that relational partners provide for one another. The exchange of goods and services (making dinner, painting a house), sexual relations, mutual support and comfort, and compliments and praise from each other are examples of instrumental rewards.

Relational rewards, produced as a result of the exchange of intimacy and relational closeness, are termed **intrinsic rewards.** These rewards include the "shared enjoyment of an activity, mutual demonstrations of affection and a sense of closeness, social involvement as a couple, and the warmth and joy associated with satisfying a partner's needs."[22]

The costs associated with a relationship are less well defined. They vary so much from one person to another that they are difficult to categorize. Hays has suggested that all relationships have certain costs, and these costs may become immaterial.[23] That is, we recognize that regardless of who we are in a relationship with, costs will be involved. Hays contends that benefits are the important factors. So long as the relationship can offer benefits that we truly value, costs become less important, regardless of whether the costs exceed the rewards.

> Jacqui is always annoyed when John leaves dirty clothes lying around and dirty dishes stacked in the sink (costs), but she is willing to overlook such inconveniences because John is so supportive of her decision to go back to college.

Stage 2: Exploratory

Let's assume that in the entry stage we have made the determination that the perceived rewards of a relationship exceed the costs, and we decide to get to know this person better. Subsequently, a great deal of information exchange will occur in order to develop the relationship further. This stage is termed *exploratory* because each person is exploring the other for new and more personalized information.

ENTRY ⟶ EXPLORATORY

As in the entry phase, we seek new, additional information about the other person so that we can reduce uncertainty about and predict behavior for that person more accurately.

Information-seeking strategies.   Berger and Bradac have suggested three methods of acquiring information that are useful in reducing uncertainty about another person: passive, active, and interactive.[24] The **passive** method of information gathering involves observing and attempting to gain information about the other person without actually interacting with him/her. A "reactivity" search is a passive information-seeking strategy. A person using it attempts to observe the targeted individual as he/she reacts to other people in a social setting, instead of as the individual reacts to passive events or objects. A second type of passive strategy is termed a *disinhibition search*. A person using this strategy is interested in observing a relational partner in informal interactions rather than in inhibiting formal ones. We expect to observe more natural and meaningful reactions in informal contexts, when people can be themselves. These informal interactions could occur at a party or a gathering that both partners are attending. Without the other person knowing it, we could observe him/her for new information.

> **Judy:** Was that Steve you were with at the church party? Why would you take him to a church function this early in your relationship? Aren't you afraid that religious differences may scare him off?
>
> **Ann:** Not really. Besides, it gave me a chance to see him react to friends of mine he had never met before. It put us in a new situation that we had not experienced. I learned a lot about him from it.

Active information-seeking procedures involve more effort on the part of the information seeker, but again, interaction does not occur between the two people in the relationship. The first type of active strategy involves asking others what they know about the target person. Their insights could give us information that could confirm or contradict our own perceptions ("Does Joe drink?" "Why did he break up with his old girlfriend?"). A second method of active information seeking is called *environmental structuring*. This strategy involves the manipulation of the environment in order to observe specific reactions by the target. For instance, we may ask a friend to engage in a conversation with the target person and bring up topics that are of interest to us. These may be topics that we are reluctant to introduce ourselves ("Do you date-around or are you a one-man woman?"), or they may be risky topics ("Do you believe in premarital sex?"). Another method might involve our restructuring the seating arrangements at a party so that we can observe the target interacting with certain people. For whatever reasons, we may actively manipulate the environment (and the person) in order to acquire previously unknown information.

Another method of gathering information about a person we are interested in is termed **interactive**. This technique involves an open discussion of topics the two people in the developing relationship are interested in. *Interrogation* is an interactive strategy that employs direct questions and answers to learn about another person in a relationship. Obviously the types of questions asked depend on the individuals involved.

Hortense: Are we going to date other people?

Herbert: Only every other weekend.

A second interactive strategy is *self-disclosure*. We discussed self-disclosure in Chapter 3. The purpose of it here is to induce the other person to reveal personal information. As we divulge personal information about ourselves, we expect that the target person will also give similar information.

Jill: I really like the way you rub my neck. It makes me feel sensuous.

Craig: That's the way I've been wanting you to feel.

Jill: I thought so, but you never told me.

All three information-seeking strategies are intended to provide us with information about the target person that we did not have previously so that uncertainty can be further reduced.

Breadth and depth of knowledge.   According to Altman and Taylor, two levels of knowledge can be exchanged in a relationship: breadth and depth. The more we know about a person's personality, attitudes, and interests, the more breadth of knowledge we have about that person. For example, we may know very little about a relational partner's feelings toward raising children but know a great deal about that person's attitudes toward higher education. The breadth of our understanding of another person depends upon our past observations of and interactions with that individual.

The depth dimension refers to the layers of personality that are revealed to others. Altman and Taylor used an onion as an analogy of how the depth dimension works in developing relationships. The outer skin of the personality (onion) contains those elements about us that are easily revealed or learned, such as biographical characteristics (race, sex, age, physical features, etc.). The intermediate layers contain our attitudes and opinions about various topics, and the central or core layers contain those aspects of our personality not readily revealed to others, such as fears, self-image, and basic values and beliefs. Most people are reluctant to share their fears and self-concepts with many people. Usually it takes trust and a highly developed relationship for two people to open up their core layers to each other.

Both of these relational dimensions are important to relational development. In order to reduce uncertainty we need to possess a storehouse of knowledge about the other person's feelings on a wide range of subjects. By the same token, we cannot really be certain of the attitude and behavior of a person unless we know that person's innermost thoughts and perceptions on these subjects. Obviously, all relationships differ in terms of their breadth and depth of knowledge. But in order for a relationship to develop to a level of closeness and intimacy both dimensions of knowledge must be addressed.

Assuming that information has been accumulating, in both the depth and breadth levels, then relational partners continue to reduce uncertainty about one another. Our predictions about the other person increase and become more accurate. As our predictions about the other person become more accurate, we become less hesitant to introduce subjects, topics, language, stories, and past histories. We predict that the other person is ready for more personalized and intimate communication and we test new communication behavior. If these tests prove to be successful initially, then we will continue the testing process. As this process continues, both our breadth and depth of knowledge about the other person increases, leading us to a new level of intimacy. Instances of emotional communication are recognized, and the relationship will contain less role communication than before because we will not any longer have to base our knowledge and predictions about the other person on sociological data. We can base our knowledge more on what we know about that person as an individual.

As in the entry phase of this model, individuals will assess the rewards and costs of the relationship. If after discovering both breadth and depth knowledge about the other person, we determine that the relationship is too costly to continue ("I give more than I receive in this relationship"), then it is likely we will exit. However, if we judge that continuing a relationship with this person is really worth our time we may decide to escalate the relationship and move to the next stage.

Stage 3: Stable

EXPLORATORY   ⟶   STABLE

The stable phase assumes that both relational partners enjoy the relationship, have experienced a great deal of information exchange at depth and breadth levels, feel that a large amount of uncertainty reduction has occurred, and know that they can be quite accurate in predicting the behavior of the other person. Because we are able to make such accurate predictions of the other person's behavior, information-seeking behavior is reduced. We don't have to overtly acquire information about the other. One reason is that we know a lot about the person already. But the other reason is that we can infer how a person will behave or react based on our knowledge of that person. For instance, if we know that our relational partner does not like small talk, then we would infer that he/she would not enjoy a formal dinner party of strangers where small talk would be required.

Wilmot has developed a conception of the stable phase of a relationship.[25] He has suggested that stable relationships demonstrate three characteristics: "(a) relationships stablize because the participants reach some minimal agreement on what they want from the relationship, (b) relationships can stabilize at differing levels of intimacy, and (c) a stabilized relationship still has areas of change occurring in it." From Wilmot's perspective, relationships continue to be dynamic even when both parties are quite certain and predictable in their assessments of each other. In fact, one person in the relationship can possess a greater perception of intimacy than the other and the relationship can still be stable. All of these factors make the study of human relationships one of the most interesting areas of study, primarily because so many different factors, combinations, and consequences can ensue from relationships that become stable.

Social support networks can contribute significantly to the development and maintenance of a stable relationship. When relational partners receive approval for the relationship from family and friends, a stronger relationship can result.[26] We reduce uncertainty about our relational partner when we receive approval from family and friends. Lingering doubts about a relational partner can be minimized when a social support network encourages the development of the relationship. When our confidence about a relational partner increases we have less need for new knowledge. Consequently, information-seeking behavior is reduced.

When information-seeking activities are reduced, the communication behavior in the stable phase of relational development involves more affective, idiosyncratic, and intimate communication than ever before. Affective communication refers to talk that endears us to another. "I love being with you, sweetie," "You're a very nice person," and "I know how you feel, and I am sorry" are instances of affective communication. Idiosyncratic communication involves interaction that only you and the other person in the relationship can understand. It may involve actual words, such as nicknames, and nonverbal behavior or particular topics that only you and your relational partner know about. For example, "Hey Snuffy, how bout a nukie?," "Let's go do our homework" (of course, meaning something else), or cute little winks meaning something only decipherable to the interactants are all instances of idiosyncratic communication.

Intimate communication is the highest level of communication a relationship can aspire to. Intimate communication involves relating your innermost thoughts about a relational partner to that person. "I love you more than anything else in the world," "I don't know what I would do without you," and "Let's get married" are examples of intimate communication. The ability of relational partners to assume a great deal about each other's understanding is also a characteristic of intimate communication. As Hornstein points outs:

> . . . the shared experience of being in a close relationship appears to allow the members of such dyads to talk together in ways that do not require full articulation of the assumptions on which their exchange is based. The use of abbreviated expressions, rapid shifting from one topic to another with little transition, and frequent ellipses are some of the features that characterize the implicit style of intimate conversation. These stylistic features are paralleled by such content characteristic as a lack of immediate reciprocity of self-disclosure.[27]

Affective, idiosyncratic, and intimate communication are possible in the stable phase of a relationship because our ability to predict our relational partner's reactions to such language is quite accurate. This type of communication makes the relationship even closer and more meaningful for both partners. The following diagram illustrates the process of developing a relationship to a meaningful level.

As the diagram indicates, the processes of information seeking and uncertainty reduction can lead to improved interpersonal communication and to enhanced relationships. However, most relationships, even in the stable phase of development, experience change, and change can cause uncertainty.[28]

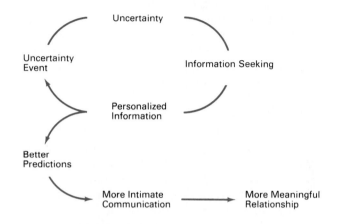

Uncertainty revisited. Events in stable relationships that produce uncertainty were studied by Planalp and Honeycutt.[29] They suggested that various actions by, or additional knowledge about, a relational partner can cause uncertainty in a relationship. For example, finding out that a relational partner betrayed your confidence or determining that your friend would rather spend Spring break with his parents than with you could increase uncertainty in a relationship. The table below reports Planalp and Honeycutt's general classes of events that can cause uncertainty, in a relationship.

Uncertainty Event	Example
1. Competing Relationships	Partner dates someone else. Friend hangs-out with other people.
2. Unexplained Loss of Closeness	Undetermined distancing from one another. Growing tired of one another without explanation.
3. Sexual Behavior	Adulterous behavior. Unexpected sexual advances.
4. Deception	Detecting a partner lying about his/her behavior. Partner misleading the other about his/her true feelings about the relationship.
5. Change in Personality/Values	Determining that a partner is a hypocrite. Finding out the partner has a double standard.
6. Betraying Confidences	Telling tales about the relationship to others. Relaying information that was to be kept confidential.

When an event causes uncertainty in a relationship, alternative scenarios are possible for the relational partners. As the table above illustrates, an event that causes uncertainty also creates a condition of doubt in which the relational partner's entire personal worth may be suspect ("If he goes out with others behind my back, there is no telling what else he might do"). According to Parks and Adelman, uncertainty in these cases may result in reduced attraction and intimacy in the relationship. This type of relational strain could cause the relationship to dissolve.[30]

On the other hand, if an event causes a state of uncertainty as the table above illustrates, it may also cause relational partners to reinvestigate one another through information-seeking strategies designed to determine why their prediction of behavior was inaccurate. In this way, the relationship can continue to develop and may perhaps even become stronger.

Secret tests.   To this point, we have discussed uncertainty reduction and information-seeking behavior from an individualistic perspective. Our goal has been to find out as much as we can about our relational partner in order to predict that person's behavior better. However, a level of uncertainty that we haven't discussed yet is the relational level. What do we know about our relational partner's attitudes, sentiments, and feelings toward the relationship itself, or as Baxter and Wilmot put it, "the state of the relationship."[31]

For many couples, talking about their relationship is very difficult, and direct and open communication about it is avoided. Instead, many couples will use "secret tests" to determine how the other partner feels about the relationship. Baxter and Wilmot discovered that relational partners will go to great lengths and use a variety of strategies to determine the state of the relationship. The following list includes fourteen different secret tests discovered by Baxter and Wilmot.

1. Asking Third Parties
2. Fidelity Checks
3. Jealousy Tests
4. Direct Questioning
5. Self-Disclosures
6. Physical Separation
7. Initiation Induction
8. Forced Choice
9. Testing Limits
10. Self-Putdown
11. Public Presentation
12. Joking
13. Escalating Touch
14. Hinting

Asking third parties involves questioning members of a social network as to what they know about a relational partner's perceptions of the relationship. In *fidelity checks* a partner will manipulate the environment in such a way as to provide a relational partner with the opportunity to be unfaithful (such as by leaving the partner alone with an attractive person). *Jealousy tests* involve either reminding a relational partner of potential competitors (old boyfriends or girl-friends) or actually dating someone else to determine the partner's reaction. While it is not a secret method, *direct questioning* is used to determine the status of a relationship.

We discussed *self-disclosure* earlier as a way of gaining information about an individual. It can also be used to obtain information about the relationship if a partner will reciprocate. A *physical separation test* can be used to see if a relationship can survive physical detachment over time. *Initiation induction* is a method of waiting out the other person to see if that person will make contact first ("If he calls first then he is serious"). In a *forced choice test* one relational partner forces the other to make a difficult choice to determine if that person really cares ("If she really loves me she won't go to that party"). In *testing limits* one person will cause a strain in the relationship to see if the other will withstand the discomfort ("If he really likes me he won't mind if I act hateful").

When one person degrades or criticizes him/herself to get a relationship partner to disagree with the self-depreciation, a *self-putdown test* is being used ("I will sound negative about myself to see if she will compliment me"). In a *public presentation test* one relational partner will publicly announce a presumed status of the relationship to see the reaction of the other person ("He introduced me as his girlfriend to his brother to see how I would react"). A *joking test* uses humor to take the edge off the real intent of the strategy, which is to find out how one partner feels about the other ("When I need to know how she feels at a certain time, I will ask her if she has decided where we will retire together"). An *escalation touch* method consists of one partner touching another in increasingly intimate ways to see how the partner will respond (to determine if the relationship is ready to progress to a more serious stage). *Hinting* is the final category of secret tests and involves indirect strategies to determine the state of a relationship (flirting, suggesting collaborative activities).

For those who have a difficult time confronting a relational partner directly about the status of a relationship, secret tests can be useful sources of information to reduce such uncertainty. Obviously, the type of test used depends on our individual personalities and on the predicted reaction of the target person. While some writers in the field of interpersonal relations would suggest that direct and open communication is an optimal means of gaining information about the state of a relationship, we suggest that in the absence of such interaction, secret tests can act as a secondary alternative.

> Jerry and Linda have been dating each other for three months and appear to have a great deal of affection for each other. During the time they have been dating neither one has mentioned the state of the relationship. Instead, Jerry on occasion will bring up the topic of his old girlfriend, which really annoys Linda. Linda, on the other hand, will test Jerry by saying how homely she is, which Jerry objects to. In their own ways they are learning how the other feels about the relationship.

Trust in an intimate relationship.   Much of our previous discussion in this chapter suggests that stable relationships contain some element of trust (in spite of how often it may be violated). In fact, trust can be a very salient factor in an intimate relationship. Trust is an advanced form of predictability. As you recall from our previous discussion, predictability is one of the goals in developing relationships. The ability to accurately predict the behavior of our relational partner can make us more successful in the relationship.

Rempel and his associates have advanced a mode of trust in interpersonal relationships.[32] Their model has three components that reflect increasing levels of attitudinal and behavioral anticipation: predictability, dependability, and faith. We have previously discussed the first level of trust, **predictability,** as the ability to anticipate the behavior of a relational partner based on reduced uncertainty. Consistent and recurring behaviors gives us a good indication that an individual will react predictably in given circumstances.

The second level of trust in a relationship is **dependability.** As relational partners get to know one another better their evaluations of each other focus more on generalized patterns of behaviors rather than specific instances or actions. Trust is attributed to the person, not to the behaviors of the person. Hence, relational partners make more encompassing assessment of one another ("Joe is a dependable guy"; "Frieda is someone I can trust").

The highest level of trust is **faith.** While faith has many religious connotations, it "reflects an emotional security on the part of individuals, which enables them to go beyond the available evidence and feel, with assurance, that their partner will be responsive and caring despite the vicissitudes of an uncertain future."[33] Obviously the process of developing trust to its highest level of faith takes time and effort. It is unlikely that higher levels of trust in a relationship can be realized except in the stable stage of relational development. Yet, when faith becomes a part of the relationship, so do love and happiness.[34]

Strategies to maintain stable relationships.   All relationships are going to experience ups and downs, good times and bad times. Perhaps it is true that only strong relationships will survive the lackluster or even dismal moments. While some may think of the stable stage of relational development as strong, even stable relationships can deteriorate and dissolve. Methods of maintaining the stability of a relationship were studied by Ayers.[35] He asked several hundred students to indicate what strategies they used to maintain stability in their intimate relationships. Ayers determined that three basic methods are used to promote stability: avoidance, balance, and directness.

According to Ayers, which of these strategies people use may depend upon whether the relationship is developing or deteriorating. The use of these strategies may also depend upon whether one person is attempting stability and the other person wants the relationship to develop further or deteriorate. For example, people who find themselves in deteriorating relationships that they want to keep stable are more likely to use balance strategies than people who are trying to stabilize a developing relationship. Furthermore, people who are trying to stabilize a relationship while their partner is trying to develop it are more likely going to use avoidance strategies.

Strategies that attempt to maintain a stable relationship are important to understand because relationships are always subject to change. If change threatens the nature of the relationship much to the dislikes of one or more of the relational partners, then these strategies may be necessary to thwart movement in the relationship.

Craig and Pam were high school sweethearts and always said they would marry upon graduation from college. Both attend State University near their home-

Method	Strategies	Example
A. Avoidance	1. Ignore things that might change the nature of the relationship.	"I try not to notice how he looks at other girls when we're out together."
	2. Avoid doing things that might change the nature of the relationship.	"I don't dare mention marriage because it will scare her off."
	3. Try to prevent partner from doing things that might change the nature of the relationship.	"I try to persuade her not to talk about our intimate activities in front of other people."
B. Balance	1. Try to maintain a constant level of emotional support.	"I try to always find time to tell him of my love and affection."
	2. Provide favors on a recurring basis for the relational partner.	"I always take her out to her favorite restaurant after her night class."
	3. Try to understand partner's moods and compensate for them.	"When I feel she is upset over school, I offer to study with her."
C. Directness	1. Directly state that the relationship should remain the way it is.	"I told him that I didn't want to date others and didn't want him to either."
	2. Remind partner about relationship decisions agreed upon in the past.	"We promised each other that we wouldn't talk about moving in with each other."
	3. Directly tell partner how you feel about the relationship.	"I love you and feel that we should be together more often."

town. After the first semester, Craig seemed to notice several changes in Pam's attitude and behavior. Pam has different friends at college who seem to influence her. Craig thinks that Pam is more aloof and likes to spend more time with her friends, which takes time away from them being together. Craig now spends a lot of his time doing favors for Pam (washing her car), always trying to cheer her up when she's bored, and continuing to tell her what a great person she is.

Rewards/costs assessment.   The stable phase of relational development is not immune from rewards/costs assessments. Even as individuals in a relationship draw closer to one another, estimations of the relative worth of the relationship are typically made. After we have gained a great deal of knowledge about a person and reduced our uncertainty about that relational partner, we have a better idea of what this person really means to us. One of the assessments that can be made in the stable phase that was more difficult to make in the earlier stages of a relationship is a comparison of the relational partner to our conception of an **"ideal other."** Sternberg and Barnes have studied the comparison of partners to ideal others and described the process in the following way:

Romantic relationships typically involve two flesh-and-blood individuals: the self and an other. Participants in such relationships, though, sometimes sense the presence of two other, elusive but nevertheless intrusive, individuals: each partner's ideal other. If each real participant in the relationship corresponds perfectly to the other's ideal, then these elusive ideal others may never make themselves known. However, if, as is often the case, one or the other individual departs in significant respects from an ideal other, the silent partners to the relationship may enter into, and possibly interfere with, the relationship in various ways.[36]

It is difficult to suggest how ideal others are formed in our minds, although we can hazard some guesses. It is likely that our attitudes and perceptions about important people in our lives can influence our conception of an ideal other. For example, we may have a lot of respect for our parents and incorporate their positive traits into our concept of an ideal other. The Oedipus complex and notions like "I want a husband just like daddy" could contribute to the composition of an ideal self. Famous and respected figures in the world, such as athletes, movie stars, and political and religious leaders, could also influence our image of the ideal other. Even certain noteworthy qualities associated with previous romantic partners may contribute to the image of the ideal other (sexual ability, kindness, sense of humor, etc.).

The comparison of an ideal other to a relational partner is important only when it affects the relationship. As Sternberg and Barnes point out, when the gap between the ideal and real other becomes large, unfavorable comparisons are made about the relational partner, and the costs of not being able to enjoy the qualities of an ideal other outweigh the benefits of the real other. Although not all relationships dissolve when one partner finds an unfavorable comparison between the ideal and real other, the chances of relational strain are improved.

Stage 4: Exit

As the model indicates, the exit stage could occur after the entry, exploratory, or stable stage. The exit phase indicates that a relationship is growing apart because the costs of continuing the relationship have exceeded the rewards.

Several reasons have been discussed for why relationships dissolve, deteriorate, and eventually terminate. A few of these reasons or causes for relational breakup include: (1) finding someone new as a relational partner; (2) having limited time for the relationship; (3) an outside friend's interference; (4) fatigue in trying to make the relationship work; (5) money; (6) a change in the relational partner; (7) poor communication between relational partners; or (8) a considerable gap between the ideal and real other. You could probably think of many other reasons why individuals decide to end relationships. Regardless of the reason for relational strain, increased uncertainty usually results, and partners must make a decision either to seek information and determine the cause of the problem (which may or may not inhibit dissolutionment) or simply terminate the relationship.

Communication in deteriorating relationships.   Communicating in a relationship that is coming apart is awkward, especially if the relationship has reached a level of stability or intimacy. Knapp has suggested that a reversal effect occurs when relationships de-escalate.[37] That is, just as a relationship becomes more intimate and personalized as it grows, it can also become more formal and less intimate as it deteriorates. Furthermore, as uncertainty increases, our predictions about the other person and his/her behavior also decrease, making relational communication less successful and more difficult.

Marital adjustment and dissatisfaction have been employed as concepts to study the communication behavior of couples who experienced relational deterioration. Both verbal and nonverbal behaviors have been studied as sources of communication that reflect the state of the relationship. Levenson and Gottman have suggested the martial dissatisfaction that can be observed when a wife will reciprocate a husband's negatively emotional communication, but a husband will not return a wife's negatively charged communication.[38] In relationships that are experiencing strain, wives are more interested in keeping communication out in the open than are husbands. Husbands have a tendency to express hostility toward the wives and subsequently retreat into silence. The wives on the other hand prefer to initiate and return hostility in order that communication can remain a viable part of the relationship.

Eye behavior is an additional indication that separates couples highly satisfied with their relationship from couples unsatisfied with it. Noller[39] studied couples well adjusted and poorly adjusted to marriage and found that those poorly adjusted looked at one another more during negative interaction than did those well adjusted. Noller suggested that well-adjusted couples have less need to observe the reactions of their partners' because they are comfortable with them, while poorly adjusted couples who are confronting one another look at each other carefully to monitor reactions to negative messages. Communication plays a very important role in the deterioration of a relationship. Many couples can work out their differences through communication. They can acquire additional information in order to reduce uncertainty so that predictions can be accurately made again (see model). However, many relationships cannot be salvaged and will terminate. Sometimes this is the best course of action.

Termination strategies.   Most of us do not intend to hurt the other person in a relational breakup. We simply want out of the relationship. But because we are aware that the other person knows us and our communication behavior well, we have to choose our communication strategies carefully to ensure that that person understands our intentions of breaking up, that we avoid the unpleasantries of the termination process, and that we consider the feelings of the other person. Obviously, this is a complicated and delicate process. How is it done? What are the best interpersonal communication strategies for accomplishing all of these goals? The next section provides some insight into these areas.

Numerous experts in the areas of relational termination have offered descriptions of the strategies that people use to dissolve, disengage, de-escalate, or otherwise break off a relationship. For example, Cody suggested that five general disengagement strategies are consistently used.[40]

Behavioral de-escalation strategies include avoidance and withdrawal, as if to let the relationship end without a confrontation. Examples of these include "I avoided contact with him/her as much as possible," "I never called the person again and never returned any of his/her calls."

Negative identity management strategies provide no justification for the breakup and do not attempt to consider the feelings of the other person. "I told him/her life was too short and that we should date other people in order to enjoy life" and "I said that I thought we might ruin our relationship altogether if we didn't start dating around a little because I was not happy" are examples of this strategy.

Justification strategies provide reasons for breaking off the relationship. Examples of these strategies are, "I fully explained my reasons for why we shouldn't see each other anymore" and "I said that I was really changing inside and I didn't feel good about our relationship anymore. I said that we'd better stop seeing each other."

De-escalation strategies suggest that the relationship has faults and that it is better to break it off and hope for a reconciliation later. Examples are, "I told him/her that I needed to be honest and suggested that we break it off for a while and see what happens" and "I said that the relationship was becoming a strain and I wanted to call it quits for a while."

Positive tone strategies are used to preserve feelings. Examples of this strategy would be, "I told him/her that I cared very, very much for him/her" and "I tried very hard to prevent us from having hard feelings about the breakup."

Recent study of relational breakups has determined that indirect termination strategies also seem quite popular. It appears that instead of facing a breakup head-on, many people would rather hint at dissolving a relationship.[41] Regardless of whether direct or indirect termination strategies are employed, relationships come to an end at a significant rate. Statistics on the divorce rate attest to the large number of relational breakups. However, just as relationships can move from the entry, exploratory, and stable phases to the exit phase, so can a relationship be reconciled and move from the exit phase to a developmental stage.

Reconciliation strategies.   Very little is known about the communication strategies associated with relational reconciliation. Krayer and O'Hair have initiated some preliminary studies on the reconciliation of relationships and have found that several different techniques are available to reenter a terminated relationship.[42] Several couples who were going through a reconciliation period were interviewed about the communication used to reconcile their broken relationship. The individuals in these relationships agreed about the type of communication strategy that was used to reconcile their differences. The figure below displays the reconciliation strategies discovered by Krayer and O'Hair.

Reconciliation Strategies

Strategy	Example
1. Martyr	"I know you're just trying to make me mad by not seeing me."
2. Innocence	"Let's talk. Let's go out and just talk."
3. Realization	"I've been wasting my time with these others."
4. Persistence	"I just can't stand to be without you."
5. Caring	"I really care for you."
6. Boastful	"I'm the best for you."
7. Denial	"Let's forget everything that happened."
8. Apologetic	"I'm sorry. You're sorry. We screwed up."
9. Directness	"Let's get married. Let's get back together."
10. Threat	"If you really don't want me now, I'll get involved with someone else."

While little information is available at this point to confidently suggest which type of reconciliation strategy works in a particular situation, we do know that they are used frequently. The reconciliation of a strained or terminated relationship is the primary reason why, in the model presented at the beginning of this chapter, the lines connecting the various stages of relational development are represented by double arrows. Relationships may move from one phase to another quite frequently. We have known relationships that were regularly characterized by instances of relational termination and reconciliation. Other relationships are less dynamic and remain relatively stable for long periods of time, even for a lifetime.

Relationships are very unique human constructions. They are hard to classify because of the unique individuals involved and the dynamic interaction that characterizes them. We do know, however, that relationships are necessary for physical and psychological health, and the study of relationships can improve our understanding of how to enjoy one another's company even more.

LOVE IN INTERPERSONAL RELATIONSHIPS

We have avoided discussing the concept of love until now because love could conceivably occur at any stage of a relationship. While love is less likely to occur in the early stages of a relationship, especially in the entry phase, perceptions of love could be evident in the exploratory phase (puppy love or Platonic love). Furthermore, love may not occur even in the most advanced stages of relationships. Many divorced people have argued that their relationship was always void of love. Even more interesting, some couples contend that they never knew they were in love until after a relational breakup, and then it was too late. Still others have not known love until they experienced relational disengagement and reconciliation. Our discussion of love will therefore apply to any stage of relational development.

The Significance of Love

Few topics of discussion are as timeless as love. The number of songs written about love exceeds the number written on any other topic. Even when music videos permeate today's music scene, love is the still the topic of choice. According to nationwide surveys, love is a very important part of almost everyone's life. Some reports claim that 97 percent of all Americans fall in love at least once before they reach adulthood. With so many experts on the topic of love, it is curious that so little solid information is available that can coherently describe what love is, what it feels like, and what it means. The easiest answer is that love is something different for everyone. For some, love means physical stimulation. For others, it provides peace of mind. For still others, it involves pain and heartache. If you were asked to describe how love feels, how would you respond?

We have often heard people in relationships question whether what they feel for someone is love or something else. "Do I really love him or just like him a lot?" "I love her, but I don't know if I'm in love with her!" Interestingly, some people will insist that others are not really in love with someone else.

Mother: You're not in love with him, you're just infatuated with him!

Daughter: You've been married three times, how would you know the difference?

It has always amazed us that others think they can tell if someone else is or is not in love. How do they know? Skin tone change? New freckles? Bad breath? Absent-mindedness? These are symptoms of college professors, not necessarily of people in love.

Studies have been carried out to determine if people have physiological reactions to love. Scientists are never wanting for topics to investigate, especially when they involve people. This point is dramatically illustrated by scientific research that sought to determine if actual chemical reactions associated with feelings of love could be verified in people's bodies.[43] Researchers have discovered that the body produces an amphetamine-like chemical in larger quantities in people who have had love affairs. The increased production of this chemical can produce the euphoria, dizziness, and appetite loss that often characterize a person who is head over heels in love. Regardless of the exact nature of the symptoms of being in love, we do know that physical, psychological, and emotional reactions can be associated with love.

Types of Love

If it is possible to have different reactions to the concept of love, is it also possible that there are different types of love? Most people would suggest that there are different types. We don't love our mother and father the same way we love our spouse, and we may not love our best friend the same way we do our sister or brother. Different relationships involve different types of love. But are there also different types of love in one basic type of relationship—heterosexual, committed relationships between lovers and/or spouses? The answer is yes, at least according to those who have investigated the types (or styles) of love.

John Lee, a Canadian scientist, first popularized the study of types of love. He suggested that there are three primary types of love corresponding to the three primary colors. Everything else is a blend of these three types. Other people interested in studying the types of love have suggested that Lee's concept was somewhat oversimplified. Lobsenz's research suggests that there are six **styles of loving.**[44]

Logical love.   Logical love is based on practical values. Those who believe in logical love will search for a love partner who fits their needs in a pragmatic way. They may also assess their own strengths and weaknesses and look for a partner who would be attracted to such offerings. "I may not be the best-looking guy in the world, but I am humorous, good-natured, and ambitious. I would like the same characteristics in a woman, and I am sure there are women out there who are looking for someone like me. I'll just look until I find one." Such logic would put a mainframe computer to shame! Logical love can exist because two people recognize this type of bonding as a worthwhile coexistence.

Game playing.   Game playing as a style of love involves one or more of the relational partners perceiving the love relationship as something that must be won or lost. For these participants, love is a challenge where each encounter involves tactics, strategies, and moves that enhances one's position in the game. For example, one partner may flirt with another person to invoke a desired response from the other partner. Game playing in a relationship usually indicates a lack of any real emotional commitment to the relationship. In fact, emotional involvement could lessen one's chances of winning the game. This style of love is usually thought to be very cynical and self-centered.

Unselfish love.   When people are willing to give of themselves physically and emotionally without asking for anything in return they are demonstrating unselfish love. Unselfish love involves caring more for the other person than for oneself. Many novels and short stories have been written about unselfish love. Examples of unselfish love could include a women enduring physical abuse from her husband simply because she loves him, or a man allowing his mother-in-law to move in because it would make his wife happy. Unselfish love is very idealistic, and while many aspire to provide partners with this type of love, it is unknown how many actually demonstrate it.

Romantic love.   Romantic love is perhaps the most prevalent style. It is passionate and all-giving. Romeo and Juliet shared romantic love. Romantics, as they are often called, hold no secrets from one another and provide all of themselves physically and emotionally to their romantic partner. Romantics dwell on the symbolic nature of emotion and strive to make their relationship perfect, both sentimentally and sensually. Flowers, cards, poems, even memories of times together are cherished by them. Romantic love exists at a heightened peak and has a tendency to abate after a period of time.

Friendly love.   Friendly love is not so fast and furious as romantic love. According to Lobsenz, friendly love is more of a recognition state.[45] That is, both parties in the relationship recognize that they have shared interests, common grounds, and similar attitudes and beliefs. Friendly lovers seem to value companionship, rapport, and mutual respect. Partners in a relationship feel more comfortable with one another and consequently do not desire to search for additional intimate relationships.

Possessive love.   The sixth style of love involves emotional behavior that becomes consuming to the point of possessiveness. It might better be called obsessive, because this type of lover wishes to totally possess his/her partner. Jealousy is a common element in this type of love and is many times carried to the point of absurdity. Possessive lovers cannot stand to think of their partner even talking to a member of the opposite sex, and sometimes do not like them talking to anyone. Some possessive lovers even try to prevent their partner from interacting with parents and relatives. Some researchers suggest that the fear of rejection is a constant source of anxiety for the possessive lover. Too many times, possessiveness is enough to cause relational strain that leads to disengagement—the fear possessive lovers had in the first place!

Effective Love in Interpersonal Relationship

While this book does not claim to be able to create passionate love in all relationships, some guidelines that others have suggested might provide guidance in making love more effective in many different types of relationships. Lobsenz synthesized the following suggestions from several scholars on love.[46]

1. Develop insight and empathy for a partner's concept of love.
2. Analyze your own and your partner's expectations of love.
3. Accept the fact that even though two people have different concepts of love, neither owns the truth.
4. Be flexible. Adapt the way you show love to meet a partner's image of loving behavior.

5. Recall what you said or did to show loving feelings in the early stages of the relationship.
6. Notice what your partner does to make you feel loved.
7. Think of change not as giving something up but as a way of getting new rewards.

IMPROVING YOUR RELATIONSHIPS

Probably every person reading this book has had a bad experience in an interpersonal relationship. Furthermore, each of us is likely involved in at least one relationship now that is not as satisfying as it could be. In light of this, we should be interested in improving our relationships. But how do we do it? Since each relationship is somewhat unique, no simple answers work for all relationships. It is difficult to give specific advice on improving relationships without some understanding of the history of the relationship and the people involved. There are, however, some guidelines that might be useful for us to follow.

The first is honesty. Relationships that do not operate with a sufficient level of honesty tend not to be very healthy. Honesty, though, is not always easy. First of all, you may not know how you honestly feel about something, so you cannot communicate that to someone else. Secondly, too much honesty in a relationship can cause a tactless bout of interpersonal ventilation between you and your partner. Honesty and tact go together in building healthy relationships. Sometimes it's better to keep your mouth shut than to disclose your negative feelings on an inconsequential topic.

Another important point is a willingness to communicate. The silent treatment, though satisfying to the silent partner, leaves the other person confused. Getting important differences of opinion out in the open is good for the relationship, especially if the partners learn more about each other in the process. Openly discussing issues helps us predict one another better.

The third point is related to the first two. Partners in a relationship should be sufficiently assertive in their communication styles so that the relationship can build itself around the feelings and needs of the people involved. Assertiveness is not be confused with aggressiveness. Rather, assertiveness refers to openly stating how you feel about something in plain talk, not in abusive language. Assertive communication is honest, tactful, and to the point. It takes account of the feelings of both parties. And if both parties understand that the intent of assertiveness is to address issues rather than to attack one another, an assertive exchange can be very rewarding.

The fourth point is that relational partners should recognize that relationships continue to evolve and develop. To experience uncertainty about a relationship is not unnatural. As we mature as individuals we change in terms of our attitudes, preferences, and behaviors. If both people in a relationship change, or if only one individual changes, information exchange must escalate in order to reduce uncertainty associated with change. In addition, relational development is a process that allows movement in and out of the various relational stages without undue hardship. A stable relationship may experience uncertainty, enter the exit phase temporarily, reconcile itself, move to the exploratory phase and back into the stable phase without major catastrophe. That is one of the advantages of interpersonal communication; being able to interact with others for the purpose of developing and continuing relationships.

SUMMARY

People are, by nature, gregarious. We prefer to associate with others, which leads to forming relationships. Involvement in relationships is beneficial to our physical and psychological well being. To a great extent, deciding which individuals we affiliate with is determined by interpersonal attraction. People of like interests, backgrounds, and attitudes seem to find each other and develop

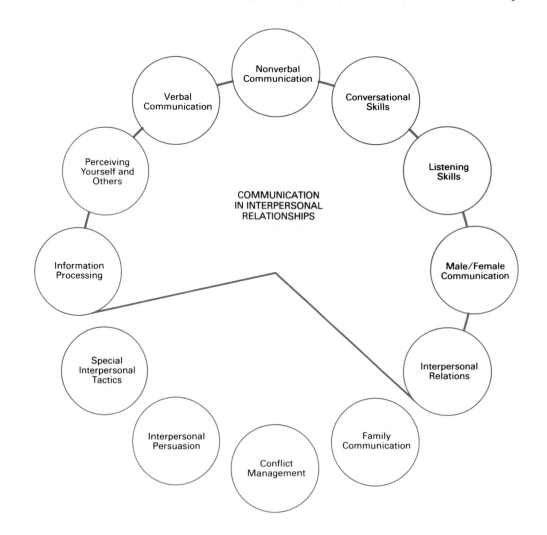

friendships. The development of relationships is somewhat involved and complex. If relationships are to evolve to an intimate level, a great deal of interpersonal communication must occur between relational partners. As we first develop a relationship, information is exchanged in order to reduce our uncertainty about the other person and about the relationship. As we reduce uncertainty, we are better able to make predictions about the other person and that person's behavior. Consequently, we become more successful in our communication with that person, and the relationship can develop into a more meaningful one. However, certain events or problems can present themselves so that uncertainty can be increased even in stable relationships. If relational partners decide to exchange additional information to reduce this uncertainty, then the relationship can remain intact or even grow. On the other hand, if relational partners decide that the costs associated with the relationship are too high or the benefits are too low then individuals may exit a relationship. Even after the relationship terminates, a reconciliation may take place if relational partners choose to reenter the relationship and attempt to reduce uncertainty in order to develop it.

THEORY INTO PRACTICE

Here are some exercises that will help you understand human relationships more fully.

Exercise 9.1: Nicknames

Purpose: To explore the role of nicknames in intimate relationships.

Materials Needed: 3×5 cards.

Time Required: 30 minutes.

Procedure: Form groups of six and secretly write on a 3×5 card a nickname that you have been called in the past. Do not sign the card or reveal whose nickname is on the card. Someone in the group should collect the cards, shuffle them, and then redistribute them, one to each member. In turn, each member should read aloud the nickname on the card. The group is to guess whose nickname it is. (If you get your own card back, don't tell anyone, just proceed normally.) Once the group members have identified the correct member, they should explain why they came to that decision.

Questions to Ask: 1) Why do people have nicknames? 2) Does a nickname tell you anything about a person? 3) What kind of person gives others nicknames? 4) Do nicknames serve to make a relationship unique? Why, or why not? 5) Why do people often drop nicknames when they reach adulthood?

Exercise 9.2: Conditions for Love

Purpose: Joseph DeVito suggests that there are four conditions which must be met in order for two people to love each other. The purpose of this exercise to explore these four things and decide their respective order of importance.

Materials Needed: None

Time Required: 40 minutes

Procedure: On the chalkboard, write the following four conditions for love:

1. When there is mutual respect.
2. When the individuals have positive self-images.
3. When there is physical attraction.
4. When the individuals are relatively free of significant problems.

Divide into four groups. Each group should be assigned to define and provide examples of one of the above conditions. After 10 minutes of group work, the class will be reassembled to hear the ideas of each group. Then the instructor will open the discussion for debate with the goal of deciding which one is the most important, next most important, etc. The final product should be a class ranking of the four conditions.

Questions to Ask: 1) Given the class's choice for #1, what can you say about the values of the class members? 2) Which of the four conditions would cause the most damage to the relationship if it were not met? 3) Which condition, if any, could we do without? 4) When relationships are approaching the exit stage, which condition has changed the most?

Exercise 9.3: Relational Strategies

Purpose: To investigate the nature of interpersonal strategies that individuals use to reestablish relationships.

Materials needed: None.

Time required: 20 minutes.

Procedure: The instructor should list the various disengagement/termination strategies discussed in the chapter on one side of the board. Beside these should be listed the reconciliation strategies that the chapter discusses. Students should decide which reconciliation strategy would be most appropriate for reestablishing a relationship depending upon the following factors: (a) who initiated termination, (b) who initiated reconciliation, and (c) which termination strategy was used. (Example: should someone who initiated termination with behavioral de-escalation use a denial reconciliation strategy in order to be effective?) Does it matter who initiates termination?

FAMILY COMMUNICATION 10

Have you ever noticed how some family members change their communication patterns depending upon who they are talking to? Grandparents may talk to grandsons and granddaughters differently than they talk to their own sons and daughters. Mothers and fathers may communicate with each other differently when in the presence of their children. Children may communicate with their divorced parents differently after the family separates. Family communication is an area of study that involves a great number of relationships. These family relationships can provide some of our more rewarding communication experiences. On the other hand, they can be some of our more disappointing ones as well. Family relationships are different from other relationships in several ways, which can make communicating in them very different as well. This chapter will explore what makes communicating in family relationships so unique.

WHAT'S AHEAD

Our task for the next several pages is to examine the nature of family communication from several different perspectives. As an organizational tool, our discussion of family communication will be developed somewhat chronologically. We will first explore intimate courtship and engagement and then proceed to various family issues such as marital satisfaction, communication in traditional and contemporary marriages, parent-child relationships, divorce, and grandparent-grandchild relationships. Family communication as a topic has benefited from a great deal of research and thinking, and our goal is to provide a synthesized view of the work completed in this area.

THE UNIQUENESS OF FAMILY RELATIONSHIPS

Our relationships with family members can differ considerably from the relationships we have with other people, partly because family relationships are initiated, developed, maintained, and sometimes dissolved because of birth or legal impetus. We have no choice who our parents, grandparents, and siblings are, and consequently our relationships differ from those that we voluntarily choose. Even marital relationships, which we usually do voluntarily choose, can differ from dating relationships simply because of the legal binding of marriage. Family relationships provide a unique study of interpersonal communication and incorporate much of the theory and research that has been discussed in earlier chapters.

Family communication can be viewed as the interaction patterns between and among those in kinship relationships. This type of interaction could include verbal and nonverbal signals exchanged among family members. Just as all relationships go through various changes over time, family relationships and the accompanying communication change as well. In the 1960s and 1970s a common complaint among parents about their offspring was, "We don't communicate any more!" Of course, parents were really saying that they thought their children had changed, and it was difficult to communicate with such changed individuals. Children, on the other hand, were saying, "You don't understand!"—which probably meant, "Yeah, I've changed—for the better: why don't you change too!"

When relational strain occurs in families, at least two factors that do not arise in nonfamilial relationships can influence the circumstances. Even through court action family relationships cannot be completely dissolved. Regardless of the quality of the relationships, we will always have parents, brothers, sisters, and so on. Even after marriages end an ex-wife or former husband continues to be a more significant relational partner than an old boyfriend or a past casual affair. The legal system ensures this.

Another factor that makes family relationships different is family history. In nonfamilial relationships our chances of becoming enmeshed in additional peripheral relationships are not nearly as great as they are in family relationships. For example, relationships with siblings are affected by relationships with parents. Spousal relationships are affected by relationships with children. Relationships with children are affected by relationships with parents or grandparents. Family relationships are complex, and as such they require a great deal of effort and understanding in order to get the most out of them.

PREMARITAL RELATIONSHIPS

Chapter 9 included a discussion of love, which, according to most contemporary and traditional thinking, is the culmination or highest reward of a close intimate relationship. For many people in love, marriage is a logical arrangement to continue a relationship that is quite satisfying. For other individuals, marriage is a relationship option that satisfies a need for convenience ("I got tired of chasing around"), security ("I was afraid of getting too old before I married"), moral necessity ("I got pregnant and we had to get married"), financial advantage ("Splitting one set of mortgage and utility bills is a real economic lift for us), companionship ("I was tired of being alone at night"), and conforming to societal norms ("All of our friends were married, and our parents were really pushing us"). Undoubtedly, there are other reasons for marriage, and any combination of the above reasons may be justification for legally binding oneself to another.

From a communication perspective, how do couples arrive at a decision to get married? Does it just happen? Or do formal negotiation strategies transpire between prospective husband and wife? While examples of both no planning and careful planning may occur, the majority of engagements probably result from events that fall somewhere in between those extremes. In the previous chapter we suggested that relationships have the opportunity to develop, remain stable, or dissolve according to four basic stages: entry, exploratory, stable, and exit. Many experts on marriage would argue that a preponderance of engagements are made in the stable phase of a relationship, when both individuals are highly intimate and are ready to make a formal commitment to one another. However, there are sufficient examples of engagements being made in the entry, exploratory, and even the exit phases (though less frequently) of a relationship ("If we don't get married now we will probably break up forever"). Still, for a great many couples, engagement is a relational topic that involves elements of both exploratory and stable types of communication. The decision to marry is a culmination of agreement on a number of issues important to both members of the relationship.

While the length of time people have in a relationship and in the engagement period have been discussed as important factors in eventual marital satisfaction, the breadth and depth of interaction between relational partners is a surer indicator of nuptial success. Galvin and Brommel[1] suggest that the period before marriage allows the couple the opportunity to discuss many of the issues that will be important after marriage. Couples would be wise to discuss issues that they feel will be important to them both as a couple and as individuals. For example, if the members of a couple feel the need for a night out with the boys or girls, they had better negotiate such an arrangement before marriage. Other topics that are common issues in marriages include the number and timing of children, relationships with in-laws, sexual patterns, methods of handling conflicts, career aspirations, religion, financial considerations, activities done together, and household duties.[2] By discussing and agreeing on many of these topics before marriage, couples should have an easier time with such issues when they actually face them. Furthermore, if a number of these issues are impossible to negotiate successfully, a couple at least has the opportunity to reexamine their desire to marry before it is too late.

The discussion of content-related marital issues is only one advantage to an intimate couple's in-depth interaction. Interaction patterns are another. By discussing various premarital topics, partners get a better idea of how each of them will handle conflict, negotiation, getting one's way, empathy, and other communication behaviors not related to content. By experiencing longer periods of serious interaction before marriage couples get a chance to undergo troublesome differences and determine their satisfaction with the eventual outcome. Simply put, we get a better opportunity to see what kind of communicator our marital partner is likely to be.

EARLY MARRIAGE

Communicating in an early marriage relationship can be an interesting experience. Some reports suggest that everything changes, especially the communication patterns, once a marriage is consummated. Others suggest that marriage itself has little effect on communication between relational partners. If a couple chose before marriage not to discuss many of the important issues likely to face them, they will most likely discuss those issues in the early marriage phase. One of the issues likely to be brought up early is the issue of **roles.**

Role Congruency

The concept of playing roles in marriage is really not that much different from assuming roles in other relationships. Many of us play such roles as student, friend, classmate, or son. Of course, the formal and generalized roles of husband and wife are rarely negotiated. However, specific roles within the marital relationship will often have to be negotiated. According to Beebe and Masterson,[3] one of the more important factors in predicting marital satisfaction is the congruence of role perceptions. When husband and wife agree on each of their duties, responsibilities, opportunities, and views in their marital relationship, then they are experiencing *role congruency*. If husbands and wives are unsure or even disagree on their marital roles, then role conflict and ambiguity may be evident.

Role expectations in a marriage may vary a great deal depending upon how marriage itself is viewed. Some husbands and wives may desire a traditional marriage while others are committed to a contemporary marriage style. A traditional style of marriage is what most of us remember our grandparents and their parents to have had. The man worked outside the house and was the primary wage earner while the women cooked, cleaned, and reared the children.

Traditional Style	Contemporary Style
Male is exclusive or primary wage earner	Male and female both contribute to outside earnings
Household responsibilities are clearly defined according to sexual stereotypes	Household responsibilities less defined according to stereotypes
Care of children a primary responsibility of female	Care of children shared by both parents

When the role expectations of a husband and a wife are congruent, marriage style is a moot point. But when one partner assumes a traditional role and the other assumes a contemporary role, problems in the marriage may arise that will diminish marital satisfaction.

George and Joyce just returned from their honeymoon, which was a delightful experience for both of them. As they settled into their new apartment, George would ask Joyce where to put such things as towels, dishes, dry goods, etc. Joyce seemed puzzled and told George to put them wherever he wanted. During one of their first nights in the new place, George asked Joyce, "What's for dinner?" Joyce replied that they could grill hamburgers outside and asked George if he would do so. On their first weekend together, Joyce went outside and mowed the yard, to George's astonishment. When Joyce bundled up their laundry she asked a surprised George when he would be ready to go to the laundry to help her. After two weeks, George asked Joyce what was wrong with their marriage.

You probably guessed that George and Joyce had different role expectations. George was interested in a traditional marriage, and Joyce wanted a contemporary one. Even more importantly, George and Joyce did not reduce uncertainty about one another in order to increase prediction accuracy (at least on these issues). George and Joyce might have been more satisfied with their marriage if they had had a frank discussion of their respective role expectations. When roles are negotiated through frank and open communication, role congruency and marital satisfaction have a greater chance of realization.

Managing Resources

Just as roles have to be negotiated in early marriage, so does the management of resources. Many couples find that there are a wide range of economic, personal, social, emotional, and relational sources that must be handled. Many couples, in early marriage, may not have discussed the management of these resources prior to marriage. However, the realities of life often force such discussions soon after the marriage vows have been completed. According to Kantor and Lehr, three resources have to be managed in marital arrangements: space, time, and energy.[4] To these we add a fourth—money.

Marital space.   According to Kantor and Lehr, couples must contend with three elements of marital space: bounding, linking, and centering. Space is an elusive term because it can refer to actual physical space as well as our feelings about space ("I need more space"). Our discussion will include both ideas.

Bounding refers to entry and exit policies of the husband and wife regarding traffic within the home. In other words, by establishing consistent practices of entry into and exit out of the home a couple establishes boundaries. For example, some husbands and wives must always tell each other where they are going and how long they will be gone each time they leave the house, while others have no such policy. Bringing friends home unexpectedly to watch a football game or to eat a meal may violate bounding rules, as might having in-laws over too often. Sometimes bounding is formally established and maintained by direct communication between the husband and wife. In other cases, bounding may be more flexible and rarely mentioned. However the negotiation of bounding occurs, it can become an important issue in marital adjustment.

Linking is a spatial matter that involves the connecting together of the husband and wife. How close a husband and wife interact together both physically and psychologically is related to linking. Some newly married couples have a difficult time in small apartments, especially when each may have come from large family dwellings. For other couples, being alone together too much or too little may be a source of difficulty in marital satisfaction. Some individuals in a marriage feel that they must have time alone with their friends, while others require that all of the couple's free time be spent together. Again, the management of spatial linking is an important consideration in many marriages.

Centering is concerned with coordinating, allocating, and monitoring the spatial resources of a couple. Who uses the hairdryer first in the mornings, where each person sits while watching television, who uses the car and who rides the bus, and what space is exclusive territory for each member of a couple are all issues in centering or coordinating of space. Some wives do not allow their husband to drive their cars or to rummage around in their sewing area. Husbands may prefer that their wives not use their tools or work at their desk. The process of centering is an important marital concern of many couples, and in many instances, mutually accommodating arrangements can only be realized through open and direct interpersonal communication.

Time

The establishment and maintenance of policies of time use in the family structure were outlined by Kantor and Lehr. They suggest three different time-related concerns that each family encounters on a regular basis: orienting, clocking, and synchronizing.

Orienting.   Time orientation refers to the temporal attitude members of a couple have toward their lives. The three basic types of time orientation are present, past, and future. Some couples prefer to adopt a future time orientation, where much of their discussion, interests, and goals are couched in futuristic terms. Many newly married or young couples embrace such a perspective because they have little marital history to look back on. Young couples usually have their lives ahead of them, and for them it is exciting to talk about the way things will be "once we get established." A time orientation that considers past events and activities is also prevalent, especially in older couples who enjoy reliving their previous good times. A present time orientation may be adopted by couples who want to experience what is happening today because the future is too uncertain, and the past may be too negative or dull.

For some couples, differing time orientations can cause problems in a marriage. For example, one spouse may want to save money for the future, but the other may be unconcerned about the future because it seems too ambiguous. In other instances, one member of a couple may always want to reminisce about old friends and times, while the other only wants to enjoy their present life together.

Clocking.   Clocking refers to how a couple uses, allocates, and sequences time. Some clocking issues are considered very important by one or both members of a marital couple. For example, the times a couple goes to bed and rises in the morning are clocking issues. Which church service to go to, how much time to devote to sexual activities, when to feed the cat, and how long one should talk on the telephone are also clocking issues. Some clocking differences between husband and wife are very minor and resolve themselves without discussion. However, for some couples a real bargaining effort may be necessary to clear up certain temporal deviations.

Synchronizing.   Synchronizing is a term used to describe how couples coordinate their individual activities and their activities as a couple in an efficient and mutually accommodating manner. Much discussion has focused on the habits of "morning" and "night" people. Some people simply cannot get anything accomplished in the morning and are at their best later in the day. Others are early risers who are most productive in the early part of the day. The synchronization of a couple that includes a morning and night person is an interesting prospect. Many couples are able to function quite effectively with such an arrangement, but it takes planning and understanding from both to make it work.

Energy

There are several ways to look at energy expenditures in a marriage. One way is to consider physical energy, attempting to determine the amount of energy and effort the members of a couple are putting into the relationship (in term of work activities, duties, etc.). The second method follows Kantor and Lehr, who considered energy as an emotional and psychological resource. They identified three aspects of it: fueling, investing, and mobilizing.

Fueling.   Just as engines must be fueled and refueled to continue functioning in an efficient manner, so must married partners be emotionally refueled. People's needs in this area are going to vary a great deal depending upon their individual preferences and the relationship they have with their partner. Some spouses can be fueled by a partner's touch or an encouraging comment. For others it may take time alone from everyone. Still others may find television a rejuvenating escape. Couples need to discuss and decide what works best for them so that refueling can be a rewarding and successful experience. Without it emotional fatigue may result.

Investing.   The effort put forth by members of a couple toward the marital relationship is an investment. Most couples invest a great deal of energy into the other person and the relationship. For some couples one member will invest more energy than the other, and whether this type of arrangement is satisfactory or not depends on the individuals and how they have negotiated the situation. Some individuals may resent their relative over-investment into the relationship, while others do not notice a discrepancy. Again, the interaction between the marital members is crucial when coming to a mutual agreement about investing energy.

Mobilizing.   Investing energy in a relationship is an individual-centered activity. That is, people invest what they desire into a relationship. With mobilizing, a couple's focus shifts from individual- to couple-centered activities, ones in which a couple together mobilize and spend their emotional energy. The effort to determine how their emotional energy should be discharged requires effective communication between the members of the couple. Do they spend their energy exchanging emotions with each other? How do they coordinate their emotions for others, such as children and relatives? Do some activities that requires a great deal of emotional energy have to be planned and saved up for? Mobilizing energy can be very difficult if a couple has different attitudes about how they should expend their emotional effort.

Money

Money has always been a salient issue in the lives of married couple, though it is difficult to say whether money is a more important issue in marital satisfaction now than in the past. However, it is known that money is a common topic of discussion in many marriages and therefore deserves treatment in this chapter. Broderick suggests that there are two main issues regarding money as a resource in marriage: providing and allocating[5] (which we will call managing).

Providing.   Providing for family finances is rapidly becoming a joint venture between husband and wife. More and more wives are earning substantial salaries outside of the home, making the two-income family more common than ever before. The providing of family finances involves two general issues: quantity and quality. The quantity of income, whether it is earned by one or two persons, can be a source of contention for many couples. The inability to make ends meet or pay the bills may cause severe difficulty for some couples. For others, having too much money to spend can be troublesome. The quality of life that results from the necessity of providing economic resources to the family is also an important issue. Such considerations as whether a member of a couple dislikes a job, whether a job takes up too much family time, and whether a job becomes the focal point of the couple's lives are all issues of quality.

Managing.   How well a family manages its economic resources is contingent on how well it communicates and negotiates its values and goals. Some family members may be more interested in investing money in material possessions, while others may be concerned about saving for a raining day. Deciding how to spend income really boils down to which needs have priority and who is dominant in the spending category. Some families find it useful to sit down and formally discuss the allocation of money. Other families rarely speak of budgeting money except on an informal, sporadic basis. In many cases, open communication about financial matters can make people uncomfortable. Unfortunately, money is a common source of marital dissatisfaction, and when families fail to communicate honestly and openly about how economic resources are to be allocated, marital unhappiness can escalate.

THE MAINTENANCE OF MARITAL RELATIONSHIPS

Someone once said, "Falling in love and getting married is easy. The hard part is keeping it that way!" When we speak of maintaining marital relationships the issue is one of marital satisfaction and stability. Many marriages that do not end in separation are not really being maintained. Many married people simply coexist in the same environment without communicating love, affection, and support for one another; they make no attempt to maintain the relationship. In this section, we are interested in examining the issues that affect marital satisfaction, stability, and adjustment.

Communication and Marital Adjustment

One of the more common conclusions from research in marital relations is that marital stability is a key to maintaining a marriage. Marital satisfaction is a major contributor to marital stability, and effective marital communication is a major influence on marital satisfaction.[6] Therefore, the path to marital stability begins with the communication between husband and wife. The following figure displays the relationship of the various components involved.

Communication ———————→ Marital Satisfaction ———————→ Marital Stability

For married couples to communicate effectively, they need to develop several communication skills. Solving problems, being open, accurately perceiving communication, and exchanging private thoughts are aspects of marital communication that contribute to satisfaction. Conveying emotions to a partner has been suggested as a crucial marital communication element. From their research Fitzpatrick and Badzinski suggest that more satisfied couples display more positive emotions during communication in many different circumstances. For example, displaying positive nonverbal behaviors, being supporting and willing to compromise, avoiding conflict, and demonstrating agreement and approval during a conversation provide couples with marital satisfaction through the communication of affect.[7]

All couples are going to face marital hardships. How these problems are handled depends to a great extent on the communication efficacy of the couple. Sometimes problems that do not relate specifically to the marital relationship can become overwhelming (unexpected pregnancy, financial hardship, career problems, etc.). However, many couples report that as long as they experience good communication in their relationship, the problems are less of a factor in predicting marital adjustment.[8] Again, communication becomes the keystone to effective marriages.

Martial Self-Disclosure

One important element of marital communication that we have not discussed is self-disclosure. As you recall from Chapter 3, self-disclosure is a method of revealing ourselves to others. The process of opening up our thoughts and perceptions to others is important to most relationships and is certainly a contributing factor to marital maintenance.

For some couples, self-disclosure is a difficult process. Wives may not want to reveal much of themselves to husbands who themselves are reluctant to talk. Some wives may not feel comfortable talking about particular topics. A study conducted in a city in the Midwest revealed that wives were reluctant to talk to husbands about "self" (worries, hurts, dreams, aspirations, etc.), feelings about in-laws, dissatisfaction with their husbands, and worries about the children.[9] These wives gave as reasons for not talking about such topics their husbands' lack of interest, a desire to protect their husbands' feelings, and the feeling that the topics themselves are difficult to talk about. Husbands reported that they were hesitant to tell wives about job dissatisfaction, bills, and the economic situation. Once a pattern of minimal self-disclosure begins in marital relationships, it is difficult to change. The trend becomes self-perpetuating: wives don't disclose to husbands who won't disclose to them, and so on.

The amount of self-disclosure in a marriage may not be as important as its quality. Disclosing large amounts of information in an attempt to gain reciprocity from another may be less effective in a marriage relationship than communicating special information and feelings. According to recent evidence, disclosing positive regard and empathy is one of the better ways of relating with one's spouse, especially when trying to open up lines of communication.[10] By revealing positive, supportive feelings and conveying notions of understanding, married couples can expect a more reciprocal communication relationship to evolve.

The Balance of Marital Power

Power and its use is a factor in most relationships. Who controls power in a marital relationship usually boils down to who makes the majority of important decisions. The balance of (or even struggle for) power is a very salient issue in many marriages. How power is negotiated depends on the interpersonal strategies each member of a marriage uses. In the past, the balance of power in a marriage was held by the husband, primarily because of his financial position as the primary provider and society's traditional expectations. In addition, for many years wives held few rights either socially or legally regarding family finances. Today, things have changed. Wives work outside of the home and often earn as much or even more than their husbands, granting them "rights to spending." Furthermore, societal constraints on wives making important decisions are no longer as strong as they once were. Consequently, the balance of power now is something decided by interpersonal bargaining.

The process of negotiating for power in a marriage can be affected by other factors. For instance, educational achievement may influence power as well as occupational prestige. Spouses with advanced college degrees may command more decision-making power than those less well educated. The balance of power could also be influenced by whether the husband's or wife's family provides more to the marriage in terms of money, advice, support, and baby-sitting chores.

The balance of power is an important consideration to the maintenance of marital relationships. Although one spouse may not have the other's educational attainment, prestigious career, economic input, and interpersonal prowess, that person may nevertheless want a share of the power in a marriage. Few people wouldn't want a share in the decision-making process. Therefore, it becomes important that married couples communicate clearly their impressions and preferences for how power is balanced. Only when marital partners agree on the balance of power can marital stability be achieved.

Cohesion/Adaptability

Cohesion and adaptability are two interpersonal behaviors that have been associated with marital satisfaction.[11] Cohesion refers to the degree of emotional bonding between spouses and can be thought of as a continuum ranging from connectedness to separateness.

Connectedness   Separateness

├────────────────────────┼────────────────────────┤

(Enmeshment)   COHESION   (Disengagement)

When a family member moves to either side of the continuum, less cohesiveness results. Someone too connected to other family members could become enmeshed in these relationships and neglect other important social relationships, or even suffocate other family members with their extreme involvement. On the other hand, family members who drift too far towards separateness might give other family members the impression that familial relationships are not important.

Adaptability is the family's ability to be flexible in its roles, rules, relationships, and even structure. Like cohesion, adaptability can be viewed as a continuum ranging from structure to flexibility.

Structure   Flexibility

├────────────────────────┼────────────────────────┤

(Rigidity)   ADAPTABILITY   (Chaos)

Again, balanced adaptability is usually optimal for marital stability. Too much structure may cause families to experience rigidity, which may stifle the spontaneous expression of ideas or even emotions. Families could then become too stuffy to function satisfactorily. On the other hand, too much flexibility could introduce chaos into the family system, which might prevent the recognition of roles and responsibilities necessary to make families function effectively.

The third element in this model involves family communication skills. If a family experiences unwanted movement toward one end of these continuums, open and clear communication could facilitate movement in directions that would allow for greater marital stability.[12]

Working Couples

In previous discussions, mention was made of the fact that more and more wives are maintaining careers outside of the home. As both husband and wife spend time away from home to pursue occupational interests, less time is available to maintain the home environment in a traditional fashion. Two-income couples, therefore, experience different pressures and contingencies than single-income households. They simply have less time to accomplish domestic duties. Consequently, the manner in which two-income couples handle their relationship is somewhat different from the way traditional families do. Inter-

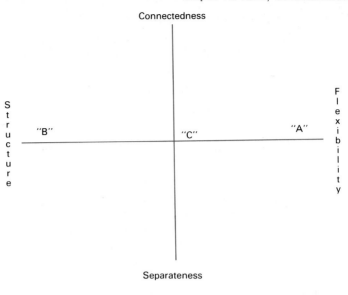

Connectedness

Structure

"B"　"C"　"A"

Flexibility

Separateness

Herb and Frieda were the parents of Susan and Billy and the entire family experienced an optimum level of cohesion. Herb and Frieda were very organized people and expected their children to be that way. Every activity and schedule was expected to be coordinated and carried out with precision. Many of the school activities which Billy and Susan participated in (band, cheerleading, ballgames) were unpredictable in terms of when they were over. Herb and Frieda were upset with the situation because they never knew when to pick up their children (and many times had to waste time waiting on them). The situation was too chaotic for them (Point A on the graph). Billy and Susan were upset because their parents were too inflexible or structured (Point B). After a great deal of open and frank discussion both parents and children agreed to strategies which would move them to a more balanced approach to their scheduling (Point C).

personal communication plays a very important part in accommodating their two-person working arrangement.

The number of two-income couples in the United States is increasing and, as a proportion of the total number of all couples, will probably continue to increase.[13] Reports of marital satisfaction with the two-income arrangement have been mixed. Both positive and negative evaluations have been reported.[14] However, one point appears clear: those couples who express positive reactions to their two-person work situation indicate that coping strategies based on open and expressive communication are necessary for marital stability.

In two-person working situations, effective communication is necessary in order to negotiate time management and role responsibilities.[15] A couple's schedule can change unexpectedly as a result of career requirements and communication may be necessary to handle these situations. Furthermore, interaction is necessary to maintain congruent values, role expectations, and life-styles.[16] Couples can talk about the quality of their lives and how they can be made better, despite the constraints from their jobs. In addition, communication can serve to confirm that the life-style they are leading is worthwhile.[17] By talking about the value of each of them having a job, marriage partners can confirm their own self-worth and the importance of their marital relationship.

RELATIONSHIPS DURING PREGNANCY AND EARLY CHILDHOOD

We have already suggested several ways in which marriage is different from other close intimate relationships. The ways in which marriage is different will be amplified with the onset of pregnancy and the birth of offspring. How to deal with such important life events is primarily a communication issue. For some couples, handling pregnancy, childbirth, and early childhood is an on-going struggle, for others it seems to come naturally. Pregnancy and childbirth achieve at least two things: the family unit is transformed from a two-person to a three-person relationship, and the interpersonal communication patterns within the family structure are likely to change.

Pregnancy and Childbirth

Once couples marry and settle into new life-styles, they may experience pressures, both from within themselves and from others, to become parents. Couples are waiting longer to have children than ever before, but they often feel subtle pressure from parents, friends, spouses, and the media even before they have discussed family planning. In our society (as in most), couples are expected to have children, and the decision not to have them is frowned upon. However, recent surveys report that some couples simply feel that they do not want to have children. Financial impositions, time constraints, and emotional hassles were reasons given for avoiding parenthood. However, most of us will have children, and our communication within a new family structure is important.

Pregnancy is an interesting period for most couples. The wife experiences psychological, emotional, and physical changes. How she handles these changes depends a lot on her relationship with her husband. Women with well-adjusted and satisfactory marriages experience fewer physical and psychological problems during pregnancy than women with less positive marriages.[18] The support and sympathy shown by a communicative and caring husband become of greater therapeutic value to a woman undergoing a significant change in her life.

During pregnancy, a couple may discuss their plans and expectations for their new child and for the family as a whole. Developing an agreement on basic values, goals, life-style changes, and role expectations are likely goals of discussion. The marriage partners will want to come to terms with each other's expectations so that a feeling of congruency exists. Pregnancy can be a very important time, one that can provide a smooth transition to a new family structure when the child arrives and begins to exert a significant influence on both parents.

Considerable evidence suggests that the arrival of a child reduces marital satisfaction. This seems especially true for wives.[19] An infant consumes a tremendous amount of a mother's as well as a father's time. Consequently, parents have less time available to them. Even when couples plan on time for themselves alone, a baby's cry or even talk of the baby may intrude into conversation meant only for them. Furthermore, parents may have a tendency to assume traditional role patterns after the arrival of a child. Husbands may assume more of the external decision-making duties (how money is spent, what car to buy, etc.) and reduce their previous domestic obligations (household chores). If these changes are not approved by their wives, marital satisfaction may diminish.

While we may be painting a somewhat gloomy picture of parenthood, we should remind you that parents who find less satisfaction in the marriage relationship may be compensated for that by their increased satisfaction in the global family relationship. Mothers and fathers experience a great deal of pride and joy with the birth of a child, and their satisfaction with the child as well as with each other as new role figures (mother and father) may more than overwhelm any reduction of satisfaction in the marital relationship.

Early Childhood Relationships

Infants are amazing in that they can form relationships with others rather quickly. They establish relationships as early as seven to eight months. Usually the first relationship is with the mother. Expressive communication is possible between mother and infant by nonverbal means. Touching, facial expressions, and body movement are forms of affection that can be recognized by infants at this age. Before the first year children begin to respond to limited amounts of verbal communication and may even begin to use language themselves. Parental support and love is critical in early childhood development, since children go through some difficult experiences, such as forming multiple relationships and learning sharing, weaning, and toilet training.[20]

Mothers' and fathers' interaction patterns with their children can differ according to sex roles. Lamb and his associates found that mothers are more likely to interact with their babies by vocalizing, showing affection, touching, and holding.[21] However, more parents are assuming nontraditional parental roles, and these distinctions may diminish as parents increasingly share responsibilities for child care. Nontraditional parents are generally better educated and have occupations with more social status. Nontraditional fathers think of themselves as independent, assertive and self-confident.[22] Both nontraditional parents feel less pressure and constraint from social norms.

Child care can be a rewarding experience for fathers. The child and the father can establish an important early attachment, one not always available in traditional parent-child relationships. Furthermore, evidence suggests that fathers are just as competent as mothers in providing attention, stimulation, health care, and other needs of a child.[23] Father-infant interaction provides benefits for the child as well. Ricks reviewed the available literature and suggests the following positive outcomes for the child from interaction with the father: (1) the infant receives additional stimulation, which improves its discriminative learning; (2) by sharing a variety of experiences, the infant improves its cognitive ability; (3) the infant has an extra opportunity to form a relationship, which makes outside relationships easier to form; and (4) the infant has a chance to improve social competence.[24]

Although both parents may care for and interact with their infant, mother and fathers differ in the type of attention they give to the child. In playing with infants, mothers are more likely to use objects (toys, books) and verbal interaction, while fathers play in a more vigorous and physical fashion (throwing baby into the air, tumbling, etc.).[25] Just as parents may behave differently toward a child, the child can behave differently depending upon which parent it is interacting with. In its first year an infant demonstrates a consistent preference for the mother, but this behavior seems to fade in the second year.[26] Also, in the presence of outsiders infants will behave in a more attached manner with the mother (touching, desire to be held, reaching), but will interact with the father in a more social manner (vocalizing, smiling, looking, laughing).[27]

The presence of a second parent can alter the interaction between child and parent. Belski suggests that the presence of a second parent has an inhibitory effect on the interaction with a child.[28] Parents appear to be more active with their children when alone than when their spouse is present. As a second parent enters into a parent-child interaction, the interacting parent may feel that exclusive communication with the infant is rude and will attempt to include the other parent. Some parents may even feel silly talking nonsense to a baby in the presence of another, even a spouse. Much of the reduction of communication with an infant in a triadic arrangement can also be accounted for by communication between spouses. Obviously, as parents communication with each other there is less time and opportunity to interact with the infant.

PARENT–CHILD RELATIONSHIPS

As infants grow the demand upon parental involvement and interaction may not decrease much, if at all. For many parents, children become the focus of the husband/wife relationship. In fact, in some families one parent may prefer and encourage primary relationships with one or more children at the neglect of the spouse. As the number of children in a family increase the amount of time each parent can spend with each decreases. Management of relationships at this multiple level is a very effortful process, and parents must decide beforehand what type of relationship they would enjoy. Obviously, the ability to communicate effectively with each child is an important element in the parent–child relationship.

Parental Communication Behavior

There appear to be two basic types of parental message strategies: support and control. Support messages involve positive parental behavior which demonstrate encouragement, affection, praise, approval, and working cooperatively with a child.[29] Control messages are designed to direct the behavior of a child according to the parent's wishes. Messages meant to control the behavior of a child include coercive, inductive, and love withdrawal tactics. Coercive messages primarily involve punitive measures such as force or punishment. Inductive messages are concerned with explanation and reasoning. Love withdrawal temporarily removes parental affection and the display of love until satisfactory behavior is restored by the child.[30]

The selection of parental messages can influence the socialization and development of children to a great extent. Gender differences have been reported which suggests that parental message strategies affect boys and girls differently. Boys seem to be more affected by control messages and girls are more strongly influenced by support messages.[31] This is consistent with previous evidence suggesting that males are more task-oriented and females are more social-oriented. Males who value an instrumental point of view are more susceptible to parental strategies which stress control and direction. On the other hand, females with a more relationally sensitive orientation would be more directly influenced by messages which approve and encourage.

Of course, most developing children need a mix of both support and control parental messages. The appropriate formula is dependent upon the special circumstances in each family unit. Factors such as the nature of the parent-child relationship, the number of children, the sex of the parent and of the child, and the saliency of the child's behavior can affect the selection of parental messages.

Parental Influence

Related to the concept of parental messages is the notion of parental influence strategies. Parents try to influence their children's behavior throughout their lives, but particularly while the children are growing up at home. Some parents want their children to behave in certain ways around outsiders, others want their children to attract and establish relationships with certain other children, and still others attempt to influence their children's educational and career decisions. Several issues are important to examine concerning parental influence, most of which revolve around the attitudes, behaviors, and perceptions of both children and parents.

In order for a parent to effectively influence a child, the child must perceive that parental attitudes and behavior are congruent. To expouse an attitude and then behave in an opposite fashion is confusing to a child. The old adage, "do as I say, not as I do" is an empty slogan for children who are still learning attitudes by examining parental behavior. Parental attitudes must be reflected in their behavior in order for them to be successful in influencing their children.[32]

A second important influence factor concerns parental perceptions of children's attitudes. In order to adopt an appropriate influence tactic parents need to understand the child's attitudes. For example, if children already hold attitudes similar to those of their parents, support messages would be effective strategies. However, if parents can determine that children hold attitudes dissimilar to theirs, control messages may be more appropriate to modify behavior. Furthermore, the correct perception of children's attitudes can provide parents with a greater understanding of why their offspring behave the way they do, regardless of their decision to try to influence them. Unfortunately, parents seem to perceive their children's attitudes fairly inaccurately, especially as the children get older.[33]

Children's perceptions of parental attitudes are also important. We mentioned earlier that children must be able to see that their parents' attitudes and behavior are congruent. Children must also correctly perceive their parents' attitudes. Influence depends not so much on what a parent thinks as what a child thinks a parent thinks.[34] Once a child perceives a parental attitude, that child will begin to internalize that attitude and make it his/her own. Obviously, parents must be careful in communicating attitudes so that children perceive real attitudes. The following example illustrates how this problem can evolve:

> Jim and Dave were college roommates and had a lot of respect for one another. Jim married after college, and he and his wife had two children. Each time Dave came over to Jim's house they would get into a discussion that put down minorities. Although Jim was not a bigot, Dave was, and Jim went along with these discussions because of his respect and affection for Dave. Of course, Jim's children observed these discussions. Jim and his wife were astonished and embarrassed one day when one of their children was sent home for harassing a minority student.

Open and frank communication about attitudes is one way of bridging the gap between perceptions and reality. Suggesting how one really feels about something and encouraging other family members to share their impressions can be effective in communicating attitudes. Some families, however, find it more convenient to skirt controversial issues in hopes of avoiding family conflict. In these cases, true attitudes may never be communicated and attempts to influence children may be ineffective.

Finally, the "irresistible force" called peer pressure is likely to emerge and meet the "immovable object", parental attitudes. When offspring start school and begin interactions with other children, pressure to take on attitudes of peer groups becomes very acute. In many cases, parental and peer attitudes conflict. Few of us have *not* heard the following exchange:

> **Daughter:** But Mother, all of the kids at school are wearing them!
>
> **Mother:** I don't care what they're wearing, your not all of the kids at school, you're my daughter!

Parental influence attempts must take into account the effect of peer pressure. By understanding how their contemporaries affect children's attitudes, parents should have a better chance of selecting appropriate influence strategies.

Offspring Influence

For a number of reasons children continually attempt to influence their parents in a desired direction. For one thing, parents control most of the resources in a family (time, space, money, etc.) and children would like to influence the allocation of such resources for their own benefit ("Would you please increase my allowance?"). Another purpose behind children's attempts to influence their parents might be to get their parents to agree with them about a particular issue, person, or relationship. For example, most children want parental support for their activities, if for no other reason than to confirm that their own participation is worthwhile. The following exchange illustrates this point:

Daughter: Are you coming to the high school football game Friday night?

Mother: Honey, you know I hate football.

Daughter: But I'm marching in the band at halftime and I want you to see me. Would you please come to the game for my benefit?

Mother: How about if I come only for the halftime show?

Gender differences may be evidenced in the attempts of children to influence their parents. For example, Leslie and his associates reported that daughters rather than sons are more likely to attempt to influence their mothers, but with less success than sons. Furthermore, daughters were also less successful than sons in influencing their fathers. Leslie concluded that mothers and fathers may believe that daughters need more protecting than sons and consequently may restrict their behaviors more.[35]

One area in which a child attempts to influence parental attitudes is in the child's relationship with another person. For the most part, children desire their parents' approval of the people they are relationally interested in.[36] In fact, without parental approval many children's relationships would not develop as quickly or as fully. Of course, children occasionally date or even marry just to spite their parents. But for the most part, parental approval can be a significant factor in the development of a child's relationship.

The methods used to influence a parent about an important relationship are varied and depend a great deal on the parent-child relationship. Some children must resort to indirect tactics that begin even before parents are aware of the dating relationship. Others are very open and direct in their influence attempts. Leslie and associates surveyed young adults and asked how they influenced their parents and how their parents attempted to influence them regarding dating relationships.[37] The following chart outlines many of those strategies.

DATING RELATIONSHIPS

Children's Influence Tactics

1. Point out my partner's strong points.
2. Tell parents how partner treats me.
3. Talk about partner's family life.
4. Ask parents to respect my judgment and opinions.
5. Tell parents how I feel about the relationship.
6. Tell parents what we do on our dates.

Parental Approval Tactics

1. Relay phone messages to child.
2. Ask about well-being of partner.
3. Be nice to partner.
4. Allow child and partner to be alone.
5. Tell child you like partner.
6. Ask about the relationship.

Parental Disapproval Tactics

1. Suggest other people child could date.
2. Ask child what he/she see in partner.
3. Nickname partner something strange.
4. Avoid interacting with partner.
5. Fix child up with other dates.
6. Tell child to wait until he/she is older.

Some of these mutual influence tactics are subtler than others, but one thing is certain: both child and parent perceive that a lot is at stake in a dating relationship, especially those that become serious. Dating relationships are usually prerequisites for marital relationships, and mutual agreement on a marital partner has important implications for both parent and child.

SIBLING RELATIONSHIPS

Most of us have experienced sibling relationships of one type or another, and it is always interesting to hear others talk about their sibling relationships. Some reports are positive, others negative, though most of us have had relationships that were a mix of both. Brothers and sisters usually spend a great deal of time together in a period of their lives that is formative. Therefore, the influence of our siblings on us is significant and probably greater than many of us are willing to admit.

To a large extent, siblings may be perceived as peers as well as family members. Some siblings form very strong attachments with one another. For example, toddlers may serve as attachment figures and provide comfort for distressed infants.[38] The amount of affection shared by siblings depends on several factors. According to Fitzpatrick and Badzinski, females report more affiliation with and attachment to their siblings than males do. Siblings of the same sex tend to be closer than those of the opposite sex. Younger children have stronger feelings for older siblings than the latter do for them. Sibling relationships also vary according to the number of children in a family.

The ability to relate well to our siblings is dependent in large part on parental behavior and the communication climate in a home. Parents who display support and control to their children in similar amounts and intensity are more likely to reduce hostility and competition among siblings for parental attention. In some large families siblings form cliques. Usually cliques form among those of similar age and gender. Some siblings resent being left out of a clique and may attempt to form a special bond with one of the parents. Regardless of the type of relationship siblings have with one another, each influences the development of the others. Older siblings in particular influence younger ones. Older brothers and sisters may serve as role models for younger siblings. By the same token, older children may learn something about themselves from younger siblings, since they may see their success as role models being manifested in their younger siblings. Actually older siblings' confidence and self-concepts could improve by seeing themselves reflected in the behavior of younger brothers or sisters.

Sibling relationships are important for another reason. As we get older we have a tendency to rely more on our families for support. Siblings can fill the need for a kind of support that can only come from contemporaries. Wives, offspring—even grandchildren are important sources of family support and communication, but people also have a need for interaction from family members who knew them when they were growing up. Siblings can provide that kind of support.

MANAGING FAMILY BREAKUP

We have waited until now to approach the issue of family breakup, primarily because it affects all of the relationships we have discussed previously. For our purposes, family breakup refers to the absence of one parent from the home. While death is one cause for parental absence, the primary reason that families experience a breakup is that spouses separate or divorce. Approximately 30 to 40 percent of all marriages end in divorce.[39] Those divorces affect more than 1 million children each year.[40] According to recent census figures, approximately 17 percent of all children live in single-parent families. Estimates indicate that one in every two infants will live in a single-parent home before reaching the age of eighteen.[41]

The effects of broken homes on children have been reported for some time. Children from families whose parents divorced appear much more likely to end their own marriages in divorce. Furthermore, children from single-parent homes seem to demonstrate lower educational, occupational, and economic achievement than those from intact homes.[42] Researchers suggest that the presence in the home of the second parent provides the role modeling, support, guidance, and affection that can be limited with only custodial visits from this parent. However, children may adjust better after a divorce than they would have had the family continued intact, with parental conflict commonplace. According to Lowery and Settle:

> *Several studies have shown that predivorce parental conflict is associated with poorer adjustment in children, and that children from intact but conflict-ridden homes have more behavior problems than do children from divorced homes where the parents no longer show a high level of conflict.*[43]

In essence, the quality of communication among family members is just as important, perhaps even more important, as the family structure.

The effects of broken homes on parent-child relationships can vary a great deal depending upon the management of the relationship between the divorced couple. While a noncustodial parent-child relationship can be enhanced by increased visitation patterns, this same relationship can be significantly affected by the quality of interaction between divorced parents.[44] If parents can communicate in an open and civil manner with one another, their relations with the children can be improved, especially for the noncustodial parent.

It is important for children to have good relationships with both custodial and noncustodial parents following divorce. A child's adjustment after divorce is highly dependent upon ties with the parents. Following divorce, strong parent-child relationships reduce the number of problems associated with family breakup and allow children the opportunity to experience the love and affection of both parents. Even if one parent-child relationship is weak or even poor, the other parent-child relationship can act as a buffer to prevent maladjustment in the child.[45]

Gender differences in the behavior of children from broken homes is fairly typical. Boys, in general, demonstrate more maladjustment and behavioral problems following divorce than girls do. For example, boys are found to be more aggressive, disobedient, and less developed than girls. Furthermore, these problems are much more prevalent and acute in son/mother than in son/father relationships. In fact, boys are generally better adjusted when custody is awarded to the father. However, many more mothers are awarded custody of children than are fathers, although current trends may be modifying this situation somewhat.

When fathers do become the custodians, they appear to demonstrate all of the appropriate behaviors for proper child development. Research suggests that when males take on the roles of both parents, they develop very strong and affectionate relationships with their children.[46]

GRANDPARENT-GRANDCHILD RELATIONSHIPS

In many family situations, a grandparent can provide us with one of the more rewarding nonmarital relationships possible. The same could be said about grandchildren, although those writing this book and most of them reading it have not had grandchildren yet! The grandparent-grandchild relationship is special, which is why so many bumper stickers proclaim, "Ask me about my grandbaby," or "If I knew grandchildren were so much fun I would have had them first!" On the other side of the coin, most of us could relate very fond memories of our relationships with grandparents. The grandparent (GP)/grandchild (GC) relationship has important communicative implications.

As people in our society live longer, the percentage of living grandparents continues to increase. Consequently, the chances of people having multiple, as well as longer, GP/GC relationships is significantly improved. Furthermore, adults are becoming grandparents at earlier ages and are therefore spending more of their time as grandparents.[47] As the opportunity to interact with grandparents increases, the importance of understanding the nature of grandparenthood and the GP/GC relationship becomes more critical.

Grandparent/Grandchild Roles

One method of understanding the nature of the GP/GC relationship is by examining the role of grandparenthood. In the previous chapter we suggested that individuals communicate according to roles (acquaintances, teachers, students, etc.) until enough information is known about someone to communicate with him/her as a unique individual. Similarly, until uncertainty is reduced between grandparents and grandchildren, role-oriented communication may be evident. While society has stereotyped grandparents as benevolent, kind, caring, and warm, the specific types of grandparent roles assumed by people depend in large part on those people's perceptions of their own grandparents' roles as grandparents.[48]

Grandparenthood is a very important role for many people. It represents an important social role for grandparents.[49] Those who understand and identify with the role of grandparent report an increased sense of well-being and self-worth. Being able to talk about, show off, and otherwise brag about a child's child is important in grandparents' conversations. The subject of grandchildren provides excellent opportunities for older adults to continue their social interaction skills with peers. Grandparents have also reported that communicating with grandchildren makes them feel younger and keeps them abreast of the latest attitudes and trends. However, evidence suggests that the importance of the grandparent role diminishes somewhat with age. Middle-aged grandparents seem most satisfied with the role, while older grandparents find the role to be more peripheral to their lives.[50]

Grandchildren also benefit from the GP/GC relationship. Grandparents can provide a source of nurturance, support, and emotional security that contributes to the emotional development of children. Grandparents appear to facilitate the development of ego identity and self-concept in children. Barranti suggests how this process works:

> . . . grandparents are in a position to offer grandchildren a form of unconditional love that parents, because of responsibilities, are unable to offer . . . The experience of being loved for simply being alive is a contribution to one's developing self-esteem and positive sense of self. Consequently, individuals who are loved grow up to be loving people who, in turn, make positive contributions to society . . .[51]

Additional benefits grandchildren receive from their grandparents have been thought to derive from the roles children see their grandparents fill. Grandparents are perceived by grandchildren as: (1) historians—they provide a sense of family history (tell stories about parents); (2) mentors—they offer wisdom and knowledge; (3) wizards—they appear magical by telling stories and encourage a child's imagination; and (4) nurturers—they provide additional emotional support.[52]

Grandparent/Grandchild Interaction

The interaction patterns between grandparents and grandchildren vary depending on several variables. While it would be impossible to mention all of the factors here, we will discuss several that have been reported by researchers on the GP/GC relationship. Gender differences appear to have some effect on GP/GC interaction. Grandmothers appear to have more interaction with grandchildren. Furthermore, evidence suggests that maternal, rather than paternal, grandmothers interact more with grandchildren.[53] Other factors include geographical closeness (it is easier to visit grandparents who are close than who far away) and a child's sense of responsibility toward the older generation (more positive attitudes toward one's elders elicit more interaction with grandparents).

Parents can also affect a child's attitude toward and subsequent communication with a grandparent. Talking positively and favorably about one's parents or in-laws in the presence of children can have a significant effect on a children's perceptions of grandparents. These perceptions and attitudes can persist for a lifetime. Another parental effect on the grandchild-grandparent relationship is divorce. Many GP/GC relationships can be negatively altered because grandparents may withdraw from grandchildren or parents may withdraw children from grandparents (especially their former spouse's parents). On the other hand, grandparents may assume an even larger role in a grandchild's life by filling the gap of the absent parent and fulfilling role responsibilities necessary for appropriate child development.[54]

SUMMARY

Family relationships are an important part of our lives. Except for relationships with marital parents we have little choice in the formation of family relationships. However, we have a great deal of latitude in determining how our familial relationships develop, grow, deteriorate, or even dissolve. Family relationships are not unlike other relationships in that a concerted effort is necessary to make them work. And the primary behavior involved in this effort is interpersonal communication. Effective communication is necessary in the premarital state of a relationship to ensure that each person in the relationship understands the motivations and expectations of the other before marriage. Relating with one another on an interpersonal level is additionally important in the early marriage phase. The management of resources and role congruency between members of a couple is facilitated when communication is open and frank.

Satisfactory communication must be employed to maintain good marital relations, which in turn lead to marital satisfaction, which produces marital stability. Marital communication can be enhanced by increasing the quality of self-disclosure by both husband and wife and by balancing cohesion and adaptability in a family. The birth of children expands the family. Consequently, the number of different relationships increases. The communication between parents may change as a result of additional family members, and new parental communication behaviors must be exerted. As children grow, mutual influence between parents and children can be observed. Children also learn to influence their siblings.

Many families break up. When they do, previous communication patterns among family members may be disrupted or modified. Children and parents (especially) must be conscientious and supportive when communicating with other family members in order to maintain previous relationships at a similar level. Boys may have a more difficult time adjusting to divorce than girls, especially when the mother is the custodial parent.

Grandparent-grandchild communication constitutes a very special form of relational interaction. Grandparenthood can offer many advantages to both grandchildren and grandparents. Each can provide supportive and nondemanding communication that may be limited in other relationships. In addition, grandparents can offer historical information, and grandchildren can bring the older generation up to date about current trends.

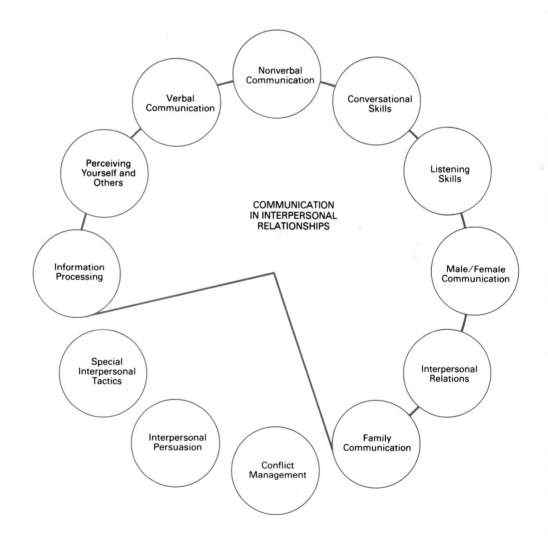

THEORY INTO PRACTICE

The following activities may be of use in more fully understanding the nature of family relationships.

Exercise 10.1: Marital Roles

Purpose: To examine marital roles as they exist within the class and society at large.

Materials needed: Chalkboard.

Time Required: 30 minutes.

Procedure: The instructor will divide the chalkboard in half (one half labeled *husband* and the other half labeled *wife*) and ask students to suggest duties, activities, and responsibilities that should only be undertaken by the husband in a marriage. Those suggestions will be put on the husband's side of the chalkboard. The same procedure will be performed for the wife's duties. Any disagreement from students on any suggestions should be starred, flagged, or otherwise noted. Once a sizable list has been accumulated for both husband and wife, the instructor should begin a discussion that could concentrate on the activities that are disputable for husband or wife, those activities that are found in both lists, and/or those activities that were clearly designated for only the husband or wife. Are traditional role styles suggested more by males or females in the class? Students should be asked how their input would be similar to or different from their parent

Exercise 10.2: Parent-Child Influence Strategies

Purpose: To examine which types of parental and child influence tactics are most effective, depending on the relationships and the circumstances involved.

Materials: None.

Time required: 60–120 minutes.

Procedure: A week before this exercise the instructor will assign each student the responsibility of gathering from any source (TV, movies, friends, personal example) examples of the most effective parental influence tactic and the most effective offspring influence tactic they ever heard. Students will bring their examples to class in the form of written scenarios that outline (a) the situation and circumstances involved, (b) the strategy used by the parent or child, (c) and why the student thought the strategy was effective in gaining compliance. The instructor will collect each student's examples and randomly distribute them back to the class. With someone else's example in hand, students will report on the examples (giving a brief summary of a, b, & c) given them and offer their own opinions of whether their examples represent effective strategies. Class discussion could follow each report. Attention should be paid to the variables or circumstances that may affect the success of an influence strategy. How different are parent and child influence tactics?

Exercise 14.3: Grandparent-Grandchild Relationships

Purpose: To explore the effects of relational communication involving grandparents, parents, and grandchildren.

Materials needed: None.

Time required: 50 minutes.

Procedure: The instructor will ask students to identify five adjectives that describe how they feel about the communication they have with their grandparents; five adjectives that describe how they think their grandparents feel about this same communication, and five adjectives that describe the communication between students' parents and grandparents. How do these three lists differ? Why? Is it positive or negative that these list might differ?

11 CONFLICT MANAGEMENT

Not long ago, we posed the following question to a group of college students: What are some of the concerns that you have about your interpersonal relationships, particularly intimate ones? An analysis of the anonymous written answers proved very interesting. The students' answers ranged from wanting more open communication to wishing that everyone would have a common perspective on life. But the three most popular answers were: 1) being accepted by others, 2) maintaining trust and honesty in a relationship, and 3) being able to express strong feelings without paying a high price for doing so. As we reflected on the answers, we realized that their common theme was compassion. That is, they wanted warm relationships that are pleasing and not stressful. In essence, they desired relationships without conflict.

Conflict is painful, especially conflict with those you care about. Furthermore, most of us long to have conflict-free relationships, which is not very likely to happen. Conflicts are inevitable. The competent communicator realizes this and has learned how to manage conflicts when they arise. Since we cannot expect to eliminate conflict in everyday life, we should work to enhance our ability to cope with it successfully.

WHAT'S AHEAD

In this chapter we will define conflict, discuss some of the social benefits of conflict, consider the phases of conflict, and evaluate some of the strategies for managing conflict. After reviewing the research on bargaining, we will offer some guidelines for improving your conflict management skills.

CONFLICTS DEFINED

By definition, a conflict occurs when two or more people have a strong disagreement that is driven by a clash of goals, perceptions, and/or values. Let's consider some examples. When workers are at odds because one of the team members refuses to finish his part of the job in a timely manner, there may be a clash of goals between one worker and others. When a married couple feuds over one another's domestic duties, they may be having a perception conflict. When two countries go to war to preserve their respective traditions and resources, their conflict may be a clash of values.

No matter what the cause of the conflict, it takes energy to engage in a conflict. This means that you have to care enough about the issue or the other person in order to enter into a conflict. Without caring, conflicts are not likely to emerge. The key to managing conflict, then, is to channel the caring feelings into constructive directions. We'll discuss how to do this later.

Conflicts, whether they are caused by a clash of goals, perceptions, or values, are serious business. Too much conflict can destroy a relationship. On the other hand, conflicts can have positive effects. There are three benefits of conflicts.

BENEFITS OF CONFLICTS

On the surface, conflicts seem to be undesirable. Most people do not like conflicts, nor do they look forward to them. Yet from a social perspective, conflicts can have beneficial effects.[1] For one thing, conflicts can create unity and open communication. International strife, for instance, can cause citizens to rally behind their country to fight off the enemy. Outside threats may cause people who would normally avoid each other to join together in the fight against the external threat. Such a situation can be seen when two employees, who normally dislike each other, behave very cooperatively when they are mutually threatened by severe budget cuts. If the budget cuts mean that they could lose their jobs, they might develop a strong working relationship as they draft a proposal defending their jobs. Likewise, stress caused by a dying family member can encourage otherwise distant family members to communicate in supportive ways. All of these are instances of how conflicts can promote unity.

There are at least two additional benefits of conflicts: issue clarification and social change/growth. Issue clarification refers to identifying and highlighting key issues that result from a healthy debate or disagreement. Such a result is especially apparent when the conflict is articulated by competent spokespersons. Too often, the points of disagreement are not clear until there is an open conflict. In fact, some issues of conflict never emerge until the time of battle.

The next benefit, social change/growth, refers to the fact that conflict sometimes moves people out of complacency and encourages new ideas that are

CASE STUDY

Buying a Car: Purchasing an automobile from a dealer is seen by many as a game of who can outdo whom. In the competitive marketplace, automobile dealers want to make as much profit as they can on each sale. On the other hand, customers want to get the most for their money. Add to this our society's expectation that you should expect to haggle over the price of the car and you have grounds for conflict. How should the customer deal with the dealer? What is the best way to reach a price that both can agree with? Several variables affect the price a dealer will agree to (customer demand for the car, sales quotas, time of the year, size of the inventory, special promotions, local competitors' prices, etc.). Likewise the customer is influenced by budget, available cash for a down payment, and personal desire for the particular car. One customer variable, however, may be more important than the others: your willingness and ability to negotiate. Many people don't like to dicker over price and as a consequence do not make the best deals possible. If you are one of those people, bring someone along with you who understands the car market, who is fair, and who enjoys dickering. With the counsel of such a person, you should have more confidence in negotiating a price.

better than old ideas. In our free enterprise system, new products are created every year because companies fear that they are not keeping up with their competitors. For instance, automobile manufacturers keep close watch on one another's products, always ready to go one better should a company produce an exciting innovation. Ironically, conflict can produce technological developments that are unexpected. The U.S. space program (initiated during early stages of Cold War) has created a microelectronics industry, making possible small hand calculators, home computers, and a myriad of other products.

All of these reasons suggest that conflicts, though often personally painful, can have social value. How much value they have is often dependent on how well we manage them.

PHASES OF CONFLICTS

Although a conflict may not be recognized until it is verbalized and out in the open, most conflicts have prior histories or stages of buildup. Pondy suggests that conflicts pass through four phases.[2] Phase one is called the *latent* conflict phase. This name refers to the beginning of most conflicts and to the conditions that provide fertile ground for a strong disagreement. In an organization, such a condition might be a budget cut that means that some people will not be funded as before, or it might be a desire for independence that causes partners to argue more than normal. Whatever the initial causes, all conflicts have them.

Phase two is labeled the *perceived* conflict phase. At this point of development, the members are becoming more aware of the problem. They sense tension even if they cannot pinpoint its origin. Phase three, the *felt* conflict phase, occurs when the conflict becomes personalized. Each person involved realizes that he/she is a principal party in the conflict and not just an observer. The fourth phase is called the *manifest* conflict phase. This occurs when the antagonistic parties strategically plan and execute acts that will frustrate their partners. According to Keltner, conflicts that reach this final phase can result in strikes, work slowdowns, and sabotage.[3] By the time a conflict reaches this stage, there is little doubt in the minds of everyone that a conflict is in progress.

STRATEGIES FOR MANAGING CONFLICTS

Given two assumptions—that conflicts show that people care and that all conflicts cannot be solved—let's enumerate some of the options available when dealing with conflicts. The strategies for managing conflicts vary according to two dimensions: cooperation (willingness to work together) and assertiveness (amount of personal initiative and aggressiveness demonstrated). Figure 11.1 illustrates how five common strategies can be plotted on these dimensions.

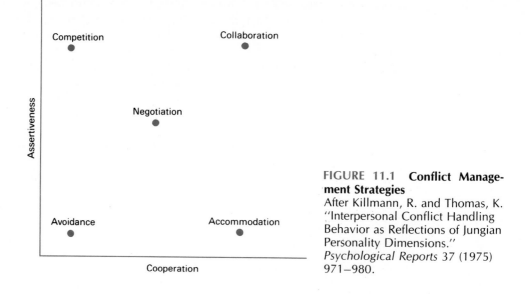

FIGURE 11.1   Conflict Management Strategies
After Killmann, R. and Thomas, K. "Interpersonal Conflict Handling Behavior as Reflections of Jungian Personality Dimensions." *Psychological Reports* 37 (1975) 971–980.

Avoidance

This strategy involves little cooperation and assertiveness. On the surface, it may not seem to be an effective strategy, but it can be, given inconsequential problems. For instance, an adult who overhears an argument between two children who are fighting over a toy may choose not to intervene because such spats tend to pass away quickly. Or an employer may not get involved in a difference of opinion between two employees because the argument is not affecting their work productivity. Or, if you have a disagreement with your physician, you can simply change doctors and avoid future confrontations. Avoidance can be a useful strategy and is only a poor one when used because a person cannot cope with conflict. Sometimes, you might want to avoid conflict, but are unable to do so. For instance, supervisors are expected to have adequate interpersonal skills to deal with problems on the job. When the boss refuses to deal with a problem, everyone suffers. People in management positions are expected to cope with interpersonal conflicts and not leave them on the desk hoping that time will make them go away.

Accommodation

This strategy involves much cooperation but little assertiveness. Such an acquiescent posture means that one person meets the needs of the other without regard to meeting his/her own needs. No power struggle is involved. Accommodation is desirable when one person has little ego involvement with the issue. This person can easily give in to the demands of the other because of his/her low ego involvement. Accommodation is also easy when one person has little to lose by acquiescing to the other. If I am wealthy and you are suing me, I may choose to settle out of court (even though I don't believe I would lose a court battle) to accommodate you and to avoid the inconvenience of going to court. Accommodation can also be used to ensure future relations. For instance, a store owner may willingly refund a customer's money when a product is returned even if the customer does not deserve the refund. This is done to encourage the customer to continue doing business with the company.

Competition

This strategy is selfish in that each person is attempting to meet personal goals at the expense of the other. It involves little cooperation, but much assertiveness. Unlike accommodation, a power struggle is involved. The competitive strategy is a win-lose strategy. When people choose this strategy they attempt to beat the opponent with greater strength and power. It is analogous to a football game: one side wins, the other loses. Competition, in interpersonal relationships, can be an effective strategy, but given that it results in winners and losers, the losers may tire of losing and choose to stop playing (abandon the relationship). In interpersonal communication, too much competition can strain relationships.

Negotiation

This is a compromising strategy that involves moderate levels of cooperation and assertiveness. It is a win-part, lose-part approach. Since most negotiations attempt to minimize losses while maximizing gains, this strategy contains some competitive aspects. In this sense, then, there is a power struggle and usually a lot of manipulation as bargaining takes place. Effective negotiating is profitable, but not simple. When negotiations become especially hardnosed, then negotiators try to outdo one another by being more stubborn, more extreme, and less cooperative. Such a reactive mode slows down the negotiation process tremendously, thereby postponing the emergence of the negotiated settlement. When you are negotiating with someone, it is important to recognize when the level of assertiveness is so high that cooperativeness is lessened to the point that you enter the competitive mode rather than the negotiation mode. When this occurs, it is a good idea to point it out and find ways to become more cooperative.

Collaboration

This strategy involves the most cooperation and assertiveness. It is a problem-solving method calling for solutions that are beneficial to all concerned. The term "collaboration" is based on "co-laboring" (people working together). To reach mutually satisfying solutions, the parties in conflict must exert a lot of effort and keep each other's welfare in mind. Because collaboration is a creative problem-solving approach, compromise is not a necessary part of it. Theoretically, there should be no need for compromising. The parties should find solutions that permit all sides to meet their goals. In actuality, many collaborated solutions involve some aspects of negotiation, especially when each side makes adjustments to its goals.

As is obvious, the first three strategies are the least dependent on communication and group problem solving. The last two are problem-solving strategies demanding a lot of interaction between the parties in conflict. As such, many attempts to sit down and work out problems fall on a continuum between negotiation and collaboration. The key to whether or not a particular communication strategy is effective depends on its effect on the relationship between the people. Those that promote the development of the relationship are called by Roloff "pro-social."[4] Those that cause a deterioration of the relationship because they are based on force or deception are antisocial, and thus less desirable. As Roloff notes, prosocial strategies require an open discussion of the issues, and negotiation and collaboration are the only strategies that encourage open discussion.

In addition, it is important that open discussions do not get out of hand, in terms of negative emotions. In a study reported in 1985, Gaelick, Bodenhausen, and Wyer found that partners (i.e., people in close relationships) tended to interact with one another in a reciprocal fashion.[5] In other words, when one person acts in a hostile way to the other, the other is likely to respond in kind. Thus, open discussions that consist of exchanging hostile remarks do little to promote negotiation or collaboration. For this reason, unchecked hostility is undesirable.

UNDERSTANDING AND AGREEMENT

Throughout the life of any relationship, issues will surface that may or may not cause conflicts. Whether or not an issue causes conflict is dependent upon the relative degree of understanding and agreement that exists between the people. Understanding refers to one's ability to predict how the other feels about an issue. Agreement refers to whether or not the two parties hold similar views on issues. (Agreement is not to be confused with settlement, which refers to a final product that binds the parties' future actions.) It is possible to have conflicts based on misunderstanding, but most conflicts center more on disagreements.

One way to conceptualize understanding and agreement is through a matrix. Figure 11.2 displays a 2 × 2 matrix of understanding and agreement between two people. For illustration purposes, let's assume that the matrix represents a set of parent's attitudes about curfew rules for their children. In square one, both parents understand each other and agree with one another. In this case, they both know each other's feelings and agree that, say, 11 P.M. is a suitable curfew. In this case, there will not be a conflict. If the situation is best represented by square two, we have another matter. In this case, the parents understand each other, but disagree about a suitable time for curfew. The father may want a 10 P.M. curfew, while the mother may favor a later one. This situation can lead to a conflict, and additional communication may or may not

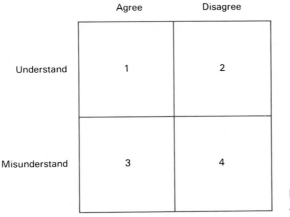

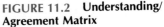

FIGURE 11.2   **Understanding/ Agreement Matrix**

lead to agreement. In square three, we have a condition wherein the parents agree about a curfew time, but do not know one another's feelings. They agree but don't realize it. Open communication, in this case, should move their situation to square one. In square four, we have a mess. The parents don't agree and don't know it, either. Under these circumstances, they might be better off not talking about the issue, thereby avoiding a potential conflict. If, however, the issue arises and they do communicate, they should discover this undisclosed disagreement.

The matrix is particularly useful for classifying states of understanding and agreement about issues, but it also serves as a reminder that more communication does not necessarily produce agreement or remove conflicts. Whenever a conflict managing strategy involves a lot of communication, we hope that it will result in more understanding and agreement between the two sides, but there is no guarantee that this will occur. With some conflicts, open communication may only generate more understanding. In these instances, agreements (really, settlements) need to be hammered out through bargaining, our next topic.

BARGAINING

Bargaining is similar to negotiating (one of the five strategies for managing conflict). Whereas negotiating is often characterized by two people starting at different ends of one continuum and then working toward a middle ground, bargaining is not so linear. Bargaining is multidimensional negotiating that does not presume a midpoint to be reached. A good example of negotiating is found in car buying. When negotiating the price that the customer will pay, the salesperson starts at one price, while the customer begins at a lower price. They proceed to exchange offers until they reach an in-between price. The agreed upon middle price is the solution. Bargaining, on the other hand, can go in many directions and can involve many different dimensions for consideration.

Price may be only one concern. Bargaining, then, is more complex than linear negotiation. Consequently, successful bargaining calls for creative communication skills. It also does not presume that one person wins, while the other loses. In fact, the bargained solution can permit both sides to win. In this sense, bargaining is more like collaborating than negotiating, but it does involve offers and counteroffers, which are characteristic of negotiations.

The main goal of bargainers in a conflict is to strategically reach a many-part solution in a stepwise manner. This means that there will be an exchange of offers and counteroffers, gradually growing in complexity. The bargainers will use several message strategies. In addition to using persuasive logic, Simons suggests that bargainers will use promises (i.e., we will do this if you do that) and threats (i.e., if you don't meet our demands, we will go on strike).[6] Putnam adds to Simons' list concessions (i.e., we are willing to reduce our demand for a 2 percent increase in wages) and commitments (i.e., we agree to return to work immediately after a settlement is reached).[7] As you can tell, bargainers employ several message strategies as they create an eventual settlement. Furthermore, bargaining can entail several agreements made along the way until the final package is agreed to.

In her review of the research in bargaining strategies, Putnam finds a number of facts about bargaining.[8] The most interesting fact is related to the quality of the conversation. Long persuasive speeches tend to get in the way of reaching a solution. Such speeches not only fail to change the opponents' mind, they can delay the process of finding a solution. On the other hand, bargainers who focus on classifying issues and on giving specific information, move the process along faster than do those who spend time trying to persuade their adversaries. The reason for this is that persuasion is seen as extraneous to the task of reaching an agreement. By clarifying issues under dispute and by detailing one's demands, the bargainers can get right down to the give-and-take aspect of bargaining. Thus, more communication does not lead to more cooperation. It is the quality of the communication that counts, especially when the parties are trying to work out a mutually beneficial solution and not just trying to negotiate a compromise.

Effective bargaining calls for careful preparation and skillful communication. Should you end up in a situation in which you will be an official bargainer for your group, you need to heed the following principles outlined by Dennis Gouran, an expert in group decision making.[9] The first few principles call for preplanning so that you do not enter the sessions unprepared. The latter ones apply to the bargaining sessions themselves. (Gouran's list includes 14 items; this list is a condensation of his.)

1. Know the issues, and have your positions clearly in mind.
2. Be sure that you have accurate information to refer to during the meetings.
3. Have an accurate assessment of your clout (power) and that of your adversary.
4. Know your bottom line (final offer), and project those of the other party.

5. Tentatively outline any concessions that you will make and what reciprocations you can expect for making them.
6. As you begin the meetings, establish the ground rules that will govern the talk.
7. Identify and discuss each issue separately (if possible).
8. Relate your offers and counteroffers to the needs of the other party.
9. Deliver on any commitments that you make.
10. Communicate in an assertive but nonbelligerent manner.

The above principles should help you prepare for bargaining and lead to productive results. But as Gouran notes, there is no substitute for experience, which means that there will be times when these principles will need to be adapted to the situation. And the experienced bargainer knows how to adapt quickly.

IMPROVING YOUR CONFLICT MANAGEMENT SKILLS

Everyday life does not bring many opportunities to exercise formal bargaining skills. But everyday life often presents situations that have conflict potential. In these situations, the competent communicator will know how to handle them through assertiveness and confrontation. Let's briefly consider each of these.

Assertiveness

When was the last time you visited your doctor. Did you arrive promptly for your appointment? How long did you wait until it was your turn to go in? Did you enjoy the delay? If you are like many people, you have experienced the frustration of killing time waiting in a reception room. Furthermore, if you are like most people, you didn't say anything about it to the doctor. Why?

The answer is related to a lack of assertiveness. When people feel that conflicts are painful, they prevent them by not speaking their minds. Assertiveness is related to self-disclosure in that assertive people willingly say what's on their minds, and they do so in a direct, nonthreatening way. Assertive people do not avoid conflicts, they deal directly with them. Assertiveness is not to be confused with aggressiveness. It is possible to be assertive without being aggressive. Let me illustrate. Suppose a friend borrowed a book of yours and hasn't returned it. The next time you see your friend you can say, "Hey, where's my book? You know I need it for the exam." This is the aggressive approach. It is openly threatening to the other person. A less aggressive and more assertive approach would be to say, "Could you please return my book by Friday? Thanks." This approach is direct and not accusing in nature. It allows you to get your book back and makes it clear to the other person what is expected.

Let's expand our analysis of assertiveness by looking at another example. Assume, for a moment, that you are a woman who has been dating a man for nearly a year. You are beginning to lose interest in the relationship, and you wish to break it off. Unfortunately, the man does not share your lack of interest. In fact, he seems to be getting more serious every day. What should you do? Do you tell him every time he calls or stops by that you are busy, hoping he'll get the message? Do you develop a case of the flu that doesn't go away? Or do you compromise your own desires and continue to see him because you don't want to hurt his feelings? Obviously, these solutions are not assertive. They do not represent your true attitudes and do not directly address the problem. Another possible reaction would be to offend your suitor by calling him a bore who can stop time with his meaningless stories. Such a response may express your attitude about the man but the aggressiveness of such an attack is more than the poor guy deserves. Overall, the best strategy would be an assertive one, one in which you honestly and tactfully explain your feelings. This is what assertiveness is all about: honesty and tactfulness.

Confrontation

Closely related to assertiveness is confrontation. Whereas assertiveness refers to a general communication style, confrontation refers to a specific communication strategy. When someone does something that is distasteful, offensive, threatening, or self-destructive, you can intervene by confronting the individual with the problem. Hamachek defines confrontation as giving constructive feedback designed to produce a change in behavior.[10] It is a form of intervention wherein one person cares enough for the other to help solve a problem. For example, if your friends drinks too much at parties and becomes socially offensive, you can look the other way or do something about it. By getting involved, you show that you care and that you are willing to stick around long enough to see a change take place.

Confrontation is difficult for most people. Countless news stories report witnesses' unwillingness to help victims of crime. For many people, the price is too high. Either the involvement may end up being too time-consuming or there may be legal entrapments in aiding strangers. Although these examples

---

CASE STUDY

Sometimes we end up in a conflict situation without anticipating it. For instance, when was the last time you drove your car into the worst line at the drive-in bank? You know the line we mean, the one in which the person in front of you is trying to cash a two-party check without having an account at the bank. The other lines seem to be moving smoothly. The one you're in is stalled by this one person. How do you feel? What do you do? The person holding up the line is probably a stranger, so there is no relationship at stake here, so why don't you step out of the car and speak your mind? What constrains us from doing so? Why is patience a virtue in this situation? Ask others in class how and why they react in this situation.

deal with helping strangers, people are even hesitant to assist their friends. David Johnson claims, though, that well-developed relationships can stand confrontations.[11] If Johnson is correct, people should be willing to confront those with whom they are intimately related. But how should it be handled? Hamachek, a counseling psychologist from Michigan State University, suggests five rules for confronting another person:[12]

1. Be sure the timing is right. Is the person ready to listen? Or is the individual too uptight to interact effectively with you? Is this the place to confront, or should you wait until later?

2. Be current by focusing on the here-and-now behavior. Don't talk about what the person did last month or last year. Focus on recent behavior. Confront the current instance, not old ones.

3. Make an effort to state your feelings or observations tentatively rather than dogmatically. People resist force, and stating your feelings forcefully will provoke resistance. Instead of saying, "You are always late, and it's rude to make people wait for you," try something like, "I wonder if your being late causes problems for others?" By asking questions, you encourage the other person to evaluate his/her behavior. This could lead to change faster than would accusations.

4. Use descriptive statements. A person's counterproductive behavior should be described in terms of its effects on the person and on others. Rather than complaining, "Quit blowing smoke in my face!" to a cigarette smoker, you might say, "When you blow your smoke, would you please do it to the side? That way it will not go in my face." The latter is more descriptive and more helpful to the other person.

5. Lastly, Hamachek says to focus on strengths rather than weaknesses. Positive feedback is more motivating than negative feedback. It is important to reinforce those aspects of the situation that the person is doing correctly, as well as to identify the negative aspects. By talking about the things that the person can continue doing as well as the things that need adjusting, you make the confrontation pill easier to swallow.

SUMMARY

Interpersonal conflicts are part of interpersonal relationships. This chapter has attempted to create a realistic attitude about conflicts so that readers are not deluded into thinking that all conflicts can be solved. The competent communicator understands the nature of interpersonal conflict and employs whatever strategies needed to manage the confront appropriately. Those strategies that engage the conflicting parties in communication are preferred over those that depend on force and unethical manipulations. But as we learned in this chapter, more communication does not ensure more agreement between people. But given our preference for communicative strategies, we should always try to settle our disputes through healthy interaction.

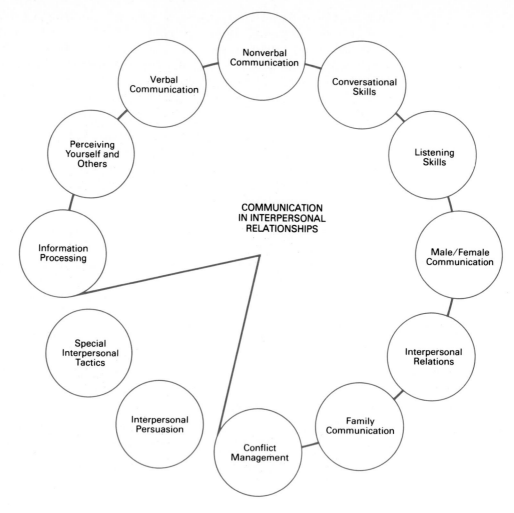

THEORY INTO PRACTICE

These exercises are designed to enhance your understanding of conflicts in interpersonal relationships.

Exercise 11.1: Taking Criticism Yourself

Purpose: Here's an exercise based on Alan Garner's book *Conversationally Speaking* (New York: McGraw-Hill, 1981). It's purpose is to help you handle criticisms when they are directed your way. Many conflicts emerge because people cannot take criticism from others. Feeling under attack, they tend to react defensively and not objectively. Alan Garner suggests that people should do two things when they are being criticized. First, ask for details. Criticisms are often vaguely stated. Therefore, you should seek specific information. Secondly, agree with the principle upon which the criticism is based. This may seem strange to you, but most criticisms are based on principles with which we can easily agree (e.g., being prompt, showing concern for others, exercising care, etc.). In doing so, you do not have to agree with the accusation ("You're always late!"), but you can agree with the principle underlying the complaint. Furthermore, your agreement in principle can defuse some of the aggressiveness of the critic, thereby minimizing the intensity of the conflict.

Materials Needed: None.

Time Required: 30 minutes.

Procedure: Along with your fellow students, develop a list of common complaints that we have all experienced. Write these on a chalkboard for all to see. Then form groups of three, choosing one of the complaints to prepare a mini-drama about. These will be performed before your classmates. The acted-out exchange may only involve two members of your group, but all three of you should prepare the script together. The mini-drama should demonstrate how a complaint should be handled. For fun, you may also include a segment on how it should not be handled.

Questions to Ask: (1) How was the original complaint stated? (2) How did the respondent react? (3) What could the respondent do to improve? (4) How should the original criticism be rephrased to avoid a defensive reaction?

Exercise 11.2: A Family Fighting Inventory

Purpose: This is a delicate but important exercise in which you will discover the extent of issues that families argue about.

Materials Needed: None.

Time Required: 50 minutes.

Procedure: On three different sheets of paper, each person (anonymously) should write down the following. On the first sheet of paper, write a number from 1–5 that describes the amount of arguing/fighting in your home as you were growing up. Use the following scale: 5, meaning you fought every day; 4, you fought more than average; 3, you fought an average amount; 2, you fought less than average; or 1, you rarely, if ever fought. On the second piece of paper, write down the most common topic of arguments, involving at least one of your parents. On the third sheet of paper, write down the topic that you feel should never have been argued about in the first place (the topic did not deserve the stress it caused). Each of these three sheets will be collected separately, and the answers will be tabulated and discussed in class.

Questions to Ask: (1) What is the class average for the first question (amount of fighting)? (2) Which are the most common topics? (3) Why were some of the topics mentioned in question three not worth fighting about? (4) What can you do to manage family fighting better?

Exercise 11.3: Male/Female Stereotypes

Purpose: To explore the perceptions that people have of one another based on gender.

Materials Needed: Two separate rooms with chalkboards.

Time Required: 40 minutes.

Procedure: Perceptions about people are often stereotypic and sometimes erroneous. This can be especially true of men's perceptions of women and women's perceptions of men. Divide the class according to sex, the women going into one room, the men going into another. In these rooms, write on the chalkboard a list of sex-related stereotypes that the other sex often believes. In other words, the women are to list those things that they think men believe about women, while the men are to list those things that they think women believe about men. (Note: The items can be positive and/or negative.) When given the cue by the instructor, the students are to switch rooms and discuss what they find on the chalkboard. Then the class will be reconvened in one room to discuss their reactions to the items listed.

Questions to Ask: (1) Which items were reasonably accurate? (2) Which were incorrect? (3) Why do the different sexes believe these things about each other? (4) Does talking about these perceptions help clarify your perceptions of men and women?

[This exercise is patterned after Joe DeVito's exercise in *The Interpersonal Communication Book* (New York: Harper & Row, 1976).]

Exercise 11.4: Male/Female Styles

Purpose: To learn more about male and female styles.

Materials Needed: None.

Time Required: 40 minutes.

Procedure: This is a role-reversal exercise. The class will be enacting a marriage counseling session involving three actors—the counselor, the wife, and the husband. The counselor can be played by a male or female. The wife must be played by a male, and the husband must be played by a female. To prepare for the role-playing session, the class will be divided into three groups. One group (comprised of men and women) will coach someone chosen from the group to be the counselor. They will help that person define the role and come up with questions that he/she will use to guide the discussion. The second group (comprised of women only) will be the husband group. They will help the woman chosen to play the husband to define the role and specify some of the problems in the marriage. The third group (men only) will choose someone to play the wife, define the role, and specify some of the problems in the marriage. Note that the husband and wife groups need to coach their players in masculine and feminine language styles as discussed on pages 137-142. After about 15–20 minutes of preparation time in the groups, the marriage counseling session will be played in front of the class. A class discussion will follow.

Questions to Ask: (1) What criteria were used in the groups to determine how the players should act and talk? (2) How well did the actors perform their roles? (3) Were the actors able to remain in their roles when caught off guard by a remark in the role-playing session? (4) What did you learn about male and female language differences by doing this exercise?

12

INTERPERSONAL PERSUASION

Recently one of the authors stopped at a rural roadside restaurant and encountered a sign on the front door requesting that patrons "leave their attitudes outside." The sign reminds us that, whenever people interact interpersonally, attitudes come into play, and sometimes these attitudes lead to arguments. How communicators feel about various topics makes a big difference in how they communicate. Attitudes are so important that people use them not only to judge objects and ideas but also to judge other people. Thus people may listen to what you say to decide if they like you. More specifically, research shows that attitudes and feelings affect our self-concepts, decision making, memory, judgments, and thinking. Furthermore, similarity of attitudes is one of the main criteria that people use to determine who they like and dislike, and with whom they initiate and build interpersonal relationships.

WHAT'S AHEAD

In this chapter you will learn the difference between values and attitudes, how the consistency principle operates, and about a number of theories of persuasion. Then you will discover how people persuade others interpersonally to comply with their requests. This will be followed by a discussion of how people resist compliance-gaining strategies.

VALUES AND ATTITUDES

In order to appreciate the role of attitudes in interpersonal communication, it is necessary to distinguish them from values. Attitudes and values are interrelated and play vital parts in how people speak and listen to one another.

Values

Closely aligned to one's self-concept and at the center of one's personality structure are values. By definition, values are enduring standards for judgment and behavior. They are similar to principles (such as freedom or pleasure) that people cling to and fight for. As criteria for thought and action, values come in two forms: instrumental values and terminal values.[1] **Instrumental** values, such as being honest, logical, and cheerful, influence one's everyday decisions. They are standards for daily application. **Terminal** values, such as world peace, happiness, and salvation, are goals to strive for. They are desirable end-states. Both instrumental and terminal values are criterial, serving as templates for behaving, making choices, evaluating, and rationalizing.[2]

Rokeach, a well-known scholar of human values, argues that values are the result of societal demands and psychological needs, and that "the number of human values are small, the same the world over, and capable of different structural arrangements."[3] Let's consider briefly these characteristics.

Values are the result of societal demands and psychological needs, which

Instrumental Values	Terminal Values
Ambitious	A Comfortable Life
Broadminded	An Exciting Life
Capable	A Sense of Accomplishment
Cheerful	A World at Peace
Clean	A World of Beauty
Courageous	Equality
Forgiving	Family Security
Helpful	Freedom
Honest	Happiness
Imaginative	Inner Harmony
Independent	Mature Love
Intellectual	National Security
Logical	Pleasure
Loving	Salvation
Obedient	Self-respect
Polite	Social Recognition
Responsible	True Friendship
Self-controlled	Wisdom

FIGURE 12.1   **Rokeach's Values**

means that values are the property of society and are learned inductively by the members of that society to meet human needs. Values are owned by a culture, but are adopted by individuals. They are rarely taught explicitly. They are learned through observing people's behavior. Values are passed from generation to generation, but can change as society changes. Those that endure are those that meet the personal needs of the individual as well as the society.

Unlike attitudes (of which we have many), the number of values is small (see Figure 12.1). Rokeach's value test includes only 18 instrumental values and 18 terminal values.[4] Furthermore, these human values, though limited in number, are known worldwide. This does not mean that every society or every person gives individual values the same priority, but we are all aware of these standards for judgment and behavior. This was brought home to me in class when I administered Rokeach's value test to my students. One student, who was Chinese, ranked "self-controlled" much higher than the other students. He explained that he was raised to believe that it is important to be self-disciplined and in control of yourself at all times. The American students certainly understood their Chinese classmate, but they ranked "responsible," "honest," and "loving" as their top choices. Even within a given society there will be differences among people in terms of how they order the values. In our class, there was diversity in rankings, especially in the terminal values, of which "happiness," "a sense of accomplishment," and "true friendship" were the most popular. In essence, people hold common human values, but arrange them (rank them) according to their cultural upbringing and individual needs and personalities. This accounts for many of the differences between people. And in interpersonal communication, realizing the differences between people is a necessity.

Attitudes

Whereas values are standards for evaluation, attitudes are *the evaluations themselves.* An attitude is a specific mental opinion about a specific object. Formally defined, an attitude is a predisposition to respond positively or negatively to a specific object, person, behavior, or idea.[5] Although, values and attitudes are both evaluative in nature, attitudes apply to specific cases. They are not generalizable standards or moods or philosophies of life. Thus, the number of attitudes that people hold is limited only by the number things they can know about and respond to. Obviously, we have many, many attitudes.

Attitudes and values support each other, are interdependent. In other words, you might value ambitiousness and courageousness and therefore have an attitude that highly speculative investments are worth the risk because that's how people get ahead in life. In this example, your values of ambition and courage directly support your positive attitude about financial investments. If these values did not have high priority for you, then your attitude toward such investing might be more cautious, especially if the value of being responsible outranks ambition and courage, thus making you hesitant about risky investments.

As illustrated with the risky investments example, attitudes and values seem to influence one another. But the same can be said for the relationship between attitudes/values and behavior. In other words, behavior should be consistent with attitudes and values. For instance, it is reasonable for a person who values an exciting life to take exotic vacations. Or it would make sense for a person who values salvation to attend church regularly. If behavior was not a reasonably reliable indicator of feelings, then we could not learn much about people by observing their actions. For sure, actions can contradict attitudes and values, but if we believe too strongly in this proposition, we end up in a dilemma when it comes time to judge others. Thus, it is better to assume that people will behave according to how they feel.

CONSISTENCY PRINCIPLE

Underlying values, attitudes, and behavior is the principle of consistency, or homeostasis, as it is sometimes called.[6] Homeostasis, an idea borrowed from the life sciences, asserts that organisms strive to maintain balance and harmony within themselves. Such thinking applies nicely to various bodily functions such as white and red corpuscles in blood. Many psychologists extend this notion (analogously), claiming that the human mind organizes and maintains values, attitudes, and behaviors in a psychologically consistent manner. Mental homeostasis is the preferred state, and when things get inconsistent, the ensuing psychological stress causes one to seek a return to consistency.

The principle of consistency is based on an inherent logic, but the logic is not an objective one with truth tables and proofs. Rather it is a subjective "psycho-logic," a logic that makes sense to the person and meets his/her needs. Such logic has no universal truth. It is a product of personal reasoning, often insulated against arguments from others. Let's consider an example.

Suppose you are at a party where things are going on that make you uncomfortable. Your discomfort is caused by the fact that your continued presence at the party may imply a tacit endorsement of the ongoing activities. Staying at the party seems inconsistent with what you believe. On the other hand, you are with friends, and you may not want to offend them by making your disapproval known. What should you do? Leave? Or stay and keep your mouth shut? No matter what you choose to do, you will have to rationalize your decision to yourself, if not to others. If you leave the party and make your reasons for doing so known to others, some of the partygoers may condemn your decision as irrational. But as long as you think that you are taking the most rational option, you can scoff at your critics and go on your way. Such instances are evidence that people are able to rationalize their choices even if the choices are unpopular. As long as you feel comfortable with your reasons, they are sufficiently logical.

Everyone may not operate with the same psychologic, but everyone seems to possess some sense of homeostasis. Thus, people often know when they are being inconsistent. When they realize this, they should work to restore balance. Surprisingly though, people have varying tolerances for inconsistency. Such differences remind us not only that people are different, but that attitudinal consistency is not an exact point. Deviation from the ideal balance point will be tolerated as long as it isn't too extreme. The process is something like a thermostat in a home. If the dial is set for 72 degrees, the unit will not start heating or cooling the house until the temperature exceeds the lower or upper tolerance limits (say, a range of 68–76 degrees). Likewise, a little attitudinal inconsistency will not cause you to act—a lot will.

THEORIES OF ATTITUDES

Research in the 20th century has spawned a myriad of theories about attitudes and attitude change.[7] Some come from sociology, but most are psychological theories of persuasion and attitude change. Each psychological theory has something to offer us in our understanding of attitudes. Let's learn about two different theories: balance theory and dissonance theory.

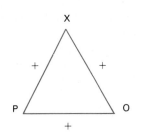

FIGURE 12.2   **Heider's P-O-X Triangles**

Balance Theory

Initially proposed in 1946 and updated in 1958, Professor Fritz Heider's balance theory posits that people try to maintain balance (harmony or consistency) in their minds and in their interpersonal relationships.[8] Heider believed that many inconsistencies have their origins in our interactions with other people. Thus he proposed the now famous *P-O-X* model of interpersonal relationships. Figure 12.2 illustrates this simple but important idea. Notice that *P* stands for a person (such as you), *O* represents the other person, and *X* is the object of consideration (in this case, "having pizza for dinner"). The plus and minus signs on each of the three lines in the triangle signify the positive/negative feelings between *P, O,* and *X*. In this example, all three are positive. *P* has a positive attitude toward *O* (*P* likes *O*). *P* likes having pizza for dinner (*X*), and *O* likes having pizza as well (*X*). This is a balanced situation. By changing the signs on the lines, eight different *P-O-X* triangles are possible, and as shown in Figure 12.3, four triangles are balanced, four are unbalanced.

Balance theory is particularly useful in studying interpersonal communication because it is applicable to relationship building. Consider the following example. You *(P)* like the Mazda RX7 automobile *(X)*, you overhear someone else *(O)* speaking favorably about the car *(X)*, this causes you to be attracted to the other person *(O)*. Notice (see Figure 12.4) that your observation of anoth-

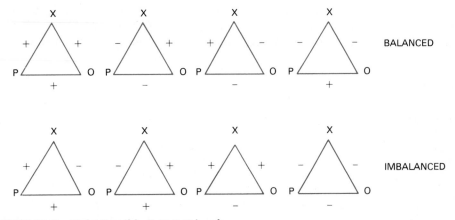

FIGURE 12.3   **Eight Possible P-O-X Triangles**

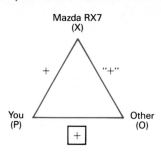

FIGURE 12.4   **Overhearing Positive Attitudes Statements**

er's communication behavior is the basis for developing positive feelings toward the other person. People often form attitudes about others by observing how they interact.

Balance theory is also applicable to interpersonal expectations. In other words, we expect people we like to like the same things we like, and vice versa. Thus, if you *(P)* like Mazda RX7s *(X)*, and if you like me *(O)*, you would expect that I too would like Mazda RX7s. (See Figure 12.5.) Consequently, if we were friends and you arrived at my house to show me your new Mazda RX7, you would be very surprised (and perhaps disappointed) if I didn't get excited over your new car.

In situations just described it is important to realize that balance/imbalance is judged from *P's* perspective. But it can also be judged from *O's* point of view. This means that a particular situation can be balanced in *P's* eyes but not in *O's* (or vice versa). Take a look at Figure 12.6. If Art *(P)* loves Julie *(O)* and knows that she likes her 4-H farm animals *(X)*, which Art can't stand, then the situation is not balanced for Art. For Julie, though, the situation is balanced because she isn't in love with Art. So although Art may be unhappy, Julie is not troubled. And if Art doesn't realize Julie's dislike for him, he might not understand why she prefers to spend her spare time with her animals and not with him. The situation can be further compounded when interpersonal balance is faked by deceptive communication. In other words, Julie, not wanting to lose Art's attention, may express positive feelings toward him, while still being unattracted to him. In this sense, balance is communicated but not actualized. If Art knew that she liked her animals more than she liked him, he would find another girlfriend. In his ignorance, though, he continues to pursue her company.

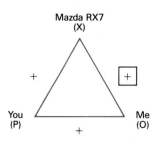

FIGURE 12.5   **Projecting Attitudes in Others**

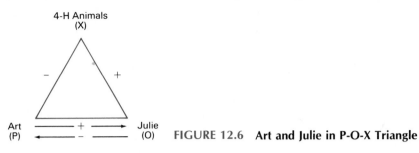

FIGURE 12.6   **Art and Julie in P-O-X Triangle**

Interpersonal balance is indeed a preferred state of affairs. When given a choice, people prefer balance to imbalance. This is what both Jordan and Feather found when they had people rate a number of situations that were differentially balanced or imbalanced. The balanced situations were consistently rated as more pleasant than the imbalanced ones.[9] Given this, we would expect that people would choose friends who provide for them interpersonal balance. As you learned in Chapter 9, this is exactly what the research on interpersonal attraction shows. People prefer balance and will choose friends who help them achieve it.

Cognitive Dissonance

Let's set up a hypothetical experiment. You have an aversion to people sticking needles in your body, but you find yourself giving blood during a blood drive. The experience was not pleasant, but you did it anyway. Suppose further that for a very nominal sum of money you agreed to convince others to give blood as well. Let's also assume (unknown to you) that other donors were paid a large sum of money to persuade people to give blood. Given the difference in payment, who will become more personally convinced of the virtues of donating blood? You, or the ones given a high reward for their efforts?

Such a question motivated Festinger and Carlsmith to conduct their famous study of cognitive dissonance, in which they discovered that people who received minimal payment for lying about the undesirable task ended up more convinced of the virtues of the task than did those who were well paid for lying about the task.[10] Those who were given a large reward for telling others that the task was worthwhile underwent little attitude change about the task itself because they lied for the money. Those who were not paid a sufficiently attractive sum of money could not justify their behavior this way. They had to reassess their negative feelings about the task and rationalize that it must have been more worthwhile than they first realized. According to Festinger and Carlsmith, the latter group experienced cognitive dissonance.

Returning to the hypothetical blood drive experiment, we would expect that if you received only minimal reward for your efforts that you would end up with more positive attitudes about donating blood than those who were paid a handsome sum of money. Whereas the others could lie for the money, you would have to reconcile yourself by changing your attitudes about donating blood or else live with the fact that you can be bought cheaply!

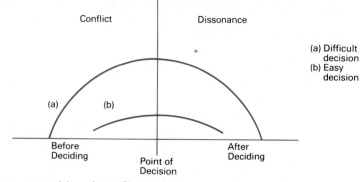

FIGURE 12.7   Intensities of Conflict and Dissonance Compared

Cognitive dissonance is an after-the-fact feeling of inconsistency.[11] It occurs when you regret doing something that must now be justified. People feel dissonance when their actions do not coincide with their values and attitudes, or when they are forced into making a tough decision. Before they act or make a decision, they experience conflict. After they act or decide, they experience dissonance. Dissonance, then, refers to the tension one feels as he/she justifies an action or decision. They are several related factors that contribute to the magnitude of the dissonance that an act or decision can create.

Amount of conflict.   The degree of dissonance that follows a decision or action is a direct function of the amount of conflict that preceded the decision or action. A difficult, agonizing decision produces mental conflict, which in turn produces subsequent dissonance. Simple decisions that generate little mental conflict result in little dissonance. So the amount of postdecisional dissonance that you will feel is related to the mental stress that you encounter before you make the decision. Figure 12.7 makes this point.

Importance of the act/decision.   People make decisions every day. Some of them are not very important. For instance, deciding which pair of socks to wear is often not a major issue in life; nor is deciding where to eat lunch. These decisions can be made without much postdecisional regret. Once these decisions are made, people don't worry about them. Thus, they do not generate much cognitive dissonance. Other decisions are more significant, causing a lot of concern. For instance, buying a new car is a significant act that breeds a lot of dissonance. Deciding to marry a particular person is also an important decision that can stimulate dissonance. Whenever the magnitude of the act or decision increases, so does dissonance.

Effort.   This principle suggests that the more effort you put into a decision, the more you will have to justify the decision after you make it. One would think that the more time you spend on making a decision, the more you would be convinced of its judiciousness, thus making unnecessary any postdecisional justification. Such is not the case. For example, if you carefully shop and compare before you buy a home computer, it will help you make an wise purchase, but it will not remove dissonance. You will still wonder about the computers that you did not buy as you enjoy your purchase. The great amounts of effort that typically go into important decisions create more dissonance than decisions involving little effort. The quality of the deliberation process that precedes an act or decision does not eliminate reflecting on the decision after it is made. Apparently, dissonance is hard to avoid.

Attractiveness of alternatives.   In addition to all the factors mentioned thus far, the relative attractiveness of the alternatives in making a choice will affect dissonance. If you are deciding between two alternatives that are equally attractive, the choice will be harder to make than if the two alternatives are not equal. Let us explain. Suppose that you are trying to decide whether to go to a party or to a football game. Assuming that it is impractical to do both, you may have a problem: it depends on the comparative attractiveness of the two alternatives. If the party is simply another weekend bash without any unusually attractive features, your decision is simple—go to the football game. On the other hand, if both the party and football game look like loads of fun, your decision is more difficult. This choice will cause more mental conflict and more dissonance than the earlier one. No matter which you choose, you will wonder what you are missing because you did not choose the other alternative. After making your choice, you might reassure yourself with some intrapersonal persuasion, noting how much fun you are having with your chosen alternative. You might even think about the negative features of the unchosen alternative to convince yourself that you made the right choice. That's the nature of cognitive dissonance. It causes us to justify your chosen alternatives, even if it means that we demean the unchosen alternative.

In conclusion, cognitive dissonance is a postdecisional state of regret that is heightened by the amount of mental conflict experienced, the importance of the decision, the effort that goes into the deciding process, and the attractiveness of the alternatives. After making a tough decision, you will experience cognitive dissonance until you adequately justify your decision, at which time you will return to the more pleasant state of homeostasis.

POWER AS A PERSUASIVE TACTIC

Several years ago, French and Raven formulated some propositions that explain the various means individuals have to influence others. French and Raven suggested that there are five "bases of power" that have the potential to influence people to do something that they would not do otherwise. These potential bases of power are: coercive, reward, legitimate, referent and expert.[12]

Bases of Power

Coercive power.   An individual's coercive power is grounded on the assumption that the actor (persuader) has the ability to punish the target (persuadee) for noncompliance with a request, order, or command. Of course, in order for coercive power to be effective the target must believe that the actor has the ability and willingness to exact punishment for noncompliance with an influence attempt. (Example: A father tells his son that if he does not go to college he will not buy him a car.)

Reward power.   Essentially, reward power is the opposite of coercive power. This power base is founded on the presumption that the actor making the request has the resources to reward a target for compliance. If a target believes that the actor has the ability and willingness to provide rewards that are perceived as valuable, and the target desires these rewards, then this type of power can be influential. (A father tells his son that if he goes to college he will buy him a new car and pay for his gas.)

Legitimate power.   Legitimate power results from the assignment of power to an actor of influence by a legitimizing authority. That is, targets of influence tactics by actors of legitimate power comply with requests because they perceive the actor to have the right to make such requests. Police officers, teachers and college professors, and parents are examples of actors who supposedly wield legitimate power. As long as the target perceives the actor to possess the right to make requests, legitimate power has the potential to influence others. (A father tells his son that *as his father* he wishes the son to attend college.)

Referent power.   The ability to influence another with referent power lies in the perception of the target to identify with the actor. That is, referent power is successful as an influence tactic because the target likes and wants to please the actor. The more a target likes and identifies with an actor of influence the more likely referent power can be successful. We comply with our friends' requests many times because we like them and want to help them out. (A father tells his son that it would please him very much to see him go to college.)

Expert power.   Expert power results from the target perceiving the actor to be intelligent, skilled, knowledgeable, or otherwise possessing abilities and talents deemed respectable and desirable by the target. Physicians, dentists, attorneys, and accountants are considered to possess expert power because of their advanced education, experience, and training. We are more likely to comply with a doctor's order if we perceive him/her to be an expert. A large number of patients (30 to 60 percent) do not hold such views of physicians and do not comply with their doctors' requests.[13] (A father tells his son that the only way to be successful like himself is to attend college.)

Power as an Interpersonal Persuasion Strategy

Educational settings.   Recent work in the area of interpersonal persuasion has revealed new insights into the use, abuse and effectiveness of power bases as sources of persuasive appeal. In educational settings, McCroskey and Richmond discovered that the use of power as an influence tactic in the classroom is perceived similarly by both teachers and students. Referent, reward, and expert power are perceived to be the predominant modes of influence in a classroom. This view was especially strong among teachers.[14] Differences in power perceptions were evident also, with teachers perceiving that they used expert power more than students thought they did, and students believing teachers used coercive power more than teachers believed they did.

One of the interesting aspects of this work concerns the relational implication of power as an influence tactic in the classroom. According to McCroskey and Richmond, power is not something a teacher can walk into a classroom with. Rather, power is something that is determined from the relationship between teacher and student. Perhaps this explains why legitimate power was not listed as a power base by either teachers or students in their study. Students are apparently unwilling to perceive power as a bonafide influence tactic unless it is relationally associated with the teacher. Observing the teacher reward appropriately, possess knowledge and skills, and identify with students are stronger bases of influence than are punishing or assigned sources of power.

The level of learning in classrooms with different types of power bases has also been examined by Richmond and McCroskey.[15] Coercive and legitimate power appear to be negatively related to learning levels, while referent and expert power are positively related to learning. Reward power does not affect learning to a significant degree. When we find someone skillful and knowledgeable, and/or we can identify with and attempt to emulate someone giving us instruction, our ability to learn is enhanced. On the other hand, when we must endure instruction from someone who insists on assigned authority or threatens and punishes us for lower achievement, our inclination for learning, and consequently our ability to learn, is inhibited.

Work settings.   Power bases as sources of influence or persuasive strategies have been studied in the workplace. Bachman and his associates conducted extensive research in over a hundred organizational units and found very definitive ideas about power as an influence tactic.[16] For example, subordinates reported that a superior's use of legitimate and expert power are the most influential strategies for inducing compliance, with coercive power being the least effective strategy. In contrast to students, workers accord superiors power on the basis of their position (legitimate) as well as on the basis of their skill and knowledge.

Thus far, we have discussed the effectiveness of power on the basis of persuading a worker to comply with a specific request. However, power can also have influence in less direct ways, such as inducing worker satisfaction and productivity. Student went further into his investigations of power in organizations and found that, while legitimate power is a major reason for complying with a superior's orders, referent and expert power are more effective in generating better worker performance overall.[17] Expert and reward power are also more satisfying forms of influence strategies. The bottom line in organizational power was offered by Bettinghaus and Cody:

> It is clear that in order to be an effective persuader in the organization one needs to develop expert and referent influence. Legitimate influence is helpful in some contexts, such as sales; but expert and referent influence are clearly to be emphasized.[18]

The ability to influence others boils down to relational issues. How we perceive others, how they perceive us, and how the relationship is viewed are critical elements in persuading others. The relational issues of interpersonal persuasion are highlighted even further in the next section.

COMPLIANCE-GAINING STRATEGIES

Recent research into persuasive strategies in everyday interpersonal communication reveals that people use a number of different, and sometimes subtle, tactics to convince others to comply with their requests. These are called compliance-gaining strategies. These specific strategies stem from the bases of powers we discussed previously, and their use is almost always dependent upon interpersonal relationship factors.

Most Popular Strategies

The most popular lists of compliance-gaining strategies are those of Marwell and Schmitt,[19] Miller et al.,[20] and Schenck-Hamlin, et al.[21] These strategies were developed further by Cody and his colleagues[22] and are synthesized into a comprehensive taxonomy here. Look closely at Table 12.1. It lists nine global strategies that people use to solicit favorable responses in interpersonal relationships. In each category of compliance-gaining strategies, an actor requests compliance from a target. (1) *Direct requests* are compliance-gaining strategies that overtly ask for compliance to a request. No additional information is supplied with the request. "Can I borrow $5 until I get my allowance?" is a direct request. (2) *Supporting evidence* involves the use of reasoning and appeals to logic or evidence as part of the compliance-gaining strategy. "If you look at the evidence you can see that I was right" illustrates a supporting argument. (3) *Exchange* strategies offer to concede, compromise, or otherwise negotiate in order to gain compliance. "I'll cook tonight if you will wash the car tomorrow" is an example of an exchange strategy. (4) *Face maintenance* strategies utilize affective appeals by casting the other person as having good qualities ("You're an expert on this subject, so would you help me out?") or bad qualities ("You're no friend, or you would let me borrow your car"). (5) When compliance-gaining strategies involve assurances of retribution or negative effects associated with noncompliance, *distributive* strategies are being used. "If you don't come to work on time, you're fired!" is an example of a distributive strategy.

(6) *Indirect tactics* are hinting strategies where compliance is requested by talking generally about a situation in hopes that compliance will be suggested by the other party (e.g., "I probably won't be able to go because I'm broke"). (7) Another category of compliance-gaining strategies is termed *empathic understanding*. With these strategies, individuals will request compliance on the basis of their love and affection for the target of the request. "If you really cared for this family you would stop drinking" is an example of this type of strategy. (8) *Referent influence* is an influence tactic that appeals to the target's identification

with the actor. That is, the actor attempting compliance-gaining will suggest how much alike the actor and target are while making a request. "This situation affects both of us so why don't we put our heads together to solve the problem" illustrates a referent influence.

(9) The final category of compliance strategies in this taxonomy is *other-benefit*. These strategies are an attempt by the actor to give targets the impression that compliance with a request is in their best interest and will benefit them. "It is best for your peace of mind that we break up" would be an other-benefit strategy.

TABLE 12.1

Categories of Tactics	Examples
1. Direct Requests	The actor asks the target to comply with a request in a direct manner. These messages do not contain any manipulation or motivation. —Can I borrow your notes until next period? —Will you have dinner with me tonight? —Dad, will you cosign my note for the car?
2. Supporting Evidence	The actor utilizes one or more reasons why the target should comply—evidence, data, logic, reasoning, appeals to rules, fairness, etc. —I provided xerox copies of the bills and cancelled checks and told him . . . —I told him that the procedures in this case were in my favor. —I thought about my arguments ahead of time and used them on her when she seemed annoyed.
3. Exchange	The actor attempts to gain the compliance of the target by offering to exchange things of value (money, services, favors, etc.). —I'll help you study if you'll go with me. —I'll agree to $1,000 if you'll throw in a radio. —I agreed not to play my stereo during study hour if he would clean up his side of the room.
4. Face Maintenance	The actor uses indirect strategies such as ingratiation (flattery, favors, attractive self-presentation, etc); or introduces topics so the target will infer or deduce the actor's intended goal. —I was sweet to him and put him in a good mood. —I told her how sad I was that I couldn't go too. —I said to him how attractive he was and how cute we look together.
5. Distributive	The actor attempts to use coercive influence or attempts to make the target feel guilt, sadness, or selfishness for not complying. —I told him that I would never see him again if he didn't stop cheating on me. —I shouted at him for not agreeing to help me. —I started crying and told him that he was the only one who could help me.

TABLE 12.1 (*Continued*)

Categories of Tactics	Examples
6. Indirect Tactics	The actor requests compliance by initiating a conversation from which the target will infer or assume the actor's real intent. —I'd hint about how much I wanted to go out with her. —I would suggest how much I valued his help in the past. —I beat around the bush about how lonely I was.
7. Empathic Understanding	Appeals to the target's love and affection for the actor are used. —If you really loved me you wouldn't drink and drive. —Dad, you know that we can't get along without you, and if you don't go for the treatment . . . —I told him how I understood his situation, but wanted him to help anyway.
8. Referent Influence	Reference to how alike and how much target and actor can identify with one another is used. —Since we're in this boat together, why don't we join forces and . . . —You and I have always thought alike, and it's only logical that we do this together. —If you are going to be popular like me, you'll have to wear these clothes.
9. Other-Benefit	Tactics similar to supporting evidence, but listed cases where the reasons benefit the target only. —I told her about the advantages of going to Europe alone. —I said to her that this car was just the right size for her. —I tried to convince her that going away for college was in her best interest.

Taken from O'Hair & Cody, "Machiavellian Beliefs and Social Influence." *Western Journal of Speech Communication*, in press.

All of the compliance-gaining strategies represent a repertoire of choices. To date, we don't even know their relative frequency in everyday interaction, but we do know that each has its time and place. As you will read in the next section, compliance-gaining strategies are not chosen at random, but rather are carefully selected for use in interpersonal persuasion contexts.

Criteria for Choosing a Strategy

Compliance-gaining strategies, though generalizable, are not applied equally in different circumstances. In other words, certain relationships and situations can increase the likelihood that some strategies will be used and that others won't. According to researchers in the area of compliance-gaining strategies, people use different strategies depending on who they are attempting to influence[23] and the factors involved in the situation.[24] This suggests that choices are affected by a dose of audience analysis and that competent communicators choose strategies that best fit the listener and the relationship.

A recent study compared strategies used on spouses and neighbors and found that people would employ compliance-gaining strategies more often in intimate relationships (with spouses) than in nonintimate ones (with neighbors).[25] Furthermore, rewarding types of strategies were more likely to be used on spouses than on neighbors. The level of intimacy with spouses enables them to be rewarded more directly than neighbors.

> **Husband:** Honey, I'll go to church with you on Sunday (reward) if instead of going to your Aunt Matilda's on Saturday you'll let me play golf with Bill (compliance-gaining attempt).

This study did suggest that compliance-gaining strategies are used selectively depending on the audience. Sometimes people hesitate to use compliance-gaining strategies when they feel that a relationship with another person does not warrant it.

The assumption that compliance-gaining strategies are selected on the basis of who the target of the strategy is and the factors involved in the situation has been extensively examined by Cody and his colleagues in a series of research projects. In one study, subjects in an experiment evaluated 12 different situations to discover the dimensions on which interpersonal situations differ from one another.[26] For example, subjects rated situations such as "persuading a professor that a test item was ambiguous" or "persuading a friend to go shopping with you." Their results showed that people distinguish situations according to intimacy (closeness of the relationship; neighbor vs. friend), dominance (how much the other person has control over you), resistance (the perceived likelihood of agreement to comply), rights (whether or not the persuader has a right to make a request), personal benefits (potential gain for the persuader), and consequences (potential effects on the future of the relationship).

Needless to say, if situations vary on this many dimensions, they are indeed complex. The decision to use any particular strategy would be a complicated one, since the persuader would be screening situations on the above six dimensions before choosing a strategy. However, as interpersonal communicators who have observed and utilized compliance-gaining strategies all of our lives, the process of selection becomes less complicated due to experience. Learning to drive a car was difficult at first because so many different decisions, both mental and physical, had to be made. After repeated driving experiences, however, many of those decisions became automatic.

Compliance-gaining situations are not always new and unique. Many of our past experiences in interpersonal persuasion situations guide us in understanding the criteria applicable in a situation and in selecting the most effective compliance-gaining strategy. Over time, we learn what works and what doesn't work in various compliance-gaining situations.

While individuals have their own ideas and perceptions of what strategies are most effective with certain people in various situations, some general guidelines have been offered to explain strategy selection. Bettinghaus and Cody[27] have summarized some of these generalizations.

(1) Direct requests are selected more often when dominance and resistance to persuasion are not factors in the situation. In interpersonal relationships

involving an actor attempting to gain compliance from a dominant target or a target who has certain rights to resist, a direct request is probably less likely to be as persuasive as a strategy that contains reasoning, justification, or appeals that can counteract such dominance.

(2) Supporting evidence strategies are used more often when persuaders feel they have rights to persuade, when they feel the receiver will be resistant, or when the two people in the situation are intimate. In each of these situations, external justification for compliance, such as supporting arguments, is perceived necessary because of the nature of the persuasive relationship between both parties. Intimacy requires careful bargaining to prevent harm to the relationship, target resistance requires additional support to gain compliance, and actor rights to persuade reduce inhibitions about employing convincing arguments.

(3) When persuaders are sure about the relationship with the other person and when the relationship is perceived to be long-term, exchange strategies are used more frequently. When actors must use compliance-gaining strategies in relationships that are enduring and long-term, they have a tendency to appear reasonable in their requests. By offering exchanges, actors can present their requests in a more legitimate manner and better preserve the nature of the long-term relationship.

(4) Persuaders will more often appeal to another's love and affection (empathic understanding) when the situation involves resistance, when consequences are long-term, and when the persuader has few rights to ask compliance. In persuasive situations where an actor has few rights to make a request, or there is perceived resistance from the target, there may be little choice than to prey on a targets's love and affection to gain compliance. Furthermore, when the relational consequences of a persuasive strategy are long-term, in that making a request may affect the relationship itself, love and affection are a preferred choice. Asking someone to move to another state with you implies long-term commitment, and appeals to love and affection seem consistent with such a request.

(5) Indirect requests occur more frequently when the persuader has a lot to gain personally from compliance. In situations where an actor can personally gain from compliance, there may be a feeling that too bold a request would appear selfish and could possible hamper the effectiveness of the request. In addition, using a more assertive strategy (direct, distributive, face maintenance, empathic understanding) in situations where the actor can personally benefit from compliance might threaten the target with perceptions of power-mongering or empire-building. When we personally benefit from compliance, hinting or beating around the bush may be more palatable types of requests, at least from the target's perspective.

(6) The use of face maintenance and distributive strategies are more difficult to predict because they involve potential costs to relationships. They are risky, since the target of these types of requests may be offended by the strategy. Not only may noncompliance result from their use, but damage to the relationship may result as well. The strategies are usually selected only when the persuader is sure that no other strategy would be effective.

PERSONALITY FACTORS IN INTERPERSONAL PERSUASION

The act of persuasion is a common activity in which all of us take part. As our previous discussion implies, a number of situational factors (e.g., relational consequences, intimacy, rights, etc.) affect how we attempt to influence others to our way of thinking. In addition, personality characteristics can cause us to attempt persuasion in different ways.

Argumentativeness and Verbal Aggressiveness

Infante and his colleagues have addressed the issue of personality and influence styles by suggesting two traits related to controversial situations in which social influence is at stake: argumentativeness and verbal aggressiveness. **Argumentativeness** is a "trait that predisposes individuals to recognize controversial issues in communication situations, to advocate positions on the issues, and to attempt refutation of the positions that other persons take."[28] This interpersonal style involves argument of the *issues* and does not attack other persons personally. On the other hand, **verbal aggressiveness** is "a personality trait that predisposes persons to attack the self-concept of other people instead of, or in addition to, their positions on topics of communication."[29]

Argumentativeness is viewed as a positive and constructive interpersonal style, while verbal aggressiveness is considered negative and destructive. When controversial issues arise, those who are able to stand up for their positions, competently refute opposing stands, and advance arguments that influence others' attitudes and feelings can gain a great deal of respect from others. Conversely, those who engage in arguments and attack others personally have much less chance of gaining respect. The distinction being made here is illustrated by the old adage, "In an argument, stick to the facts and leave personalities out of it." In many cases, an attack on someone personally will cause reciprocation and the argumentation level will be lowered to one of mudslinging. Many politicians are guilty of verbal aggressiveness when argumentativeness is the more desirable alternative. The following argument between two friends illustrates how verbal aggressiveness can reduce the quality of communication:

Jack: How could you possibly believe that the tuition rate is "about right"?

Jim: If you had any sense you would know that tuition here is the lowest anywhere within 500 miles.

Jack: I guess if I were a zit-face like you I would have more sense.

Jim: It's better than being a homosexual nerd!

Several explanations have been offered for why someone would be verbally aggressive instead of argumentative.[30] While frustration, social learning, and psychopathology are suggested as reasons for verbal aggressiveness, the one explanation we find most intriguing is *argumentative skill deficiency*.[31] Verbal aggressiveness may be some people's only perceived option for dealing with others in a persuasive situation because those people lack the ability to argue effectively or advocate their position rationally. Individuals may feel helpless when losing an argument and decide to attack the person instead of that person's arguments.

This point was made clear by a friend of ours who once remarked that she seldom engaged in discussions involving controversial issues with a friend of hers because the argument always ended in name-calling and vicious attacks on one another. She felt that being a college debater and knowing how to formulate arguments objectively intimidated her friend, who subsequently resorted to verbal aggressiveness as a means of fighting back.

If a lack of argumentative skill is a reason for verbal aggressiveness, the development of communication skills in the area of debate and argumentation could obviate the need for someone to attack people instead of issues. Becoming more aware of the facts and figures of the issues under discussion could also provide confidence in the points that someone makes during a controversy. Avoiding the trap of verbal aggressiveness can enhance our image as an effective interpersonal cummunicator.

Machiavellian Beliefs and Compliance-Gaining

Machiavellianism is a personality characteristic with which many students are quite familiar. Traditionally the Machiavellian is someone who manipulates others in order to pursue personal goals. A Machiavellian would subscribe to the view that "the ends justify the means." Two encompassing traits have been associated with the Machiavellian personality: a cynical view of human nature and a willingness to utilize manipulative strategies in interpersonal settings. More recent research has suggested that the Machiavellian personality is composed of four different characteristics: immorality, cynicism, deceit, and flatttery.[32] Furthermore, individuals may possess only one, two, or three of the Machiavellian traits, but not necessarily all of them. That is why more recent study of the concept subscribes to a view of individual Machiavellian beliefs instead of the concept of a comprehensive Machiavellian personality. O'Hair and Cody found the first three Machiavellian beliefs (immorality, cynicism, deceit) to be closely related to the selection of particular compliance-gaining strategies.[33] These will be discussed below.

Immorality.   Immorality is characteristic of individuals who believe that others are bad, unkind, and immoral. Consequently, these individuals place little trust in others and de-emphasize relational importance in their dealings with others. In compliance-gaining situations, immoral actors use distributive strategies more often and exchange strategies less often than actors with higher moral beliefs. Furthermore, actors with immoral beliefs are more likely to employ referent influence on their superiors (teachers, bosses), while actors with moral beliefs are more likely to utilize the same tactic on their peers and co-workers.

Actors with immoral beliefs, in contrast to their more moral counterparts, appear to view compliance-gaining situations as opportunities to achieve goals, with little regard for preserving relationships. This is evidenced by their willingness to use coercive and relationally negative tactics and a reluctance to employ more prosocial strategies such as exchange. Only when influencing superiors do they appear relationally oriented (referent influence), and the situation probably requires such for compliance to be successful. Since actors with immoral beliefs views others negatively, it is not surprising that they choose the type of strategies that they do.

> **Actor (with immoral beliefs), to superior:** Hey, Mr. Josten, didn't I see you at the country club on Saturday night? Yeah, great time. Say, since you understand the importance of socializing, I was wondering if I could have the day off to develop some contacts for the business.

> **Actor (with immoral beliefs), to peer:** Listen Jones, if you don't cover for me while I'm gone you're going to be real sorry!

Cynicism.   Cynical individuals possess a jaded view of humanity as well, except that their beliefs are somewhat different from those of immoral actors. Cynical individuals do not trust others, believe that others are vicious and unlawful, feel that they should keep their true intentions hidden from others, and have defensive and rigid attitudes toward others. When attempting to gain compliance from equals, such as peers and coworkers, cynical actors tend to use distributive tactics more often than do less cynical actors. In addition, cynical actors are more likely to make use of indirect strategies, especially when persuading superiors.

Cynical actors, who believe others to be untrustworthy, vicious, and defensive, apparently place little faith in relational concerns during compliance-gaining and consequently have little hesitation to employ distributive tactics. Furthermore, because cynical actors prefer to keep their true intentions hidden during compliance-gaining, they are more prone to employ indirect tactics for persuasive purposes. Less cynical persuaders are more trusting in others and are more likely to use influence tactics that are sensitive to the other person and the relationship.

> **Cynical actor:** Look, if you go out on me while I'm out of town, we're through.

> **Noncynical actor:** I hope that we'll stay faithful to one another while I'm gone. We seem to be a good couple.

Deceit.   Persons with a highly deceitful orientation believe that honesty is not always the best policy, that being important is better than being honest, and that there are legitimate reasons for lying to someone. In effect, deceit is a personality trait that reflects an actor's willingness to win and succeed even if it involves manipulation of truth. When persuading others, deceitful actors are more likely to use supporting evidence and other-benefit tactics, especially when the relational consequences associated with the request are short-term. Additionally, actors with deceitful orientations are less likely to employ exchange tactics during persuasion than their more honest counterparts.

Deceitful compliance-gaining actors will pursue their goals regardless of the ratio of truth/falsehood involved in the influence tactic because winning is so important to them. Accordingly, compliance-gaining strategies that are more easily manipulated are ready tools for the work of a deceitful persuader. For example, supporting evidence tactics can always be molded to fit the goals of the deceitful actor. The old adage, "Figures don't lie, but liars can figure" can be applied here. Furthermore, other-benefit tactics can also be manipulated by deceitful actors to give the impression that the target has a lot to gain from compliance, when this fact may not necessarily be true ("You'll feel so good about yourself after you lend me $100"). Compliance-gaining strategies that are less apt to involve manipulation, such as exchange tactics, are not common choices among deceitful actors. In addition, exchange tactics involve a concession on the part of the actor, and winning is too important to the deceitful actor for him/her to give up or concede part of the spoils.

> **Deceitful actor:** Hey, it's your turn to wash dishes, I've washed the last six out of nine times, and I've cooked the last eight of eleven times.

> **Nondeceitful actor:** I'll tell you what; if you'll wash dishes, I'll cook. How's that for a deal?

An individual's Machiavellian beliefs can affect the selection of compliance-gaining strategies just as situational factors can (rights, consequences, etc.). Some people may possess only one belief, while others view human nature using several beliefs. Regardless of the number of beliefs a person possesses, how we think about others and the world has a bearing on our persuasive style and the strategies we choose to influence others.

Apparently, people are resourceful enough to take each situation as unique and adapt their strategies accordingly. All of this points to people's amazing flexibility in altering their persuasive strategies to account for the other person and the particular situation. Furthermore, we seem to be able to do so spontaneously in everday interaction. This means that persuasion permeates not only well-planned campaigns, but is also prevalent in our daily interpersonal communication.

COMPLIANCE-RESISTANCE STRATEGIES

Thus far, we have discussed the methods of influencing others and attempts to get them to comply with our requests. However, as we mentioned before, communication is an interactive process that involves the back-and-forth nature of speaking. Accordingly, we must address the issue of people's responses to compliance-gaining attempts. If the target of a compliance-gaining attempt complies, then the request is successful. However, this is not always the case. If a target decides not to comply with a compliance-gaining attempt, then a response denying compliance usually occurs. Such a response is termed

compliance-resistance. McLaughlin, Cody, and Robey[34] studied compliance-resisting behavior and found that targets of compliance-gaining strategies will utilize strategies in order to indicate that a request cannot be granted. Most of the communication strategies we employ to resist others' compliance-gaining requests do not involve simple denial. Rather, we provide additional information, evidence, or reasoning why we will not comply.

In their study, McLaughlin and her colleagues determined that four basic strategies are used to resist compliance-gaining attempts. Table 12.2 lists the four strategies with examples. *Identity management strategies* are "indirect strategies in which the image of the agent, the target, or both is manipulated." *Negotiation strategies* are "exchange strategies in which the target proposes to engage in an alternative behavior to that proposed by the agent and/or empathic understanding strategies in which the target solicits discussion conducive to mutual accommodation." *Justifying strategies* are tactics "in which the target justifies his/her unwillingness to comply on the basis of potential outcomes, positive or negative, to self or to others, of compliance or noncompliance." Finally, *non-negotiation strategies* are "straightforward, unapologetic strategies in which the target overtly declines to comply with the agent's request."

TABLE 12.2   Compliance-Resistance Strategies

Identity Management
1. "I would point out to the other person I have never made a request like this one of him/her."
2. "I would tell him/her that no reasonable person would make the request."
3. "I would plead with the other person not to make me go along with the request."
4. "I would let the other person know how hurt I was that he/she made the request."
5. "I would act surprised and astonished so that he/she would feel bad about making the request."

Negotiation
1. "I would tell the other person we should have mutual talks and work it out."
2. "I would suggest to the other person that both of us could give in a little bit and reach a compromise."
3. "I would ask the person to explain his/her reasons for making the request."
4. "I would offer to make some sort of concession rather than go along with the request."

Non-negotiation
1. "I would simply refuse to go along with the request."
2. "I would tell the other person that I don't want to discuss it."
3. "I would make it clear to the person that I have no obligation to go along with the request."

Justification
1. "I would explain to the person the negative consequences to me of my complying with the request."
2. "I would explain to the person how I would personally benefit from not complying with the request."

(From McLaughlin, Cody & Robey, 1980)

Compliance-resisting strategies, like their compliance-gaining counterparts, are rarely selected at random by interpersonal communicators. The attitudes of the person attempting compliance, perceptions of the situation, and the effects of compliance or noncompliance can affect compliance-resisting strategy selection. For example, McLaughlin and her colleagues determined that identity management strategies are used most frequently when communicators are more intimate. She suggested that identity management strategies are deemed less effective when refusing nonintimates because a relational commitment does not exist. It is more difficult to prey on other people's emotions when individuals do not have an established intimate relationship.

Of all the strategies, negotiation strategies are the ones most likely to be used, especially in intimate situations. It is apparently easier to compromise and negotiate a compliance-gaining-resisting situation when you know the other person well. Justification strategies seem to be used more prevalently in situations where the relational consequences of not complying with a request are more long-term. Non-negotiation strategies are the least popular of the strategies to use when resisting compliance-gaining attempts. A flat ''no'' seems to carry negative relational overtones, and most individuals would rather give some reasons for noncompliance. While the body of knowledge representing compliance-resisting strategies is considerably smaller than that for compliance-gaining strategies, we do know that many of the criteria used to select a compliance-gaining strategy are also used to resist compliance. Saying no is an important relational event and involves careful interpersonal communication.

STRATEGIES FOR OVERCOMING RESISTANCE

What happens when you have carefully selected a compliance-gaining strategy in order to persuade a friend to do something for you, only to receive a compliance-resisting strategy in return? Some people will respect the wishes of the target to refuse the original compliance-gaining strategy and attempt to achieve their ambition in some other way (convince someone else to help you with your calculus homework). However, in many cases ultimate compliance by the target is the only way to accomplish your goal (persuading your roommate to be quiet while you are studying). In instances such as this strategies for overcoming compliance-resistance behavior become necessary.

Repeated Attempts

Repeated attempts to change the mind or action of resistant targets were studied by deTurck.[35] He found that individuals who try to gain compliance from resistant, nonintimate others (strangers and acquaintances who initially refused to comply) are more likely to use punishment-oriented (e.g., coercive, negative identity management) strategies and less likely to use reward-oriented strategies (e.g., exchange, ingratiation, appeals to love and affection) in subsequent compliance-gaining attempts. However, in situations involving friends, actors are most likely to use reward-oriented strategies and to some extent punishment strategies when the target initially refuses to comply.

Reward strategies may be a more optimal choice for compliance-gaining when dealing with friends because of the relational implications involved. Friends may not appreciate being threatened or coerced even though they may not be willing to go along with the compliance-gaining request. Our concern for the relationship tempers the selection of compliance-gaining strategies in such a way that the persuasive attempt does not adversely affect our friendship with the target. In contexts involving strangers or acquaintances, the unfavorable relational consequences associated with punishment strategies may not be as important as the goal we are trying to achieve, and consequently punishment strategies are the preferred choice.

In most interpersonal persuasion situations (compliance-gaining, compliance-resisting, overcoming resistance), the goals we are trying to achieve and the relationship we have with the target of our compliance request are balanced against each another. When our concern for the relationship is paramount, our choices for persuasive strategies become more limited. However, when relational concerns are deemed less important, our repertoire of persuasive strategies becomes much larger. The importance of the relationship is one of those factors we mentioned previously that affect our choice of persuasive strategies.

Sequential Requests

In many planned campaigns where gaining compliance from others is the focused activity (sales, charitable donations, etc.), compliance-resistance is expected initially, and sequential requests are actually designed with this in mind. Two compliance-gaining techniques where sequential requests are an intrinsic part of the persuasive strategy are "foot-in-the-door" and "door-in-the-face."

In "foot-in-the-door" (FITD) strategies, a person makes a small request that most people would agree to (getting his/her foot in the door), and upon compliance, asks for a larger request that is the person's actual goal.[36] Start with something small, get them in the complying mood, and subsequently make a larger request is the outline of the FITD technique. This technique operates on the assumption that people will recognize that they have already performed similar behavior by complying with the initial request and do not want to appear inconsistent by refusing to comply with the second request (even though it is larger).

"Door-in-the-face" (DITF) strategies are basically the opposite of FITD strategies. A DITF technique asks for a very large request initially, one that most people would refuse, and is followed by a smaller subsequent request. As with the FITD technique, the second request is the actual goal of the persuasive attempt.[37] According to Cialdini and colleagues,[38] in order for the DITF technique to work effectively the target of the requests must perceive that the requester has made a concession (given up something) with the second request and feel obligated to make a concession as well. Furthermore, by not pressing the issue with the first large request, the persuader is demonstrating a concession that may motivate the target to reciprocate by complying with the smaller second request.

The success of FITD and DITF techniques were analyzed by Dillard and his colleagues, who statistically examined a number of studies involving these strategies.[39] They concluded that neither technique is effective if the request is self-serving or self-oriented. These techniques work best if the requests involve important issues. Asking to borrow $100 from your father in an initial request, and then asking for $50 after being turned down is not as persuasive as employing the same technique to raise money for the March of Dimes.

Dillard and his colleagues also concluded that FITD appears to have more lasting effects than DITF if there is an anticipated delay between requests. In fact, DITF is more effective when the requests are made in a single episode. Apparently, the latency period between requests inhibits persuasiveness more if a large request is made followed by a smaller one than if the reverse occurred. This is intuitively logical, in that, over time, we are more apt to yield to someone who we remember made a reasonable request that we complied with initially than we are to yield to someone who we recall made a more unreasonable request and now wants to compromise. The act of concession is more salient when it is recognized as an honest way to achieve goals. A delay between requests with the DITF technique may make the requestee wonder what has happened in the meantime to suggest a concession.

Finally, Dillard and his colleagues determined that another problem associated with DITF strategies is that the initial request could be too large. When requests are made that are obviously beyond the range of compliance for anyone, most people will question the legitimacy of the strategy and refuse to comply even with a smaller request. The researchers suggest that such unreasonable requests may pose a threat to the self-image of the requestee ("Does he think I'm stupid, or what?"). For the DITF technique to work the request must be large enough to compromise later for a concession, but not too large to make the request look absurd.

IMPROVING YOUR PERSUASIVENESS

The task of improving your interpersonal persuasiveness is not so much a matter of learning new strategies and techniques as it is of learning to exercise your choices more effectively. You probably overuse some strategies and underuse others. People get into the habit of using one or two strategies in many circumstances. The first thing to do, then, is to take inventory of your own behavior. Do you tend to rely too often on a limited number of strategies? Do you take into account the situational factors involved? Do you find yourself being verbally aggressive when argumentativeness is considerably more appropriate? Which strategies should you consciously try to employ more often? Do you rely on certain types of power too often? Honest answers to these questions can go a long way in making you a more effective communicator.

Resistance strategies should also be developed. For instance, many people have difficulty saying no to phone solicitors or other peddlers. Many people find it hard to say no to friends who take advantage of them. Learning to say no without guilt or regret is an important skill, one which we all should possess. Too often, however, we overestimate the price of saying no. If personal insecurities lead you to believe that you will lose friends or become unpopular for saying no, you should realize that other people say no and don't always lose friends for doing so. Many times we can gain new respect by standing up for ourselves. By recognizing that several different types of compliance-resisting strategies are available, you can select the appropriate one for a particular situation and free yourself from obligations you do not want to make.

When encountering resistance to an initial compliance-gaining request, it might be well to remember that reward-type strategies are more preferred than punishing strategies. In addition, when anticipating resistance, remember that "foot-in-the-door" and "door-in-the-face" techniques work differently depending upon several factors, but on balance chances of success are greater with the FITD technique.

SUMMARY

The act of persuading others is a prevalent interpersonal communication activity. People persuade people every day, and it doesn't seem to make much difference whether the people are in formal or informal situations. Our ability to maintain our own, or change others', attitudes and values seems to permeate many communicative situations. While many people strive to maintain consistency in their attitudes and actions, they also work to maintain consistency in their interpersonal relationships. Despite the goals interpersonal communicators have in persuading others, they also keep in mind the status and health of relationships in their persuasive attempts.

In this chapter, you learned that values are general standards for behavior, whereas attitudes are specific mental opinions. We looked at how balance theory and cognitive dissonance theory contribute to our understanding of attitude change. Certainly the attitude change process is complicated, but these theories help sort out some of the basic principles underlying persuasion in everyday life. The bases of power were introduced as an influence technique in interpersonal encounters, and we discussed how different types of power are effective in educational and work settings.

We also discovered how communicators use compliance-gaining strategies to get their friends and associates to comply with their requests. We discussed several factors that influence which strategies are preferred for particular situations. Compliance-resistance strategies were also introduced to reveal how targets of compliance-gaining attempts say no to a request. Finally, we reported interpersonal influence strategies that can be used when our initial persuasive strategy was denied or resisted. The competent communicator understands the different strategies and applies them appropriately.

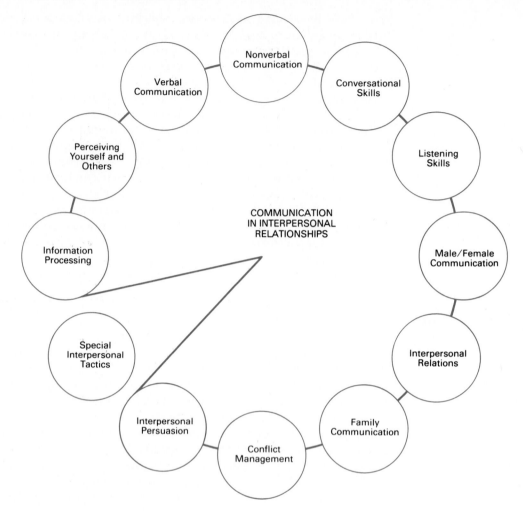

THEORY INTO PRACTICE

The following are exercises designed to demonstrate how attitudes and values work in everyday affairs.

Exercise 12.1: Analyzing Advertisements

Purpose: To learn how advertisers gear their ads to fit certain attitudes and values.

Materials Needed: Two magazine advertisements.

Time Required: 50 minutes.

Procedure: Bring to class two advertisements taken from two distinctly different magazines. Meet in groups of five, and share one another's ads. Discuss the merits of each ad, and then choose two that the group will analyze in detail by determining the characteristics of the target audience. By analyzing the ad it-self, determine who the typical buyer is in terms of:

  a. age
  b. marital status
  c. level of education
  d. occupational class
  e. income
  f. leisure time activities
  g. political party preference
  h. religiousness

Once your group has agreed on the target audience's characteristics for each ad, trade ads with another group and try to figure out how they analyzed their ads. Compare your answers with theirs. Afterwards, a class discussion will be held.

Questions to Ask: (1) What specifically did the advertiser do to make the adver-tisement appeal to a specific audience? (2) What are the attitudes and values of each audience? (3) In what ways do the advertisements that you like best reflect your own attitudes and values?

Exercise 12.2: Value Role-Playing

Purpose: To reinforce our understanding of human values.

Materials Needed: None.

Time Required: 40 minutes.

Procedure: Values are most often learned by observing the actions of others. Divide into groups of five, and choose one of Rokeach's instrumental values (see pages 229–230) and develop a 1–2 minute nonverbal skit (pantomime) that members of your group will act out for the rest of the class. The class will try to guess which value you are pantomiming. If you have time, repeat this ex-ercise, using one of the terminal values.

Questions to Ask: (1) Why did your group choose a particular value? (2) Which part of the pantomime was most revealing? (3) How much behavior do chil-dren need to observe to learn any particular value?

Exercise 12.3: The Case of the Restaurant Owner

Purpose: To investigate how much a particular situation influences compliance-gaining choices.

Materials Needed: None.

Time Required: 50 minutes.

Procedure: Read the case study presented below and then divide into groups of five to discuss the case and to choose strategies that Mr. Lyle might employ.

In a nice neighborhood is a long-established convent that is closing down to move to another location. The nuns in the convent need to sell their property before they can move. A buyer has offered to purchase the convent property for a handsome price if the city will rezone the property to permit him to erect an apartment complex designed for singles. The nuns have no problem with the potential rezoning of the property because it will expedite the sale of the property. The surrounding neighbors, living in suburban ranch-style homes, however, do not want the property rezoned. The nuns in the convent were quiet neighbors and caused no problems. On the other hand, a large apartment complex would increase noise and traffic in the neighborhood. Thus, the neighbors are against rezoning.

The neighborhood also includes a nice restaurant owned and operated for more than 20 years by Mr. Lyle. Over the years, he has made friends with both the nuns and the neighbors in the residential homes. He is well liked by all. Although he will miss his convent friends when they move, the apartment complex would provide more potential diners for his restaurant.

Mr. Lyle's real problem comes when the nuns enlist him to circulate a rezoning petition among the neighbors. In essence, he has agreed to solicit signatures from the neighbors allowing the property to be rezoned. As he goes around the neighborhood seeking signatures, what compliance-gaining strategies should he use?

After about 20–25 minutes, the class will reconvene to share the groups' decisions. Be prepared not only to announce your group's decisions, but to explain them as well.

Questions to Ask: (1) How do you see the situation in terms of intimacy, dominance, resistance, rights, personal benefits and long-term consequences? (See page 243 for definitions of these terms.) (2) What specifically led you to choose certain strategies? (3) Which strategies would not work in this situation?

SPECIAL INTERPERSONAL TACTICS

This chapter is designed to acquaint you with some interpersonal communication situations that are commonly encountered every day, but that are extremely awkward. The previous chapters in this book have discussed major topics that suggest how people can become better interpersonal communicators. There are special situations or instances that only briefly have been touched upon, and a fuller discussion of the interpersonal communication issues involved would be worthwhile. Each of the topics discussed in this chapter has important implications for communicating in interpersonal relationships. Detecting deception, accounting for our actions, and handling compliments and insults are important communication strategies that can affect our relationships with others.

WHAT'S AHEAD

This chapter will explore several interpersonal communication situations that communicators encounter or at least observe on a frequent basis. Specifically, we will discuss detecting deception, accounting for our actions, and giving and receiving compliments and insults. Detecting deception, or determining when someone is lying, is a skill that can have several important implications. This chapter will take up the issue of deception and the ways in which we can become better human lie detectors. This chapter will also discuss the ways in which we account for our actions. Making excuses or explaining why we did something is an interpersonal tactic that we have to use occasionally. It is, therefore, important for us to know the facets of accounting behavior. Compliments and insults are special interpersonal communication tactics that involve specific intentions. Most individuals do not compliment or insult others lightly, without having a motive in mind. We expect that much of what you read in this chapter will remind you of your own and others' actions. You may also be surprised to learn new interpersonal tactics that appear to be more successful in some situations than in others.

DETECTING DECEPTION

You can probably recall many instances where someone lied to you. You may even be able to remember situations in which you were forced to lie to someone else. It is difficult to find anyone who hasn't engaged in deception at least a few times. Unfortunately, deception is a prevalent interpersonal communication behavior in our society. Many reasons are given for the use of deception, but seldom has anyone advocated that lying is a preferred communication strategy. Deception involves the manipulation of truth and fact and as such is highly susceptible to being discovered. Many factors work against successful deception, especially in the long run. Our fear of detection is one of the reasons that deception is such an awkward communication situation.

Except in few cases, deception is an inappropriate form of interpersonal communication behavior. Several reasons justify our position, all of which will become apparent as this part of the chapter unfolds. At this point we will contend that deceptive communication distorts the entire process of interpersonal communication. Trust is a critical ingredient in any type of relationship, and deception is a primary cause of relational mistrust. As you recall from Chapter 8, trust involves predictability, dependability, and faith. As deception enters into relationships, trust will diminish, and relationships will suffer. As we develop our discussion of deception and methods of detection we hope that you will understand our position.

Deception Defined

Deception has been defined as "the conscious alteration of information a person believes to be true in order to significantly change another's perceptions from what the deceiver thought they would be without the alteration."[1] For the purposes of this chapter we have described deception as lies or lying behavior. Hopper and Bell have taken exception to this description of deception because they believe that deception involves more than just concealing or distorting truthful information.[2] They prefer to broaden the notion of deception to include actions or behavior that do not reflect our true feelings or beliefs (smiling at people we dislike, hiding our emotions, acting busy to avoid more work) or engaging in "identity pretense" (wearing a hairpiece, getting face-lifts, wearing falsies, acting important when you're not). While it may be true that many of us have examined deception from a myopic viewpoint, a narrow focus can lead to generalizable findings. Furthermore, the space limitations of this chapter do not allow us to devote attention to a broadened description of deception. We will focus therefore on interpersonal lying behavior.

Prevalence of Interpersonal Deception

A friend of ours once remarked, "We have become a society of liars." What a drastic statement. We are often naive enough to believe that deception is not widespread, yet we are not so naive to believe that all people are honest all of the time. Interpersonal deception is prevalent in social interaction. Sometimes we believe that we are forced to lie in order to produce a better outcome (protecting someone's feelings, preventing someone from getting into trouble, etc.). In other cases, we may just stretch the truth in an attempt to attain goals ("Let me borrow your car, I'm a great driver!"). In still other cases, instances of withholding the truth may seem appropriate (e.g., remaining silent when someone asks about an unfortunate incident).

Outright, bold-faced lies are also common. The reasons to commit such blatant interpersonal deception are numerous and difficult to categorize. Some general reasons for overt deception include flattery ("I just love your new nose job"), self-gain ("I am one of the more talented people you could meet"), avoiding embarrassment ("I wasn't the one who spilled the beer"), and avoiding trouble ("I wasn't aware that I had to pay state income tax"). We are sure that you could probably think of other categories. The point is, deception is prevalent in our society, and recognition of its widespread use is important.

White Lies

Most of us are familiar with what people mean by white lies. White lies are forms of deception used in social interaction in order to avoid unpleasant circumstances. Camden, Motley, and Wilson suggest that white lies are somewhat socially acceptable and have the potential for generating little or no negative consequences for those involved.[3] According to a large survey, this type of deception is quite frequent in social interaction.[4] When people were asked to determine the truthfulness of their own statements made in previous conversations, only 39 percent of the statements were judged to be completely honest. Given that white lies are prevalent in interpersonal communication, it is appropriate to discuss the reasons for the use of such a strategy.

You can probably think of several reasons why it might be appropriate to tell a white lie. Camden and his associates have studied white lies and have suggested several reasons why someone would be motivated to use them.[5] They suggest that white lies can be described in two dimensions: rewards and targets. The **reward** dimension involves the basic motivation behind committing a lie (what the liar hopes to gain from the lie). The reward dimension is divided into four categories: (a) basic rewards—obtaining material possessions, (b) affiliation rewards—social interacting goals, (c) self-esteem rewards—promoting self-image or self-concept, and (d) other rewards—a general category involving dissonance reduction, jokes, and exaggeration.

The **target** dimension involves the person that the lie is intended to benefit. There are three parties who could possibly benefit from a white lie: (a) the liar—self-benefit, (b) the other party—benefit to the person being lied to, and (c) a third party—benefit to someone outside of the interaction.

Based on their category system, Camden, Motley, and Wilson examined the frequency of each type of lie to determine if lies are selfishly motivated or if they are largely told for altruistic reasons. Their analyses revealed that most white lies are instigated from selfish desires. Only 24 percent of the lies studies in their survey were told for the benefit of people other than the liar. White lies, therefore, may play an important role in communicators' attempts to attain personal goals and less of role in benefiting the lives of others.

Obviously many interpersonal situations present opportunities for telling white lies. In fact, some circumstances that you face almost dictate that you tell white lies. For example, in many interpersonal settings, white lies are a more tactful form of communication ("Yes, I like your new boyfriend"—when you know he is a creep). In other situations, white lies can help to develop and maintain a relationship ("I never felt this way about another person"— only three others in the past two years). Whatever the excuses for them, white lies are prevalent and are used with justification and ease by many people.

Being able to recognize the various types of white lies improves our understanding of interpersonal communication even further. We are not saying that white lies are appropriate, and we do caution that white lies may lead to bigger, blacker lies. Recall Shakespeare's *Macbeth* or the Watergate scandal for examples of one lie being used to cover up a previous lie. Furthermore, the distinctions between white lies and other types of deception are quite relative. One person's exaggeration may be another person's deceit and hypocrisy. White lies may be just as dangerous as they are useful.

Why Deception Is Detectable

When individuals engage in deception they know that several risks are involved. There is the risk that they will be caught up in the lie later; the risk that they will have to tell another lie in order to cover up the first lie; the risk that they will damage their own self-concept ("I am an honest person"); and the risk that that they will be immediately confronted with the lie ("I don't believe it—prove it!"). For these and perhaps other reasons individuals become aroused and nervous when telling a lie. Furthermore, deceptive behavior is not normal for most people. Except for the occasional pathological liar whom we have all known, we are not used to lying. If you couple nervousness (arousal) with unaccustomed behavior, the result is eccentric interpersonal communication (behavior that is not normal for the individual). The following formula illustrates the relationship:

$$\text{Arousal (Stress)} + \text{Unaccustomed Behavior} = \text{Eccentric Interpersonal Communication}$$

When we communicate in ways that are not normal for us, others who know us perceive that something strange is taking place. They may become suspicious and begin to scrutinize our behavior even more than normal. Of course, we may experience even more stress during deception if we think others suspect us of lying. Deception is detectable because this abnormal or eccentric interpersonal behavior is recognizable through various verbal and nonverbal clues. This is the reason polygraphs (lie detectors) work so reliably. When individuals are subjected to lie detector tests, the person monitoring the polygraph looks for eccentric or abnormal physical behaviors that are caused by the arousal or stress associated with deception. Of course, the behaviors polygraph monitors look at are blood pressure, skin perspiration, respiratory changes, and pulse rate. Polygraph tests provide obvious support for the idea that behavior changes during deception, since they are reported to be 95 to 99 percent accurate.

Deception Cues

As human lie detectors, we have to rely on deception clues other than physiological changes. Several behavioral clues or cues are purported to be associated with deceptive communication. The term *cue* refers to verbal or nonverbal behaviors that leak out *unintentionally* during deceptive communication. We will divide our discussion into the verbal and nonverbal cues that are generally association with deception.

Verbal deception cues.   Knapp, Hart, and Dennis conducted research into verbal cues of deception and found that liars display more vagueness, dependence, uncertainty, and reticence than people who tell the truth.[6] Cody and his colleagues discovered that deceivers' messages seem less plausible and their verbal behavior contains more errors and lack of fluency ("ugh," "ah") than those who tell the truth.[7] Liars also seem to talk less and talk slower than those who tell the truth.[8] Information that is personally relevant (personal accomplishments, honors, etc.) appears to be more detectable than nonpersonal information (facts, data, etc.).[9]

Nonverbal deception cues.   Several different nonverbal cues have been associated with deception. One of the more obvious cues is eye contact. For some time, we have been told that "liars won't look you in the eye." This assumption has been reliably proven in several experimental studies. For example, one of your authors and his colleagues found liars to avoid eye contact much more than those who told the truth about their grade point averages.[10] Smiling has been found to vary when people lie. Some research has found deceivers to smile more than nondeceivers,[11] and other studies have found liars to smile less than those telling the truth.[12]

Some studies have found that liars have a tendency to engage in more leg and foot movement than their honest counterparts.[13] Deceivers also seem to shift posture more while they are lying than truthful people.[14] Perhaps this squirming is related to the stress that deceivers experience when having to lie. Liars have also been observed to produce more self- and object-adapters when lying than truthful people.[15] As you recall from Chapter 5, adapters are nonverbal behaviors that are produced almost subconsciously and occur in response to stress or arousal. Liars may exhibit more adapters in response to their uneasiness about interpersonal deception. More hand/shrug emblems and fewer illustrators[16] by deceivers have also been reported.

It should be noted that these behaviors should be considered as generalized findings rather than specific signs of deception. The basic method of detecting deception is to look for changes from normal behavior.

Types of Lies

Not all lies are the same. The content and form of lies can be modified as the needs, goals, and motivations of the deceiver change. In this section will discuss four types of deception: factual deception, emotional concealment, prepared lies, and spontaneous lies, each of which is quite distinct.

Factual deception.   In factual deception, the deceiver falsifies information or data. Factual deception could include lying about accomplishments, past experiences, or even personality traits. Research has indicated that lies about factual information were best detected from movements near the head area.[17] Apparently, certain facial expressions and eye or head movements alert others to deception when factual information is involved.

Emotional concealment.   Emotional concealment is a type of deception where the underlying emotional state of the individual is distorted or misrepresented. Emotional concealment could occur when we try to be serious when we actually find something humorous or when we try to mask our disappointment, sadness, or fear. In contrast to factual deception, during emotional concealment most deception cues are leaked from the body rather than the head. Lying about one's emotional feelings causes our bodies to fidget and move about, thereby sending signals that we are lying. On the other hand, lying about factual information produces telltale signs in our head movements and facial expressions.

Prepared lies.   Prepared lies are those that deceivers have a chance to think about or even rehearse before they actually use them. The following senario, which was related to one of us by a student, illustrates prepared lying.

> A friend of mine was going out of town for the weekend and asked me to keep an eye on her boyfriend while she was gone since she is the suspicious type. Since I was friends with her boyfriend as well, I didn't mind. In fact, we went out for drinks on Saturday night. The boyfriend kept asking other girls to dance and ended up going home with one of them for the night. Later I saw him, and he asked me not to say anything to his girlfriend (my friend) because he really loved her and one mistake shouldn't ruin a relationship. Besides, he didn't want to hurt her. I agreed, and since I knew she would ask about him, I prepared a lie. I've never been so nervous or scared with a friend of mine.

Prepared lies differ from spontaneous lies in that the deceiver has had time to worry about how the lie will come off. Anxiety, arousal, and stress will probably be greater for those using prepared lies because the anticipation of telling the lie allows stress to build. O'Hair, Cody, and McLaughlin found that while telling prepared lies, deceivers answered questions more quickly, gave shorter answers, nodded at the questioner more, smiled less, and produced more body adapters than people who told the truth.[18] The nervousness associated with prepared lies obviously produces eccentric behavior in liars. It is interesting that deceivers who use prepared lies answer more quickly and give shorter answers. These behaviors probably result from the fact that liars who are prepared will have a response ready. When they are called upon to produce the lie they are eager to get it over with. In addition, liars, who are already self-conscious, may be afraid that if they wait people will think they are trying to think something up and consequently may give a quick response. By the same token, prepared lies may be abnormally short because liars have already prepared the proper response, one that will not reveal too much information that can be contradicted.

Spontaneous lies.   Spontaneous lies are those produced on the spur of the moment. No advance warning, and consequently no preparation, accompanies spontaneous deception. Rather, spontaneous liars must come up with a plausible-sounding message in an impromptu fashion. The following example from a friend of ours illustrates the nature of spontaneous lies.

Some time ago I told a friend of mine that I would let him borrow my car any-time he wanted. Since then he has had two wrecks in other friends' cars and has started drinking quite heavily. Recently, he came up to me and asked to borrow my car to go to a party. I blurted out, "My car is in the shop." As I did, I felt my face blush, and I wouldn't look him in the eye, because my car was sitting at home in perfect condition. I felt really bad about lying to him, but I didn't want him using my car.

We mentioned previously how prepared and spontaneous lies differ. While spontaneous lies do not engender the same level of anticipatory arousal as prepared lies, they do produce enough stress to cause eccentric behavior. Spontaneous lies have been associated with an elevated level of body adaptors. As with prepared lies, deceivers rub, scratch, and squeeze themselves while telling spontaneous lies.

Cues and Deceiver Characteristics

Physical or personality characteristics may cause liars to differ in how they display cues related to deception. For example, gender differences have been examined in relation to deception cues. While males have been found to suppress normal leg/foot movement when telling prepared lies, females seem to suppress leg/foot movement during spontaneous lies. In addition, male liars exhibit a greater number of illustrators during prepared lies than female liars. Furthermore, males have more of a tendency to employ facial adapters when lying in a prepared fashion than males who tell the truth.[19]

The level of communicator dominance has also been shown to affect the display of nonverbal cues during lying. Dominance in communication is characterized by more assertive and direct styles of verbal and nonverbal behavior. Research by Cody and O'Hair determined that liars who are more dominant in their communication style replied to questions with spontaneous lies more quickly than dominant communicators who tell the truth, and less dominant communicators sit in more rigid positions and shift their posture less during prepared and spontaneous lies than less dominant truthful people. Apparently, the nervous gestures exhibited by less dominant communicators are a reflection of their inability to completely cope with the task of lying. Consequently, they give themselves away with nonverbal cues.

Control of Deception Cues

Most people are aware that certain cues can give them away when they are lying. Therefore, they may attempt to control these cues, especially in situations where they have forewarning and can prepare the lie. Control of deception cues can be difficult, because determining which of your cues are obvious to people is difficult. Unless you can look in the mirror while lying or have someone tell you what are typical deception cues for you ("You always scratch your head when lying"), you would have to rely on what is generally known about deception cues (as this chapter illustrates). Hocking and Leathers[20] have suggested that deceivers may be motivated to prevent detection and avoid looking like liars by suppressing deception cues that they think are typical of deceivers. Such behaviors as leg and foot movements, illustrators, postural shifts, and adapters are thought to be indicative of deception, and as such liars may attempt to suppress these behaviors to avoid detection. Perhaps that is why an abnormal reduction of some of these behaviors occurs when people lie (see above). Deceivers, in an attempt to avoid looking like liars, may make matters worse by appearing more stilted or rigid than they normally do when telling the truth. This evidence proves that lie detection may not be so much looking for an increase or decrease in particular cues, but rather looking for differences from normal behavior.

Detection Skills

Given that honesty and trust are important in interpersonal communication, it makes sense that dishonesty can seriously flaw a relationship. It is naive to think that people are always honest. The ability to detect deceptive communication is important in many circumstances. Unfortunately, people are not that good at doing so. For the most part, the untrained observer has only a 50-50 chance of detecting when someone is lying. Certain conditions can increase these odds, but most research finds that people have only a 40 to 60 percent chance of accurately identifying a lie.

Although untrained observers are not skilled at detecting deception. Under certain conditions they can improve their detection. Knapp and Comadena[21] conclude that the accurate detection of deception is a function of the motivation of the observer and the past experience that the observer has with the deceiver. To successfully identify a lie, the observer must pay close attention to the behavior of the liar and have a dependable model of the liar's honest behavior to compare the current behavior with. The observer must be alert and know the other person well. This explains why mothers can often tell when their children are lying. Their extensive experience with their children allows them to notice deviations from normal behavior. Detecting dishonesty, then, involves knowing what signs to look for and observing shifts from normal patterns.

Conclusions

Interpersonal deception is an interesting, though troublesome, area of interpersonal communication. Most of us have engaged in it, and the behaviors associated with it are potentially detectable. We know that a person's normal behavior can differ when that person is lying, but which behaviors change and how they change depends on the individual. Detecting lying necessitates knowing the person you suspect of lying well. If someone you suspect of lying displays fewer illustrators, less leg/foot movement, and fewer postural shifts than normal, you may have cause to wonder about the veracity of that person's communication. Remember, most individuals are anxious and show stress when they are lying. These feelings lead to behavior that is atypical or abnormal for them.

For many of us, engaging in deception or recognizing (detecting) deception is very awkward. Having to tell a lie is awkward because it is unnatural, and we are probably anxious about the possibity of getting caught. Detecting deception is awkward because we may not be sure what to do about it. If we confront the deceiver, it could harm our relationship with that person. On the other hand, if we keep silent it may encourage future deception or cause us internal grief because our relational partner cannot be trusted. It may be argued that improving detection skills only enhances the chance of relational strain. However, the exception to this idea is that if we are unaware of others' lies, we may be taken advantage of more often. Harm to the relationship could result from this state of affairs. Seldom is the pursuit of honesty in relationships a failing grace.

ACCOUNTING FOR OUR ACTIONS

When we give others reasons for why we behaved or didn't behave in certain ways we are accounting for our actions. **Accounting behavior** has been around as long as humans have. For example, Adam, and subsequently Eve, accounted for their misbehavior in the Garden of Eden.[22] As humans, we expect that when others commit an act or a behavior that may be considered inappropriate, they need to account for that behavior. *Excuse* is the commonly used term for communication strategies that explain our behavior. However, as we will discover, excuses are only one type of accounting behavior. For many of us accounting for our actions is a very awkward situation. It is difficult enough to explain our behavior in normal circumstances, but to provide reasons and justifications for our untoward actions is even more difficult. That is why we have included this situation in this chapter.

Accounting behavior is an important part of our interpersonal communication behavior. As an interpersonal communication strategy, accounting provides opportunities for relationships to grow or deteriorate. If we are able to explain our actions effectively to others, they have a better idea of our intents and motivations, even when our behavior may have been less than appropriate. Other people will have a better idea of how to predict our actions in the future, which will allow relationships to grow (recall Chapter 9). However, if we handle accounts poorly and do not communicate well why we reacted or behaved in a certain way, others may lower their opinions of us, and our relations may become strained. Effective accounting behavior is a relational strategy that can benefit all of us who are less than perfect.

Several researchers have offered similar models of the sequence of events involved in accounting behavior.[23] These models involve four basic steps or actions: (1) the failure event (someone's inappropriate actions), (2) the reproach (to rebuke, assess blame, or find fault with someone's actions), (3) the account (the reply to a reproach), and (4) the evaluation (the evaluative response to the account).[24] Figure 13.1 graphically illustrates the accounting sequence.

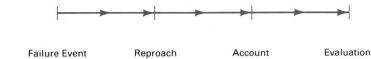

Failure Event   Reproach   Account   Evaluation

FIGURE 13.1   **The Process of Accounting for Our Actions**

Failure Event

An offense[25] or **failure event**[26] occurs when "an untoward or unexpected act is committed or an anticipated act or obligation is not fulfilled."[27] Some offenses are more serious than others, and more serious failure events require more accounting than less serious ones. McLaughlin, Cody, and Rosenstein have proposed that four different types of offenses are possible in initial interactions with strangers.[28] We will adopt these and add a fifth of our own in order to broaden the category of offenses to include most accounting situations.

(1) **Taste/attitude/belief.** Offenses of this type customarily involve issues related to the way people think or feel. Examples of these offenses could include dressing inappropriately for an important occasion, being politically conservative, having atheistic beliefs, being a male chauvinist, etc. (2) **Personal identity.** This category of offenses refers to the type of person the individual happens to be. Being lazy, always putting things off until the last minute, being romantic, liking sick horror movies, and being car sick are examples of personal identity offenses. (3) **Work/school.** Work/school offenses involve failure events where our major work or occupation is concerned. Included in this category are such examples as working overtime, studying too hard, never getting promoted, making poor grades, and not standing up to the boss. (4) **Interaction.** The interaction category of offenses involves how someone communicates. Individuals are sometimes criticized for failure to interact in an expected and appropriate manner. For example, not understanding a joke, asking silly questions, not listening carefully, not remembering what someone has said, and interrupting people while they are talking could all constitute an interaction failure event. To these four offense types, we add a fifth category. (5) **Relational.** These offenses involve behavior that adversely affects relationships between people, and these could have the most lasting impact. Relationship offenses embrace such instances as flirting with another person, forgetting another's birthday or anniversary, not providing enough affection, attention, or complimentary behavior, making callous or disparaging remarks, and ignoring a relational partner in front of others.

Reproach

As we mentioned earlier, reproaches are the second phase in the accounting sequence and involve the placement of blame or criticism on an inappropriate act or behavior. Several different categories of reproaches have been suggested by McLaughlin and her colleagues.[29] It is important to understand the nature of reproaches and their categorical groupings because the type of reproach used in a situation can determine the type of account to follow. In established relationships McLaughlin, Cody, and O'Hair have outlined six different types of reproaches.

(1) **Silence.** In this type of reproach nothing is said or done by the reproacher. Silence itself may be enough of a signal to indicate that the failure event was significant. The cold shoulder treatment is an example of silence as a reproach strategy. (2) **Behavioral cues.** This reproach is signaled by the nonverbal behavior or cues of the person fixing blame. Frowns, raised eyebrows, shaking of the head, and intense staring could be signs of reproachment. The intent of the nonverbal behavior is usually quite obvious. (3) **Projected concession.** Projected concessions are reproach strategies that imply that an apology or restitution is in order. "The least you could do is say you're sorry" and "So this is what I get for putting you through school for the past four years" are examples of projected concessions. (4) **Projected excuse.** In a projected excuse, the reproacher allows the actor in trouble to take advantage of making an excuse or denying responsibility for the inappropriate behavior. For example, "I suppose you are going to tell me that you overslept again" or "What's the matter, did you have car trouble again?" are instances of projected excuses. (5) **Projected justification.** In this reproach, the person fixing blame or criticism requests that the actor minimize or reduce the impact of the failure event. "I'll bet you're going to say that you really didn't mean it!" is one such projected justification. (6) **Projected refusal.** The reproacher in this situation implies that the actor may deny guilt, deny the reproachable behavior, or even deny the right of the reproacher to complain about the behavior. "Now, I want you tell me the truth, this time" or "Don't tell me that you didn't do it" or "I most certainly do have the right to expect satisfaction in this case" are examples of projected refusal. Again, the previous categorical scheme refers to reproach types in ongoing, established relationships.

Accounts

Accounts have been defined as "statements made by social actors to relieve themselves of culpability for untoward or unanticipated acts."[30] Buttny is even more specific: "An account is a speech act used to change meanings of the event through explanatory statements in order to relieve oneself of full responsibility."[31] A category system of accounting behavior has been outlined that includes most of the strategies individuals will utilize in the face of a failure event followed by a reproach.[32] There are five different types of accounts: concessions, excuses, justifications, refusals, and silence.

(1) **Concessions.** In concessions, the accounter admits guilt or wrongdoing, apologizes, and may even offer restitution for the failure event. "I'm sorry, I was wrong to do it, let me make it up to you" would be an example of a concession. (2) **Excuse.** An excuse is an account in which the actor admits that the offense occurred, but denies that he/she had any control over it. "I'm late to the meeting because my parents are in town and wanted to go to lunch"

and "I missed the exam because I was sick" are typical excuses. (3) **Justification.** When actors attempt to minimize or even dismiss the reproach or failure event, they are using justification strategies. Illustrations of justification accounts include "Getting loaded every once and a while is not so bad," "My grades are not as bad as yours," and "I know you're upset that we broke up, but I'm not so sure that it wasn't for the best anyway." (4) **Refusal.** Refusals, like account strategies, involve uncooperative behavior on the part of the actor. Actors reject responsibility for the offense, deny that the offense occurred, or refuse to acknowledge that the reproacher deserves an account. Refusals could be risky to a relationship. The following exemplify refusals: "I'm not the one who always has to order the most expensive item," "I don't know what you're talking about, the light was yellow, not red," and "I don't owe you an apology, you started it, you always start it." (5) **Silence.** When actors feel that "no response is a good response" they utilize silence as an account strategy. In some instances, actors may feel that talking about the offense or responding to the reproach would just make matters worse, and therefore maintaining silence seems the best strategy.

Evaluation

The final step in this sequence of events is the evaluation of the account. According to McLaughlin, Cody, and Rosenstein, the reproacher has four possible evaluation options: honor, retreat, reject (or reinstate reproach), and drop/switch topic.[33] Which evaluation strategy a person chooses depends on the nature of the offense, the type of reproach used, and the resulting account offered by the actor. We will briefly discuss each of these evaluation types.

(1) **Honor.** When a reproacher honors an account by the actor, he/she is indicating that an ample response has been made and acceptance of the account is tendered. Honoring can take many forms, such as laughter, nodding, verbal acknowledgement, smiling, and indicating appreciation for the account ("It was nice of you to give an explanation, I feel so much better!"). (2) **Retreat.** A retreat strategy evaluates an account in a less overtly positive way. Retreats could involve partial honoring (acknowledging that some part of the account is acceptable), withdrawing the reproach, or even assisting the actor in making excuses for the offense. Examples could include, "Now that you've explained it I see your side of it" and "I wish now I hadn't said anything about it." (3) **Reject.** If the reproacher is not satisfied with the account, he/she may reject, take issue with, or reinstate the original reproach. "I don't care what you say, you cannot make up a speech without an audience" and "That is the flimsiest excuse I ever heard" are examples of rejection. (4) **Drop/switch topic.** The last evaluation type can be accomplished by just dropping the issue or topic. The reproacher could decide that a continued discussion of the failure event, reproach, or account is simply not worth the effort and elect to drop the subject. Furthermore, the actor may select this option as well and hope that the issue will die on the vine.

Implications of the Model

Recall that the model of accounting behavior involves four sequential steps: offense, reproach, account, and evaluation. The model is informative in that we can learn a great deal from it about the nature of social interaction management. However, even more knowledge about this process can be gained by examining the relationships between the four elements in the model. Specifically, what are the most widely used accounts? What effect does that offense have on the type of reproach used? What is the relationship between the reproach style and the account employed? Does the type of account affect evaluation? Though many of the answers to these questions are in preliminary stages of investigation, we will nevertheless discuss several of them.

Excuses seem to be the most popular type of accounting behavior. McLaughlin et al. have suggested that the wide use of excuses "may simply reflect the fact that most people in judging their own behavior attribute failure to the circumstances of the situation rather than to their own bad intentions."[34] The type of reproach is many times related to the account strategy. For instance, a concession is more likely to result from an actor when the failure event was severe, when the reproacher was silent, or when the reproacher utilized a projected-concede type of reproach.[35] Silence on the part of a reproacher also seems to elicit justification strategies from the actor.

Refusal, as an account strategy, appears more often when the actor denies the offense or when projected refusal and projected concession are employed by the reproacher. Behavioral cues do not appear to be related to any specific type of account strategy.[36] As McLaughlin et al. suggest, nonverbal cues can be interpreted as reproaches, but the specific type may be ambiguous. Consequently, several types of accounts are associated with behavioral cues.

While very little evidence exists on the connection between accounts and evaluation in established relationships, we do have information in this area regarding initial encounters, which we will cautiously generalize to many types of relationships. First, excuses are honored more than other types of accounts. Second, retreats are likely to be communicated after concessions and justifications are offered as accounts. Third, rejections or reinstatements of the reproach seem to occur most when the actor has offered a justification, maintains silence, or when he/she refuses to account. When an actor chooses to maintain silence as an account strategy, the reproacher may also be likely to drop the topic.[37]

Conclusion

Accounts are a prevalent type of communication strategy in social interaction, although for many people they involve very awkward situations. We have attempted to sort out the elements involved in the process of accounting behavior. It is our hope that the model and the accompanying information provide some clues about the highly complex and interactive nature of accounts. It is obvious that several factors work in conjunction with one another to effect the process of repairing a failure event or offense. Relationships can be significantly affected by failure events (grounds for divorce, breakup, etc.), and the satisfactory completion of the accounting process after an offense has occurred (reproach, account, evaluation) is necessary to maintain healthy relationships. The accounting process may even cause the relationship to grow.

COMPLIMENTS AND INSULTS

How did you feel the last time you received a compliment? Did you experience pride, embarrassment, joy, or humbleness? How did that feeling differ from the one you experienced after the last insult you received? Compliments and insults are communication strategies that emanate from certain intentions and motives that people have toward goals or desires. Recall the last time you gave someone else a compliment. What was your purpose in doing so? We all have a wide range of reasons for complimenting others. We also have a number of reasons why we might insult another person. Compliments and insults are communication events that involve a great deal of awkwardness for many people. It is just as difficult for someone to respond to a compliment as it is for others to reply to an insult. In this section we will take up the issue of compliments and insults and attempt to ascertain the nature of each of these potentially awkward interpersonal communication tactics.

Compliments

Compliments, as a communication behavior, are quite common in social interaction. Although some individuals are more prone to give compliments than others, most of us give compliments from time to time. Compliments are a politeness strategy[38] that express admiration, approval, and encouragement.[39] It has been said that compliments indicate what we value.[40] If we compliment people on their clothes, we may be indicating that attire is important to us. If we compliment others on their athletic prowess, we may be indicating our interest in sports and competition.

Compliments are probably very important for relational development. In fact, compliments can be effective conversation starters, as well as strategies for getting to know someone better. There are numerous types of compliments, to say the least. Any aspect of behavior, appearance, accomplishment, personal possessions, and relational affiliation (to name a few) are subject to compliments. However, some aspects of an individual may be more prone to compliments, especially depending on the relationship between the compliment giver and the recipient.

Knapp, Hopper, and Bell conducted an elaborate study designed to enable them to better understand compliment behavior.[41] They proposed a category system to account for most of the compliments that individuals give to one another. The following list describes compliments that fall into the categories.

Category	Description	Examples
Performance	Comments on individual skill or ability.	"I loved your piano recital."
Personality	Reference to aspects of one's personality.	"You are a brave person."
Appearance	Recognition of physical features.	"I love the way you fix your hair."
Possessions	Compliments about items of possession.	"Your house is the prettiest on the block."
Attire	Reference to clothing and other artifacts.	"That is a beautiful sweater."
Helping/Service	Compliments about help or service to others.	"It is so nice of you to serve on the United Way campaign."

Knapp, Hopper, and Bell found that the most frequent types of compliments were, in order, those given for appearance/attire (combined into one category), performance, personality, and possessions. The respondents in their study reported that compliments about personality were the most meaningful to the recipient. In addition, compliments about another's appearance or attire were more likely to be made by persons under 30 years of age, and compliments about performance were more likely to be communicated by those over 30 years of age.

Compliment responses are usually made after receiving a favorable comment from another person.[42] A category system, outlined below, has been proposed to account for the various responses people will make to someone giving them a compliment.[43]

Compliment Response	Description	Example
Ritualistic acceptance	Acknowledgement without elaboration.	"Thank you."
Pleased acceptance	Expression of pleasure with the compliment.	"I'm glad you think so."
Embarrassment	Behavior associated with embarrassment.	Blushing, loss of words, etc.
Tempered acceptance	Acknowledgement with a disclaimer.	"Thanks, but my son did the work."
Return compliment	Reciprocation of a compliment.	"I like yours, too."
Magnified acceptance	Expands the original compliment.	"If you think this is good, wait until you see me snow ski!"
No acknowledgement of topic or switches topics.	Ignores the compliment.	Continues the previous topic.

Compliment Response	Description	Example
Solicits confirmation	Asks for confirmation of original compliment.	"Do you really think so?"
Denial	Rejects the compliment or complimenter.	"You're crazy."

The frequency of compliment responses was studied by Knapp, Hopper, and Bell, who found that about half of the responses to compliments were accepted (ritual acceptance, pleased acceptance, and embarrassed acceptance), and approximately one-third of compliment responses were minimized in some way (tempered acceptance, return compliment, or solicit confirmation). There seemed to be very few instances of denial or no acknowledgement, and no instances of magnified acceptance. Furthermore, return compliments were most likely to occur when the recipient was complimented on appearance or attire. Compliments on performance seemed to elicit the most instances of embarrassment and no acknowledgement.

Pomerantz has suggested that compliments are problematic for some individuals.[44] Several reasons may account for the inability of those people to accept compliments. Some individuals may feel that they will appear conceited if they accept a compliment from another person. Some people are preoccupied with the image that they present and will reject compliments that distort that image (humbleness, etc.). Other individuals have a difficult time fully accepting compliments because they do not feel the compliment is deserved.[45] That is, their self-concept does not allow the compliment to be accepted when they feel that it is an inaccurate portrayal of them or their behavior. As the previous research demonstrates, these problems are not widespread.

The personal characteristics of those who send and receive compliments have been studied to determine their effect on the selection of and reaction to compliments. Compliments from individuals with higher status (bosses, for example) seem to be more favorably received than those from individuals with lower status.[46] If someone who has status over us takes the trouble to compliment us we are usually impressed. We may suspect that people with lower status are trying to ingratiate themselves with us to enhance themselves. We would also expect that compliments from people who are experts or have credibility in a particular area are more readily received and enjoyed. For example, to receive a compliment on attire from a fashion expert means more than receiving the same compliment from someone who doesn't know fashion from fascism. Likewise, being commended on our outstanding work is more meaningful from rigorous rather than indulgent instructors.

Sex differences and compliment behavior have been studied, and it is generally assumed that women receive more compliments than men.[47] Women, in turn, reciprocate or return compliments more than men.[48] It also seems that more compliments are generated in mixed-sex rather than in same-sex interactions.[49] Two explanations for this effect have been suggested. Women may not feel that compliments from other women are sincere and consequently will not give their female counterparts a great number of compliments. Men, on the other hand, may feel that complimenting other men is not part of the masculine role model and will avoid doing so.[50] Other research has observed that the effect of compliments on people of the opposite sex is not so pronounced.[51]

Fake compliments (or false praise) are usually recognized by the recipient. Many individuals will compliment others in order to establish themselves as an authority on a particular subject. Their motive is to enhance their own position rather than to provide a true compliment ("Congratulations on your new grant, I received several like that when I was in your position"). In other instances, compliments may be given to actually put someone down ("You're so lucky; I remember how simple things were when I was a poor degraded college student"). False compliments may also occur as a result of jealousy or envy ("Well, I guess you are really proud that you got a new car for Christmas and the rest of us didn't"). Finally, fake compliments may be generated as the result of social politeness. That is, regardless of our true feelings, we may give someone else a compliment because we know that that person is expecting it ("Oh grandmother, I just love the way they bronzed your hair").

The inappropriateness of compliments can also become a problem for many people. This problem was pointed out by Cheris Kramarae.[52] She took issue with public compliments that men give to women they do not even know (street hassling). Examples of male compliments include, "Hey baby, where did you get that pretty smile?" "Great body, honey!" and "Hey sugar, I like your style." Seldom do you hear a reciprocation of these compliments from women. "Hey stud-muffins, are you ever cute!" or "What a hunk of flesh!" Kramarae suggested that street hassling or sexist compliments are really more like insults, and steps should be taken to prevent unwanted and untoward compliments.

Insults

Insults can introduce a great deal of awkwardness in an interpersonal situation. Insults are very much different from compliments, not only in content and form, but also in the motives and intentions associated with them. Insults can be characterized as behavior that is insolent, degrading, contemptuous, or otherwise rude. One of the primary purposes of an insult is to arouse the emotions of the person insulted. Consequently, responses to insults can take many forms. In this section we will discuss the nature of insults, responses to insults, and the psychology of insults.

The nature of insults.   Theoretically, very little is known about insults as a communication strategy. We do know that for the most part insults are viewed as antagonistic behavior. Insults may be used as a last choice of verbal criticism. That is, when nothing else has worked in attempting to change inappropriate behavior, an insult may be advanced. The comment, "Look, creep, I told you over and over not to stack the dishes that way. You must have bricks for brains," indicates the frustration of a restaurant owner toward a busboy. Drill sargents in the armed services may use insults as a strategy to gain respect from new recruits (whom they may call scrotum-heads, sweet-peas, maggots, wimps, or panty-waists). Some football coaches have copied this technique.

In other instances insults may be used as signs of affection. Some close friends will assign somewhat derogatory names to each to indicate their liking for one another. "Hello, fart-sniffer, how's it going?" "Fine, sewer-breath, how about you?" is an exchange one of us heard between two friends who were indicating that their relationship was close enough to engage in verbal play, which was superficially insulting in this case.

In still other situations insults are used as gaming. If you have ever engaged in or heard of one-upmanship, playing the dozens, wolfing, or sounding, you know we are referring to a contest of insulting behavior. The object of the game is to see who can get the best of the others through insults. While the "dozens" is typically associated with black males, games of insults are not restricted to a particular class or gender. The dozens is typified by the "your mama" stem and several different combinations can ensue. For example, consider this exchange between two people playing the dozens:

Blaine: "You mama wears army boots."

Dan: "Your mama's got funky drawers."

Blaine: "Your mama's drawers's got so many holes that she whistles when she walks."

Dan: "Your mama don't wear drawers in the summer so she can get a good breeze."

Insult gaming does not have to include the "your mama" reference, as the following exchange illustrates:

Dan: "You've got Buster Brown shoes. Brown on the top and all busted on the bottom."

Blaine: "You're so skinny, I put a Cheerio over you and say hula hoop, hula hoop."[53]

Responses to insults.   When we are insulted for reasons other than relational fun or gaming, we have several responses available to us. We can *ignore* the insult (as our mothers told us to do) and hope that the matter will die. Unfortunately, there is very little interpersonal satisfaction involved with that alternative. We usually feel that we have been taken advantage of when we are insulted and make no response. Another alternative is to *return* the insult with a similar one. That is, the insulted individual can indicate that the nature of the insult is also applicable to the insulter. Replies such as, "You're one to talk," "That's like the kettle calling the pot black," or "At least I'm not as bad as you are" illustrate such responses.

Still another response to insults could be a return that attempts to *devastate* the insulter. This type of insult response is an insult itself, one that goes for the throat. This response is intended to inflict more damage to the insulter than that person had intended. In this way, the insulter will think twice about future transgressions. *Second-party* responses, responses by persons other than the insulted individual, are another method of replying to insults. These responses are fairly common because insults to other people made in our presence are embarrassing, we have less to lose by defending the other person than if we were defending ourselves, and they give us the chance to be heroic. We may be more likely to defend others than ourselves after an insult.

The psychology of insults.   In examining the psychological implications of insults, we are faced with answering several questions. Does the insulted person believe the insult to be true? Does the insulted person perceive the insulter to believe the insult to be true? Who else was present when the insult occurred? What is the status relationship between the insulter and insulted person? The ways in which these questions are answered will determine the behavior of the insultee in responding to the original insult. An insult that the insulted person knows is true or is warranted may precipitate a milder response than one that the insulted person knows is false. If an insulted person thinks that the insulter may not know for sure that the insult is warranted, a stronger response could result. If friends, subordinates, superiors, or impressionable people are present during the insult, a strong and competent response may be in order. Finally, insults from superiors may elicit no response from us, while insults from peers may generate a devastating reciprocation.

Insults are a form of interpersonal communication that is problematic for most of us. Fortunately, we do not have frequent interaction with others who are prone to insulting behavior. However, when we do encounter insults, we should understand that appropriate measures are available to counteract them, especially when they are unwarranted.

SUMMARY

This chapter has examined four interpersonal situations that are typically awkward for communicators: deception detection, accounting behavior, compliment behavior, and insults. While each of these communication events is distinct from the others, if not in motive, then at least in form, they all have one thing in common. They can best be handled by someone who is an effective and knowing interpersonal communicator. By reading this chapter you have already accumulated knowledge about these situations that most people do not have. You may not be able to prevent someone from lying to you, but you may be in a better position to detect lying when it occurs. It may be difficult for you to avoid insults from other people, but at least you are acquainted with the nature of insults and strategies for handling them. You may commit offenses in the future, but you are now aware of the sequence of accounting behavior and can handle the aftereffects of failure events more competently. Finally, you are now more knowledgeable about compliment behavior and can better tell which compliments elicit certain responses from particular people. This chapter

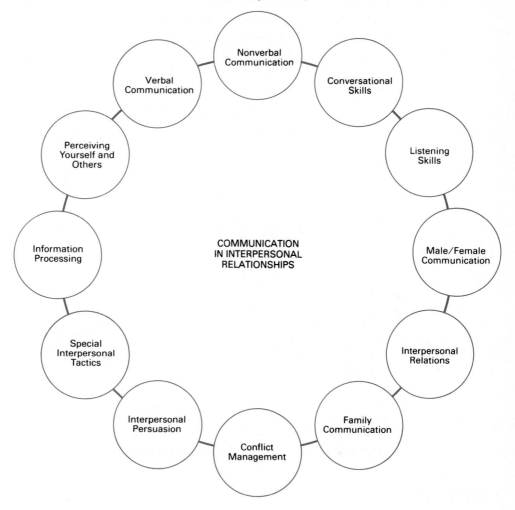

has been devoted to making you a more skilled and knowledgeable interpersonal communicator. We hope that the awkwardness of these four situations will be minimized for you in the future.

THEORY INTO PRACTICE

The following exercises are provided to give you the opportunity to develop better skills in special interpersonal tactics.

Exercise 13.1: Detecting Deception

Purpose: To get firsthand knowledge of cues that are associated with deception.

Materials needed: None.

Time required: 30 minutes.

Procedure: Ask students to relate those deception cues they have noticed in their friends, family, or other people. Draw attention to the similarities in the cues discussed. How did the cues that were observed differ from normal behavior? What cues do students think they commit when they lie? How do they attempt to avoid detection of deception? Are there special techniques that members of this class use to detect deception?

Involve the class in a discussion of *why* people engage in interpersonal deception. What are other people's motives for lying? What are their own motives for lying? What circumstances, if any, lead to justifiable lies? Are lies justified for national security or criminal justice reasons? Why or why not?

Exercise 13.2: Accounting Behaviors

Purpose: To better acquaint students with the process and nature of accounting behavior.

Materials needed: None.

Time required: 30 minutes.

Procedure: Begin a discussion of accounting behavior by asking students about the last time they gave an excuse to someone else. How much planning went into forming the right strategy so that the account would be accepted? Which types of accounts seem to be most acceptable to college students, professors, parents, girlfriends or boyfriends, etc.? How much does the evaluation of the account mean to the person responsible for the failure event? How often are people willing to admit that they made a mistake?

Exercise 13.3: Understanding Compliment Behavior

Purpose: To equip students with a realistic understanding of the theory involved in compliment behavior.

Materials needed: None.

Time required: 20 minutes.

Procedure: In this exercise, students will be asked to recall the last compliment they received that they knew was fake. How did they know the person didn't really mean the compliment? How did it make them feel? How did they respond to the fake compliment? When was the last time they gave someone a fake compliment? How much complimenting do they normally do? Are there interpersonal communication advantages to complimenting others?

Exercise 13.4: Understanding Insults and the Appropriate Responses to Them

Purpose: To explore the reasons why people insult others and to understand the characteristics of insults and responses to insults.

Materials needed: None.

Time: 20 minutes.

Procedure: A class discussion should begin by suggesting reasons that some people insult others. How does criticism differ from insults? When was the last time students in class were insulted? What precipitated the insults? How did they students respond? Is returning an insult an effective method of handling the situation? Are there justifiable reasons for insulting others? Why are insults sometimes humorous to observe (such as those of Don Rickles)?

EPILOGUE

Back in Chapter 1, on pages 13–16, you were encouraged to explore your feelings about yourself and about others. The test was not designed to find out how much you knew about interpersonal communication, but to test your attitudes. We know that your attitudes about your abilities as a communicator significantly affect your willingness to communicate with others. Those who are confident in themselves often communicate more effectively than those who are not.

Now that you have completed this text, you know that there is more to effective interpersonal communication than just being confident in yourself. Your future success in interpersonal communication should be guided by your new educated perspective. You now know more about interpersonal communication than most people. At the same, you should now appreciate the complexity of interpersonal communication more than ever.

More knowledge does not necessarily make for better communicators. You still have to apply what you have learned. To help you do this and to help maximize your success in interpersonal communication, we leave you with two thoughts: dialogue, not debate, and choosing strategies.

DIALOGUE, NOT DEBATE

Successful interpersonal communication is often a matter of style. Think about the people you admire the most. Oftentimes they are effective communicators with effective styles. In interpersonal communication, it doesn't make much sense to develop a grand speaking style that is more appropriate for the pulpit than for everyday conversations. Yet you can develop a smooth and attractive interpersonal communication style. Such a style places a premium on listening and is geared toward understanding others and building relationships.

The style we are talking about is called *dialogue*. It is best understood when contrasted with debate. Successful communicators are typically good listeners, ones who explore topics with others in a positive way. They are not argumentative or bullish in their methods. There are times when a little bullishness is needed, but such times occur infrequently in most of our interpersonal conversations.

When people have debate mindsets, they tend to argue a lot, defend themselves, hate losing, and see their success in life related to defeating others. They also tend to be involved in more time-consuming interpersonal conflicts than others. However, it takes more time to resolve a conflict than to start one. On the other hand, a person who thinks in terms of dialogue discusses more than argues, asserts him/herself tactfully, and sees success as at least partially dependent on cooperation with others. As a result, many time-consuming conflicts can be minimized. Effective communicators who wish to maximize cooperation with others should be mindful of the following:

Debate	Dialogue
Defend your position	Listen to other positions
Give answers	Explore options
Think "either-or"	Think "more or less"
Correct others	Respect differences
Use "me," "you"	Use "we," "us"

If you make an effort to do the things listed on the dialogue side of the chart, you should find that your overall interpersonal effectiveness will increase. People will like you more, enjoy talking with you, and consider you a valued friend.

CHOOSING STRATEGIES

We have covered a lot of different strategies in this text. It will do little good for you to memorize all of them. You can, however, develop some guidelines for choosing one strategy over another. Whether you are involved in male-female communication, family communication, or exploring different compliance-gaining strategies, you should always evaluate your choices based on the three considerations introduced in Chapter 1:

1. *The importance of the relationship.* Ask yourself how important this relationship is to you. All relationships you have are not of equal value. But for very important relationships, you need to carefully monitor what you say and do. Remember your actions, along with your partner's, determine the quality of your relationship.
2. *The intimacy of the relationship.* The perceived closeness of the communicators should determine how they communicate with each other. Your strategies with strangers should be different from the ones you use with your most intimate associates. At the same time it is important not to take our intimate relationships for granted. By this, we mean that people should be just as considerate in their communication strategy choices with those they care about a lot as with others that they may not be as intimate with.
3. *The consequences of each strategy.* Whenever you make choices about what to say and how to say it, you need to pause and reflect about the possible outcomes of your choices. Relationships live on how communicators talk with one another. So, be careful how you talk. Keep in mind the positive and possible negative consequences of your choices.

REFERENCES

Chapter 1

1. Naisbitt, J. *Megatrends.* (New York: Warner Books, 1984).
2. Bennett, J., and Olny, R. "Executive Priorities for Effective Communication in an Information Society," *Journal of Business of Communication 23* (1986) 13–22.
3. Beck, C., and Beck, E. "The Manager's Open Door and the Communication Climate," *Business Horizons 29* (1986) 15–19.
4. Nussbaum, J., and Scott, M. "Instructor Communication Behaviors and Their Relationship to Classroom Learning." In D. Nimmo, ed., *Communication Yearbook III* (New Brunswick: Transaction Press, 1979); Norton, R. "Teacher effectiveness as a function of communicator style. In B. Rubin, ed., *Communication Yearbook I* (New Brunswick: Transaction Press, 1977).
5. Cattermole, J., and Robinson, N. "Effective Home/School Communication—From the Parents' Perspective," *Phi Delta Kappan 67* (1985) 48–50.
6. Engel, G. "The Need for a New Medical Model: A Challenge for Biomedicine," *Science 196* (1979) 129–130; Smith, D. "Essence of Medicine," *Pennsylvania Medicine 83* (1979) 5.
7. Gillum, R., and Barsky, A. "Diagnosis and management of patient non-compliance," *Journal of the American Medical Association 228* (1974) 1563–1567.
8. DiMatteo, M., and Hays, R. "The Significance of Patients' Perception of Physician Conduct: A Study of Patient Satisfaction in a Family Practice Center," *Journal of Community Health 6* (1563–1567).
9. Bochner, A. "Perspectives on Inquiry: Representation, Conversation, and Reflection." In M. Knapp and G. Miller, eds., *Handbook of Interpersonal Communication* (Beverly Hills: Sage, 1985).
10. Miller, G. "The Current Status of Theory and Research in Interpersonal Communication," *Human Communication Research* (1977).
11. Fisher, B. *Perspectives on Human Communication* (New York: Macmillan, 1978).

Chapter 2

1. Anderson, P., Garrison, J., and Anderson, J. "Implication of a Neurophysiological Approach for the Study of Nonverbal Communication," *Human Communication Research 6* (1979) 74–89.
2. Burgoon, J., and Saine, T. *The Unspoken Dialoque.* (Boston: Houghton-Mifflin Co., 1978).
3. Woodall, W., and Folger, J. "Encoding Specificity and Nonverbal Cue Context: An Expansion of Episodic Memory Research," *Communication Monographs 49* (1981) 39–53.
4. Kennedy, G. *The Art of Persuasion in Ancient Greece.* (Princeton, NJ: Princeton University Press, 1963).
5. Lindsay, P., and Norman, D., *Human Information Processing* (New York: Academic Press, 1977).

6. Tulving, E. "Episodic and Semantic Memory." In *Organization of Memory*, E. Tulving and W. Donaldson, eds. (New York: Academic Press, 1972).

7. Housel, T., and Acker, S. "A Comparison of Three Approaches to Semantic Memory: Network, Feature Comparison and Schema Theory," *Communication Quarterly 29* (1981) 21–31.

8. Goss, B. *Processing Communication* (Belmont, CA: Wadsworth Publishing Co. 1982).

9. Calvin, W., and Ojemann, G. *Inside the Brain*. (New York: Mentor Books, 1980).

10. Herrman, D., and Neisser, U. "An Inventory of Everyday Memory Experience." In M. Grunberg, P. Morris, and R. Sykes, eds. *Practical Aspects of Memory*. (London: Academic Press, 1978).

11. Loftus, E., and Palmer, J. "Reconstruction of Automobile Destruction: An Example of the Interaction between Language and Memory," *Journal of Verbal Learning and Verbal Behavior 13* (1974) 585–589.

12. Loftus, E., Burns, H., and Miller, D. "Semantic Integration of Verbal Information into a Visual Memory," *Journal of Experimental Psychology: Human Learning and Memory 4* (1978) 19–31.

13. Hayes, D., and Birnbaum, D. "Preschoolers' Retention of Televised Events: Is a Picture Worth a Thousand Words?" *Developmental Psychology 16* (1980) 410–416.

14. Levin, J., and Berry, J. "Children's Learning of All the News That's Fit to Picture," *Educational Communication and Technology 28* (1980) 177–185.

15. Stauffer, J., Frost, R., and Rybolt, W. "Recall and Learning from Broadcast News: Is Print Better?" *Journal of Broadcasting 25* (1981) 253–262.

16. Kelly, G. *The Psychology of Personal Constructs*. (New York: Norton, 1955).

17. Schroeder, H., Driver, M., and Streufert, S. *Human Information Processing* (New York: Holt, Rinehart & Winston, 1967).

18. Littlejohn, S. *Theories of Human Communication*. 2nd ed. (Belmont, CA: Wadsworth Publishing Co, 1983).

19. Hale, C. "Cognitive Complexity-Simplicity as a Determinant of Communication Effectiveness," *Communication Monographs 47* (1980) 304–311.

20. Crockett, W. "Cognitive Complexity and Impression Formation." In B. Maher, ed. *Progress in Experimental Personality Research. (New York: Academic Press, 1965)*.

Chapter 3

1. Goss, B. *Processing Communication*. (Belmont, CA: Wadsworth Publishing Co., 1982).

2. Mead, G. *Mind, Self, and Society*. (Chicago: Univ. of Chicago Press, 1934).

3. Pavlov, I. *Conditioned Reflexes*. (Translated by G. Anrep). London: Oxford Univ. Press, 1927): or see any current introductory psychology textbook.

4. McCroskey, J. "Oral Communication Apprehension: A Summary of Recent Theory and Research," *Human Communication Research 4* (1977) 78–96.

5. Maslow, A. *Toward a Psychology of Being*. (New York: Van Nostrand, 1968).

6. Berger, C., and Roloff, M. "Social Cognition, Self-Awareness, and Interpersonal Communication." In B. Dervin and M. Voight, eds., *Progress in Communication Sciences*, vol. 2. (Norwood, NJ: ABLEX Publishing Corp, 1980).

7. Ibid.

8. King, S. *Communication and Social Influence*. (Reading, MA: Addison-Wesley Publishing Co. 1975).

9. Gibbon, F., and Wicklund, R. "Selective Exposure to Self," *Journal of Research in Personality 10* (1976) 98–106.

10. Scott, M., and Powers. W. *Interpersonal Communication: A Question of Needs.* (Boston: Houghton-Mifflin Co., 1978).

11. Cohen, A. "Some Implications of Self-Esteem for Social Influence." In C. Hovland and I. Janis, eds., *Personality and Persuasibility*, vol. 2. (New Haven, CT: Yale University Press, 1959).

12. Goss, B., Thompson, M., and Olds, S. "Behavioral Support for Systematic Desensitization for Communication Apprehension," *Human Communication Research 4* (1978) 158–163.

13. Leventhal, H., and Perloe, S. "A Relationship between Self-Esteem and Persuasibility," *Journal of Abnormal and Social Psychology 64* (1968) 383–388.

14. Jourard, S. *Self Disclosure: An Experimental Analysis of the Transparent Self.* (New York: Wiley-Interscience Publishers, 1971).

15. Miller, G., and Steinberg, M. *Between People.* (Palo Alto, CA: Science Research Associates, 1975).

16. Powell, J. *Why Am I Afraid to Tell You Who I Am?* (Niles, IL: Argus Communication, 1969).

17. Hosman, L., and Tardy, C. "Self-Disclosure and Reciprocity in Short and Long Term Relationships: An Experimental Study of Evaluational and Attributional Consequences," *Communication Quarterly 28* (1980) 20–30.

18. Archer, R., and Berg, J. "Disclosure Reciprocity and Its Limits: A Reactance Analysis," *Journal of Experimental Social Psychology, 14* (1978) 526–540.

19. Lynn, S. "Three Theories of Self-Disclosure Exchange," *Journal of Experimental Psychology, 14* (1978) 466–479.

20. Lange, J., and Grove, T. "Sociometric and Autonomic Responses to Three Levels of Self-Disclosure Dyads," *Western Journal of Speech Communication, 45* (1981) 355–362.

21. Ibid.

22. Chelune, G., and Figueroa, J. "Self-Disclosure Flexibility, Neuroticism, and Effective Interpersonal Communication," *Western Journal of Speech Communication, 45* (1981) 27–37.

23. Rawlins, W. "Openness as Problematic in Ongoing Friendships: Two Conversational Dilemmas," *Communication Monographs 50* (1983) 1–13.

24. Wheeless, L. "Self Disclosure and Interpersonal Solidarity: Measurement, Validation, and Relationships," *Human Communication Research 3* (1976) 47–61.

25. Wheeless, L. "A Follow-up Study of the Relationships among Trust, Disclosure, and Interpersonal Solidarity" *Human Communication Research, 4* (1978) 143–157; Tardy, C., Hosman, L., and Bradac, J. "Disclosing Self to Friends and Family," *Communication Querterly 29* (1981) 263–268.

26. Bochner, A. "On the Efficacy of Openness in Close Relationships." In M. Burgoon, ed. *Communication Yearbook 5* (New Brunswich, NJ: Transaction Books, 1982).

27. Goss, B. *Communication in Everyday Life.* (Belmont, CA: Wadsworth Publishing Co., 1983).

28. Berger, C. "Interpersonal Communication Theory and Research: An Overview." In B. Ruben, ed., *Communication Yearbook 1* (New Brunswick, NJ: Transaction Books, 1977).

29. Hymes, D. *Foundations in Sociolinguistics.* (Philadelphia: University of Pennsylvania Press, 1974).

30. Shimanoff, S. *Communication Rules: Theory and Research.* (Beverly Hills: Sage Publications, 1980); Frentz, T., and Farrell, T. "Language-Action: A Paradigm for Communication," *Quarterly Journal of Speech, 62* (1976) 333–349; Delia, J. "Constructivism and the Study of Human Communication," *Quarterly Journal of Speech 62* (1976) 333–349; Delia, J. "Constructivism and the Study of Human Communication," *Quarterly Journal of Speech 63* (1977) 66–83; Searle, J. *Speech Acts: An Essay in the Philosophy of Language.* (London: Cambridge University Press, 1969).

31. Wiemann, J. "Explication and Test of a Model of Communicative Competence," *Human Communication Research 3* (1977) 195–213.

32. For an excellent review of the communication competence research, see Spitzberg, B., and Cupach, W. *Competence in Communicating: Approaches and New Directions.* (Beverly Hills: Sage Publications, 1983).

33. Spitzberg, B. "Performance Styles, Interpersonal Communication Competence, and Communicative Outcomes: An Empirical Examination." Paper presented at the Western Speech Communication Association Convention, Denver, 1982.

34. Glaser, S. "Interpersonal Communication Instruction: A Behavioral Competency Approach," *Communication Education 32* (1983) 221–225.

Chapter 4

1. Chomsky, N. *Aspects of the Theory of Syntax.* (Cambridge, MA: The M.I.T. Press, 1965).

2. Dale, P. *Language Development,* 2d. ed. (New York: Holt, Rinehart, & Winston, 1976).

3. Berlo, D. *The Process of Communication.* (New York: Holt, Rinehart & Winston, 1960).

4. Greenberg, J. *Universals of Language,* 2d. ed. (Cambridge, MA: The M.I.T. Press, 1966).

5. Hockett, C. "The Problem of Universals in Language." In *Universals of Language,* 2d. ed. (Cambridge, MA: The M.I.T. Press, 1966).

6. Foss, D., and Hakes, D. *Psycholinguistics: An Introduction to the Psychology of Language.* (Englewood Cliffs, NJ: Prentice-Hall, Inc., 1978).

7. Searle, J. *Speech Acts.* (London: Cambridge University Press, 1969).

8. Ellis, D. "Language and Speech Communication." In M. Burgoon, ed., *Communication Yearbook 6.* (Beverly Hills, CA: Sage Publications, 1982).

9. Dale, P., loc. cit.

10. Goss, B. *Communication in Everyday Life.* (Belmont, CA: Wadsworth Publishing Co., 1983).

11. Smith, F. *Comprehension and Learning.* (New York: Holt, Rinehart, & Winston, 1975).

12. Osgood, C., Suci, G., and Tannenbaum, P. *The Measurement of Meaning.* (Urbana, IL: Univ. of Illinois Press, 1957).

13. Rosch, E. "Cognitive Representations of Semantic Categories, *Journal of Experimental Psychology 104* (1975) 192–233.

14. Bowers, J. "Language Intensity, Social Introversion, and Attitude Change," *Speech Monographs 30* (1963) 345–352.

15. Bradac, J., Bowers, J., and Courtright, J. "Three Language Variables in Communication Research: Intensity, Immediacy, and Diversity," *Human Communication Research 5* (1979) 257–269.

16. Mulac, A. "Effects of Obscene Language upon Three Dimensions of Listener Attitude," *Communication Monographs 43* (1976) 300–307.
17. Bradac, J., Bowers, J., and Courtright, J., op. cit.
18. Gilbert, S., and Horenstein, D. "The Communication of Self-Disclosure: Level versus Valence," *Human Communication Research 1* (1975) 316–322.
19. Burgoon, M., Jones, S., and Stewart, D. "Toward a Message-Centered Theory of Persuasion: Three Empirical Investigations of Language Intensity," *Human Communication Research 1* (1975) 240–256.
20. Hovland, C., Janis, I., and Kelley, H. *Communication and Persuasion.* (New Haven, CN: Yale University Press, 1953).
21. Bradac, J., Bowers, J., and Courtright, J., op. cit.
22. DeVito, J. *The Psychology of Speech and Language.* (New York: Random House, Inc., 1970).
23. Street, R., and Jordan, W. "Lexical Diversity and Rhetorical Interrogatives as Adaptations to Communication Environments: A Research Note," *Communication Quarterly 29* (1981) 276–282.
24. Sherblom, J., and Reinsch, Jr., N. "Stylistic Concomitants of Persuasion in Conversations," *Communication Quarterly 29* (1981) 55–63.
25. Bradac, J., Bowers, J., and Courtright, J., op. cit.
26. Giles, H., and Powesland, P. *Speech Style and Social Evaluation.* (London: Academic Press, 1975).
27. Giles, H., and St. Clair, R. *Language and Social Psychology.* (Baltimore: University Park Press, 1979).
28. Goss, B. "The Effect of Sentence Context on Ambiguous, Vague and Clear Nouns," *Communication Monographs 39* (1972) 286–289.
29. Williams, M., and Goss, B. "Equivocation: Character Insurance," *Human Communication Research 1* (1975) 265–270.
30. Bruner, J. "Going Beyond the Information Given." In *Contemporary Approaches to Cognition.* (Cambridge, MA: Harvard University Press, 1957).
31. Bransford, J., and Franks, J. "The Abstraction of Linguistic Ideas," *Cognitive Psychology 2* (1971) 331–350.
32. Loftus, E., and Zanni, G. "Eyewitness Testimony: The Influence of the Wording of a Question," *Bulletin of the Psychonomic Society 5* (1975) 86–88.
33. Allport, G., and Postman, L. *The Psychology of Rumors.* (New York: Holt, Rinehart and Winston, 1948).

Chapter 5

1. Knapp, M. "The Field of Nonverbal Communication: An Overview." In C. J. Stewart and B. Kendall, eds., *On Speech Communication: An Anthology of Contemporary Writing and Messages.* (New York: Holt, Rinehart and Winston, 1972).
2. Argyle, M. *Bodily Communication.* (New York: International Universities Press, 1975).
3. Ekman, P. "Communication through Nonverbal Behavior: A Source of Information about an Interpersonal Relationship." In S. S. Tomkins and C. E. Izard, eds., *Affect, Cognition, and Personality.* (New York: Springer, 1965).
4. Burgoon, J., and Koper, R. "Nonverbal and Relational Communication Associated with Reticence," *Human Communication Research 10* (1984) 601–626.
5. Trager, G. "Paralanguage: A First Approximation," *Studies in Linguistics 13* (1958) 1–12.

6. Ibid.

7. Reardon, R. "Individual Differences and the Meaning of Vocal Emotional Expressions," *Journal of Communication 21* (1971) 72–82.

8. Ekman, P., Friesen, W., and Ellsworth, R. *Emotion in the Human Face: Guidelines for Research and an Integration of Findings.* (New York: Pergamon Press, 1972).

9. Boucher, J., and Ekman, P. "Facial Areas of Emotional Information," *Journal of Communication 25,* (1975) 21–29.

10. Ekman, P., and Friesen, W. "Felt, False, and Miserable Smiles," *Journal of Nonverbal Behavior 6* (1982) 238–253.

11. Burgoon, J., Buller, D., Hale, J., and deTurk, M. "Relational Messages Associated with Nonverbal Behaviors," *Human Communication Research 10* (1984) 351–378.

12. Coutts, L., and Schneider, F. "Affiliative Conflict Theory: An Investigation of the Intimacy Equilibrium and Compensation Hypothesis," *Journal of Personality and Social Psychology 34* (1976) 1135–1142.

13. Henley, N. *Body Politics.* (Englewood Cliffs, NJ: Prentice-Hall, 1977).

14. Romano, J., and Bellack, A. "Social Validation of a Component Model of Assertive Behavior," *Journal of Consulting and Clinical Psychology 48* (1980) 473–490.

15. Ekman and Friesen, 1982.

16. Ibid.

17. Ekman, P. "Universal and Cultural Differences in Facial Expressions of Emotions." In Nebraska Symposium on Motivation, ed. J. K. Cole (Lincoln: University of Nebraska Press, 1971).

18. Ibid.

19. Argyle, M., and Ingham, R. "Gaze, Mutual Gaze, and Proximity," *Semiotica 6* (1972) 32–49.

20. Modigliani, A. "Embarrassment, Facework, and Eye-contact: Testing a Theory of Embarrassment," *Journal of Personality and Social Psychology 17* (1971) 15–24.

21. Fromme, D., and Schmidt, C. "Affective Role Enactment and Expressive Behavior," *Journal of Personality and Social Psychology 24* (1972) 413–419.

22. Jurick, A., and Jurick, J. "Correlations among Nonverbal Expressions of Anxiety," *Psychological Reports 34* (1974) 199–204.

23. Kendon, A. "Some Functions of Gaze-Direction in Social Interaction," *Acta Psychologica 26* (1967) 22–63.

24. Rubin, Z. "Measurement of Romantic Love," *Journal of Personality and Social Psychology 16* (1970) 265–273.

25. Beebe, S. "Effects of Eye Contact, Posture, and Vocal Inflection Upon Credibility and Comprehension," *Australian SCAN: Journal of Human Communication 7–8* (1980) 57–70.

26. LaFrance, M., and Mayo, C. *Moving Bodies: Nonverbal Communication in Social Relationships.* (Monterey, CA: Brooks/Cole, 1978).

27. Ellsworth, P., Carlsmith, J., and Henson, A. "The Stare as Stimulus to Flight in Human Subjects: A Series of Field Experiments," *Journal of Personality and Social Psychology 21,* (1972) 302–311.

28. Werner, A., and Reis, H. "Do the Eyes Have It? Some Interpersonal Consequences of the Stare." Paper presented at the meeting of the Eastern Psychological Association, Chicago, 1974.

29. Ekman, P., and Friesen, W. "The Repertoire of Nonverbal Behavior: Categories, Origins, Usage, and Coding," *Semiotica 1* (1969) 49–98.

30. Hall, E. *The Silent Language.* (New York: Doubleday, 1959).

31. Patterson, M. "Compensation in Nonverbal Immediacy Behaviors: A Review", *Sociometry 36* (1973) 237–252.

32. Mehrabian, A. "Inference of Attitude from the Posture, Orientation, and Distance of a Communicator," *Journal of Consulting and Clinical Psychology 32* (1968) 296–308.

33. Burgoon et al, 1984.

34. Riess, M., and Rosenfeld, P. "Seating Preference as Nonverbal Communication: A Self-Presentational Analysis," *Journal of Applied Communications Research 8* (1980) 22–28.

35. Willis, F. "Initial Speaking Distance as a Function of the Speaker's Relationship," *Psychonomic Science 5* (1966) 221–223.

36. Strube, M., and Werner, C. "Interpersonal Distance and Personal Space: A Conceptual and Methodological Note," *Journal of Nonverbal Behavior 6* (1982) 163–170.

37. As cited in Kanpp, M. *Nonverbal Communication in Human Interaction* 2nd ed. (New York: Holt, Rinehart and Winston, 1978); Malandro, L., and Barker, L. *Nonverbal Communication.* (Reading, MA: Addison-Wesley Publishing Co., 1983).

38. Jones, S., and Yarbrough, A. "A Naturalistic Study of the Meanings of Touch," *Communication Monographs 52* (1985) 19–56.

39. Nguyen, T., Heslin, R., and Nguyen, M. "The Meaning of Touch: Sex Differences," *Journal of Communication 25* (1975) 92–103.

40. Rytting, M. "Self-Disclosure in the Development of a Heterosexual Relationship" (Doctoral Dissertation, Purdue University, 1975). *Dissertation Abstracts International 36* (1976) 3582–B. (University Microfilms No. 76–584).

41. Heslin, R., Nguyen, T., and Nguyen, M. "Meaning of Touch: The Case of Touch from a Stranger or Same Sex Person," *Journal of Nonverbal Behavior 7* (1983) 147–157.

42. Henley, N. *Body Politics: Power, Sex and Nonverbal Communication.* (Englewood Cliffs, NJ: Prentice-Hall, Inc., 1977).

43. Major, B., and Heslin, R. "Perceptions of Cross-sex and Same-sex Nonreciprocal Touch: It Is Better to Give than to Receive," *Journal of Nonverbal Behavior 6* (1982) 148–162.

44. Knapp, 1978.

45. Altman, I. *The Environment and Social Behavior.* (Belmont, CA: Wadsworth, 1975).

46. Lyman, S., and Scott, M. "Territoriality: A Neglected Sociological Dimension," *Social Problems 15* (1967) 235–249.

47. Westin, A. *Privacy and Freedom.* (New York: Atheneum, 1967).

48. Burgoon et al., 1984.

49. Halberstat, A. "Family Expressiveness Styles and Nonverbal Communication Skills," *Journal of Nonverbal Behavior 8* (1983) 14–26.

50. Brauer, D., and DePaulo, B. "Similarities between Friends in Their Understanding of Nonverbal Cues," *Journal of Nonverbal Behavior 5* (1980) 64–68.

51. Ibid.

52. Zuckerman, M., and Larrance, D. "Individuals Differences in Perceived Encoding and Decoding Abilities." In R. Rosenthal, ed., *Skill in Nonverbal Com-*

munication: Individual Differences. (Cambridge, MA: Oelgeschlager, Gunn, and Hain, 1979).

53. Ibid.

Chapter 6

1. Motley, M., Baars, B., and Camden, C. "Experimental Verbal Slip Studies: A Review and Editing Model of Language Encoding," *Communication Monographs 50* (1983) 79–101.
2. Brown, E., and Deffenbacker, K. *Perception and the Senses.* (New York: Oxford University Press, 1979).
3. Foss, D., and Hakes, D. *Psycholinguistics: An Introduction to the Psychology of Language.* (Englewood Cliffs, NJ: Prentice-Hall Inc., 1978).
4. Goss, B. *Processing Communication.* (Belmont, CA: Wadsworth Publishing Co., 1982).
5. Deese, J. "Thought into Speech," *American Scientist 66* (1978) 314–321.
6. Lashbrook, W., and Lashbrook, V. *Proana5: A Computer Analysis of Small Group Communication.* (Minneapolis: Burgess Publishing Co., 1975).
7. Motley, Baars, and Camden, op. cit.
8. Miller, G., and Hewgill, M. "The Effects of Variations in Nonfluency on Audience Ratings of Source Credibility," *Quarterly Journal of Speech 50* (1964) 36–44.
9. DeVito, J. *The Psychology of Speech and Language.* (New York: Random House, 197).
10. Street, R., and Brady, R. "Speech Rate Acceptance Ranges as a Function of Evaluative Domain, Listener Speech Rate, and Communication Context," *Communication Monographs 49* (1982) 290–308.
11. Ellis, D., Hamilton, M., and Aho, L. "Some Issues in Conversation Coherence," *Human Communication Research 9* (1983) 267–282.
12. Lee, I. *Language Habits in Human Affairs.* (New York: Harper and Row, 1941).
13. Grice, H. P. "Logic and Conversation." In D. Davidson and G. Harman, eds., *The Logic of Grammar.* (Encino, CA: Dickenson Publishing Co., 1975).
14. Tracy, K. "The Issue-Event Distinction: A Rule of Conversation and its Scope Condition," *Human Communication Research 9* (1983) 320–334.
15. Pearce, W. B. "The Coordinated Management of Meaning: A Rules-Based Theory of Interpersonal Communication." In G. Miller, ed., *Explorations in Interpersonal Communication.* (Beverly Hills, CA: Sage Publications, 1976).
16. Littlejohn, S. *Theories of Human Communication.* (Belmont, CA: Wadsworth Publishing Co., 1983).
17. Schenklein, J. *Studies in the Organization of Conversational Interaction.* (New York: Academic Press, 1978).
18. Nofsinger, R. "The Demand Ticket: A Conversational Device for Getting the Floor," *Speech Monographs 42* (1975) 1–9.
19. Knapp, M. *Social Intercourse: From Greeting to Goodbye.* (Boston: Allyn and Bacon, 1978).
20. Schegloff, E. "Sequencing in Conversational Openings." In J. Gumperz and D. Hymes, ed., *Directions in Sociolinguistics.* (New York: Holt, Rinehart & Winston, 1972).
21. Ervin-Tripp, S. "On Sociolinguistic Rules: Alternation and Co-occurence." In J. Gumperz and D. Hymes, eds., *Directions in Sociolinguistics.* (New York: Holt, Rinehart & Winston, 1972).

22. Sacks, H., Schegloff, E., and Jefferson, G. "A Simplest Systematics for the Organization of Turn Taking for Conversation." In J. Schenklein, ed., *Studies in the Organization of Conversational Interaction*. (New York: Academic Press, 1978).

23. Coulthard, M. *An Introduction to Discourse Analysis*. (Essex: Longman Group Limited, 1977).

24. Jacobs, S., and Jackson, S. "Strategy and Structure in Conversational Influence Attempts," *Communication Monographs 50* (1983) 285–304.

25. Ibid.

26. Ramsay, R. "Speech Patterns and Personality," *Language and Speech 11* (1968) 54–63.

27. Kennedy, C., and Camden, C. "A New Look at Interruptions," *Western Journal of Speech Communication 47* (1982) 45–58.

28. Flammer, A., and Kintsch, W. *Discourse Processing*. (Amsterdam: North-Holland Publishing Co., 1982).

29. Quasthoff, U., and Nikolaus, P. "What Makes a Good Story?: Towards the Production of Conversational Narratives." In A. Flammer and W. Kintsch, eds., *Discourse Processing*. (Amsterdam: North-Holland Publishing Co., 1982).

30. Garner, A. *Conversationally Speaking*. (New York: McGraw Hill, 1980).

Chapter 7

1. Goss, B. "Listening as Information Processing," *Communication Quarterly 30* (1982) 304–307.

2. Sanford, A., and Garrod, S. "Towards a Processing Account of Reference." In A. Flammer and W. Kintsch, eds., *Discourse Processing*. (Amsterdam: North-Holland Publishing Co., 1982).

3. Lundsteen, S. *Listening: Its Impact on Reading and the Other Language Arts*. (Illinois: NCTE/ERIC, 1971).

4. Craik, F., and Lockhart, R. "Levels of Processing: A Framework for Memory Research," *Journal of Verbal Learning and Verbal Behavior 11* (1972) 671–684.

5. Honeycutt, J., Knapp, M., and Powers, W. "On Knowing Others and Predicting What They Say," *Western Journal of Speech Communication 47* (1983) 157–174.

6. Aronson, D. "Stimulus Factors and Listening Strategies in Auditory Memory: A Theoretical Analysis," *Cognitive Psychology 6* (1974) 108–132.

7. Brown, J., and Carlsen, G. *Brown-Carlsen Listening Comprehension Test*. (New York: Harcourt, Brace, and World, 1955); Beery, A. *Sequential Tests of Educational Progress: Listening Comprehension*. (Princeton, NJ: Educational Testing Service, 1957).

8. Kelly, C. "An Investigation of the Construct Validity of Two Commercially Published Listening Tests," *Speech Monographs 30* (1963) 152–156; Devine, T. "Listening," *Review of Educational Research 37* (1967) 152–158.

9. Sticht, T. "Learning by Listening." In R. Freedle and J. Carroll, eds., *Language Comprehension and the Acquisition of Knowledge*. (Washington DC: V. H. Winston and Sons, 1972).

10. Tzeng, O., Alva, I., and Lee, A. "Meaning Specificity in Sentence Processing," *British Journal of Psychology 70* (1979) 127–133.

11. Hulse, S., Deese, J., and Egeth, H. *The Psychology of Learning*, 4th ed. (New York: McGraw-Hill Book Co., 1975).

12. O'Hair, D., and Goss, B. "Recalling Conversations Under Stress." Paper presented at the International Communication Association, Boston, 1982.

13. Marlen-Wilson, W., and Welsh, A. "Processing Interactions and Lexical Access during World Recognition in Continuous Speech," *Cognitive Psychology 10* (1978) 29–63.

14. Lesgold, A., Roth, S., and Curtis, M. "Foregrounding Effects in Discourse Comprehension," *Journal of Verbal Learning and Verbal Behavior 18* (1979) 291–308.

15. Lindsay and Norman, *Human Information Processing,* op. cit.

16. Wolvin, A., and Coakley, C. *Listening.* (Dubuque, IO: W. C. Brown Co., 1982).

17. Orr, D. "Time Compressed Speech—A Perspective," *Journal of Communication 18* (1968) 288–292.

18. Floyd, J. *Listening: A Practical Approach.* (Glenview, IL: Scott Foresman and Co., 1985).

Chapter 8

1. Jespersen, O. *Language: Its Nature, Development, and Origin.* (London: Allen and Unwin. Ltd., 1922).

2. Ickes, W. "Sex-Role Influences in Dyadic Interaction: A Theoretical Model." In C. Mayo and N. Henley, eds., *Gender and Nonverbal Behavior.* (New York: Springer-Verlag, 1981); Eakins, B., and Eakins, R. *Sex Differences in Human Communication.* (Boston: Houghton Mifflin Company, 1978).

3. Sherriffs, A., and McKee, J. "Qualitative Aspects of Beliefs about Men and Women," *Journal of Personality 25* 451–464.

4. Montgomery, B., and Norton, R. "Sex Differences and Similarities in Communicator Style," *Communication Monographs 48* (1981) 121–132.

5. Eakins and Eakins, loc. cit.

6. Merrit, F., and McCallum, R. "Sex-related Differences in Simultaneous-Successive Information Processing," *Clinical Neuropsychology 5* (1983) 117–119.

7. Birdwhistle, R. "Masculinity and Femininity as Display." In *Kinesics and Context.* (Philadelphia: University of Pennsylvania Press, 1970).

8. Mayo, C. and Henley, N. "Nonverbal Behavior: Barrier or Agent for Sex Role Change?" In C. Mayo and N. Henley, eds., *Gender and Nonverbal Behavior.* (New York: Springer-Verlag, 1981).

9. Birdwhistell, loc. cit.

10. Eakins and Eakins, loc. cit.

11. Ibid.

12. Ibid.

13. Ibid.

14. Mulac, A., Bradac, J., and Mann, S. "Male/Female Language Differences and Attributional Consequences in Children's Television," *Human Communication Research 11* (1985) 481–506.

15. Mulac, A., and Lundell, T. "Differences in Perceptions Created by Syntactic-Semantic Productions of Male and Female Speakers," *Communication Monographs 47* (1980) 111–118.

16. Selnow, G. "Sex Differences in Uses and Perceptions of Profanity," *Sex Roles 12* (1985) 303–312.

17. Ibid.

18. Mulac, A. "Effects of Obscene Language upon Three Dimensions of Listener Attitude," *Communication Monographs 43* (1976) 300–307.
19. Eakins and Eakins, loc. cit.
20. Eakins and Eakins, loc. cit.; Lakoff, R. "Language and Women's Place," *Language in Society 2* (1973) 45–79.
21. Lakoff, loc. cit.
22. Crosby, F., Jose, P., and Wong-McCarthy, W. "Gender, Androgyny, and Conversational Assertiveness." In C. Mayo and N. Henley, eds., *Gender and Nonverbal Behavior.* (New York: Springer-Verlag, 1981).
23. Martin, J., and Craig, R. "Selected Linguistic Sex Differences During Initial Social Interactions of Same-Sex and Mixed-Sex Student Dyads," *Western Journal of Speech Communication 47* (1983) 16–28.
24. Eakins and Eakins, loc. cit.
25. Ibid.
26. Ibid.
27. Dubois, B., and Crouch, I. "The Question of Tag Questions in Women's Speech: They Don't Really Use More of Them, Do They?" *Language and Society 4* (1975) 289–294.
28. Baumann, M. "Two Features of 'Women's Speech?' " In *Papers in Southwest English IV: Proceedings of the Conference on the Sociology of the Languages of American Women*, eds., B. Dubois and I. Crouch. (San Antonio: Trinity University Press, 1979).
29. Siverman, E., and Zimmer, C. "The Fluency of Women's Speech." In *Papers in Southwest English IV: Proceedings of the Conference on the Sociology of the Languages of American Women*, eds., B. Dubois and I. Crouch. (San Antonio: Trinity University Press, 1979).
30. Eakins and Eakins, loc. cit.
31. Landis, M., and Burt, H. "A Study of Conversations," *Journal of Comparative Psychology 4* (1924) 81–89.
32. Haas, A., and Sherman, M. "Reported Topics of Conversation Among Same-Sex Adults," *Communication Quarterly 30* (1982) 332–342.
33. Ibid.
34. Lewin, J., and Arluke, A. "An Exploratory Analysis of Sex Differences in Gossip," *Sex Roles 12* (1985) 281–286.
35. Eakins and Eakins, loc. cit.
36. Grigsly, J., and Weatherley, D. "Gender and Sex-role Differences in Intimacy of Self-Disclosure," *Psychological Reports 53* (1983) 891–897.
37. Petronio, S., Martin, J., and Littlefield, R. "Prerequisite Conditions for Self-Disclosing: A Gender Issue," *Communication Monographs 51* (1984) 268–273.
38. Ibid.
39. Eakins and Eakins, loc. cit.
40. Crosby et. al., loc. cit.
41. Eakins and Eakins, loc. cit.
42. Eakins and Eakins, loc. cit.; Strodtbeck, F., and Mann, R. "Sex Role Differentiation in Jury Deliberations," *Sociometry 19* (1956) 3–11.
43. Ellyson, S., Dovidi, J., and Fehr, B. "Visual Behavior and Dominance in Women and Men." In C. Mayo and N. Henley, eds., *Gender and Nonverbal Behavior.* (New York: Springer-Verlag, 1981).
44. Eakins and Eakins, loc. cit.; Mayo and Henley, loc. cit.
45. Smith, H. "Same-sex Versus Cross-sex Observational Recognition: An Effect of Attention or Recall?" *Perceptual and Motor Skills 57* (1983) 380–382.

46. Haviland, J., and Malatesta, C. "The Development of Sex Differences in Nonverbal Signals: Fallacies, Facts, and Fantasies." In C. Mayo and N. Henley, eds., *Gender and Nonverbal Behavior*. (New York: Springer-Verlag, 1981).

47. Fugita, B. N., Harper, R. G., and Wiens, A. N. "Encoding-Decoding of Nonverbal Emotional Messages: Sex Differences in Spontaneous and Enacted Expressions," *Journal of Nonverbal Behavior 4* (1980) 131–145.

48. Ibid.

49. LaFrance, M. "Gender Gestures: Sex, Sex-role, and Nonverbal Communication." In C. Mayo and N. Henley, eds., *Gender and Nonverbal Behavior*. (New York: Springer-Verlag, 1981).

50. Eakins and Eakins, loc. cit.

51. Eakins and Eakins, loc. cit.; LaFrance, loc. cit.

52. Davis, M., and Weitz, S. "Sex Differences in Body Movements and Positions." In C. Mayo and N. Henley, eds., *Gender and Nonverbal Behavior*. (New York: Springer-Verlag, 1981).

53. Ibid.

54. Peterson, P. "An Investigation of Sex Differences in Regard to Nonverbal Body Gestures." In B. Eakins, G. Eakins, and B. Leib-Brilhart, eds., *Siscom '75: Women's (and Men's) Communication*. (Falls Church, VA: Speech Communication Association, 1976).

55. Eakins and Eakins, loc. cit.

56. Ibid.

57. Davis and Weitz, loc. cit.

58. Ibid.

59. Major, B. "Gender Patterns in Touch Behavior." In C. Mayo and N. Henley, eds., *Gender and Nonverbal Behavior*. (New York: Springer-Verlag, 1981).

60. Clay, V. "The Effect of Culture on Mother-Child Tactile Communication," *Family Coordinator 17* (1968) 204–210.

61. Major, loc. cit.

62. Gifford, R. "The Experience of Personal Space: Perception of Interpersonal Distance," *Journal of Nonverbal Behavior 7* (1983) 170–178.

63. Eakins and Eakins, loc. cit.

64. Daly, J., Hogg, E., Sacks, D., Smith, M., and Zimrig, L. "Sex and Relationships Affect Social Self-Grooming," *Journal of Nonverbal Behavior 7* (1983) 183–189.

65. Williams, J., and Bennet, S. "The Definition of Sex Stereotypes Via the Adjective Check List," *Sex Roles 1* (1975) 327–337.

66. Daly et. al., loc. cit.

67. Eakins and Eakins, loc. cit.

68. Burgoon, M., Dillard, J., and Doran, N. "Friendly or Unfriendly Persuasion: The Effects of Violations of Expectations by Males and Females," *Human Communication Research 10* (1983) 283–294.

69. Bradley, P. "Sex, Competence and Opinion Deviation: An Expectation States Approach," *Communication Monographs 47* (1980) 101–110.

70. Sprecher, S. "Sex Differences in Bases of Power in Dating Relationships," *Sex Roles 12* 449–461.

71. Coleman, M., and Ganong, L. H. "Love and Sex Role Stereotypes: Do Macho Men and Feminine Women Make Better Lovers?" *Journal of Personality and Social Psychology 49* (1985) 170–176; Balkwell, C., Balswick, J., and Balkwell, J., "On Black and White Family Patterns in America: Their Impact on the Expressive Aspect of Sex-role Socialization," *Journal of Marriages and the Fam-*

ily 40 (1978) 743–747; Balswick, J., and Avertt, C. "Differences in Expressiveness: Gender, Interpersonal Orientation, and Preceived Parental Expressiveness as Contributing Factors," *Journal of Marriage and the Family 39* (1977) 121–127.

72. Firestone, S. *The Dialectic of Sex.* (New York: Bantam Books/William Morrow, 1970).

73. Holter, H. *Sex Roles and Social Structures.* (Oslo, Norway: Universitetsferlaget, 1970).

74. Bayer, A. E. "Sexist Students in American Colleges: A Descriptive Note," *Journal of Marriage and the Family 37* (1975) 391–400.

75. Voelz, C. J. "Effects of Gender Role Disparity on Couples' Decision-Making Processes," *Journal of Personality and Social Psychology 49* (1985) 1532–1540.

76. Wheeless, V., and Berryman-Fink, C. "Perceptions of Women Managers and Their Communicator Competencies," *Communication Quarterly 33* (1985) 137–148.

77. Liden, R. "Female Perceptions of Female and Male Managerial Behavior," *Sex Roles 12* (1985) 421–432.

78. Palmer, D. "Personal Values and Managerial Decisions: Are There Differences Between Men and Women?" *College Student Journal 17* (1983) 124–131.

79. Baird, J., and Bradley, P. Styles of Management and Communication: A Comparative Study of Men and Women," *Communication Monographs 46* (1979) 101–111.

80. Mayo and Henley, loc. cit.; Porter, N., and Geis, F. "Women and Nonverbal Leadership Cues: When Seeing Is Not Believing." In C. Mayo and N. Henley, eds., *Gender and Nonverbal Behavior.* (New York: Springer-Verlag, 1981).

81. Mayo and Henley, loc. cit.

Chapter 9

1. Schacter, S. *The Psychology of Affiliation.* (Stanford, CA: Stanford Univ. Press. 1959).

2. Reis, H. T., Senchak, M., & Solomon, B. "Sex Differences in the Intimacy of Social Interaction: Further Examination of Potential Explanations," *Journal of Personality and Social Psychology 48* (1985) 1204–1217; McAdams, D. P., & Vaillantg, G. E. "Intimacy Motivation and Psychosocial Adjustment: A Longitudinal Study," *Journal of Personality Assessment 46* (1982) 586–593.

3. Pearson, J. *Interpersonal Communication.* (Glenview, IL: Scott, Foresman and Co., 1983).

4. Patzer, G. "Source Credibility as a Function of Communicator Physical Attractiveness," *Journal of Business Research 11* (1983) 229–241.

5. Benassi, M. "Effects of Order of Presentation, Primacy, and Physical Attractiveness on Attributions of Ability," *Journal of Personality and Social Psychology 43* (1982) 48–58.

6. Fisher, B. *Small Group Decision Making.* (New York: McGraw-Hill, 1980).

7. Bercheid, E., and Walster, E. *Interpersonal Attraction.* (Reading, MA: Addison-Wesley Publishing Co., 1969).

8. Roloff, M. *Interpersonal Communication: The Social Exchange Approach* (Beverly Hills, CA: Sage Publications, 1981).

9. Matarazzo, J., Saslow, G., Wiens, A., Weitman, M., and Allen, B. "Interviewer Head-nodding and Interviewer Speech Deviations," *Psychotherapy 1* (1964) 54–63.

10. Clore, G., and McGuire, H. "Attraction and Conversational Style." Paper presented at the Society of Experimental Social Psychology, Urbana, IL, 1974.

11. Byrne, D. "Interpersonal Attraction and Attitude Similarity," *Journal of Abnormal and Social Psychology 62* (1961) 713–715.

12. Berger, C., Weber, M., Munley, M., and Dixon, J. "Interpersonal Relationship Levels and Interpersonal Attraction." In B. Ruben, ed., *Communication Yearbook 1*. (New Brunswich, NJ: Transaction Books, 1977).

13. Swann, W., and Predmore, S. "Intimates as Agents of Social Support: Sources of Consolation or Despair," *Journal of Personality and Social Psychology 49* (1985) 1609–1617.

14. Giffin, K., and Patton, B. *Personal Communication in Human Relations*. (Columbus, OH: Charles E. Merrill, 1974).

15. Villard, K., and Whipple, L. *Beginnings in Relational Communication*. (New York: John Wiley and Sons, 1976).

16. Altman, I., and Taylor, D. *Social Penetration*. (New York: Holt, Rinehart and Winston, Inc., 1973); Miller, G., and Steinberg, M. *Between People*. (Chicago: Science Research Associates, Inc., 1975); Knapp, M. *Social Intercourse*. (Boston: Allyn and Bacon, Inc., 1978).

17. Altman and Taylor.

18. Miller and Steinberg.

19. Berger, C., and Bradac, J. *Language and Social Knowledge: Uncertain in Interpersonal Relations*. (London: Edward Arnold, 1982).

20. Miller and Steinberg.

21. Rempel, J., Holmes, J., and Zanna, M. "Trust in Close Relationships," *Journal of Personality and Social Psychology 49* (1985) 95–112.

22. Ibid.

23. Hays, R. "A Longitudinal Study of Friendship Development," *Journal of Personality and Social Psychology 48* (1985) 909–924.

24. Berger & Bradac.

25. Wilmot, W. "Relationship Stages: Initiation and Stabilization." In J. Civikly, ed., *Contexts of Communication*. (New York: Holt, Rinehart, and Winston, 1981).

26. Parks, M., and Adelman, M. "Communication Networks and the Development of Romantic Relationships: An Expansion of Uncertainty Reduction Theory," *Human Communication Research 10* (1983) 55–79.

27. Hornstein, G. "Intimacy in Conversational Style as a Function of the Degree of Closeness between Members of a Dyad," *Journal of Personality and Social Psychology 49* (1985) 671–681.

28. Baxter, L., and Wilmot, W. " 'Secret Tests': Social Strategies for Acquiring Information about the State of the Relationship," *Human Communication Research 11* (1984) 171–201.

29. Planalp, S., and Honeycutt, J. "Events That Increase Uncertainty in Personal Relationships," *Human Communication Research 11* (1985) 593–604.

30. Parks and Adelman.

31. Baxter and Wilmot.

32. Rempel, et al.

33. Ibid.

34. Ibid.

35. Ayers, J. "Strategies to Maintain Relationships: Their Identification and Perceived Use," *Communication Quarterly 31* (1983) 62–67.

36. Sternberg, R., and Barnes, M. "Real and Ideal Others in Romantic Relation-

ships: Is Four a Crowd?'' *Journal of Personality and Social Psychology 49* (1985) 1586–1608.

37. Knapp.

38. Levenson, R., and Gottman, J. "Physiological and Affective Predictors of Change in Relationship Satisfaction," *Journal of Personality and Social Psychology 49* (1985) 85–94.

39. Noller, P. "Gaze in Married Couples," *Journal of Nonverbal Behavior 5* (1980) 115–129.

40. Cody, M. "A Typology of Disengagement Strategies and an Examination of the Role Intimacy, Reactions to Inequity and Relational Problems Play in Strategy Selection." *Communication Monographs 49* (1982) 148–170.

41. Baxter, L. "Self-Disclosure as a Relationship Disengagement Strategy," *Human Communication Research 5* (1979) 215–22; Baxter, L. "Relationship Disengagement: An Examination of the Reversal Hypothesis," *Western Journal of Speech Communication 47* (1983) 85–98.

42. Krayer, K., and O'Hair, D. "The Development of a Typology of Reconcilation Strategies," Unpublished manuscript, (1986).

43. Lobsenz, N. *Men and Women—What We Know about Love.* (New York: Public Affairs Pamphlets, 1981).

44. Ibid.

45. Ibid.

46. Ibid.

Chapter 10

1. Galvin, K., and Brommel, B. *Family Communication.* (Glenview, IL: Scott, Foresman and Company, 1982).

2. Adapted from Galvin and Brommel.

3. Beebe, S., and Masterson, J. *Family Talk: Interpersonal Communication in the Family.* (New York: Random House, 1986).

4. Kantor, D., and Lehr, W. *Inside the Family: Toward a Theory of Family Process.* (San Francisco: Jossey-Bass, 1975).

5. Broderick, C. *Marriage and the Family.* (Englewood Cliffs: Prentice-Hall, 1979).

6. Fitzpatrick, M., and Badzinski, D. "All in the Family: Interpersonal Communication in Kin Relationships." In M. Knapp and G. Miller, eds., *Handbook of Interpersonal Communication.* (Beverly Hills: Sage Publications, 1985).

7. Ibid.

8. Meeks, S., Arnkoff, D., Glass, C., and Notarius, C. "Wives' Employment Status, Hassles, Communication and Relational Efficacy: Intra- versus Extra-Relationship Factors and Marital Adjustment," *Family Relations 34* (1985) 249–255.

9. Hurvitz, N., and Komarovsky, M. "Husbands and Wives: Middle-Class and Working-Class." In C. Greenblat, P. Stein, and N. Washburne, eds., *The Marriage Game: Understanding Marital Decision Making,* 2d ed. (New York: Random House, 1977).

10. Schumm, W., Barnes, H., Bollman, S., Jurich, A., and Bugaighis, M. "Self-disclosure and Marital Satisfaction Revisited," *Family Relations 34* (1985) 241–247.

11. Anderson, S. "Cohesion, Adaptability and Communication: A Test of an Olson Circumplex Model Hypothesis," *Family Relations 35* (1986) 289–293;

Olson, D., Russell, C., and Sprenkle, D. "Circumplex Model of Marital and Family Systems: VI. Theoretical Update." *Family Process 22* (1983) 69–83.

12. Anderson, 1986.

13. Spicer, C. "Special Report Careers and Relationships: The Interpersonal Intricacies of Maintaining a Dual-Career Relationship," *Southern Speech Communication Journal 51* (1986) 256–259.

14. Smith D., "Wife Employment and Marital Adjustment Culmination of Results," *Family Relations 34* (1985) 483–490.

15. Meeks, et al, 1985.

16. Wood, J. "Maintaining Dual-Career Bonds: Communicative Dimensions of Internally Structured Relationships," *Southern Journal of Speech Communication 51* (1986) 267–273.

17. Ibid.

18. Fitzpatrick & Badzinski, 1985.

19. Ibid.

20. Galvin & Brommel, 1982.

21. Lamb, M., Frodi, A., Hwang, C-P, Frodi, M., and Steinberg, J. "Mother– and Father–Infant Interaction Involving Play and Holding in Traditional and Nontraditional Swedish Families," *Developmental Psychology 18* (1982) 215–221.

22. Ricks S., "Father–Infant Interactions: A Review of Empirical Research," *Family Relations 34,* (1985) 505–511; Russell, G. "Highly Participant Australian Fathers: Some Preliminary Findings," *Merrill-Palmer Quarterly 28* (1982) 137–156.

23. Swain, D. and Parke, R. "Fathers' Affectionate Stimulation and Caregiving Behavior with New Infants," *Family Coordinator 28* (1979) 509–519.

24. Ricks, 1985.

25. Ibid.

26. Lamb, M. "Effects of Stress and Cohort on Mother– and Father–Infant Interaction," *Developmental Psychology 12,* (1976) 435–443.

27. Ibid.

28. Belski, J. "Mother–Father–Infant Interaction: A Naturalistic Observational Study," *Developmental Psychology 15,* (1979) 601–607.

29. Fitzpatrick & Badzinski, 1985.

30. Ibid.

31. Gecas, V., and Schwalbe, M., "Parental Behavior and Adolescent Self-Esteem," *Journal of Marriage and the Family 48* (February 1986) 37–46.

32. Ibid.

33. Thompson, L, Acock, A., and Clark, K., "Do Parents Know Their Children? The Ability of Mothers and Fathers to Gauge the Attitudes of Their Young Adult Children," *Family Relations 34* (1985) 315–320.

34. Ibid.

35. Leslie, L., Huston, T., and Johnson, M., "Parental Reactions to Dating Relationships: Do They Make a Difference?," *Journal of Marriage and the Family 48* (February 1986) 57–66.

36. Ibid.

37. Ibid.

38. Fitzpatrick & Badzinski, 1985.

39. Thornton, A., and Freedman, D. "The Changing American Family," *Population Bulletin 38* (1983) 1–44.

40. Lowery, C., and Settle, S. "Effects of Divorce on Children: Differential Impact of Custody and Visitation Patterns," *Family Relations 34* (1985) 455–463.
41. Mueller, D., and Cooper, P. "Children of Single Parent Families: How They Fare as Young Adults," *Family Relations 35* (1986) 169–176.
42. Ibid.
43. Lowery and Settle, 1985.
44. Ibid.
45. Ibid.
46. Risman B. "Can Men "Mother"? Life as a Single Father," *Family Relations 35* (1986) 95–102.
47. Barranti C. "The Grandparent/Grandchild Relationship: Family Resource in an Era of Voluntary Bonds," *Family Relations 34* (1985) 343–352.
48. Ibid.
49. Kivett, V. "Grandfathers and Grandchildren: Patterns of Association, Helping, and Psychological Closeness," *Family Relations 34* (1985) 565–571.
50. Neugarten, B., and Weinstein, K. "The Changing American Grandparent," *Journal of Marriage and the Family 26* (1964) 199–204.
51. Barranti, 1985.
52. Ibid.
53. Ibid.
54. Ibid.

Chapter 11

1. Frost, J., and Wilmot, W. *Interpersonal Conflict.* (Dubuque, IA: W. C. Brown and Co., 1978); Miller, G., and Simons, H. *Perspectives on Communication in Conflict.* (Englewood Cliffs, NJ: Prentice-Hall, 1974); Filley, A. *Interpersonal Conflict Resolution.* (Glenview, IL: Scott, Foresman and Co., 1975).
2. Pondy, L. "Organizational Conflict: Concepts and Models," *Administrative Science Quarterly 12* (1967) 296–320.
3. Keltner, J. *Interpersonal Speech Communication.* (Belmont, CA: Wadsworth Publishing Co., 1970).
4. Roloff, M. *Interpersonal Communication: The Social Exchange Approach.* (Beverly Hills, CA: Sage Publications, 1981).
5. Gaelick, L. Bodenhausen, G., and Wyer, R., "Emotional Communication in Close Relationships," *Journal of Personality and Social Psychology 49* (1985) 1246–1265.
6. Simons, H. "The Carrot and Stick as Handmaidens of Persuasion in Conflict Situations." In G. Miller and H. Simons, eds., *Perspectives on Communication in Conflict.* (Englewood Cliffs, NJ: Prentice-Hall, 1974).
7. Putnam, L., and Jones, T. "The Role of Communication in Bargaining," *Human Communication Research 8* (1982) 262–280.
8. Ibid.
9. Gouran, D. *Making Decisions in Groups.* (Glenview, IL: Scott, Foresman and Co., 1982).
10. Hamachek, D. *Encounters with Others.* (New York: Holt, Rinehart and Winston, 1982).
11. Johnson, D. *Reaching Out: Interpersonal Effectiveness and Self-Actualization.* (Englewood Cliffs, NJ: Prentice-Hall, 1972).
12. Hamachek, loc. cit.

Chapter 12

1. Rokeach, M. *Beliefs, Attitudes, and Values: A Theory of Organization and Change.* (San Francisco: Jossey-Bass Publishing Co., 1968).
2. Williams, R. "Change and Stability in Values and Value Systems: A Sociological Perspective." In M. Rokeach, ed., *Understanding Human Values.* (New York: The Free Press, 1979).
3. Rokeach, M. *Understanding Human Values.* (New York: The Free Press, 1979).
4. Rokeach, M. *Value Survey.* (Sunnyvale, CA: Halgren Tests, 1967).
5. McGuire, W. "The Nature of Attitudes and Attitude Change." In G. Lindzey and E. Aronson, eds., *The Handbook of Social Psychology,* 2d ed. (Reading, MA: Addison-Wesley Publishing Co., 1969).
6. Abelson, R., Aronson, E., McGuire, W., Newcomb, T., Rosenberg, M., and Tennenbaum, P. *Theories of Cognitive Consistency: A Sourcebook.* (Chicago: Rand McNally and Co., 1968).
7. Smith, M. *Persuasion and Human Action.* (Belmont, CA: Wadsworth Publishing Co., 1982).
8. Heider, F. "Attitudes and Cognitive Organization," *Journal of Psychology 21* (1946) 107–112; Heider, F. *The Psychology of Interpersonal Relations.* (New York: John Wiley and Sons, 1958).
9. Jordan, N. "Behavioral Forces That Are a Function of Attitudes and of Cognitive Organization," *Human Relations 6* (1953); Feather, N., "A Structural Balance Analysis of Evaluative Behavior," *Human Relations 18* (1965) 171–185.
10. Festinger, L. and Carlsmith, J. "Cognitive Consequences of Forced Compliance," *Journal of Abnormal and Social Psychology 58* (1959) 203–210.
11. Festinger, L. *The Theory of Cognitive Dissonance.* (Stanford, CA: Stanford University Press, 1957).
12. French, J., and Raven, B. "The Bases of Social Power." In D. Cartwright, ed., *Studies in Social Power.* (Ann Arbor: University of Michigan, 1959).
13. Becker, M., and Maiman, L. "Strategies for Enhancing Patient Compliance," *Journal of Community Health 6* (1980) 113–132.
14. McCroskey, J., and Richmond, V. "Power in the Classroom I: Teacher and Student Perceptions," *Communication Education 32* (1983) 175–184.
15. Richmond, V., and McCroskey, J. "Power in the Classroom II: Power and Learning". *Communication Education 33* (1984) 125–136.
16. Bachman, D., Bowers, D., and Marcus, P. "Bases of Supervisory Power: A Comparative Study in Five Organizational Settings." In A. Tannenbaum, ed., *Control in Organizations.* (New York: McGraw-Hill, 1968).
17. Student, K. "Supervisory Influence and Work-Group Performance," *Journal of Applied Psychology 52* (1968) 188–194.
18. Bettinghaus, E., and Cody, M. *Persuasive Communication.* (New York: Holt, Rinehart and Winston, (1986).
19. Marwell, G., and Schmitt, D. "Dimensions of Compliance Gaining Behavior: An Empirical Analysis," *Sociometry 30* (1967) 350–364.
20. Miller, G., Boster, F., Roloff, M., and Seibold, D. "Compliance-Gaining Message Strategies: A Typology and Some Findings Concerning Effects of Situational Differences," *Communication Monographs 44* (1977) 37–51.
21. Schenck-Hamlin, W., Wiseman, R., and Georgacarakos, G. "A Model of Compliance Gaining Strategies," *Communication Quarterly 30* (1982) 92–100.
22. Bettinghaus and Cody, loc. cit.; O'Hair, D., and Cody, M. "Machiavellian Beliefs and Social Influence," *Western Journal of Speech Communication,* in press;

Cody, M., and McLaughlin, M. "Perceptions of Compliance Gaining Situations: A Dimensional Analysis", *Communication Monographs 47* (1980) 132–148.

23. Sillars, A. "The Stranger and the Spouse as Target Persons for Compliance Gaining Strategies: A Subjective Expected Utility Model", *Human Communication Research 6* (1980) 265–279.

24. Cody and McLaughlin, loc. cit.

25. Sillars, loc. cit.

26. Cody and McLaughlin, loc. cit.

27. Bettinghaus and Cody, loc. cit.

28. Infante, D., and Gorden, W. "Superiors' Argumentativeness and Verbal Aggressiveness as Predictors of Subordinates' Satisfaction," *Human Communication Research 12* (1985) 117–125.

29. Infante and Gorden, loc. cit.; Infante, D., and Wigely, C. "Verbal Aggressiveness: An Interpersonal Model and Measure," *Communication Monographs 53* (1986) 61–69.

30. Infante and Wigely, loc. cit.

31. Infante and Wigely, loc. cit.

32. Hunter, J., Gerbing, D., and Boster, F. "Machiavellianism Beliefs and Personality: Construct Invalidity of the Machiavellian Dimension," *Journal of Personality and Social Psychology 43.* (1982) 1293–1305.

33. O'Hair and Cody, loc. cit.

34. McLaughlin, M., Cody, M., and Robey, C. "Situational Influences on the Selection of Strategies to Resist Compliance-Gaining Attempts," *Human Communication Research 7* (1980) 14–36.

35. deTurk, M. "A Transactional Analysis of Compliance-Gaining Behavior: Effects of Noncompliance, Relational Contexts, and Actors' Gender," *Human Communication Research 12* (1985) 54–78.

36. Dillard, J., Hunter, J., and Burgoon, M. "Sequential-Request Persuasive Strategies: Meta-Analysis of Foot-in-the-Door and Door-in-the-Face," *Human Communication Research 10* 461–487.

37. Ibid.

38. Cialdini, R., Vincent, J., Lewis, S., Catalan, J., Wheeler, D., and Darby, B. "Reciprocal Concessions Procedure for Inducing Compliance: The Door-in-the-Face Technique," *Journal of Personality and Social Psychology 31* (1975) 206–215.

39. Dillard et al., loc. cit.

Chapter 13

1. Knapp, M., and Comadena, M. "Telling It Like It Isn't: A Review of Theory and Research on Deceptive Communication," *Human Communication Research 5* (1979) 270–285.

2. Hopper, R., and Bell, R. "Broadening the Deception Concept," *Quarterly Journal of Speech 79* (1984) 287–302.

3. Camden, C., Motley, M., and Wilson, A. "White Lies in Interpersonal Communication: A Taxonomy and Preliminary Investigation of Social Motivations," *Western Journal of Speech Communication 48* (1984) 309–325.

4. Turner, R., Edgely, C., and Olmstead, G. "Information Control in Conversation: Honesty Is Not Always the Best Policy," *Kansas Journal of Sociology 11* (1975) 69–89.

5. Camden, et al., loc. cit.

6. Knapp, M., Hart, R., and Dennis, H. "An Exploration of Deception as a Communication Construct," *Human Communication Research 1* (1974) 15–20.

7. Cody, M., Marston, P., and Foster, M. "Deception: Paralinguistic and Verbal Leakage." In R. Bostrom, ed., *Communication Yearbook 8.* (Beverly Hills, CA: Sage Publications, 1984).

8. Mehrabian, A. "Nonverbal Betrayal of Feeling," *Journal of Experimental Research 5* (1974) 64–73.

9. Kraut, R. "Verbal and Nonverbal Cues in the Perception of Lying," *Journal of Personality and Social Psychology 36* (1978) 380–391.

10. McClintock, C., and Hunt, R. "Nonverbal Indicators of Affect and Deception in an Interview Setting," *Journal of Applied Social Psychology 5* (1975) 54–67.

11. Mehrabian, loc. cit.

12. McClintock and Hunt, loc. cit.

13. Ekman, P., and Friesen, W. "Nonverbal Leakage and Clues to Deception," *Psychiatry 32* (1969) 88–106.

14. McLintock and Hunt, loc. cit.

15. Ekman, P., Friesen, W., and Scherer, K. "Body Movement and Voice Pitch in Deceptive Interaction," *Semiotica 16* (1976) 23–27.

16. Ekman, P., and Friesen, W. "Hand Movements," *Journal of Communication 22* 353–374.

17. Hocking, J., Bauchner, J., Kaminski, E., and Miller, G. "Detecting Deception from Verbal, Visual, and Paralinguistic Cues," *Human Communication Research 6* (1979) 33–46.

18. O'Hair, H. D., Cody, M., and McLaughlin, M. "Prepared Lies, Spontaneous Lies, Machiavellianism, and Nonverbal Communication," *Human Communication Research 7* (1981) 325–339.

19. Cody, M., and O'Hair, H. D. "Nonverbal Communication and Deception: Differences in Deception Cues Due to Gender and Communicator Dominance," *Communication Monographs 50* (1983) 175–192.

20. Hocking, J., and Leathers, D. "Nonverbal Indicators of Deception: A New Theoretical Perspective," *Communication Monographs 47* (1980) 119–131.

21. Knapp and Comadena, loc. cit.

22. McLaughlin, M., Cody, M., and O'Hair, H. D. "The Management of Failure Events: Some Contextual Determinants of Accounting Behavior," *Human Communication Research 9* (1983) 208–224.

23. McLaughlin, M., Cody, M., and Rosenstein, N. "Account Sequences in Conversations Between Strangers," *Communication Monographs 50* (1983) 102–125.

24. Schonbach, P. "A Category System for Account Phases," *European Journal of Social Psychology 10* (1980) 195–200.

25. Blumstein, P. "The Honoring of Accounts," *American Sociological Review 39* (1974) 551–566.

26. Schonbach, loc. cit.

27. McLaughlin, Cody, and O'Hair, op. cit., p. 208.

28. McLaughlin, Cody, and Rosenstein, loc. cit.

29. Ibid; McLaughlin, Cody, and O'Hair, loc. cit.

30. Scott, M., and Lyman, S. "Accounts," *American Sociological Review 33* (1968) 46–62.

31. Buttny, R. "Accounts as a Reconstruction of an Event's Context," *Communication Monographs 52* (1985) 57–77.

32. McLaughlin, Cody, and O'Hair, loc. cit.; Schonbach, loc. cit.

33. McLaughlin, Cody, and Rosenstein, loc. cit.

34. McLaughlin, Cody, and O'Hair, loc. cit.

35. Ibid.

36. Ibid.

37. Ibid.

38. Brown, P., and Levinson, S. "Universals in Language Usage: Politeness Phenomena." In E. Goody, ed., *Questions and Politeness: Strategies in Social Interaction.* (Cambridge: Cambridge University Press, 1978).

39. Wolfson, N. "Compliments in Cross-Cultural Perspective," *TESOL Quarterly 15* (1981) 117–124.

40. Knapp, M., Hopper, R., and Bell, R. "Compliments: A Descriptive Taxonomy," *Journal of Communication 34* (1984) 12–31.

41. Ibid.

42. Pomerantz, A. "Compliment Responses: Notes on the Co-operation of Multiple Constraints." In J. Schendein, ed., *Studies in the Organization of Conversational Interaction.* (New York: Academic Press, 1978).

43. Knapp, Hopper, and Bell, loc. cit.

44. Pomerantz, loc. cit.

45. Ibid.

46. Catano, V. "Relation of Improved Performance through Verbal Praise to Source of Praise," *Perceptual and Motor Skills 41* (1975) 71–74; Colman, A., and Oliver, K. "Reactions to Flattery as a Function of Self-Esteem: Self-Enhancement and Cognitive Consistency Theories," *British Journal of Social and Clinical Psychology 17* (1978) 25–29.

47. Araki, S., and Barnlund, D. "Intercultural Encounters: The Management of Compliments by Japanese and Americans." Paper presented at the Speech Communication Association convention, Anaheim, CA, 1981.

48. Turner, R., and Edgley, C. "Reciprocity Revisited: The Case of Compliments," *Human Mosaic 8* (1974) 1–13.

49. Ibid.

50. Ibid.

51. Knapp, Hopper, and Bell, loc. cit.

52. Kramarae, C. "Speech Crimes which the Law Cannot Reach or Compliments and other Insulting Behavior." In *Proceedings of the Women and Language Conference.* Berkely Women and Language Group, in press.

53. Both examples adapted from Labov, W. *Language in the Inner City: Studies in Black English Vernacular.* (Philadelphia: University of Pennsylvania Press, 1972).

GLOSSARY

Accommodation. A highly cooperative way to handle conflict. It is not very assertive, in that you simply give people want they ask for.

Accounting behavior. Explaining our actions to someone else. Offering reasons for why we do things.

Accounts. Statements made by social actors to relieve themselves of culpability for untoward or unanticipated acts.

Adaptability. The amount of flexibility available in performing roles in relationships.

Adapters. Gestures or other nonverbal signs which show that a person is emotionally aroused. Nervous tics, such as scratching where you really don't itch, or pulling your earlobe may be signs of emotional arousal.

Adjency pairs. Two conjoint utterances in a conversation, one initiating, the other responding. Common pairs are question–answer, request–comply, etc.

Affect displays. Showing affection by hugging, kissing, or holding hands.

Affection. One of two main dimensions upon which relationships can be described. It refers to the degree of love and caring that exist between relational pairs.

Affective communication. Refers to talk that endears us to another. "I love being with you, sweetie," "You're a very nice person," and "I know how you feel, and I am sorry" are instances of affective communication.

Ambiguity. When a word or expression refers to two or more unrelated meanings.

Anonymity. A type of privacy where one attempts to lose his/her personal identification.

Argumentativeness. The tendency to enjoy debating controversial issues. Focus is on the issues, not on the people.

Assertiveness. Not aggressiveness, but rather it refers to tactful expressions of your concerns. Assertiveness training teaches people how to di-rectly, but politely, make their points known to others.

Assimilation (information distortion). When people incorporate newly learned information with information they already know.

Attitudes. Specific mental opinions about specific objects, ideas, people, or places.

Avoidance. A conflict management strategy that ignores the problem and makes no attempt to deal with it directly. This method is not very cooperative, nor it is it very assertive.

Balance. A form of consistency that applies to our interpersonal relationships. It refers to the notion that we tend to like those people who like the things we like.

Bargaining. Similar to negotiating, it usually involves more lines of settlement than negotiation. Bargaining often leads to package deals, rather than settling on one thing, such as price.

Bounding. Bounding refers to the entry and exit policy of the husband and wife regarding traffic within the home. In other words, by establishing consistent practices of entry into, and exit out of the marital domicile a couple establishes boundaries.

Centering. Centering is concerned with coordinating, allocating, and monitoring the spatial resources of a couple.

Clocking. Clocking refers to how time is used, allocated, and sequenced by a couple. When a couple goes to bed and/or rises in the morning is a clocking issue.

Coercive power. Exerting influence over others by threatening to punish them if they do not comply.

Cognitive complexity. The number of features (variables) through which people mentally organize their world. Ranges from simple black–white thinking to more complex multifaceted thinking.

Cognitive differentiation. The number of different features a person takes into consideration when observing differences between two or more objects, places, and people.

Cognitive dissonance. Doubts that follow making an important decision in which you wonder whether or not you made the right choice. Dissonance follows the decision, it does not precede it.

Cohesion. The degree of emotional bonding between couples.

Collaboration. A conflict management strategy that calls for a lot of assertiveness and cooperation. The conflicting parties discuss the problem and jointly seek creative, multifaceted solutions.

Communication competence. One's overall ability to communicate effectively with others. Among other things, it is a measure of your proficiency at saying the right thing at the right time.

Competition. A conflict management strategy wherein the two conflicting parties are in a win–lose battle. To win, you must beat your opponent and be highly assertive, and not cooperative.

Compliance gaining. Interpersonal methods of persuasion. Convincing others through informal means to believe what you believe, or to do what you request.

Compliance resistance. Strategies used to resist the compliance-gaining attempts by another person.

Compressed speech. Speech that has been artificially speeded up and compressed by a speech compressor machine. Used primarily in scientific research.

Conditioning. The way people learn new thoughts and behaviors. The two most prominent kinds of conditioning are classical conditioning and operant conditioning. (See chapter 3.)

Consistency principle. The idea that people strive to maintain a congruent set of attitudes in their minds, and when they experience inconsistency, they work to restore consistency.

Contamination. This is a type of territorial encroachment that refers not to the presence of another, but to the after-effects or remains of another's encroachment.

Convergence (language style). Occurs in ongoing conversations. It is when two people begin to talk alike as evidence in their use of similar words, phrases, and sentences.

Conversational narratives. Stories or extended explanations that occur in a conversation.

Deception. Lying. Altering, concealing, or distorting information to disguise the truth.

Deception cues. Refers to verbal or nonverbal behaviors that "leak out" unintentionally during deceptive communication.

Display rules. Adapting one's facial expressions to meet the social demands of the immediate situation (e.g., smiling when you are introduced to someone).

Dominance. One of two dimensions upon which relationships can be described. It refers to the relative status/power that one person may exercise over his/her partner.

Door-in-the-face strategies. Interpersonal persuasion strategies that involve making a very large request initially, one which most people would refuse, and are followed by a smaller subsequent request.

Emblems. A nonverbal gesture or sign that can stand alone. It is like a word, in that people know what it means without comment.

Emotional concealment. A type of deception where the underlying emotional state of the individual is distorted or misrepresented. Emotional concealment could occur when we are trying to be serious, when we find something humorous, or when we try to mask our disappointment, sadness, or fear.

Environmental factors. A theory that suggests that differences in communication behavior between males and females are based on learned behavior by observing the environment.

Episode (conversations). A part of a longer conversation in which a sequence of utterances can be seen as forming a complete set. Often organized around distinct topics. Any particular conversation can contain one or more episodes.

Episodic LTM. The part of long term memory that stores our recollections of events and other sequentially ordered information. Contains such things as your memory for songs, dance routines, steps for starting your car, and so forth.

Evaluation. The final step in the accounting behavior sequence of events. Evaluation of the account is made by the one considered to be offended. There are four possible evaluations: honor, retreat, reject and drop topic.

Expert power. Having influence with people because of your qualifications or known expertise. Physicians have expert power in medical matters.

Factual deception. Situation in which the deceiver falsifies information or data. Factual deception could include lying about accomplishments, past experiences, or even personality traits.

Failure event. An "offense" or failure event occurs when an untoward or unexpected act is committed or an anticipated act or obligation is not fulfilled.

False smiles. Facial expressions that are used to convince others that we are experiencing positive emotion when we actually aren't. There are three types of false smiles: phony smiles, masking smiles and dampened smiles.

Family expressiveness styles. A nonverbal communication theory that states that family members develop similar encoding skills and opposite decoding skills based on family role models.

Feedback. In interpersonal communication, it refers to how others respond to your messages. We use feedback from others to gauge how our messages are being received.

Felt smiles. These are true facial expressions that reflect positive emotion such as happiness, amusement, or delight. This type of smile is probably an automatic reflex, especially when we are in a good mood.

Foot-in-the-door strategies. Interpersonal persuasion strategies that involve making a small request, one which most people would agree to, and upon compliance making a larger request that is the actual goal of the requester.

Forecasting (listening). Predicting what the speaker is going to say before it is said.

Foregrounding. Setting the context for what you are trying to say. Giving your listeners preliminary information before you make your main point.

Friendly love. Considered to be a less intense type of relationship. Both parties in the relationship recognize that they have shared interests, common grounds, and similar attitudes and beliefs. Friendly lovers seemed to value companionship, rapport, and mutual respect from each other.

Fueling. A concept referring to the revitalizing nature of marital energy. Just as engines must be fueled and refueled to continue functioning in an efficient manner, so do marital members have to be emotionally refueled. Without it, emotional fatigue may be the result.

Game-playing. A style of love that involves one or more of the relational partners perceiving of the love relationship as something which must be won or lost. Playing the game of love is a challenge for these participants where each encounter involves tactics, strategies, and moves which enhance one's position in the "game."

Gender differences. A general group of contentions, theories and hypotheses that attempt to account for the behavioral differences which are sometimes apparent between members of the opposite sex.

Gender role preference. How men and women in relationships "divide the labor" based on their preferences for certain tasks, taking into consideration gender variables.

Idiosyncratic communication. A type of interaction that only you and the other person in the relationship can understand. It may involve actual words, such as nicknames, and nonverbal behavior or particular topics which only you and your relational partner know about.

Illocutionary force. Refers to the communicative intent of the utterance. It is what the speaker is doing when he/she says something. Utterances can be used as commands, questions, criticisms, jokes, and so forth.

Illustrators. Nonverbal gestures or signs that serve to reinforce or support the words the speaker is saying.

Inferences. Going beyond what is said to arrive at conclusions not presented in the original input. Inferences can be true or false.

Information processing. The way people mentally handle information. How they gather it, save it in memory, and recall it later.

Instrumental values. Those values that guide your daily decision making and behavior (e.g., honesty, loving, logical, etc.).

Interpersonal attraction. The degree to which others wish to affiliate with you. How much you draw people to you.

Interpersonal communication. The process of exchanging verbal and nonverbal messages in order to understand, develop, and influence human relationships.

Interpersonal conflict. When two or more people have a strong disagreement that is driven by a clash of goals, perceptions, and/or values.

Interpersonal relationships. A linking bond between people. It begins when two or more people sense a "go-togetherness" between them and communicate with their relationship in mind.

Interperson trust. Believing that the other person will not cause you personal harm when you are vulnerable, and at other times for that matter. Being confident in the other person's concern for your welfare.

Intimacy. A type of privacy where a dyad or small group of people attempt exclusion from others to communicate privately.

Intimate communication. The highest level of communication a relationship can aspire to. Intimate communication involves relating your inner-most thoughts about a relational partner to them. Communication in intimate relationships is also reflected by the ability of relational partners to assume a great deal about the others' understanding.

Invasion. This is a type of territorial encroachment and constitutes a comprehensive and on-going type of territorial take-over.

Investing. The idea that the effort (energy) put forth by members of a couple toward the marital relationship is an investment. Most couples invest a great deal of energy into the other person and the relationships. For some couples one member will invest more energy than the other.

Kinesics. The study of how people use gestures, and other body movements to communicate.

Language competence. Your knowledge of the languages you use. Your formal understanding of the sounds, syntax and vocabulary of any language you use.

Language distortion. Confusion created by linguistic ambiguity and vagueness. In addition, verbal messages become distorted when people make faulty inferences about what speakers mean and when they change the content of the original message when relating it to others.

Language openness. Refers to the portability of words, which when combined with other words can be used to construct many different messages.

Language performance. The actual sentences/utterances that you produce based on your knowledge of the language.

Language style. How people combine words, phrases, and sentences when they communicate. The way we organize our sentences.

Language universals. Common features of languages found around the world. Similarities in structure and function among different languages.

Legitimate power. The ability to influence someone because of the position or occupation you hold. Policemen have legitimate power in law enforcement matters.

Leveling. Making a message shorter when repeating it to someone who hasn't heard it yet. Commonly found in rumors.

Lexical diversity. Variety in word choice. The range of different words which occur in a given message.

Lexical intensity. The degree to which word choice reflects a speaker's attitudes about the topic. More extreme words should reflect more extreme attitudes in the speaker.

Lexicon. Vocabulary, your mental dictionary of words.

Like-Look paradigm. Essentially what this implies is that we look longer at those whom we like, and those who look more are liked better. Along similar lines, familiarity with someone causes more eye gaze.

Linking. Linking is a spatial matter that involves the connecting together of the husband and wife. How close a husband and wife interact together both physically and psychologically is related to linking.

Listening. A perception/comprehension process of taking what you hear and organizing it into units to which you assign meaning.

Literal processing. The second phase of listening involving the assignment of meaning to the message. Inferences are minimal at this point.

Logical love. A type of love based on practical values. Those who believe in logical love will search for a "love partner" who fits their needs in a pragmatic way. They may also assess their own strengths and weaknesses and look for a partner who would be attracted to such offerings.

Long term memory (LTM). Compared to short term memory, LTM is a fairly permanent memory which contains information organized semantically and episodically. (See Semantic LTM and Episodic LTM.)

Machiavellianism. The act of manipulating others (in primarily subtle ways) to attain one's own goals. Communication skills are often used in this way.

Meanings. All the learned experiences that you have associated with the usage of words, phrases, gestures, and so on. Includes formal, functional, affective, and prototypical understanding. (See chapter 4.)

Mental economy. A human preference for simplifying our psychological perceptions of places, things, and people. Characterized by closure, familiarity, and expectations. (See chapter 2.)

Miserable smiles. Facial expressions that are exhibited when negative emotion is experienced and no attempt is made to cover up our feelings. Miserable smiles are used to convey that we are unhappy.

Mobilizing. This refers to a marital energy concept where the focus goes from individual- to couple-centered energy expenditures, that is, how a couple together mobilize and spend their emotional energy. The effort to coordinate how their emotional energy should be discharged requires effective communication between the couple.

Negotiation. A method of handling conflicts that is moderately cooperative and moderately assertive. It is a give-and-take, win-some, lose-some approach to dealing with differences of opinion.

Nonverbal communication. The process of signalling meaning through interpersonal behavior that does not involve spoken words.

Occulesics. The study of how people use eye contact when communicating.

Orienting. Time orientation refers to the temporal mind-set members of a couple have toward their lives. The three basic types of time orientation are present, past, and future.

Other-oriented. Communicating with the receiver in mind. Being aware of your conversational partner's feelings and point of view.

Paralanguage. Tone of voice, or how something is said rather than what is said.

Possessive love. A style of love involving emotion and behavior that becomes consuming to the point of possessiveness. It might better be called obsessive because this type of lover can think of nothing more than totally possessing his/her partner.

Predictions (relational). One of the components of relational development. Relational partners attempt to reduce uncertainty in order to increase their predictions about the other. The ability to make predictions about another person allows us to be more successful communicators in the relationship. We can avoid saying the wrong things, and emphasize communication strategies that are more appealing when we can accurately predict the behavior of another person.

Prepared lies. Lies in which deceivers have a chance to think about or even rehearse before their actual enactment.

Propositional content. The literal content of a message. What it says. The total idea being proposed by a statement.

Proxemics. The study of how people use space when they communicate. Distances between communicators, privacy, and territoriality are concerns of proxemics.

Qualifying terms. Words or phrases that soften or modify the degree of confidence or assertiveness in a sentence. Examples would be "In my opinion . . . ," or "Perhaps I can . . ."

Reciprocity (self disclosure). When your partner tells you something intimate about him/herself after you have done so. When both communicators share personal information.

Reconciliation. A stage in interpersonal relationships where disengaged couples attempt to repair their severed relationships.

Referent power. The ability to influence people because you know that they want to please you.

Reflective processing. The deepest level of listening in which the listener reflects on the meaning of the message, perhaps trying to identify why the message was spoken. Inferences are more extensive at this level.

Regulators. Nonverbal gestures and signs designed to control the flow of communication. Raising your hand to speak, and getting up from your chair to encourage a person to leave are examples of regulators.

Reinforcement. The way rewards and punishments are handed out. In interpersonal communication, it refers to how what we say encourages or discourages our colleagues from continuing any act of behavior. (See Feedback.)

Relational de-escalation. A stage that many relationships experience where intimacy and involvement become reduced and relational breakup may occur.

Relational stages. Different periods of developments for relationships. There are four stages through which relationships may pass—entry, exploratory, stable, and exit.

Reproach. Considered as the second phase in the accounting sequence and involves the placement of blame or criticism on a perceived inappropriate act or behavior.

Reserve. A type of privacy where one attempts to construct psychological barriers to avoid communicating with others.

Reward power. Exerting influence over others by promising rewards if they perform appropriately.

Rewards/costs determinations. This refers to the activity of sizing up the potential rewards of further interaction or relational development with another person and weighing these against the costs perceived to be related with a further association with the person.

Role congruency. When both partners in a relationship understand and agree to each others' duties and responsibilities.

Romantic love. Perhaps the most prevalent style of love. Romantic love is passionate and all-giving. Romantics, as they are often called, hold no secrets from one another and provide as much as they can of themselves physically and emotionally to their romantic partner. Romantic love performs at a heightened peak and has a tendency to abate after a period of time.

Schemata. Bundles of information stored in memory about particular topics of conversation. Potentially, everything that you know about a place, person, or idea. You refer to your schemata as you converse with others.

Secret tests. Indirect methods of finding out about a relationship of which you are a member, such as asking a third party about your partner's feelings.

Self concept. Your mental picture of yourself. It is composed of your atttitudes about yourself, your observations of your attributes, and how you see others responding to you.

Self disclosure. Telling others information about you that is personal, private, and intimate.

Self esteem. Your feelings about your overall worth. Your global assessment of your value. Low self esteem is very undesirable.

Self monitoring. Your ability to observe yourself in action. Being able to see your behaviors as others see them.

Semantic LTM. Your conceptual memory system. Your memory for words, categories, and other concepts that can be expressed linguistically.

Semantics. The study of meanings. A part of all languages, in addition to sounds and syntax.

Sharpening. Highlighting a select set of details of an event or message when retelling it to someone else. Occurs in rumors.

Short term memory (STM). Unlike long term memory, STM is a brief memory system designed to hold information temporarily until it is stored in LTM or put to immediate use. Information in STM must be rehearsed if it is to stay there.

Signal processing. The first stage of listening wherein the auditory signal is recognized as speech and segmented into its linguistic parts.

Social influence. The ability to persuade others.

Solitude. A type of privacy where one attempts to be completely alone.

Speech. The joining of voice and language. Speech is spoken language. It is not just making vocal noises. It is oral communication structured by the speaker's knowledge of the language.

Spontaneous lies.   Lies that are produced on the spur of the moment. No advanced warning, and consequently no preparation, accompanies spontaneous deception. Rather, spontaneous liars must come up with a plausible sounding message in an impromptu fashion.

Spontaneous speech.   Making up your sentences while you are talking.

Supportiveness.   Providing understanding, loyalty, liking, concern, etc. to others in order to show that you care for them and your relationships.

Synchronizing.   Synchronizing is a term used to describe how a couple coordinate their individual- and couple-related activities in an efficient and mutually accommodating manner.

Syntax.   The grammar of a language. The rules for contructing grammatically correct sentences.

Tactile communication.   Touching behavior. How people use physical contact to communicate with one another.

Tag questions.   Brief questions tagged on the end of an utterance which seeks agreement from the listeners. An example would be "It goes over here, right?"

Terminal values.   Those values which are ends to which you are striving (e.g., happiness, self-respect, freedom, etc.). They are desirable end-states.

Territoriality.   Actions that suggest that people claim certain areas of physical space. People will often defend territory they feel is theirs.

Territories (types).   The types of territories are grouped according to the degree of control or ownership of the territory by an individual or group. The first type of territories, termed primary territories, involve exclusive ownership. Secondary territories involve territories that are not controlled exclusively by any one person, but others generally relate the territory to one person or group. Public territories involve areas which are available to anyone.

Traits vs. states.   Competing theoretical explanations for human behavior. The trait approach argues that people display consistent patterns of behavior because of their fixed personality traits. The states approach says that people's behavior is influenced by the immediate setting they find themselves in, and that the demands of the situation will govern their behavior.

Uncertainty event.   Events occurring in stable relationships that produce uncertainty. Various actions by, or additional knowledge about a relational partner can cause uncertainty in a relationship.

Uncertainty reduction.   Seeking reliable information about others which will help you understand how to communicate with them.

Unselfish love.   When someone is willing to give of themselves physically and emotionally without asking for anything in return they are demonstrating unselfish love. Unselfish love involves caring more for the other person than for oneself.

Vagueness.   When it is unclear what the speaker is referring to because the words do not have easily identifiable referents. When the meaning itself is unclear.

Verbal aggressiveness.   The tendency to attack another's self concept as well as arguing the topic of a conversation.

Violation.   This is a type of territorial encoachment that refers to the unauthorized use of another's territory.

Vocal fluency.   The extent to which a speaker's speech is free from unnecessary pauses, verbal errors, nonfluencies, and false starts.

White lies.   Forms of deception that are used in social interaction in order to avoid unpleasant circumstances. Considered somewhat socially acceptable because of their potential for generating little or no negative consequences for those involved.

AUTHOR INDEX

SUBJECT INDEX

COMPUTER BOOK SERIES FROM IDG

Internet For Dummies®, 5th Edition

Cheat Sheet

Fill In Information about Your Internet Account

Your e-mail address:

_____

@ _____

Your Internet provider's data phone number (the number your software dials):

_____

Your Internet provider's technical-support phone number (if you want to talk to a human being): _____

Your Internet provider's technical-support department's e-mail address:

_____

@ _____

For PPP and SLIP accounts

Your IP address (you may not have one assigned): _____

Your Internet provider's DNS (domain name server): _____

Your Internet provider's SMTP mail gateway (for outgoing mail): _____

Your Internet provider's POP mail server (for incoming mail): _____

Your provider's news server (for Usenet newsgroups): _____

Hostname Zones

This list shows you the three-letter last word of Internet hostnames; for two-letter country codes, see the Web page http://net.gurus.com/countries.

com	Company or individual
edu	Educational institution
gov	U.S. federal government
mil	U.S. military
net	Network organization
int	International organization
org	Nonprofit or other noncommercial organization

Netiquette Tips

Remember that everyone else on the Net is human, too.

Don't respond in anger or insist on getting the last word.

DON'T TYPE IN ALL CAPS! It's shouting.

Don't post messages to mailing lists if you don't have something new to add.

Don't pass along chain letters, make-money-fast messages, avoid-this-virus warnings, or other bogus mail.

Acronyms to Know

BTW	By the way
RTFM	Read the manual
IMHO	In my humble opinion
ROFL	Rolling on floor, laughing
TIA	Thanks in advance
YMMV	Your mileage may vary
TLA	Three-letter acronym

IDG BOOKS WORLDWIDE

...For Dummies: #1 Computer Book Series for Beginners

COMPUTER BOOK SERIES FROM IDG

Internet For Dummies®, 5th Edition

Cheat Sheet

Useful Web Pages

http://www.yahoo.com	Yahoo! Web directory
http://altavista.digital.com	AltaVista Web search page
http://www.infoseek.com	Infoseek Web directory
http://www.tucows.com	The Ultimate Collection of Windows Software (also for Macs)
http://cws.internet.com	Stroud's Consummate Winsock Applications
http://www.infobeat.com	Sign up to get news via e-mail
http://www.liszt.com	Liszt Directory of E-mail Mailing Lists
http://www.unitedmedia.com/comics/dilbert	Dilbert
http://www.four11.com	Four11 phone and e-mail directory
http://www.usps.gov	U.S. Postal Service zip codes and postage rates
http://mail.yahoo.com and http://www.hotmail.com	Free e-mail via the Web
http://net.gurus.com	Updates to this book

Types of URLS

file://*pathname*	File stored on local computer
ftp://*hostname*/*pathname*	File on FTP server
http://*hostname*/*pathname*	World Wide Web page
mailto:*address*	E-mail address
telnet:*hostname*	Computer to log in to using telnet program

E-Mail Mailing Lists

To find a list, go to http://www.liszt.com.

To subscribe, send a message to the administrative address (usually with username LISTSERV, ListProc, or Majordomo) containing the line "subscribe *listname yourname*" (for Majordomo, omit *yourname*) in the text of the message.

Read and save the welcome message you receive.

To sign off, send a message to the administrative address containing the line "signoff *listname*" (for LISTSERV and ListProc) or "unsubscribe *listname*" (for Majordomo) in the text of the message.

E-Mail Addresses

To Send To	With This Address	Type This:
AOL	SteveCase	stevecase@aol.com
AT&T WorldNet	TedVail	tedvail@worldnet.att.net
CompuServe	77777,7777	77777.7777@compuserve.com
FIDONET	MarySmith 1:2/3.4	mary.smith@p4.f3.n2.zl.fidonet.org
MCI Mail	555-2468	5552468@mcimail.com
MSN	BillGates	billgates@msn.com
Prodigy Classic	ABCD123A	abcdl23a@prodigy.com
Prodigy Internet	dummies	dummies@prodigy.net

...For Dummies: #1 Computer Book Series for Beginners